PETER JOYCE

SOUTH AFRICA in the 20th century

chronicles of an era

PETER JOYCE

SOUTH AFRICA in the 20th century

chronicles of an era

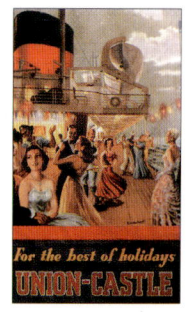

First published in 2000 by Struik Publishers (Pty) Ltd
(a member of Struik New Holland Publishing (Pty) Ltd)

London • Cape Town • Sydney • Auckland

24 Nutford Place
London W1H 6DQ
United Kingdom

14 Aquatic Drive
Frenchs Forest
NSW 2086, Australia

80 McKenzie Street
Cape Town 8001
South Africa

218 Lake Road
Northcote, Auckland
New Zealand

Reg no: 54/00965/07

2 4 6 8 10 9 7 5 3 1

Copyright © 2000 in published edition:
Struik Publishers (Pty) Ltd
Copyright © 2000 in text: Peter Joyce
Copyright © 2000 in photographs and illustrations
rests with the photographers and/or their agencies
as credited on pages 246–7.

Managing editor: Annlerie van Rooyen
Concept and cover design: Janice Evans
Editor: Lesley Hay-Whitton
Assistant designers: Tracey Mackenzie
and Illana Fridkin
Researcher: Jocelyn Convery
Research assistant : Sonya Meyer
Picture researcher: Carmen Watts
Proofreader: Gill Gordon
Indexer: Sarah Maddox

ISBN 1 86872 309 7

Reproduction by Hirt & Carter Cape (Pty) Ltd
Printed and bound by CTP Book Printers (Pty) Ltd,
Caxton Street, Parow 7500, Cape Town

All rights reserved. No part of this publication
may be reproduced, stored in a retrieval system or
transmitted, in any form or by any means,
electronic, mechanical, photocopying or otherwise,
without the prior written permission of the
publishers and copyright holders.

Every effort has been made to trace the copyright holders and we apologize
in advance for any unintentional omissions or errors. We would be pleased to
insert the appropriate acknowledgments in any subsequent editions of this
publication. Please write to: The Editor, *South Africa in the 20th Century*,
Struik Publishers, PO Box 1144, Cape Town 8000.

ACKNOWLEDGMENTS

Many organizations and individuals helped in the compilation of this book, most notably by locating, identifying and providing pictures. The publishers and author are especially grateful to the following for their courteous assistance: The National Library, Cape Town, and in particular John Dwyer, Peter Coates, Marius Fortune, Enver Ebrahim and Najwa Hendrickse; the Campbell Collections of the University of Natal, Durban; the Cape Town Archive Repository; the *Cape Times* and *Cape Argus*, Cape Town; the Cory Library, Grahamstown; the C.P. Nel Museum, Oudtshoorn; Nicola Fick; International Press Agency, Cape Town; the Local History Museum's Collection, Durban; MuseumAfrica, Johannesburg; the National Archives, Pretoria; Picturenet Africa, Johannesburg; and René van der Westhuizen.

Contents

1900s
pages 6–27

1910s
pages 28–49

1920s
pages 50–75

1930s
pages 76–93

1940s
pages 94–111

1950s
pages 112–37

1960s
pages 138–59

1970s
pages 160–79

1980s
pages 180–99

1990s
pages 200–23

2000
pages 224–31

Index 232–45
Picture credits 246–7
Further reading 248

1900s

DIED
1901: Queen Victoria, Britain's longest reigning monarch.
US president William McKinley, assassinated; he is succeeded by Theodore Roosevelt.
1902: SA tycoon and politician Cecil Rhodes.
1904: Paul Kruger, former Transvaal president, in Switzerland.

CROWNED
1902: Edward VII, as king of England.
1908: Infant Pu Yi, as Chinese emperor.

WAR IN SOUTH AFRICA
1900: British forces relieve besieged Kimberley, Mafeking and Ladysmith, and occupy Bloemfontein, Johannesburg and Pretoria. Orange Free State and Transvaal become colonies; Boer guerrilla commandos take to the field; British establish concentration camps.
1901: Kitchener launches 'scorched earth' campaign.
1902: Treaty of Vereeniging ends the war.

POST-WAR RECOVERY
1903: Milner establishes his 'Kindergarten' to oversee reconstruction.
1904: Chinese labourers brought in to work on gold mines.

REBELLIONS
1900: Boxers' uprising (against foreigners) in China.
1903: Turks massacre 50,000 Bulgarians.
1904: Hereros rise against German settlers in South West Africa.
1905: Russian workers revolt; first soviet (workers' council) founded.
1906: Bambatha rebellion breaks out in Natal.

BREAKTHROUGHS
1901: First transatlantic wireless message sent (UK).
1903: Wright brothers complete first powered flight (US). Ford motor company produces its first cars (US). Physicist Marie Curie becomes first woman to win Nobel Prize (France).
1904: Johannesburg's first 'urban location', Pimville, established. First large ocean-going vessels enter Durban harbour. Trans-Siberian railway completed (Russia).
1905: Johannesburg gets its first waterborne sewerage system. Einstein publishes 'special theory of relativity' (Switzerland).
1906: World's first wireless broadcast of music and voice (US). Johannesburg gets its first electric trams. First SA rugby squad tours Britain.
1907: First SA oil company, Vacuum, established.
1908: Cecilia Makiwane is SA's first black woman admitted to nursing register. First SA motor show held, at Wanderers, Johannesburg. Henry Ford unveils the Model T (US).
1909: French aviator Bleriot becomes first to fly the English Channel.

DISCOVERED
1905: Cullinan diamond, largest ever unearthed, near Pretoria.

DESTROYED
1906: Much of San Francisco (US), by earthquake.
1908: Part of the Siberian tundra, by a gigantic meteorite. Most of Messina, Sicily, by earthquake.

DEFEATED
1905: Russia's army (in Manchuria) and navy, by the Japanese.

CONQUERED
1909: The North Pole, by American explorer Admiral R.E. Peary.

VANISHED
1909: The liner *Waratah*, off SA's south-east coast. No traces of the wreckage, or of the 211 people on board, could be found.

POLITICS AND PROTEST
1903: SA Native Affairs Commission appointed. Suffragist (women's vote) movement gains momentum in Britain.
1905: Lagden report recommends racial segregation in SA. Het Volk party founded in Transvaal colony. Second Afrikaans language movement launched.
1906: Transvaal colony gains self-government.
1907: Selborne Memorandum recommends unified 'native policy' in SA. Black political bodies, including the African Peoples' Organisation, meet in Queenstown to plan opposition to Union proposals. Orange River colony granted self-government. White miners strike against importation into SA of Chinese labour; 50,000 Chinese repatriated. Gandhi defies Transvaal government on issue of fingerprinting for identity documents.
1908: SA Indians launch massive anti-pass campaign; Gandhi imprisoned.
1909: South Africa Act passed by British House of Commons, paving way for Union. Eight-man non-white SA delegation visits London to protest.

6 The Hundreds

SOUTH AFRICA in the 20th CENTURY — 1900s

1900

MAFEKING SURVIVES SIEGE

Boer forces continue to besiege the towns of Mafeking, Kimberley and Ladysmith until well into the year.

The siege of Mafeking begins on 24 October 1899, lasts 217 days and, romanticized by British newspapers and magazines, makes an instant celebrity of its commanding officer, Colonel Robert Baden-Powell. Reports tell tales of heroic battle and bravery, but in reality the garrison troops and civilian residents are well protected by Baden-Powell's ingenious system of trenches, earthworks and dug-outs and, in the commander's words, have only to 'sit and wait for them [the Boers] to go'.

Mafeking soup kitchen: barely sustaining life.

Daily life goes on much as usual during the long periods between the occasional bombardment: polo, cricket, football and pony-racing, musical evenings and theatre shows feature on the social calendar.

Not so lucky are the town's 7,000 black inhabitants. Their rations are cut to levels that barely sustain life; Baden-Powell has a number executed, and others flogged, for stealing food. A visiting reporter writes that 'words could not describe the scene of misery…. I saw them fall down on the veldt and lie where they had fallen, too weak to go on their way. Hunger had them in its grip, and many were black spectres and living skeletons'.

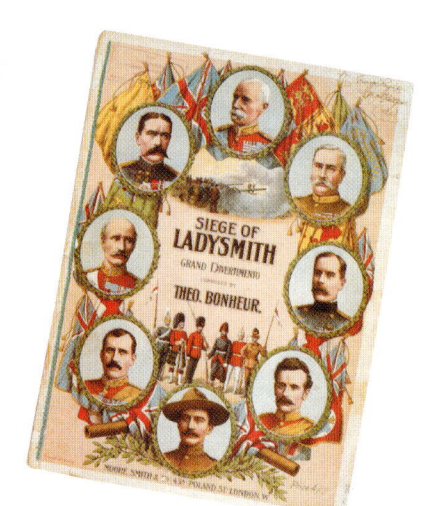

BOERS CAPTURE SPIOENKOP

24 January. One of the bloodiest engagements of the war is fought on the slopes of Spioenkop, near the Tugela River in Natal – a battle witnessed by three men who will later leave their imprint on the course of human affairs. Present during the battle are Louis Botha, Winston Churchill and Mohandas Gandhi, who leads a team of stretcher-bearers (morbidly known as 'body-snatchers').

General Buller's British troops, in command of the hill, are subjected to such murderous fire from Boer artillery, snipers and advancing infantrymen that they are forced to fall back across the river. One Englishman later recalls the 'great bearded warriors charging up the mountain, taking death as nothing… there was something godlike in those men: their faces change to iron and they seem like Fate itself'. So bitter has the fighting been – more than 2,000 soldiers are killed or wounded – that the Boers start to pull back, occupying the summit only when dawn breaks and they can see, to their surprise, that the heights are clear.

Nevertheless, Buller eventually manages to breach the Tugela line and, on 28 February, relieves the beleaguered garrison of Ladysmith. The town

The Mafeking court in session: black residents suffered grievous punishment for minor offences.

SOUTH AFRICA in the 20th CENTURY

Boer sharpshooters pose in ambush mode.

has suffered grievously: shortage of food and polluted water have consigned 2,000 patients to a hospital designed to hold 300; many have died.

Meanwhile, a massively reinforced British army under Lord Roberts rolls up the central front, occupying Bloemfontein on 13 March, Johannesburg on 31 May and Pretoria a week later. Paul Kruger, president of the Transvaal republic, flees to Europe and into exile. The war, it seems, is over.

YOUNG WINSTON BACK IN THE SADDLE

Winston Churchill, the young former special correspondent for the London *Morning Post*,

Churchill the newsman.

takes part in the relief of Ladysmith as an officer in the South African Light Horse. Some three months ago he was taken prisoner, in Natal, when forces commanded by General Louis Botha ambushed the armoured train in which he was travelling. He later made a daring escape from confinement at the Staatsmodelskool in Pretoria, hid himself on an eastward-bound goods train, received sanctuary from a pro-British mine official and eventually made his way to Lourenço Marques.

ANCIENT CULTURE DISCOVERED

The modern world catches its first glimpse of an ancient civilization when British archaeologist Arthur Evans unearths relics of what will become known as the Minoan culture, at Knossos, Crete. Among the most exciting discoveries are fragments of inscribed pottery (yet to be deciphered) and a throne, which might have belonged to King Minos.

UNION-CASTLE LINE IS LAUNCHED

It is announced that the Union Line and tycoon Sir Donald Currie's Castle Mail Packets Company, fierce rivals for the lucrative South African trade for the past 30 years, will merge to form the Union-Castle Mail Steamship Company.

The Union Line began life in 1853 as the Southampton Shipping Company, carrying coal from the Welsh collieries before it changed its name and, three years later, launched its first liner, the Cambrian, which had been built specially for the Cape route. Sir Donald, who had made a fortune in diamonds and gold (and owned a fleet of sailing ships, all named after English castles), entered the Cape trade in 1872.

British dead on the summit of Spioenkop.

SOUTH AFRICA in the 20th CENTURY 1900s

The Castle Line's flagship hotel, the Mount Nelson in Cape Town, opened its doors just a few months ago. Designed to provide the ultimate in elegance and luxury, its early guest list features such luminaries as financier and politician Cecil Rhodes, the writers Conan Doyle and Rudyard Kipling (a regular visitor to the Cape), Field Marshal Lord Roberts and his successor, General Kitchener, young Winston Churchill and his American-born mother, the beautiful Lady Randolph Churchill.

A pioneer cameraman records the Anglo-Boer War.

FIRST WAR SCENES ON SCREEN
Audiences in Cape Town and England are astonished and, at times, shocked by flickering scenes of the Anglo-Boer War, the first major conflict to be captured on film. The newsmen, most notably William Dickson (sponsored by the British Biograph and Mutoscope Company) and Joseph Rosenthal (Warwick Trading Company), follow the troops and, well briefed by commanders in the field, manage to produce a wealth of descriptive and, occasionally, dramatic sequences. These intrepid men, though, are not always in the right place at just the right time, and incidents sometimes have to be re-enacted for their benefit.

TWO BOOKS FOR CHILDREN
New titles include Beatrix Potter's *The Tale of Peter Rabbit* and L. Frank Baum's *The Wonderful Wizard of Oz* (the title occurred to the author by happy accident: at a loss for a name, his gaze rested on a row of office files labelled O–Z). Adult readers welcome Joseph Conrad's *Lord Jim*. Conrad, a 43-year-old Polish-born writer, served for 16 years as an officer in the British merchant navy. He also visited the Belgian territory of the Congo, an experience which inspired his puzzling but powerful *Heart of Darkness*.

Turn-of-the-century elegance: guests stroll in the graceful grounds of Cape Town's new Mount Nelson hotel.

BORN
International: Screen actor Spencer Tracy; jazz musician Louis Armstrong; American composer Aaron Copland. **South Africa:** Author Lawrence Green.

DIED
International: Irish playwright, author and convicted homosexual Oscar Wilde, in poverty-stricken exile in Paris; German philosopher Friedrich Nietsche; Italy's King Umberto, shot by an anarchist; writer and art critic John Ruskin; composer Sir Arthur Sullivan. **South Africa:** Boer politician and commandant-general Piet Joubert. Also American engineer George Labram, who, at Cecil Rhodes' urging, built the field gun known as 'Long Cecil' for the defence of Kimberley. This was so successful that the Boers brought up their own Creusot 'Long Tom' artillery piece, one of whose first shells killed Labram.

WHAT'S NEW IN 1900

- The **Paris Métro** (underground railway) opens; a **moving stairway** (escalator) is demonstrated at the Paris Exhibition.
- The phrase **concentration camp** enters the English language after the British military in South Africa set up civilian internment centres.
- The **paper clip** is invented by German-based Norwegian Johann Waaler.
- **Tennis:** The Davis Cup is inaugurated; the US beats Britain 3-0.
- First **book of postage stamps** is issued.
- George Eastman markets his **Box Brownie** camera.
- **Sigmund Freud** publishes his *The Interpretation of Dreams*.
- **Puccini's** opera *Tosca* premieres in Rome.
- Max Planck formulates his **quantum theory**.

SOUTH AFRICA in the 20th CENTURY

1901

QUEEN VICTORIA DIES: END OF AN EPOCH

February. Millions mourn as Queen Victoria, longest reigning of England's monarchs, is laid to rest in the family vault at Windsor. The Queen is succeeded by her eldest son, Edward, the pleasure-loving Prince of Wales. Victoria, who came to the throne as a young girl of 18, in 1837, presided over the full flowering of the Empire: by the turn of the century her domain stretched across one quarter of the earth, and Britain ranked as the world's foremost industrial and military power. That status, however, is now being challenged as both Germany and the United States flex their economic muscles.

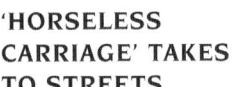

The aged queen.

'HORSELESS CARRIAGE' TAKES TO STREETS

A new era in road transport dawns with the opening, in Cape Town, of two motor workshops. The country's first motor car, a fragile little single-cylinder, 1.5-horsepower Benz Voiturette, was introduced to Oom Paul Kruger and a wonderstruck crowd of onlookers at Pretoria's Berea Park four years ago. Posters proclaimed it 'The Invention of the Age.... The Motor, or Horseless Carriage' which would 'supersede all locomotion before the end of this century'. It hasn't quite done that, but cars are becoming an increasingly familiar sight on the country's dusty streets.

Garlicks of Cape Town opened a successful dealership in the late 1890s; the Johannesburg Motor Car Company will begin advertising the Cudell in 1902, followed shortly afterwards by the city's Continental Garage, holder of the De Dion franchise.

> 'It is a generally accepted fact that smoking is a great protection from the plague. That being the case, the public are strongly advised to smoke Taddy's Myrtle Grove cigarettes.'
> *Advertisement in the* Cape Times

MUSIC RECORDED ON DISC

The Consolidated Talking Machine Company, based in New Jersey, USA, begins marketing a new 10-inch circular disc that records sound to a far higher quality than the wax cylinders used in Thomas Edison's phonograph. The single-sided discs, with title labels at the centre, carry three minutes of music and can be stored in albums, a boon to those who are building up collections of recorded music.

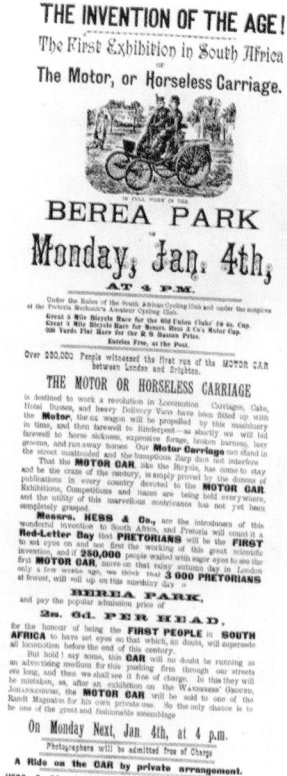

The Benz Voiturette, first car seen in South Africa, on display in Pretoria's Berea Park.

SOUTH AFRICA in the 20th CENTURY — 1900s

BOERS FIGHT ON

After the set-piece victories of 1900, and the military occupation of major northern centres, British commanders can be forgiven for thinking the war is won. But the Boers have other ideas: they take to the great spaces of the interior to carry on the fight. Inspired by such gifted leaders as Louis Botha, Jan Smuts, Koos de la Rey and Christiaan de Wet, their highly mobile guerrilla commandos – living off the land and helped by their kinfolk – launch lightning hit-and-run raids on isolated British detachments, railway lines, bridges. De Wet, the most audacious of the Boer generals (his exploits are widely reported in Britain, where he is regarded as something of a hero) is singled out by Imperial fighting forces but their 'great De Wet hunts', involving thousands of troops, fail to capture the elusive Freestater.

The Boer 'Long Tom' gun in action during the Anglo-Boer War.

Koos de la Rey, among the finest of Boer commanders.

Inmates of a concentration camp; 26,000 die.

KITCHENER SCORCHES THE EARTH

Harassed to distraction by Boer guerrilla tactics, British commander-in-chief Lord Kitchener launches a savage scorched-earth campaign to starve the guerrillas into submission. His occupation forces burn 30,000 farmsteads to the ground, destroy crops and cattle, and deport tens of thousands of rural Boer families and their black workers to internment centres, or 'concentration camps'. Author Denys Reitz is later to write of a 'driven' area his commando passed through, 'leaving behind us only blackened ruins and trampled fields, so that our course lay through a silent, unpeopled waste across which we navigated our wagon like a lonely ship at sea'.

The camps are designed to intern civilians and not, as Hitler's would be two generations in the future, to exterminate them. But they still take a terrible toll: some 26,000 incarcerated Boers – most of them women and children – die of enteritis, dysentery and epidemics of measles. So too do a great many Africans, but nobody bothers to count their number (the official figure is later put at 14,154, almost certainly much too low an estimate). In Britain, Liberal leader David Lloyd George predicts, with some accuracy, that 'a barrier of dead children's bodies will rise up between the British and Boer races in South Africa'.

A Boer family on the move. Altogether, 30,000 homesteads are torched.

SOUTH AFRICA in the 20th CENTURY

RADIO SIGNAL OPENS WAY TO FUTURE

In an experiment that promises to revolutionize communications, the inventor Guglielmo Marconi sends a wireless signal (the letter S in Morse code) 3,200 kilometres across the Atlantic – from his transmitter in Cornwall, England, to Newfoundland, Canada. Scientists are at a loss to explain how the signal overcame the problems posed by the curvature of the earth to reach its destination.

DEATH OF A HERO

After suffering two weeks of brutal torture at the hands of a Boer commando, Abraham Esau is taken into the veld near Calvinia and shot. Esau, a coloured man and blacksmith by trade, was passionately pro-British but his attempts to enlist with the Imperial forces were rejected as the war is considered a 'whites only' affair. Nevertheless he raised a local militia (armed with swords) and organized an intelligence network covering much of the northern Cape. His unit was eventually defeated and taken prisoner. Esau refuses to betray his agents despite the torture, nor does he renounce his allegiance to the British cause. A Union Jack drapes his coffin.

Abraham Esau, a patriot who retains his honour and gives his life for the British cause.

Thousands of Boer prisoners-of-war are dispatched to far-off lands by their British captors – to St Helena, to the Bermudas, to Portugal, India and Ceylon – where they wait out the war in sadness and in reasonable comfort. The camps are self-sufficient little societies, some with church, school, newspaper, home industries, craft shops, brewery, clubs, theatre, sports field, graveyard. Pictured is an instrumental band in one of St Helena's two exile communities, which also boasts a string quartet, a piano trio and a minstrel troupe.

CAPE CARS SHOW THE WAY

The newly formed Automobile Club of South Africa (six founder members, headed by Sir Alfred Hennessy) holds its first rally. The route runs from Cape Town to Kalk Bay; all contestants arrive safely.

WHAT'S NEW IN 1901

- **US:** President William McKinley is assassinated by a young Polish immigrant; vice-president Theodore Roosevelt succeeds to the presidency.
- **Australia** becomes a Commonwealth.
- **US:** Booker T. Washington is the first black man to be invited to the White House.
- **Sport:** Netball is invented, in Kent, England; boxing is legalized under the Marquess of Queensbury rules (in Britain, but not yet in the US).
- First **Nobel prizes** awarded.
- **Motor industry:** The Cadillac Motor Company is founded in Detroit, US; the first Mercedes car is produced by Germany's Daimler (it is named after the daughter of the first customer, Emile Jellinek); a car features for the first time in a bank robbery, in Paris; Louis Fournier sets a speed record when he drives one mile in 52 seconds, in the New York area.
- **The law:** The world's first file of criminal fingerprints is established at New Scotland Yard, London.
- **New products:** The throw-away 'safety' razor blade is developed by Mr King Gillette in the US, and soon replaces the standard cut-throat; instant coffee makes its debut, in Buffalo, New York.
- **Cosmetic surgery:** The first facelift operation is performed, in Berlin.

SOUTH AFRICA in the 20th CENTURY 1900s

BORN
International: Hollywood actors Gary Cooper and Clark Gable; German actress Marlene Dietrich; animation king Walt Disney.
South Africa: Poet Roy Campbell; politician Hendrik Verwoerd.

DIED
International: Operatic composer Giuseppe Verdi; painter Henri Toulouse-Lautrec; 400 die in New York heatwave.
South Africa: Thembu schoolteacher Enoch Sontonga (probably in this year), composer of 'Nkosi Sikelel' iAfrika' (God Bless Africa), the beautiful hymn that, much later, becomes part of South Africa's national anthem.

Electric trams: now a familiar presence in Cape Town's Adderley Street.

A SONG IS BORN

What is to become white South Africa's best-known 'folk song' emerges, from a homestead near Vryheid, when soldiers of Louis Botha's commando, gathered informally around the piano, adapt the American 'slave ballad' 'Ellie Rhee' (also known as 'Carry me back to Tennessee') to produce 'Sarie Marais'. The lady so commemorated was in all likelihood a Saré Marais from Uitenhage, who married young and in romantic circumstances, settled on a farm 'in die wyk van die Mooirivier' (in the Mooi River area), bore 11 children and died, in childbirth, at the age of 37.

QUICK TRAVEL FOR CAPETONIANS

Electric trams are now providing South Africa's city dwellers with their main means of transport. The first ones – ten massive, noisy double-deckers imported from the United States – appeared in 1896, offering a fast and regular service between Cape Town's Adderley Street and Mowbray Hill; last year the Cape Electric Tramways Company, which also runs the Port Elizabeth system, carried more than 16 million passengers. Comfort, apparently, is low on the company's priority list: the trams are open at front and back and along the sides of the upper deck. Johannesburg's first trams will take to the rails in 1906, Pretoria's only in 1910, by which time petrol-driven motor vehicles will begin to compete seriously for the urban carrier trade.

THE ARTS SCENE

♦ Painter Pablo Picasso holds his first exhibition, in Paris.
♦ Anton Chekhov's play *The Three Sisters* is staged.
♦ Books published include Rudyard Kipling's *Kim*.
♦ Scottish-born Andrew Carnegie sells his US business empire (for $447 million) and sets up the Carnegie Trust.

Saré Marais, from Uitenhage.

> 'Dear Sir: I wish to inform you that I have agreed to a rugby match taking place between you and us. I from my side will agree to order a cease-fire tomorrow afternoon from 12 o'clock until sunset.
> *Boer field general S.G. 'Manie' Maritz, to Major Edwards*

SOUTH AFRICA in the 20th CENTURY

1902

AT LAST, THE GUNS FALL SILENT

Pretoria, 31 May. After nearly three years of brutal battle, Boer and Briton finally sit down to negotiate an honourable peace. Both sides are ready to talk: the war is proving hugely expensive to the British exchequer and has become unpopular with the voting public at home; the Boers in the field are exhausted, starving, many reduced to wearing grain-bags for clothing.

The Treaty of Vereeniging, signed by the delegates meeting in Pretoria's elegant Melrose House, ends the hostilities and, although it returns the Transvaal and Orange Free State to the colonial fold, also guarantees them eventual self-government, recognizes Boer property rights, safeguards the Dutch language, promises relief to war victims – and denies black South Africans their political rights. Indeed, it has been a white man's war all along, and in the end it is a white man's peace. Writes one objective observer: 'Of all who have suffered by the war, those who have endured the most and will receive least sympathy, are the [blacks] of the country places of the Transvaal...'.

News of the peace (see left) is announced to assembled Pretorians.

'BREAKER' MORANT EXECUTED

Towards the end of hostilities a British court martial finds Australians Harry 'Breaker' Morant, Peter Handcock and George Witton guilty of war crimes: they had pursued and shot a suspected informer. It later becomes clear that the trial is politically motivated: circumstances demand that a gesture be made towards Boer sensitivities. Morant and Handcock are executed by firing squad; Witton is reprieved after representations by Cape politicians.

English-born Morant, who fought with the Bushveldt Carbineers, earned the nickname 'Breaker' while working as a horse-breeder in Australia.

WHAT'S NEW IN 1902

- **Films:** Georges Melies' *A Trip to the Moon* breaks cinematic ground with its advanced special effects.
- **Crowned:** King Edward VII is crowned.
- **China:** Authorities ban the practice of foot-binding.
- **Egypt:** First Aswan Dam opened.
- **Art Nouveau** takes off after Paris Exhibition.
- **Thomas Edison** invents the electrical storage battery.
- **London School of Economics** opens.
- **US:** First coin-operated vending machine is installed, in Philadelphia.

THE PASSING OF A COLOSSUS

Muizenberg, 26 March. Cecil John Rhodes, financial baron, visionary and one-time Cape premier, dies, aged 49, in his cottage at this small seaside village near Cape Town. His body is taken by train northwards along his dreamed of (but unfinished) Cape-to-Cairo route, across the Limpopo and into a country founded by and named after him (Rhodesia), and interred on World's View, a quiet place on the commanding heights of his beloved Matopo Hills, near Bulawayo.

Rhodes, whatever his faults – and there were many – was inarguably a powerful force in the shaping of the subcontinent during the latter part of the Victorian era. He bequeathed most of his vast fortune, made initially on the early Kimberley diamond fields, to the nation, his memory soon to be honoured in the classical-style 'temple' – the work of his friend and architect Herbert Baker – built beneath Devil's Peak on the slopes of Table Mountain. The monument's fine equestrian statue will be inscribed with part of Rudyard Kipling's personal tribute to 'the immense and brooding spirit.... Living he was the land, and dead, his soul shall be her soul'.

Rhodes strides the continent.

SOUTH AFRICA in the 20th CENTURY 1900s

Anglo-Boer War heroes De Wet, De la Rey and Botha.

BOERS TRIUMPH IN EUROPE

Shortly after peace is concluded a trio of Boer leaders – generals Christiaan de Wet, Koos de la Rey and Louis Botha – visit Britain and Europe on a whirlwind fund-raising tour. They are received everywhere as heroes; in London, hostesses vie for their presence at society functions, and on their last night they dine with Royalty at Buckingham Palace. They are also offered knighthoods but, good republicans that they are, decline the honour.

DIARY ADVISES ON DOMESTICS

Among the most popular local books published in 1902 are Hildagonda Duckitt's *Diary of a Cape Housewife*, in which this well-connected spinster offers volumes of advice to the Edwardian homemaker. For the general-purpose domestic – whose hours are long (dawn to late), the work arduous – Miss Duckitt recommends a starting wage of £1 rising to a maximum of £2 a month. The richer English-speaking South African families, however, have tended to employ whole platoons of more specialized, better paid servants – lady's maids, parlourmaids, butlers, full-time cooks, head gardeners, governesses for their children, coachmen – whom in many cases they imported from an ancestral country their employers still regard as 'home'.

Edwardian child and nursemaid.

BENZ BLAZES THE TRAIL

French motoring pioneer Georges Chapart completes the first car journey from Durban to Amanzimtoti. His imported Benz has to be pushed up every rise in the road, but covers the 40-mile stretch in a single day.

THE PUBLISHING WORLD

Edgar Wallace, who will later make his name as a popular novelist, is appointed editor of *Rand Daily Mail*. Books published during the year include:

- Joseph Conrad's *Heart of Darkness*;
- Rudyard Kipling's *Just So Stories* and *Puck of Pooks Hill* (written in Cape Town);
- Arthur Conan Doyle's *The Hound of the Baskervilles* (Doyle receives a knighthood for his book *The War in South Africa*).

SONGS OF THE DAY
- A Bird in a Gilded Cage
- Goodbye Dolly Gray
- Beer, Beer, Glorious Beer

1903

TALENTED YOUNGSTERS GET THE COUNTRY GOING

Lord Milner and his brilliant young administrators (the 'Kindergarten') make splendid progress in returning South Africa to normality after the devastation of the Anglo-Boer War. Their priorities are to get the gold mines working again, repatriate displaced Boer families, launch farming, forestry and irrigation schemes, and import large numbers of British immigrants. They are succeeding admirably in all but this last, though the five-year drought that now begins will delay the recovery of the land.

Lord Milner's clever young 'Kindergarten'.

SOUTH AFRICA in the 20th CENTURY

WHAT'S NEW IN 1903

- *Motoring:* First Ford motor cars (Model A) go on sale, in the US; top speed is 48 mph.
- The *Harley-Davidson* motorcycle company is founded, in the US.
- *Pepsi-Cola* is introduced to soft-drinks market.
- A Dutch scientist invents the *electro-cardiograph*.
- *Pierre and Marie Curie* share the Nobel physics prize (with a third scientist, Henri Becquerel) for their work on radioactivity. Madame Curie will later (in 1911) win the Nobel prize for chemistry.
- The *thermos flask*, invented by a Scottish scientist in 1892, is finally patented – in Germany.
- The word *clone* is added to the English language.

Wilbur Wright.

WOMEN'S LEAGUE ENTERS THE LISTS

Social worker and teacher Charlotte Maxeke returns from the United States of America to found the Bantu Women's League, later to be renamed the African National Congress Women's League. Maxeke, the first African woman ever to gain a university degree in South Africa, will go on to lead vigorous campaigns (in 1918 and 1919) protesting the extension of the pass laws to women. She will also co-found the All Africa Convention in 1935.

LOCAL RUGBY MAKES STRIDES

The national rugby team, wearing green jerseys provided by the Old Diocesans club, wins the series against Mark Morrison's touring British side, drawing the first two Test matches and emerging victorious from the third. The outcome is more than creditable since the South Africans are still relatively new to the game: they entered the international arena in 1891, when they lost all 19 matches (including three Tests) against W.E. Maclagan's tourists. However the second British touring party, led by John Hammond, arrived in 1896 and found the going much tougher: although South Africa lost the first three internationals, they triumphed (5-0) in the fourth, played at Newlands.

WRIGHT BROTHERS IN HISTORIC FIRST FLIGHT

17 December. Bicycle makers Orville and Wilbur Wright make aviation history when Orville pilots their primitive flying machine over the windy dunes of Kitty Hawk, North Carolina, to complete humankind's first-ever powered heavier-than-air flight under controlled conditions. The craft covers 36 metres, and is airborne for 12 seconds. In a later test it remains aloft for 59 seconds.

Wilbur Wright watches as brother Orville takes off.

Pioneers of Motoring

The 'horseless carriage', introduced to South Africans in the later 1890s, begins to take to the roads in earnest during 1903. The year sees the country's first motor endurance test, a run from Cape Town over the precipitous Sir Lowry's Pass to Houw Hoek. The winner is a Mr S. Benjamin, driving a De Dion. Earlier in the year the Green Point cycle track hosts the inaugural motor race, and Arthur Youlden of Johannesburg imports the first of Henry Ford's new Model As to leave America.

South Africa's first serious motor accident also takes place during 1903: Cape Town's Charles Garlick and two friends drive their 24-horsepower Darracq onto the railway line in Maitland and are hit by the Johannesburg express. All are injured (and all, including the car, recover well).

As the decade unfolds, the motor car becomes an increasingly familiar sight on city streets and country roads. Ford introduces its renowned Model T in 1908, the hugely popular 'car of the people', in which year South Africa's first motor show attracts enthusiastic crowds to the Wanderers Club, Johannesburg.

The 1901 Benz owned by Port Elizabeth mayor William Alcock.

The Shimwell family's De Dion, Durban's first motor car.

Charles Garlick's Darracq, victim of the first serious accident.

Johannesburg's Albert Piel in his 25-horsepower Talbot-Darracq in 1908. His daughter is driving.

The sturdy Model T Ford, introduced in 1908. Ninety-two years later it is adjudged 'Car of the Century'.

SOUTH AFRICA in the 20th CENTURY
The Hundreds

NEW TIVOLI OPENS ITS DOORS

Cape Town's new Tivoli Theatre, its elaborately decorated cream, blue and gold auditorium equipped with electric lights (still a novelty) and 'the latest form of tip-up chair', opens. The theatre will host many of the greats of Edwardian vaudeville and musical hall, among them Harry Lauder, George Robey and the inimitable Marie Lloyd, before the demolishers move in in 1932.

DOYLE BRINGS HERO BACK TO LIFE

Sherlock Holmes makes a welcome return to the best-seller lists after his creator, Arthur Conan Doyle, resurrects the pipe-smoking sleuth. Holmes made his debut in *A Study in Scarlet* (1887) but, after regular appearances in *The Strand Magazine* (1891–93), Doyle tired of his hero and tried to kill him off. Popular

BORN
International: Authors Evelyn Waugh, George Orwell, Nathanael West, Georges Simenon and Erskine Caldwell. South Africa: Writer Alan Paton.

DIED
International: Painters Paul Gauguin and James McNeill Whistler; 50,000 Bulgarians are massacred by Turkish soldiers; the king and queen of Serbia are assassinated by army officers.

Cape Town's grand new Tivoli Theatre (opposite the Post Office, far right), viewed from the Parade.

pressure, however, has prompted the publication of *The Return of Sherlock Holmes*.

STAGE AND SCREEN

The fledgling American film industry's first Western, *The Great Train Robbery*, is screened – new cinematic techniques and a good story-line spellbinds audiences; 578 people die when Chicago's Iroquois Theatre burns down; Italian tenor Enrico Caruso makes his debut in Verdi's *Rigoletto*, at New York's Metropolitan Opera House; among the year's new plays is G.B. Shaw's *Man and Superman*. *The Wizard of Oz*, the stage musical of Frank Baum's enormously popular book, captivates New Yorkers when it opens on Broadway.

1904
DEATH OF A PATRIARCH

Former Transvaal president Paul Kruger dies in exile, in Clarens, Switzerland, on 14 July at the age of 79. Affectionately known to his people as 'Oom Paul', and more seriously as 'the father of the Afrikaner nation', Kruger was a boy of ten when his family set out on the Great Trek, was present at the historic 1852 Sand River Convention which conferred independence on the Transvaal, helped draw up the republic's constitution and, as commandant-general, played a vital role in unifying the country during its early, faction-ridden days. He was elected president of Transvaal in 1883, shortly before the discovery of the Witwatersrand's fabulous gold fields – an event which, in 1899, led to outright war with a Britain bent on forcing the newly rich Transvaal into the Imperial fold. Kruger fled to Europe in 1900.

Paul Kruger in later life.

SOUTH AFRICA in the 20th CENTURY — 1900s

WHAT'S NEW IN 1904

- **Russia:** Trans-Siberian railway completed.
- **UK:** The submarine makes its inaugural underwater voyage – from Portsmouth to the Isle of Wight.
- **Rolls-Royce** motor company founded.
- The word **hangover** is added to the English language.
- **US:** Tea-bags go on sale for first time.
- **US:** The first newspaper colour photo appears, in The Daily Illustrated Mirror.
- **Henry Ford** breaks the world land speed record with a run of 146 km/h.
- **US:** Maryland prohibits blacks from voting.

FASHIONS FOR THE FEW

For the more privileged woman, the Edwardian era is an age of extravagant elegance, fashions taking much of their inspiration from the Art Nouveau movement and its emphasis on organic, flowing lines. Her dress is voluminous, sweeping the ground, girded about with frills, flounces and trimmings; indoor outfits are of opulent silks, chiffons, voiles, laces, muslins, crepes de chine worn over whalebone stays and acres of taffeta petticoat; street wear tends to be of less flamboyant cut, velvet and linen the favoured materials; necklines remain modestly high by day but plunge to surprisingly sexy depths in the soft ambience of a candlelit evening.

Accessories – the word was coined in 1901 – are many and imaginative: spacious reticules, a parasol to keep the harsh African sun away from delicate skin; muffs in the winter and kid gloves for all other times; ostrich feathers everywhere, embellishing fans, headbands, cloaks, boas and, of course, hats. These last are wide, high and handsome affairs topped with feathers, flowers, even fruit.

BOERS TAKE THE WAR TO AMERICA

Circus impresario Frank Fillis takes his spectacular Boer War Show to the United States; his cast includes former generals Piet Cronjé and Ben Viljoen and what are billed as '1,000 veterans' of the battles. The entertaining pageant tours American cities – including St Louis, which is hosting the Great World Fair – enacting dramatic scenes from a conflict still fresh in most people's memories. Cronjé, who besieged Mafeking and later surrendered to the British at Paardeberg, returns to South Africa a bitter and lonely man. Viljoen, victor of the Elandslaagte, stays on to take out US citizenship. He also writes two books; becomes involved in Mexican revolutionary politics; serves as military adviser to Francisco Madero, who will overthrow the dictator Porfirio Diaz in 1911; seeks (but fails) to establish an Afrikaner settlement in Mexico, and, in an attempt to broker a peace treaty between the government and the Yaqui Indians of Sonora, becomes the first white man ever to enter the Yaqui stronghold.

CHINESE 'INVASION' OF THE RAND

During the year large numbers of Chinese begin to arrive on the Witwatersrand. Known as the 'Celestials', they are Lord Milner's answer to the crippling shortage of labour – African workers, scattered by the winds of war, have been slow to return to the mines and the country desperately needs the income from gold production.

The Chinese presence triggers bitter controversy. Locally, wild (and largely unfounded) rumours of crime and banditry circulate within the white community. In Britain, the government is accused of encouraging slavery and brutality. Indeed the 1906 British general election will be fought on the issue. Thereafter, the Chinese of the Transvaal are progressively repatriated, the last leaving South Africa's shores in 1910.

ARTS AND ENTERTAINMENT

- Puccini's opera *Madama Butterfly* premieres in Milan, Italy.
- James Barrie's *Peter Pan – or The Boy Who Wouldn't Grow Up* is the talking point of the London theatre season.
- Dublin's famed Abbey Theatre opens.

HIT SONGS
- After the Ball
- Bill Bailey Won't You Please Come Home
- Land of Hope and Glory (Edward Elgar)
- Give My Regards to Broadway

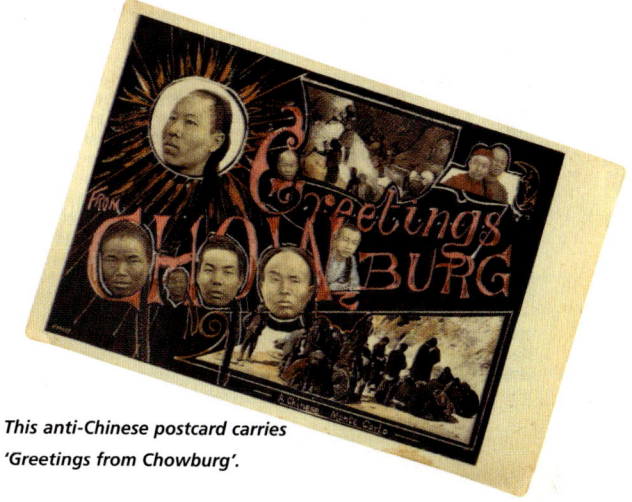

This anti-Chinese postcard carries 'Greetings from Chowburg'.

SOUTH AFRICA in the 20th CENTURY

Hunger stalks the Herero people.

German settlers in action against the Hereros.

HEREROS IN BLOODY REBELLION

The Herero people of German South West Africa rise in revolt against their colonial rulers, and in so doing trigger one of the most horrific chapters in the annals of southern Africa. The rebellion will last almost four years, lead to the loss of many German lives and in the end, after 88 bloody engagements, to the extermination of three-quarters of the Herero nation.

1905

REPORT A BLUEPRINT FOR DISASTER

Sir Godfrey Lagden, chairman of the Inter-Colonial South African Native Affairs Commission (SANAC), produces his crucial report on 'native policy' – a document that will prove disastrous for future race relations. Based on the assumption that white people are of 'superior intellect', it recommends (among many other things) the formal separation of races and the creation of reserves for the black groups. Future generations of white politicians will use the report to justify a growing arsenal of apartheid-type laws.

MASSIVE DIAMOND DISCOVERED

The world's largest diamond is found at the Premier mine near Pretoria. Named the Cullinan after mine-owner Patrick Cullinan, it weighs a massive 3,025 carats, measures 100 millimetres across and is believed to be just part of a much larger stone. The diamond is bought by the Transvaal government, presented to England's King Edward VII on his birthday in 1907 and later cut into 96 brilliants, seven gems, the 530-carat Star of Africa and the 317-carat Lesser Star of Africa. The latter two will rank among the best-known elements of the crown jewels.

SMOKERS CHANGE THEIR HABITS

The United Tobacco Companies (UTC) become South Africa's leading and most modern cigarette manufacturing enterprise when they open a factory in Cape Town's Kloof Street. The plant is electrically driven, power-cleaned with compressed air and incorporates dust-removal appliances as well as rolling machines. Other new factories soon make their appearance in Johannesburg and elsewhere – all of which has

BORN
International: Actor Cary Grant (birth-name Archibald Leach); band-leader Glenn Miller; jazzman Count Basie; crooner Bing Crosby; authors Graham Greene and Christopher Isherwood; photographer Cecil Beaton; actor and swimmer Johnny Weissmuller, the screen's first Tarzan.

DIED
International: Explorer Henry Morton Stanley of 'Dr Livingstone, I presume' fame; Russian dramatist Anton Chekhov (his play *The Cherry Orchard* premieres in Moscow during the year); Theodor Herzl, founder of modern Zionism; composer Antonín Dvořák.

The Star of Africa.

Early Springbok cigarettes.

SOUTH AFRICA in the 20th CENTURY 1900s

a profound effect on both growers and consumers. Farmers can now sell their crops, for cash, direct to the manufacturer, and are encouraged to cultivate cigarette tobacco (hitherto imported; local producers have catered exclusively for the pipe and snuff markets); cigarettes become cheaper, and a lot more popular.

FEATHERS MAKE FORTUNES FOR LOCALS

The Little Karoo town of Oudtshoorn and its surrounds continue to prosper from the world-wide, fashion-led boom in ostrich feathers;

Feathered fashion.

The hazards of country travel: drivers must also be mechanics.

local ostrich farmers and businessmen make fabulous fortunes and, some of them, build splendid mansions for themselves – multi-roomed, ostentatious 'feather palaces' of turrets, gables, marble floors and cast-iron trimmings. The larger farms sustain around 600 of the big birds; at the height of the bonanza a pound of prime white feathers fetches up to £110 on the London market.

DRIVERS UNDER DURESS

Motor cars are now a familiar if not yet common sight on city streets. Rules of the road, though, remain rudimentary: you can drive on either side unless approaching an oncoming vehicle, when you keep to the left; most urban centres have imposed a maximum speed limit of around 15 mph, some allow a high 20 mph. Cape Town will continue (until 1912) to restrict its drivers to 8 mph. In this year, in fact, the city's Charles Rorich becomes the first South African motorist to be fined for speeding. Country roads are still untarred, rough, pot-holed, with central ridges that can be a foot high, and a myriad farm gates make them, if not impassable, tedious to negotiate. Car tyres are small, unreliable, prone to punctures, their pressures 60 pounds per square inch. Outside the cities, a blacksmith will fix damaged springs or a broken axle, but for the rest the driver has to be his own mechanic. Petrol stations are a rarity: one still buys fuel, for about £1 10s. 0d a drum, from general dealers.

WHAT'S NEW IN 1905

- **Gastronomy:** The pizza, Italy's budget meal, makes its US debut, at Lombardi's restaurant in New York.
- **IQ** (intelligence quotient) tests are devised, in France.
- First **Rotary Club** meets, in Chicago.
- **Russia:** Leon Trotsky presides over the first soviet, or worker's council of delegates, in St Petersburg.
- **Britain:** Aspirin is introduced to the market.
- The words **depression** and **smog** (a mix of smoke and fog) are added to the language.
- The **Simplon tunnel** (through the Alps) opens.

BORN
International: Screen stars Greta Garbo, Bob Hope and Henry Fonda; writer and philosopher Jean-Paul Sartre; eccentric tycoon Howard Hughes; fashion guru Christian Dior.
South Africa: Writers Herman Charles Bosman and Joy Packer; anti-apartheid campaigner Helen Joseph.

DIED
French fantasy writer Jules Verne; actor Sir Henry Irving; most of Russia's 200,000-strong army in Manchuria, in battle with Japanese; the Russian navy also suffers heavy losses: 35 of 38 ships are sunk or seriously damaged by the Japanese fleet.

SOUTH AFRICA in the 20th CENTURY
The Hundreds

KOCH WINS NOBEL PRIZE

The world's leading bacteriologist, Robert Koch, is awarded the Nobel prize for medicine for identifying (in 1882) the tuberculosis bacillus. He is also famed for his pioneering work on cholera, anthrax, sleeping sickness and bubonic plague.

RUSSIAN TZAR FACES REVOLT

Popular unrest forces the Russian Tzar to promise a series of reforms, most notably the establishment of a *duma* (parliament) – although he later reverses his decision. Earlier (in January), 500 striking workers were shot by Imperial troops. In the port of Odessa, mutiny spreads through the Black Sea fleet after sailors raise the red flag of rebellion aboard the battleship *Potemkin*; protesters also take to the streets of St Petersburg, many to be cut down by charging Cossacks. A revolt in Moscow is also crushed.

TRENDS

The look: The Gibson Girl's cupid-bow mouth, sultry eyes and carelessly high-piled hair.
The dance: The Cakewalk.
For lady cyclists: Knickerbockers.
For enjoying city spaces: Roller skates.

BORN

International: Irish playwright Samuel Beckett; Greek shipping tycoon Aristotle Onassis. *South Africa:* Artist Walter Battiss; actor André Huguenet; writer Laurens van der Post.

PASSING OF A PIONEER

John Household.

Among those who die during the year is John Goodman Household, the South African aviation pioneer. Three decades ago Household built a primitive glider, which he launched from the slopes of Karkloof, near Howick in Natal. He remained airborne for some 230 metres – a remarkable feat which, inexplicably, failed to arouse any interest at the time. Other deaths recorded at home and abroad are those of financier Alfred Beit; Jotello Soga, first South African-born veterinary surgeon (he qualified, in Edinburgh, in 1886); French artist Paul Cézanne and Norwegian playwright Henrik Ibsen.

1906

BAMBATHA LEADS ZULU REVOLT

Zulu tribesmen rise in rebellion after Bambatha, a minor chieftain, refuses to pay the government's hut-tax – a levy that is forcing villagers to work on the coal and gold mines and on white farms in order to raise the money.

The death in February of a white farmer and two policemen provides the actual trigger for violence. Bambatha flees to the Nkandla forests from where, with the help of other chiefs, he wages a 'war of liberation' for six weeks before his guerrillas are ambushed at Mome Gorge. He and more than 500 of his warriors die in the action; Bambatha's severed head is carried through the countryside by the victors. The rebellion, however, spreads to other parts of the colony and troops, despite savage reprisals, manage to restore order only when paramount chief Dinuzulu, though innocent of conspiracy, is arrested. Dinuzulu is later tried, convicted and sentenced to four years in prison. Altogether, some 3,000 Zulu lose their lives in the strife.

Zulu chief Dinuzulu.

Collecting hut tax: trigger for Zulu unrest.

Colonial troops burning rebel villages during the Bambatha rebellion.

SOUTH AFRICA in the 20th CENTURY 1900s

Percy Sherwell.

Sir Pelham 'Plum' Warner.

SOUTH AFRICAN CRICKET COMES OF AGE ...

The Wanderers, Johannesburg. South African cricketers record their finest victory to date in the first of five Tests against Sir Pelham 'Plum' Warner's MCC (English) tourists. Batting poorly in the first innings and needing 258 runs to win the match, the home side lose their first six wickets for just 104, but a splendid 121-run partnership between Gordon White and Dave Nourse bring them within striking distance of the target, a prospect that suddenly dims with the loss of three quick wickets. But Nourse and last-man-in Percy Sherwell, the South African captain, manage to hold on, precariously, and scramble the last of the 45 runs needed to win. Sherwell later recalls 'an outburst of cheering which has never been equalled before or since on the Wanderers'. Nourse scores a gutsy 93, for which the crowd collect a £111 'plate'. Other heroes of the triumph are Aubrey Faulkner, Albert Vogler, Reginald Schwarz and B.J. Snooke.

... AND RUGBY PLAYERS TRIUMPH

The national rugby squad embarks on its first-ever overseas tour – to Britain. And it is an historic trip, one which establishes South Africa as a true rugby-playing country: led by the legendary Paul Roos, the colonials trounce the opposition in all but two of the 29 matches. They win two of the four Tests, draw one and lose one, scoring a total of 608 points and conceding just 84.

It is on this inaugural tour, too, that the South Africans adopt the Springbok as their national emblem. Dressing-room debate came up with several names (including, of all things, the 'Mimosas'), but Roos himself finally settles the argument, and the animal duly appears as a pocket-badge on the green-and-gold blazer.

JOHANNESBURG'S NEW OASIS OF COMFORT

Johannesburg's new Carlton Hotel opens its doors to set new standards in luxury and hospitality. The 300-bedroom complex offers everything the heart of the hedonist can wish for: the finest of food in its oak-panelled Grill Room, an oyster bar, a Smoke Room panelled in pigskin, tea-dances in its glass-roofed Palm Court, a ballroom that will host the grandest of social occasions, Turkish baths, a hairdressing salon, thick pile carpets everywhere. Over the following half-century many of the world's rich and famous, including royalty, are to feature on its guest-list. Prices range from a 25/- daily inclusive tariff to 35/- for a three-room suite; an ordinary Turkish bath costs 7/6, one with 'scientific massage' a hefty 21/-.

Luxury on offer.

MASSIVE QUAKE DESTROYS SAN FRANCISCO

18 April. A cataclysmic three-minute early-morning earthquake devastates the city of San Francisco, killing more than a thousand people and rendering two-thirds of the city's population homeless. Many buildings collapse during the initial shock; much else is destroyed by the huge fires that follow.

WHAT'S NEW IN 1906

- William Kellogg invents **cornflakes**, in the US.
- The letters **SOS** become the international Morse code distress signal, in Berlin.
- **In the home:** The first electric washing machine appears on the market, in the US.
- **Shipping:** The Lusitania, the world's biggest passenger liner, is launched in Glasgow, Scotland.
- The phrase **hot dog** is introduced to the language.

> 'Everyone has the right to go to hell in his own way.'
> Colonial secretary Lord Elgin, commenting on the Transvaal government's new Pass Law restricting the free movement of Indians.

SOUTH AFRICA in the 20th CENTURY

1907

GANDHI FIGHTS PASS LAW

Mohandas Gandhi, campaigner for Indian rights in South Africa, puts his refined philosophy of *satyagraha*, loosely translated as 'passive resistance' (it more correctly means 'keeping firmly to the truth'), to practical test when he urges his followers to disobey the Transvaal's new Pass Law. Among other things, this measure requires all Asians to carry a registration document bearing their thumbprint. Gandhi rejects the law, and during the next few months more than 3,000 Indians and Chinese burn their registration books.

Gandhi is eventually sent to jail, but his presence behind bars proves – as it will so many times in the future – more of an embarrassment to the authorities than his freedom, and after secret meetings with Transvaal colonial secretary Jan Smuts a compromise is reached on the issue.

Lawyer and activist Mohandas Gandhi (seated centre), later to be known as 'the Mahatma', with some of his associates.

THE RISE AND FALL OF A FIGHTER

Andrew Jeptha, the young coloured boxer from the slums of Cape Town, fights his way to the top ranks when he defeats British welterweight champion Curley Watson. But Jeptha's story is destined to end in tragedy: he is soon forced into a punishingly demanding schedule of fights, which tire his body and damage his eyes. He will eventually return to the Cape where, poverty-stricken and blind, he will die.

SELF-GOVERNMENT FOR BOER COLONIES

The movement for responsible government in the former Boer republics culminates in victory for Het Volk in the Transvaal colony. The party, founded by generals Louis Botha and Jan Smuts in 1905, fights the election on two main issues: the unpopular presence of Chinese labourers on the mines, and British 'domination' of post-war South Africa and especially its assault on Afrikaner culture – Lord Milner, for example, launched a strong bid to attract settlers from Britain (the campaign failed) and to 'anglicize' education ('Dutch should only be used to teach English, and English to teach anything else', he stated).

Het Volk wins 37 of the 69 seats in the Transvaal legislative assembly. Its counterpart in the Orange River Colony, the Orangia-Unie, also sweeps to victory. Both parties have opened their doors to English-speakers; reconciliation between South Africa's two politically dominant groups, and between Afrikanerdom and Britain, is almost complete. 'What we now need', says Smuts, 'is a supreme national authority to give expression to the national will of South Africa.' By that he means the will of the white tribes.

'B-P' LAUNCHES BOY SCOUT MOVEMENT

Robert Baden-Powell, hero of the Mafeking siege and newly promoted to the rank of major-general in the British Army, founds the Boy Scout Association. The scheme was inspired by his experiences as commander of the Mafeking garrison, where he employed young boys as military 'runners'. Later, he states publicly that 'we ought really not to think too much of any boy, even though a cricketer and footballer, unless he can aim and shoot, and will therefore be useful as a soldier'.

JOCK BECOMES A BESTSELLER

Among the most popular books published during the year is Sir Percy FitzPatrick's *Jock of the Bushveldt*. This delightful work recalls the author's experiences as a transport rider plying his rugged way between the goldfields of Barberton and the Indian Ocean port of Delagoa Bay, journeys he undertook with his terrier dog Jock – the runt of the litter who became the bravest of hunters and the most resourceful of companions. FitzPatrick originally told the stories to his children, but was eventually persuaded to publish them by his friend Rudyard Kipling. The book is an immediate bestseller.

Jock, bravest of dogs.

SOUTH AFRICA in the 20th CENTURY

ADVANCES ON HEALTH FRONT

Medical science takes two big steps forward with the introduction of blood transfusions (different blood groups were first recognized, and classified, in 1901) and chemotherapy – in Germany, for the treatment of venereal disease. The Salvation Army launches the world's first suicide counselling service, in the US.

THE WRITTEN WORD

◆ Rudyard Kipling, author of Empire and a familiar visitor to the Cape, becomes the first Briton to win the Nobel Prize for literature.
◆ Books published during the year include Joseph Conrad's *The Secret Agent*.
◆ Among new plays are J.M. Synge's *The Playboy of the Western World* and G.B. Shaw's *Major Barbara*.

WHAT'S NEW IN 1908

◆ *Invented:* Paper cups (in the US) and cellophane (by a Swiss chemist).
◆ *Aviation:* Henri Farman pilots the first passenger aeroplane, in France.
◆ *US politics:* Oklahoma is annexed to become the 46th state of the Union.
◆ *Motoring:* Buick and Oldsmobile merge to form General Motors, in the US.
◆ *Religion:* The Gideon company launches a drive to leave a Bible in every hotel room.
◆ *Drinking:* Georgia and North Carolina ban alcohol.
◆ *Wedding:* Winston Churchill, Britain's rising young politician and president of the Board of Trade, marries Clementine Hozier.
◆ *Votes for women:* The British suffragette movement continues to gain impetus in the UK; 200,000 women gather to protest the denial of their political rights.

1908

CONVENTION BEGINS CHARTING THE FUTURE

Durban, 12 October. White delegates from the Cape, Transvaal, Orange River Colony and Natal meet as the National Convention to deliberate the creation of a united South Africa.

One of the Convention's chief tasks is to reconcile the racial views of the relatively liberal Cape politicians with those of the Transvaal hard-liners (supported by the Orange River and Natal representatives), who have made it clear they will under no circumstances accept a black vote.

In due course a compromise, proposed by Jan Smuts and the Cape's John X. Merriman, is adopted: each colony will retain its existing franchise system. Only the Cape and, to a very minor extent, Natal have extended voting rights to people of colour.

WALKER SPRINTS TO VICTORY

South Africa officially takes part in the Olympic Games for the first time when a team of 14 men travels to London's splendid new White City stadium. Among them is Reggie Walker, who was overlooked by the selectors. His supporters rallied around to raise the funds to send him over – a gesture well rewarded when he streaks to victory in the 100 metres (time: 10.8 seconds). The real drama of the Games, however, is played out in the marathon. Italian Dorando Pietri, literally on his last legs, is the first to stagger into the stadium. He collapses four times on the final lap but, inspired by the roaring crowd, manages to pick himself up each time to reach the finish line – only to be disqualified: track officials helped him over the last few metres. The US runner John Hayes, second across the line, is awarded the gold (time: 2 hours, 55 minutes, 18 seconds). South African Charles Hefferon takes the silver.

Champion Reggie Walker.

BELGIUM TAKES OVER THE CONGO

The Congo Free State, ruled by King Leopold II as a private fiefdom since 1884, is sold to his government for £5 million to become the Belgian Congo. Leopold's personal tenure over the mineral-rich territory has been blighted by brutality, and he is forced to relinquish control when European states learn the full extent of the atrocities his administration has committed over the years.

INSTANT SUCCESS FOR TWO NEW BOOKS

◆ Special among the year's new titles is Kenneth Grahame's *The Wind in the Willows*, a delightful children's tale of the English countryside and its animals.
◆ During the year, too, unknown Canadian author Lucy Maud Montgomery publishes her first novel, *Anne of Green Gables*, the story of a headstrong young orphan girl. The manuscript was turned down by a number of other publishers.

SOUTH AFRICA in the 20th CENTURY

GIANT METEORITE HITS EARTH

30 June. The largest meteorite in modern times crashes to earth in the Tungusta area, in the wastes of northern Russia. The massive explosion devastates the countryside for 30 miles on all sides. The force of the impact is detected all around the world.

'TIN LIZZY' HITS THE ROAD

Henry Ford takes a giant step towards his ambition to create a vehicle that everyone can afford – 'a motor car for the great multitude' – when the first of his Model Ts rolls off his Detroit production line. Known as the 'Tin Lizzy', the Model T is a tough, no-nonsense roadster made largely of vanadium steel and distinguished by its squarish brass radiator. New mass-production techniques, including moving assembly lines, keep costs down; the cars – available only in black for the time being (black enamel dries quickly) – are priced at $900 apiece.

SPORT: GRACE BOWS OUT, JOHNSON BECOMES CHAMPION

◆ The great English cricketer W.G. Grace finally retires from the first-class game – at the age of 59. Grace made his debut, for the Gentlemen of England against the Players, in 1864 at the age of 16, went on to represent Gloucester and, during his unbroken 44-year career, scored 54,896 runs (including 126 centuries) and took 2,876 wickets.

◆ Jack Johnson defeats Canadian Tommy Burns to become the first black boxer to wear the world heavyweight crown. Burns takes so savage a beating that police have to intervene, in the 14th round, to stop the bout.

BORN
International: Actress Bette Davis; 'James Bond' creator Ian Fleming.
South Africa: Harry Oppenheimer, son of Sir Ernest Oppenheimer, founder of Anglo American Corporation.

1909

'FLYING MATCHBOX' TAKES TO THE AIR

Albert Kimmerling, a Frenchman, pilots his 'Flying Matchbox' – a flimsy 50-horsepower Voisin aircraft – six metres above the countryside near East London to complete the first-ever controlled powered flight to be recorded in South Africa. Three months later a Thomas Thornton pays Kimmerling £100 to become the country's inaugural air passenger, joining the pilot on his flight from the top of Sydenham Hill near Johannesburg. Shortly afterwards Miss Julia Stansfield, social editor of the *Rand Daily Mail*, steps

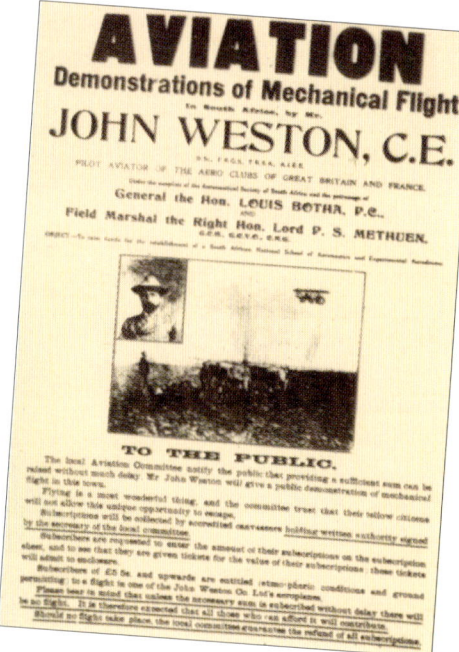

aboard and into history as 'the first lady to leave South Africa's soil in an aeroplane amid the plaudits of assembled thousands'.

Later in the year local aviation pioneer John Weston takes his wholly South African plane – he built it in Brandfort, in 1909, and flew it in France – to the air over Kimberley. Afterwards his elated female passenger, pantomime actress Cessie Leonard, recalls 'a mighty rushing wind, a feeling of entire mental detachment from everything mundane – that is what I felt'.

Meanwhile, Louis Bleriot, another Frenchman, becomes the first pilot to fly the English Channel when he takes off from Sangatte, close to Calais, and lands his fragile, 20-kilogram wooden monoplane on a field near Dover Castle. The flight takes 43 minutes.

Kimmerling's 'Matchbox' soars above Orange Grove, Johannesburg.

SOUTH AFRICA in the 20th CENTURY — 1900s

SOUTH AFRICA'S POLITICAL FUTURE MAPPED OUT

The British government accepts the recommendations of the National Convention in their entirety to pass the South Africa Act, despite strong protests from non-white groups and a powerful appeal by former Cape Prime Minister William Schreiner. An eight-man deputation to London in July fails in its bid to have the draft Act amended; Britain's measured and negative response, says delegate Abdullah Abdurahman, is 'the most hypocritical piece of humbug I have ever listened to'.

Schreiner: strong protest.

The Act gives legal framework to the union of the four South African colonies. This makes provision for, among other things, a 'Westminster system' of a sovereign, all-white central parliament comprising an upper chamber (Senate) and lower chamber (House of Assembly), and the recognition of English and Dutch as the country's official languages. A governor-general will represent the Crown.

In the interests of Boer-Briton reconciliation, the institutional spoils will be divided among Cape Town (legislative capital), Pretoria (administrative capital) and Bloemfontein (judicial capital). Natal, much of its white citizenry still passionately royalist in sentiment, gets nothing.

Blacks, coloureds and Asians have not been directly represented at the Convention. Those in the Transvaal, Orange River and Natal colonies will be denied voting rights; the Cape non-white franchise will remain, enshrined in an entrenched clause. Of great significance to the future is the weighting of the white rural vote: country constituencies will have 15 percent fewer voters than the norm; urban ones 15 per cent more. In due course this will ensure Afrikaner dominance at the polls.

CIVIL-RIGHTS BODY LAUNCHED

New York. A new organization to fight for the American black man's civil rights is launched at a city convention. The National Association for the Advancement of Coloured People (NAACP), founded by W.E.B. DuBois, holds its first meeting on 1 June.

Abdurahman: 'humbug'.

SONGS OF THE DAY
- Give My Regards to Broadway
- Shine On, Harvest Moon
- I Wonder Who's Kissing Her Now
- I Do Like to be Beside the Seaside
- Has Anyone Here Seen Kelly?
- Moonstruck

BORN
International: Jazzman Benny Goodman, actress Katherine Hepburn. *South Africa:* Artist Gregoire Boonzaier, long-distance runner Wally Hayward.

DIED
International: Native-American leader Geronimo, who had led his Apache people against US troops and settlers in New Mexico and Arizona; British poet, playwright and critic Algernon Swinburne. *South Africa:* Politician and publisher Jan Hendrik Hofmeyr, affectionately known as 'Onze Jan'.

WHAT'S NEW IN 1909

- **Products:** The electric toaster is introduced (US); bakelite, the first commercial plastic, is developed by Leo Baekeland (Belgium).
- **Naval base:** The US government makes plans to build a naval base at Pearl Harbor, in mid-Pacific, to deter possible Japanese attack.
- **Transport:** The first double-decker buses appear on city streets, in Britain.
- **Beatified:** Legendary French heroine Joan of Arc, known as the Maid of Orleans, is beatified in Rome, 478 years after her capture and execution by the English.
- **Medical breakthrough:** Biologist Alexis Carrel performs the first organ transplant, from one animal to another, in France.
- The world's most prolific recorded mass murderer, **Madame Popova**, is arrested and charged with 300 individual killings, in Russia.
- The word **gene**, the basic unit of heredity, is added to the English vocabulary.

Heroine Joan.

1910s

Smuts calls for volunteers, during the Great War, 1915.

DIED
1910: King Edward VII; is succeeded by George V.
1918: Millions around the world in the great 'flu epidemic; one third of the Reef's black miners die.
1919: South African premier Louis Botha; is succeeded by Jan Smuts.

UNITED
1910: Cape, Natal, Transvaal and Orange Free State, to form the Union of SA.

ESTABLISHED
1910: The SA Railways & Harbours administration. Wireless telegraphy station, Durban. SA College of Music, Cape Town.
1912: SA Native National Congress (SANNC, later ANC). SA Land Bank. *SA Ladies' Pictorial* magazine.
1913: *African Mirror* newsreel. National Botanical Gardens, at Kirstenbosch, Cape Town.
1915: Nasionale Pers, in Cape Town; *Die Burger* becomes National party mouthpiece.
1916: SA Native College (later Fort Hare University). *Huisgenoot* magazine.
1917: Anglo American Corporation.
1918: Afrikaner Broederbond. Universities of Cape Town, Stellenbosch and South Africa constituted.
1919: National Socialist (Nazi) party in Germany.

CONQUERED
1911: The South Pole, by Roald Amundsen.
1912: The Olympic marathon (in Stockholm) by SA runners.
1919: The Atlantic Ocean, by British aviators Alcock and Brown.

SUNK
1912: The liner SS *Titanic*, on her maiden voyage; 1,513 drown.

DESTROYED
1910: Millions of head of cattle in southern Africa, by East Coast fever.

FIRST
1910: Hollywood film (D.W. Griffith's *In Old California*).
1911: Air mail transported in SA, between Kenilworth and Muizenberg. Lipton Cup yacht race.
1914: Charlie Chaplin films.

OPENED
1915: The Panama Canal.

THE GREAT WAR
1914: Europe's armies march into battle. SA declares war on Germany, provoking a rebellion by leading Boer generals; the uprising is crushed.
1915: SA invades German South West Africa; Germans surrender. Union government raises volunteer force for service in Europe. Cape Coloured Corps formed.
1916: SA Brigade virtually annihilated at battle for Delville Wood, France. Union expeditionary force, under Smuts, begins long campaign against Germans in East Africa.
1917: USA declares war on Germany.
1918: Armistice signed in November; Germans in East Africa surrender two weeks later. US president Wilson proposes his 'Fourteen Points', paving way to formation of League of Nations.

OVERTHROWN
1917: Russia's Tzarist regime, in a workers' revolution led by Lenin; Tzar Nicholas II and family later executed.

NEGOTIATED
1919: The Treaty of Versailles, at Paris peace conference. Botha and Smuts attend; the SANNC sends a delegation.

GRANTED
1919: To the Union of SA: an international mandate to govern South West Africa.

POLITICS AND PROTEST
1910: Louis Botha forms first Union government.
1911: Botha and Smuts form the South African Party. Mines and Works Act passed; blacks excluded from most skilled jobs.
1913: Natives Land Act passed. Black women in Orange Free State choose jail rather than carry passes. Gandhi launches 'passive resistance' campaign in Natal; Indians march en masse into Transvaal.
1914: Barry Hertzog forms National Party.

Welcoming the Union, 1910.

SOUTH AFRICA in the 20th CENTURY **1910s**

Cape Town's Adderley Street in festive mood.

1910

MUTED CELEBRATIONS WELCOME UNION

31 May. 'Glorious weather ushered in Union Day in the capital,' reports Johannesburg's newspaper *The Star*. '[Pretoria] ... was astir early... flags and bunting draped the chief stores and buildings.'

In truth, though, the celebrations of white South Africa's move to unity are more muted than was expected, in deference to the Royal bereavement: King Edward VII had died suddenly, on 6 May. The new Union's first general election is held on 15 September. General Louis Botha's South African Nationalist Party gains a 67-59 parliamentary majority over L.S. Jameson's Unionists. Shortly afterwards the Duke of Connaught opens the first Union parliament.

The Duke of Connaught.

Britannia launches the new ship of state: the cover of the Cape Times supplement on Union day.

Ironically, General Botha himself is defeated in the largely English-speaking Pretoria East constituency by Sir Percy FitzPatrick (this despite all the good intentions to avoid a straight Boer-Briton contest). Botha later enters parliament through the back door, sneaking in via a by-election to take office as the Union's first prime minister.

Paris Sets the Style

Ladies' fashions during the early years of the decade are dictated by Paris, and by the great beauties of stage and high society. Waists are still small, sleeves puffed at the shoulder, skirts hip-hugging but widening lower down; one popular outfit is the long, tightly fitting jacket; 'merry-widow' hats are wide-brimmed, gorgeously trimmed with ostrich plumes and sometimes flowers.

Bustlines at the beginning of the century were low, but these rise to give women a prouder silhouette; hemlines also rise (in 1908), though only to the ankle; the narrowest of hobble skirts come into fashion around 1910, condemning their wearers to the most awkward of gaits.

Around this time, too, the master Parisian couturier Paul Poiret introduces his 'lampshade' tunic, and, taking his inspiration from the wonderful colours and oriental settings of the Ballet Russe, creates (among much else) the harem skirt and the minaret skirt, using bright and beautiful prints. For evening wear, he chooses the glittering richness of lamé.

Poiret also revolutionizes under garments, waging a largely successful war against the suffocating corsets and stays (and thus the freakishly tiny waists) of the time. Lighter foundation wear comes into vogue, the looser, freer look giving birth to what becomes derisively known – among the conservatives – as 'the debutante slouch'.

Then, in 1912, the dressmaker Madeleine Vionet launches a softly enveloping fashion which emphasizes line and cut rather than trimming, a stylistic priority that has endured ever since.

SOUTH AFRICA in the 20th CENTURY 1910s

Some of the 'bioscope' equipment on sale in South Africa.

THE CINEMA TAKES OFF

'Bioscope fever' takes firm hold of the South African paying public. Last year the impresario Frederick Mouillot launched his short-lived chain of 'electric theatres' around the country; these were a motley collection of auditoriums in which vaudeville featured as prominently as the silver screen. These are South Africa's first permanent cinemas.

Others quickly follow, most notably Wolfram's grand 565-seat Bioscope, which opens in Cape Town in 1910 and is the first to employ a permanent pianist to accompany the film's action.

Wolfram also raises the quality of the entertainment. Up to now most of the films imported have been cheap and vulgar shorts, prompting anger among the socially conscious. One of them – showing the fight between the black boxing champion Jack Johnson and James Jeffries – is banned in July 1910 for fear of race riots.

Wolfram gives his audiences longer, better fictional features – such as *Nero*, or *The Burning of Rome*, and the hugely popular racecourse drama *The Trainer* – and a more sophisticated environment in which to enjoy them. Comfortable, even plush movie theatres soon replace the assortment of sordid little halls, warehouses and barns that have hitherto done duty. The great age of the 'picture palace' has arrived.

> 'Four spectres haunt the poor: old age, accident, sickness and unemployment. We are going to exorcise them.'
> *British chancellor of the exchequer David Lloyd George*

CRIPPEN CAUGHT BY WIRELESS

31 July, off the Canadian coast. British police officers arrest physician and suspected murderer Dr Hawley Crippen and his mistress, Ethel le Neve,

Crippen's mistress, Ethel le Neve, disguised as a boy.

aboard the passenger liner SS *Montrose* after wireless messages are exchanged between the ship's captain, Henry Kendall, and Scotland Yard, London. The fugitive couple appeared on the ship's passenger list as 'Mr Robinson and son'. This is the first time wireless has been used to bring a criminal to justice.

TANGO OFFENDS ELDERS

During the year a new dance, the Tango, becomes all the rage among the younger set the world over for its sensuality and the close bodily contact it prescribes. Older people condemn the dance, which originated in South America, as indecent and immoral.

Professor and Mrs Sparman demonstrate the sensational Tango.

SOUTH AFRICA in the 20th CENTURY
Nineteen Tens

Agnes Baden-Powell (centre) and some of her lieutenants.

'The Natives Land Act breaks our people and puts them back in the rearing of their stock and ruins what they term their bank. It causes our people to be derelict and helpless. There is winter in the Act. In winter the trees are stripped and leafless ....'
T.M. Dambuuzu, a leader of the SA Native National Congress

GIRL GUIDES MAKE DEBUT
London. Mafeking hero General Robert Baden-Powell and his sister Agnes found the Girl Guides movement on 31 May. The Guides, female counterpart of the Boy Scouts conceived and launched by Baden-Powell three years earlier, have their own uniform. Training focuses on feminine skills (cookery, mothercraft, needlework) and, like the Scouts, on self-discipline, clean living and the capacity to 'keep good homes and bring up good children'. South Africa's first Guide troop is launched, in Johannesburg, in 1910.

JUDGE IS ELEVATED TO PEERAGE
Mr Justice Johann de Villiers, president of the National Convention that prepared the way for Union, is created a baron of the British realm. De Villiers, 68, was appointed chief justice of the Cape Colony in 1873 (he held the post for a record 40 years), acted as peace-maker in the Transvaal war of 1880–81, later turning down offers to become president of both the Transvaal and Orange Free State. In 1896 he became a member of the Privy Council, the first colonial judge to achieve that status.

LAST WORD ON TWAIN
Among those who die during the year is American writer Mark Twain, author of *Adventures of Tom Sawyer* and *Adventures of Huckleberry Finn*. Twain (real name Samuel Langhorne Clemens) visited South Africa with his wife and daughter in 1896, recounting his experiences in the book *Following the Equator*, published in the British edition as *More Tramps Abroad*. His many, often wry descriptions included that of the Cape's house of assembly, of which he wrote: 'They [the members] quarrelled in two languages... and agreed in none.' He was especially harsh on Dr L.S Jameson and his raid into the Transvaal.

PIONEERS CHALLENGE THE POLES
There are two historic assaults on the polar regions during the year. US driver Oscar Tamm crossed the Arctic region by automobile, and British explorer Captain Robert Falcon Scott boarded the vessel *Terra Nova* to begin his attempt on Antarctica.

The infant Hollywood.

HOLLYWOOD IS BORN
Film-maker D.W. Griffith sets Hollywood on its way to becoming the capital of the motion-picture industry when he establishes a studio in the sleepy little village of Hollywood (population 4,000, and recently annexed as a suburb of the city of Los Angeles) for the production of his fiml *In Old California*.

Lord de Villiers in his 15-hp Napier.

SOUTH AFRICA in the 20th CENTURY 1910s

WHAT'S NEW IN 1910

- **Germany:** *Rayon (artificial silk) stockings.*
- **Thomas Edison's** *first, experimental talking movies.*
- **Radium,** *isolated by Marie Curie.*
- **France:** *The seaplane takes off on its maiden flight.*
- **Father's Day** *is first celebrated, in the US.*

Physicist Curie.

BORN
International: Mother Theresa; ocean explorer Jacques Cousteau.
South Africa: Govan Mbeki, a future leader of the liberation movement; rugby king Danie Craven; artist Gerard Bhengu.

1911

PARLIAMENT PASSES RACE LAWS

The new Union parliament loses no time in enacting statutes that further divide the races. Laws passed include the Black Labour Regulation Act, which criminalizes the breaking of a workplace contract; the Dutch Reformed Churches Union Act, which denies black people full membership of the Church; and the far-reaching Mines and Works Act.

This last, a refinement of the law introduced seven years earlier by the British administration in the Transvaal, excludes blacks from a wide range of skilled jobs within the mining industry, and on the railways, on the grounds of 'competency'. It will become the cornerstone of job reservation.

Black leader Pixley ka Isaka Seme, condemning the conflicts that are dividing the African people, makes an impassioned plea for unity in the face of this legislative onslaught. 'The demon of racialism must be buried and forgotten,' he says. 'It has shed among us sufficient blood. We are one people. These divisions, these jealousies, are the cause of all our woes and of our backwardness and ignorance today.'

Seme: 'Demon of racialism'.

Amputee Nesbitt.

MURROGH'S LONG ROAD TO AVALON

A tale of lifelong courage and fortitude begins when 13-year-old Murrogh Nesbitt, of Jagersfontein, has both legs amputated after a railway accident at the local diamond mine. The boy grows up to become a notable wheelchair athlete, to found a rehabilitation centre (near Tulbagh in the Cape) and to describe his trauma and spiritual recovery in a moving book, *The Road to Avalon*.

GENERALS GET TOGETHER

Prime Minister General Louis Botha joins forces with General Jan Smuts to form the South African Party (SAP). The new party finds little backing among either die-hard Afrikaners or British loyalists but draws substantial support from those who favour reconciliation between the two language groups – and who resent British imperial meddling. In short, the SAP stands for a broad 'South Africanism' among white people.

LOCAL FILM INDUSTRY MAKES A START

The first full-length feature film to be made in South Africa – a melodrama, produced by the Springbok Film Company, about a massive diamond – is shown to theatre audiences over the Christmas period. Entitled *The Star of the South*, it receives poor notices, critics describing it as 'amateurish'.

MAIL DELIVERED BY AIR

27 December. Evelyn Driver, piloting his Bleriot monoplane, completes South Africa's first airmail flight when he carries 729 specially designed postcards (now valuable collector's items) from

Taking the first aerial post aboard.

SOUTH AFRICA in the 20th CENTURY
Nineteen Tens

One of the first airmail postcards.

Scott's party, using man-pulled sledges, disappears into the snowy wastes in November, and is not heard from again. It is later revealed that it did indeed reach the Pole, but a full month after Amundsen, and had perished on the return journey.

The Norwegian puts his success down to his well-trained team of tough, speedy husky dogs.

BOOKS OF THE YEAR
- G.K. Chesterton's *The Innocence of Father Brown*
- D.H. Lawrence's *The White Peacock*
- Edgar Wallace's *Sanders of the River*
- James Barrie's *Peter Pan*
- Olive Schreiner's *Women and Labour*, a feminist landmark.

BORN
International: Actor and politician Ronald Reagan; actress-comedienne Lucille Ball; playwright Tennessee Williams; racing driver Juan Fangio; author William Golding.
South African: Churchman and Afrikaner nationalist Stephanus du Toit; artist Alexis Preller.

WHAT'S NEW IN 1911

◆ **Motoring:** Chevrolet Motor Car Company founded in Detroit, USA.
◆ **Aviation:** An Italian pilot of a Bleriot aeroplane mounts the first air raid when he drops bombs on Turkish troops in Libya.
◆ The lost **Inca city** of Machu Picchu, hidden in the Peruvian mountains for 500 years, is discovered.
◆ **Paris:** Leonardo da Vinci's masterpiece, the *Mona Lisa*, is stolen from the Louvre.
◆ England's **King George V** is crowned at Westminster Abbey; eldest son Prince Edward is invested as Prince of Wales shortly afterwards.
◆ The word **jinx** is added to the English language.

The Mona Lisa.

Kenilworth racecourse to Muizenberg near Cape Town. The 12.8-kilometre journey takes seven and a half minutes. Driver, an experienced 'instinctive navigator', previously served with Britain's trail-blazing Royal Mail Aerial Service.

THE PASSING OF A PATHFINDER
Nursing pioneer Henrietta Stockdale dies during the year at the age of 64. Stockdale, an Anglican nun, settled in Bloemfontein in 1874, later moving to Kimberley, where she worked among the people of the rugged diggers' camps before launching a wide-ranging training programme, and establishing a maternity home and a nursing school. It was largely due to her efforts that, in

Nursing pioneer Stockdale.

1891, the Cape colonial parliament formally recognized nursing as a profession, setting a precedent that other countries were soon to follow.

NORWEGIAN GAINS POLE POSITION
Captain Robert Scott fails in his bid to be the first to reach the South Pole: he is beaten to the post by Norwegian Roald Amundsen.

1912
BLACK SOUTH AFRICANS UNITE
On 8 January some hundreds of black delegates from all parts of the country gather in Bloemfontein to form the South African Native National Congress (SANNC). They sing Tiyo Soga's moving hymn 'Lizalise Dinga Dingalako tixo We Nyaniso' (Fulfil Thy Promise, God of Truth) and are then addressed by the charismatic Pixley ka Isaka Seme, who condemns the Act of Union as an arrangement for whites only, one in which Africans can serve only as hewers of wood and drawers of water. The proposal to establish the SANNC is accepted enthusiastically, and unanimously.

SOUTH AFRICA in the 20th CENTURY 1910s

The conference then elects the Rev. John Dube as its first president. Dube, a churchman and teacher, received part of his training in the US, where he was influenced by the one-time slave and leading educationist Booker T. Washington (whose teachings, which accepted the separation of the races, are later to be rejected by the American civil rights movement). On his return from the USA Dube founded the influential Zulu-language newspaper *Ilanga Lase Natal* (in 1903).

John Dube (centre), leader of the later (1914) SANNC delegation to London. Flanking him are, from left to right: Walter Rubusana, Thomas Makipela, Sol Plaatjie and Saul Msane.

MIGHTY LINER SINKS IN ICY SEA

North Atlantic, 15 April. The world's newest and most luxurious ocean liner, the White Star Line's 'unsinkable' *Titanic*, strikes an iceberg and sinks with the loss of more than 1,500 lives.

Passengers, many of them wealthy and well-born, have little to fear when they board the great vessel for her maiden voyage from Southampton to New York: she has been built in 16 watertight compartments which, they are assured, will enable her to survive any collision or other disaster.

The *Titanic*'s lifeboats are too few in number, and are not filled to capacity: some are cast off too soon; others ignored by passengers who feel safer on deck. Most of those aboard show commendable courage, remaining calm as the stricken ship tilts alarmingly. The band plays on to the last, its final number the lively tune 'Autumn'.

First rescue ship to reach the scene is the *Carpathian*, which picks up some hundreds of survivors. Among them is Bruce Ismay, chairman of the White Star Line.

STARS SHINE AT OLYMPICS

July. In a double triumph, Potchefstroom policeman Kenneth McArthur wins the marathon gold

Medallist McArthur.

medal at the Stockholm Olympics, to be closely followed to the finish by another South African, Christopher Gitsham. Remarkably, Gitsham has never before competed over the distance.

Star of the Games, though, is undoubtedly the American Indian (Native American) athlete Jim Thorpe, who wins the decathlon (ten different track and field events), the

Thorpe throws the javelin.

pentathlon (long-distance running, shooting, horseback riding, swimming, wrestling), the 200 metres and the 1,500 metres. Along the way he breaks a number of records. He also comes fourth in the high jump. A year later, however, the US Amateur Athletic Union finds out that Thorpe had played professional baseball, takes away his amateur status and forces him to return his Olympic medals.

TOMMY TRIES IT ON

A highway robbery of comic-opera dimensions takes place among the lovely hills of the eastern Transvaal. Tommy Dennison 'arms' himself with a pair of simulated pistols (he carves them from wood), adopts a phoney American accent (a dead give-away), and takes £129 in small change from the Lydenburg coach. Next day he spends the money in the bar of the Royal Hotel, Pilgrim's Rest, and is promptly apprehended. He is sentenced to serve five years in jail. Later, on his release, he returns to Pilgrim's Rest to open the Highwayman's Garage, above whose doors he nails his wooden pistols. Robber's Pass, which links the village with the Lydenburg-Ohrigstad road, is named in celebration of his ineptitude.

MISS WATSON CONQUERS ALL

April. Pint-sized, leather-booted Miss E.L.C. Watson, a Scottish mathematics

SOUTH AFRICA in the 20th CENTURY
Nineteen Tens

Queen of the road Watson.

teacher, astonishes press and public alike when she completes a solo motor-cycle ride from Cape Town to Durban via Johannesburg. The obstacles en route would intimidate even experienced motoring pioneers of the male gender: roads, where they exist, are rugged, ill-signposted and, in many places, blocked by drifts. But the intrepid Miss Watson overcomes all with the help of her reliable 2½ horsepower machine, a set of tools and true British grit.

BORN
International: Singer, dancer and actor Gene Kelly; rocket scientist Werner von Braun. **South Africa:** Political leader Walter Sisulu.

NEW THEORY ON CONTINENTS
Scientists have dismissed as 'crackpot' the theories of German geologist Alfred Wegener, who claims that at one time in the hugely distant past all the world's continents were joined together, slowly separating as they floated on inner-Earth's molten rock to create the land masses we know today. As evidence, Wegener points to the shapes of the continents and the way they would fit neatly together if rejoined. Moreover, the plants, animals and rock formations of 'related' parts of the Earth bear striking ancestral similarities. He calls the process 'continental drift'.

SCIENTISTS HOAXED BY 'DISCOVERY'
The scientific world is confounded by the remarkable discovery, by British lawyer and amateur fossil-hunter Charles Dawson, of the skull and jawbone of a hitherto unknown hominid species. The press hails the find as that of the long-sought 'missing link' between *Homo sapiens* and his long-gone simian ancestors.

The remains, found in a gravel pit on Piltdown Common in Sussex, are thought to be more than half a million years old – but, to experienced palaeoanthropologists, they make little sense: the skull appears to belong to modern man,

Re-creation of Piltdown Man.

the jaw much like that of an ape. The hominid is named *Eoanthropus* ('dawn man') *dawsoni*.

Much later – in 1953, by which time accurate chemical tests have been developed – Piltdown Man is found to have been a massive hoax. The skull is indeed that of a modern human, the jawbone that of an orangutan; both have been ingeniously stained and aged by, it is assumed, the late Charles Dawson.

HIT SONGS
- I'm Twenty One Today
- Roamin' in the Gloamin
- Oh You Beautiful Doll
- When Irish Eyes Are Smiling

WHAT'S NEW IN 1912

New president Woodrow Wilson.

- **Inventions:** British engineer Charles Belling invents the electric stove; neon signs make their debut – advertising Cinzano, in Paris.
- **France:** Coco Chanel opens her first fashion salon in Deauville.
- **Medicine:** For the first time a physician, James Herrick of Chicago, diagnoses a heart attack; a 'cancer microbe' is discovered by French doctor Gaston Odin.
- **US Aviation:** First parachute jump from aircraft.
- The first movies from **Keystone Films** (to become famed for its bumbling-cop comedies) are screened.
- **Britain:** Royal Flying Corps formed.
- **Publishing:** Britain's socialist *Daily Herald*, Russian Bolsheviks' *Pravda* (banned by the Tsar) founded.
- **Balkans:** Turks routed in and expelled from Balkans; armistice signed between Turkey, Bulgaria, Serbia and Montenegro.
- **US politics:** Woodrow Wilson is elected president.
- The word **blues** is added to the musical lexicon.

SOUTH AFRICA in the 20th CENTURY 1910s

Striking miners on the streets during riots on Johannesburg's Reef.

A full team of Morkels.

1913

WHITE MINERS RIOT ON RAND

Johannesburg, 4 July. Violence spreads through central Johannesburg after some 18,000 white mineworkers, employees of 63 of the 69 Reef gold mines, down tools in support of five sacked colleagues. Rioters set Johannesburg's Park Street station on fire, attack the premises of *The Star* newspaper, and battle troops of the newly formed Union Defence Force in the streets. More than 100 strikers and bystanders are killed in the clashes. Many of the seeds of conflict have been sewn by the mine-owners, who are determined to replace English-speaking miners with Afrikaners (on the false assumption that the 'poor white' element will prove more docile) and, more inflammatory, employ cheap African labour for semi-skilled work. Mine boss Lionel Phillips sums up the hard-nosed attitude of his colleagues when he tells his London principals that 'a general strike would of course be a serious matter from a dividend-paying standpoint. I do not think, however, that it could last very long and, if it does happen, we must make up our minds once and for all to break the unions here'.

It is the mine-owners, though, who cave in. The workers are reinstated, and by 12 July the strikers are back at work. In the following year, in a bid to prevent similar outbreaks, government steers the Riotous Assemblies Bill through parliament.

CONTRARY MARY ON THE WARPATH

Among those arrested during the labour riots in Johannesburg is feisty feminist Mary FitzGerald, who is taken into custody for inciting striking white workers to burn down the Park Street station and *The Star*'s printing works. Known as 'Pickhandle Mary' after leading a militant group of miners' wives two years ago – they had armed themselves with pickhandles – FitzGerald will also be in the vanguard of the 1914 labour troubles. She will later publish the journal *Voice of Labour* and serve as Johannesburg's first woman city councillor.

RUGBY FAMILY MAY TAKE ON THE BEST

There is speculation in rugby quarters that a team comprised entirely of members of the Morkel family, of Somerset West in the Cape, will travel overseas next year to take on one or more of the Home Unions. At this time a full 22 Morkels are playing at first-team level; on occasions more than half the Western Province side is made up of Morkels (ten of them earn Springbok colours between the years 1903 and 1928). Gerald Morkel captains the national side on its 1912–13 tour of Britain. But the war clouds gathering over Europe will eventually put paid to the scheme.

WHITES GRAB MOST OF THE LAND

The Natives' Land Act, passed on 16 June, is a major landmark on the bleak road to apartheid. The Act confirms the status of existing 'tribal' lands and sets aside some 7.5 percent of South Africa for exclusive occupation by black people (who

Women volunteers deliver Johannesburg's mail.

37

SOUTH AFRICA in the 20th CENTURY

Nineteen Tens

Natal Indians, called to action by Gandhi, march into the Transvaal.

make up 67 percent of the population), much of it in the already overcrowded Transkei and Ciskei regions and in what is to become KwaZulu. Africans are prohibited from buying and owning land outside the designated areas.

INDIAN LEADER JAILED
Mohandas Gandhi, the lawyer and campaigner for Indian rights in South Africa, draws a nine-month prison sentence after organizing massive protests. Up to now Gandhi's approach has been somewhat elitist, but this year he seeks and gains support from the labouring classes. Strikes on the northern Natal coalfields spread to the sugar industry and other areas; there are riots and incidents of arson, and on 1 November Indian workers, inviting arrest, begin moving en masse across the Natal border into the Transvaal.

Gandhi.

BARRY HERTZOG QUITS
Former guerrilla leader General J.M.B. 'Barry' Hertzog and his supporters resign from the governing South Africa Party. Hertzog, co-founder of the Orangia-Unie in the Orange Free State and a member of the first Union government (but excluded from the 1912 cabinet), leaves in protest against premier Louis Botha's conciliatory policies towards English-speaking whites. He goes on to found the National Party.

TIPPERARY TAKES OFF
The new song 'It's a Long Way to Tipperary', first rendered during the year by British music hall artiste Florrie Forde, gains instant popularity. The jaunty number with its poignant undertones will be sung, and whistled, by countless columns of marching soldiers during the coming war with Germany.

DEATH AT THE DERBY
4 June, Ascot. The suffragette movement, which has campaigned long, hard and courageously for the women's vote in Britain, gains a martyr when Emily Davidson runs out from the crowd to grab the reins of the King's horse, Anmer, in the Derby. She is swept beneath its hooves and dies instantly. The British movement was launched (in 1905) and led by Emmeline Pankhurst and her Women's Social and Political Union.

BOOKS OF 1913
- Arthur Conan Doyle's *The Lost World*
- D.H. Lawrence's *Sons and Lovers*
- Thomas Mann's *Death in Venice*

BORN
International: US politician Richard M. Nixon; athlete Jesse Owens; Algerian-French author Albert Camus. *South Africa:* Anti-apartheid campaigner Fr Trevor Huddleston; artists Gerard Sekoto and Russian-born Vladimir Tretchikoff.

DIED
South Africa: Zulu paramount chief Dinuzulu.

British suffragettes honour one of their dead.

SOUTH AFRICA in the 20th CENTURY 1910s

Archduke Franz Ferdinand and his wife.

> 'I have come to Sarajevo on a friendly visit and someone throws a bomb at me. It is outrageous.'
> *Archduke Franz Ferdinand, just after a failed assassination attempt – and a hour before a second attempt succeeded*

1914
EUROPE GOES TO WAR

As the balmy days of July come and go the great powers of Europe mobilize their armies and, early in August, march against each other, so beginning a conflagration in which millions are to die.

The trigger for the Great War is a relatively minor incident. On 28 June the Archduke Franz Ferdinand, heir to the Austro-Hungarian (or Habsburg) throne, is shot dead by Gavrilo Princip, a 19-year-old Serbian nationalist, in the streets of Sarajevo, capital of the Balkan state of Bosnia and part of the Austro-Hungarian empire. His wife, the Duchess of Hohenberg, is also gunned down.

The underlying causes of the war, however, go much deeper – to the rise of Germany as an industrial and military giant. On one side are the nations of the so-called Triple Entente (Britain, France, Russia), on the other the Central Powers – Germany, Austria-Hungary and Turkey. German troops, moving on Paris, are stopped short along the line of the Marne River, and dig themselves into defensive trenches. So, too, do the French infantry and their allies, the British Expeditionary Force.

Britons marching to glory.

The reality of war: mud and death.

It is to be a war of attrition, fought in the mud of Flanders, by foot-soldiers who go 'over the top' in endless sacrificial waves to advance, across the open, against murderous rifle and machine-gun fire.

For the next four years the armies will battle titanically, at tragic cost in human life, for each yard of shell-torn, corpse-laden ground.

A German officer reads the declaration of war.

Early days: British 'Tommies' help two wounded Germans.

39

SOUTH AFRICA in the 20th CENTURY
Nineteen Tens

German guns open up on the Western Front.

> 'The lamps are going out all over Europe. We shall not see them lit again in our lifetime.'
> *Sir Edward Grey, shortly before the nations go to war*

A BRIEF LIGHT IN THE DARKNESS

'It will all be over by Christmas', says Sir John French as his British Expeditionary Force prepares for war. But hopes soon fade as the armies become bogged down. For a brief moment, though, peace and goodwill shines through the darkness of war: on Christmas Day 1914 German and British soldiers, resigned to the stalemate, emerge from their trenches to play football in the bleak no-man's land that separates them.

BOER REBELS TAKE UP ARMS

September. More than 10,000 Boers, with the tragedies of the South African war still fresh in their memories, take up arms in open rebellion against prime minister Louis Botha's decision to declare war on Germany. Rebel leaders include former guerrilla commanders Christiaan de Wet and Christiaan Beyers, and Union Defence officers Manie Maritz, J.C.G. Kemp and Jopie Fourie.

Probably the only man who could stop the conflict is Botha's political opponent, the influential Koos de la Rey, but he is accidentally killed at a police roadblock just before the insurrection erupts. De la Rey was on his way to a crucial meeting to resolve the crisis. At the time the police were on the look-out for the notorious Foster gang of criminals.

Fourie: executed by firing squad.

However, the rebels attract little popular support and, lightly armed and poorly organized, prove no match for disciplined government troops. The uprising is quickly crushed. Beyers, formerly commandant-general of the Union Defence Force, drowns while trying to cross the Vaal River (that is the official story; he may have been 'executed' by government agents); De Wet is imprisoned; Fourie is led before a firing squad and dies bravely, singing the hymn 'Als wij de doodvallei betreen' (Though we walk in the Valley of Death).

CORNERED FOSTER GANG TAKES QUICK WAY OUT

A large crowd gathers outside the cave in Kensington, Johannesburg, to watch the final act of a drama that has captured the headlines. Inside are ex-convicts William Foster, Carl Mejar and John Maxim, an American gunman on the run.

Earlier, the three broke out from their Cape Town prison to embark on an orgy of robbery and murder before being cornered. Police allow Foster's wife Peggy, carrying the couple's child and accompanied by his father, to enter the cave to reason with the fugitives. They fail in their mission; the old man re-emerges with the child; Peggy stays inside, and shots are heard. When detectives enter they find four corpses.

ENTER THE TRAMP

Allied troops on the battlefronts of Europe are enchanted by short films featuring Charlie Chaplin, the bow-legged little tramp with the toothbrush moustache, bowler hat and cane. He made his debut last year, in a movie called *Making a Living*.

Early foundation garments.

FASHION FIRSTS

The new zip fastener makes life a little easier for US troops (who are not yet at war). The civilian clothing industry shows little interest.

America also sees the birth of the bra when wealthy Mary Phelps Jacob, determined to conquer the constrictions of wrap-round whalebone, contrives a 'backless brassière' from two handkerchiefs and a ribbon. She patents her invention.

BIGGEST CRATER CLOSES

Kimberley's Big Hole, largest of the world's man-made craters, finally comes to the end of its long and hugely productive life. Over the years it has reached a depth of 1,097 metres and yielded over three tonnes (14,504,375 carats to be exact) of diamonds.

SOUTH AFRICA in the 20th CENTURY — 1910s

WHAT'S NEW IN 1914

- **Colour photography**, developed by the Eastman Kodak company.
- **US:** First commercial airline, in Florida.
- **Books:** James Joyce's *Dubliners* published.
- The term **birth control** enters the language.
- First aerial **'dogfight'**, on the Western Front.

BORN
International: Actors Alec Guinness and Tyrone Power; actress Loretta Young; boxer Joe Louis; poet Dylan Thomas; explorer Thor Heyerdahl; baseball maestro Joe DiMaggio. *South Africa:* Activist Archie Gumede.

DIED
International: Field Marshal Lord Roberts; Pope Pius X. *South Africa:* Cape Astronomer Royal (1879–1907) Sir David Gill.

1915

SA FORCES RECORD 'FIRST COMPLETE TRIUMPH'

February. Generals Louis Botha and Jan Smuts leave the political arena to lead South African soldiers against the German colonial forces in German South West Africa. Botha's 12,000-man army lands at Swakopmund, Smuts's 6,000 at Lüderitiz Bay. Other South African troops – more than 30,000 of them – march in from the Orange River in the southeast. By May it is all over. The invaders are numerically superior; their chief enemies prove to be the heat, the hostile desert terrain, the vast distances, the mines and booby traps the retreating Germans have laid and the drinking wells they poisoned. The formal surrender is accepted on 9 July; the peace terms are generous. Reports *The Times* of London: 'To the youngest of the sister nations belongs the glory of the first complete triumph of our arms …'.

MOBS RAMPAGE AFTER SINKING OF LUSITANIA

7 May. A total of 1,198 passengers die when the ocean liner *Lusitania*, pride of the Cunard shipping line, is torpedoed by a German submarine off the Irish coast. The 32,000-tonne vessel, which is carrying a cargo of ammunition, goes down within minutes of being struck.

The sinking inflames anti-German sentiment in South Africa; rampaging mobs destroy German (and some non-German) property in Johannesburg and elsewhere after reports that residents of German stock 'gleefully celebrated' the disaster. Many citizens bearing Teutonic sounding names place newspaper advertisements disclaiming German nationality.

POISON GAS USED FOR FIRST TIME

23 April, Western Front. Masked German troops make a swift 4-mile advance at Ypres after releasing deadly, windborne chlorine gas over Allied positions. Most severely affected are French Zouave units, who retreat in disorder. The deadly yellow-green substance attacks the lungs and eyes. Pending the issue of gas masks, Allied soldiers will go into battle holding wet cloths to their faces.

South African troops sail for South West Africa.

POET RESTS IN FOREIGN FIELD

Among the casualties of the doomed Dardanelles expedition is Rupert Brooke, the handsome young poet who captured the minds and hearts of the English-speaking world with his *Poems* (published in 1911) and later war sonnets. Brooke, a naval officer, dies of blood poisoning on the Aegian island of Skyros. His prophetic poem 'The Soldier' anticipated his death with the lines 'If I should die, think only this of me: that there's some corner of a foreign field that is forever England.'

ON THE SHELVES
- John Buchan's *The 39 Steps*
- W. Somerset Maugham's *Of Human Bondage*
- Joseph Conrad's *Victory*
- Edgar Rice Burroughs's best-selling *Tarzan of the Apes*

Rupert Brooke.

SOUTH AFRICA in the 20th CENTURY

> 'Patriotism is not enough. I must have no hatred or bitterness towards anyone.'
> *Nurse Edith Cavell, just before she is executed by the Germans*

NURSE CAVELL EXECUTED
12 October. Edith Cavell, the British matron of a Red Cross hospital in Brussels, is executed by firing squad after a German military court finds her guilty of helping Allied soldiers escape from occupied Belgium. The trial lasts two days; Cavell admits to aiding 130 fugitives.

Edith Cavell.

ON THE SILVER SCREEN
African Mirror, one of the world's earliest news-reel productions (founded in 1913), breaks new ground when its cameramen accompany South African units bound for East Africa.

Farther afield, cowboy actor William S. Hart is adjudged Hollywood's most popular screen personality. The new Western genre proves a huge box-office success; Hart stars in 18 of the feature films released in 1915. Mary Pickford is the top female drawcard.

The year's most notable film, and destined to become a classic (despite its blatant racial prejudice), is D.W. Griffith's *The Birth of a Nation*.

SONGS OF THE DAY
- You Made Me Love You
- Keep the Home Fires Burning
- Pack Up Your Troubles in Your Old Kit Bag
- Back Home in Tennessee

BORN
International: Pope Pius X; singers Edith Piaf, Billie Holiday, Frank Sinatra and Nat 'King' Cole; British politician John Profumo; actors Orson Welles, Hedy Lamarr and Ingrid Bergman; playwright Arthur Miller; footballer Stanley Matthews; and Israeli soldier Moshe Dayan. *South Africa:* Politician B.J. Vorster; churchman and human-rights campaigner Beyers Naudé.

DIED
International: US black leader Booker T. Washington.

The devastation at Delville Wood.

1916

GREAT SOMME OFFENSIVE LAUNCHED; SA TROOPS HOLD DELVILLE WOOD

1 July, Western Front. After a week-long artillery barrage, thousands of heavily laden Allied soldiers go 'over the top' in a massive offensive against German positions near the Somme River. The barrage, however, serves merely to warn the enemy, and the advancing regiments are cut to ribbons. More than 20,000 British are killed on the first day, another 40,000 wounded.

South African troops play a small but remarkably courageous part in the great battle.

By the middle of July 121 officers and 3,032 men of the South African Brigade of the 9th Division have advanced to the fringes of Delville Wood, a key tactical position. On the 15th, they storm the wood, which they then hold for almost a week in the face of ferocious artillery bombardment and infantry counter-attack. Just five officers and 750 men survive unwounded.

German Kaiser Wilhelm II later says: 'If all divisions had fought like the 9th, I would not have any troops left.' Author John Buchan describes the battle as 'an epic of terror and glory scarcely equalled in the entire campaign'.

The Somme offensive lasts five months. By November, the Allies have advanced just five miles, at a cost of

SOUTH AFRICA in the 20th CENTURY 1910s

420,000 British, 190,000 French and 650,000 German lives.

It has proved impossible to break the two-year stalemate, largely because the means of defence – machine guns, barbed wire, trenches – have outstripped offensive capability. Realizing this, the British launch a brand new weapon, an armoured vehicle they call a 'tank' (the name is deliberately deceptive: for security reasons, the vehicles are shipped to France in crates marked 'water tanks'). They enjoy immediate success, but are mechanically unreliable and there are too few of them to make any real difference to the outcome of this particular battle.

The terrible loss of life, though, hasn't been entirely wasted. The fighting along the Somme prevents a German breakthrough farther to the south, at Verdun. Here, the French armies have been pounded by 1,400 German guns concentrated along a front of just eight miles.

COKE PATENTS NEW BOTTLE

The Coca-Cola Company launches its new, distinctively curvaceous bottle design and its 'hand-written' logo in a bid to halt commercial piracy. The dark-coloured fizzy drink originally (in the later 1800s) contained both cocaine and caffeine, and was marketed as a health beverage. The cocaine was later omitted, but the drink's 15 other special ingredients (including one known only to two or three insiders) ensured its continued popularity.

TREKKER SAGA FILMED

The first home-grown epic film, *De Voortrekkers*, premieres on 16 December, anniversary of the battle of Blood River. The two-hour feature has been scripted by the noted writer and cultural leader Gustav Preller, produced by American import Harold Shaw and created at the newly established Killarney Studios in Johannesburg.

It attracts full houses for weeks, and wins critical acclaim both for its narrative breadth and its historical accuracy. One sequence, indeed, is rather too authentic: hundreds of workers from the ERPM mine, hired to play Zulu warriors and armed with assegais (20,000 of these were specially made), carry on their charge and a real battle threatens to develop. The scene is re-shot.

Writer Gustav Preller.

Jabavu and son.

FIRST 'BLACK' UNIVERSITY OPENS

John Tengo Jabavu, the prominent newspaper editor and human rights campaigner, realizes a longstanding ambition with the opening of the South African Native College in the eastern Cape. The college will later be renamed the University of Fort Hare.

Jabavu, only the second black South African to matriculate, launched the newspaper *Imvo Zabantsundu* (Black Opinion) in 1884, opposed British policy during the Anglo-Boer War, and later supported the Cape's white liberals – which placed him on a collision course with the more radical elements of the fledgling African resistance movement. His determination to open the doors of higher learning to young blacks gained strength when his own son was refused entry to a 'white' school.

TWO BIG-NAME DEATHS

War leader Lord Kitchener, remembered in South Africa for his brutal 'scorched earth' policy and concentration camps, drowns when the troopship in which he is sailing to Russia is torpedoed by a German submarine. Kitchener's has probably

Among the songs of the time is 'Good-bye Dolly Gray', a sentimental ballad of the Anglo-Boer War evoking the heartbreak of parting.

43

SOUTH AFRICA in the 20th CENTURY

Nineteen Tens

been the most familiar face in the British Isles: it has appeared, with pointing finger, on countrywide recruiting posters to help persuade more than three million Britons to fight for king and country.

On 16 December Rasputin, the drunken, sexually ravenous Russian monk who cast his spell over Tsar Nicholas II and his Tsarina, is murdered by two relatives of the royals. Rasputin's power at court lay partly in his apparently successful efforts (they involved the use of hypnosis) to keep the haemophiliac heir to the throne, Prince Alexei, from bleeding to death. The mad monk's hold on his own life proves tenacious: over the hours the murderers stab, poison and shoot him and then throw him into freezing waters of the Neva River, where he finally drowns.

Mad monk Rasputin.

BORN
South Africa: Politician P.W. Botha; businessman and philanthropist Anton Rupert.

> 'To me, the real hero of the East African campaign is the South African citizen soldier. Disease and hunger sapped them on long marches ... they kept marching on.'
> *General Jan Smuts*

Lenin addresses the workers.

1917
BOLSHEVIKS SEIZE POWER

Russia's Tsar Nicholas abdicates in March, handing power over to a provisional government headed initially by Prince Lvov and then by Socialist lawyer Alexander Kerensky. However, opposition to the disastrous war with Germany, and to economic hardships at home, opens the door to the small Bolshevik Party, led by Vladimir Ilyich Ulyanov, otherwise known as Lenin.

Over the next few months popular support for the Bolsheviks grows, most importantly among disaffected soldiers of the hard-pressed Russian armies at the front. An attempted right-wing coup by their commander in chief heightens tension, swelling the ranks of the Left. In September the Bolsheviks, promising 'peace, land and bread', win clear and enthusiastic majorities in the Moscow and Petrograd soviets, or workers' councils.

On 7 November Lenin masterminds a revolutionary seizure of power, and bands of armed Bolsheviks occupy key points in Petrograd, including the Winter Palace. The palace housed the provisional government, which is taken captive.

'DOUGHBOYS' ENTER WAR

6 April. The United States, appalled at the toll taken by hostilities in Europe (and fearing vast investment losses) declares war on Germany. Young American soldiers, fresh and enthusiastic, inject much-needed vigour into the ranks of the exhausted Allied armies. Indeed, their intervention will eventually tip the balance in favour of the Allies.

SMUTS INVADES EAST AFRICA

South African troops are in the vanguard of Imperial forces that, by September, have occupied most of German East Africa.

Fresh and keen: American 'doughboys' in training.

SOUTH AFRICA in the 20th CENTURY 1910s

South African forces on the road in East Africa.

General Jan Smuts, appointed commander-in-chief of the Allied army in February last year, has driven the enemy from their strongholds in Kenya and pushed steadily southwards.

However, the Germans, led by the brilliant Paul von Lettow-Vorbeck, stand their ground to the south of the Rufiji River. In November, short of ammunition and supplies, they retire into Portuguese East African territory to carry out cross-border raids. Next year one such raid will take Von Lettow-Vorbeck as far into the interior as the Abercorn area of Northern Rhodesia, at which point he surrenders – two weeks after the armistice is formally signed in Europe.

For the ordinary South African foot-soldier, the campaign has been notable more for its natural hazards than for the bullets he faces. Writes one officer: 'Here we have 17 rivers in 18 miles, with mud and black turf in between. A motor lorry goes at the rate of three miles a day in such country. Then you get a stretch of desert where there is no water ...'. Troops are placed on reduced rations; dysentery, malaria and various tropical diseases take a heavy toll.

HIT SONGS
- If You Were the Only Girl in the World
- For Me and My Gal
- Over There
- Yankee Doodle Boy
- Give My Regards to Broadway

DISASTER STRIKES BLACK REGIMENT

February. In one of the war's biggest single tragedies, more than 700 members of the South African Native Labour Corps die when their ship, the *Mendi*, strikes a German mine in the English Channel. The vessel was transporting the men to the battlefields of the Western Front.

In an eerie turn of events, news of the disaster reaches the victims' families in southern Africa before the official announcement.

Altogether, more than 80,000 black South African volunteers have enlisted in the Corps, over 25,000 of whom serve in France.

GERMANS BOMB LONDON

13 June, London. Aerial warfare takes on a new dimension on 13 June when 14 German Gotha aircraft appear over the centre of the city, dropping bombs which kill 162 people and injured a further 432.

IN FASHION

- Bobbed hair, prompted by the safety needs of increasingly female factory workforces.
- Silk stockings (by 1915, hemlines had risen slightly to reveal ankles).
- Larger handbags, often covered in tapestry, for the newly mobile woman and her greater variety of personal effects, including comb, mirror, pale face-powder, perfume, lip-salve.

Soldiers of the African Native Labour Corps in France.

SOUTH AFRICA in the 20th CENTURY
Nineteen Tens

MATA HARI SHOT FOR SPYING

15 October, France. Celebrated Dutch-born exotic dancer Mata Hari is executed by firing squad. Mistress and confidante of men in high places (she numbered the Dutch premier and the French foreign minister among her close friends), she had been arrested by French authorities and brought before an Allied court martial on charges of espionage. She protests her innocence to the end, but the prosecution uses her flamboyant lifestyle with damning effect.

Sultry siren Mata Hari.

BORN
International: Indian premier Indira Gandhi; US president John F. Kennedy; jazzman Dizzie Gillespie; actor Robert Mitchum; British authors Arthur C. Clarke and Anthony Burgess. *South Africa:* Political leader Oliver Tambo; politician Helen Suzman; golfer Bobby Locke.

DIED
International: French sculptor Auguste Rodin; US law-man Colonel William Cody, otherwise known as Buffalo Bill. *South Africa:* Politician and 'raider' Leander Starr Jameson.

WHAT'S NEW IN 1917

- The first **million-dollar film contract** is signed, by UK-born comic actor Charlie Chaplin.
- **Liquid nail polish** is marketed for the first time, by Cutex.
- The first **Pulitzer prizes** are awarded.
- The word **camouflage** enters the English language.
- **UK:** The British royal house changes its family name from Saxe-Coburg to Windsor.
- **Germany:** Bayerische Motoren Werke (better known as BMW), the car and motorcycle manufacturing company, is founded.

1918
VICTORY FOR THE ALLIES; ARMISTICE SIGNED

In March General Erich von Ludendorff launches his armies westwards in a massive offensive that pushes the Allies back at several points. It is a desperate, last-ditch effort to win the war for Germany before more of America's finest – the 'doughboys' that have been setting sail for the front in their thousands – arrive in force. But the Allied naval blockade has created a critical shortage of supplies, German reserves have been bled dry, and Ludendorff is unable to capitalize on the initial breakthroughs.

In the early hours of 11 November, German and Allied representatives meet inside a railway carriage set among tall trees in the forest of Compiegne, near Paris, to negotiate an armistice.

> 'We lived like rats, fed like rats, and died like rats.'
> *South African veteran of the Western Front*

The German delegates acknowledge defeat, agree to evacuate all conquered territories, surrender military hardware, repatriate all Allied prisoners, and remove Germany's armed forces to the west of the Rhine River.

Hostilities formally cease at 11 o'clock on the eleventh day of the eleventh month. At last, all is quiet on the Western Front. The 'war to end all wars' is over.

The home-coming.

End of the 'war to end all wars'.

SOUTH AFRICA in the 20th CENTURY **1910s**

COLOURED UNIT CAPTURES HILL

19 September. Men of the Cape Corps, serving with General Allenby's forces in Palestine, record a notable victory in the last months of the war when they fight the Turks to a standstill to take the tactically important Square Hill position. Before the battle, according to one of their officers, the men 'sang, made their wills, said their prayers and washed their teeth. At the immediate prospect of a scrap at close quarters they were high spirited and full of vim'.

The Cape Corps, a coloured military unit, has a long and honourable history: it was formed in 1795 to help defend the Cape against British invasion, and revived when two infantry battalions were raised earlier in the Great War. The coloured community responded so enthusiastically to the call to arms that government had to halt recruitment.

LAWRENCE ENTERS DASMASCUS

Shortly before the Armistice in Europe, T.E. Lawrence – 'Lawrence of Arabia' – helps lead Prince Feisel of Mecca's Arab Liberation Army into Damascas ahead of Lord Allenby's advancing troops. This is the culminating triumph in the young soldier's two-year-long campaign – waged mainly through sabotage and hit-and-run raids – to oust Turkish occupying forces from the Middle

T.E. Lawrence.

East region. His capture of the southern port of Aqaba last year, after a massed cross-desert camel charge, contributed much to Allenby's successful advance on Palestine.

WHAT'S NEW IN 1918

◆ **UK:** Women (those over 30) vote for the first time in a general election.
◆ **Royal Air Force** founded. Jan Smuts, as chairman of the founding committee, is a key figure in its creation.
◆ **US:** First electric food mixer goes on sale.
◆ **Russia:** The Bolsheviks rename themselves the Russian Communist Party.

RUSSIAN ROYAL FAMILY MURDERED

16 July. Tsar Nicolas II of Russia, his wife Alexandra, their son, four daughters and a number of their servants are shot to death by a Bolshevik execution squad. The murders, carried out on the orders of the Urals soviet, take place in the cellar of a mansion in Ekaterinburg. The bodies are dismembered, burnt and buried in a nearby forest. Later, there is speculation that one of the daughters, Anastasia, survives the massacre.

'SPANISH LADY' KILLS THOUSANDS

The great influenza pandemic sweeping the world claims 140,000 South African lives – according to the official figures. Many more deaths are unrecorded. The first case of what has been dubbed 'the Spanish Lady' (the initial outbreak occurred in Spain) is reported from Durban on 14 September; soon thousands are laid up, shops and factories close, hospital wards overflow, many of the dead are buried in mass graves.

Tsar Nicolas and his family in happier times.

HIT SONGS
● Oh, Oh, Oh, It's a Lovely War
● Till We Meet Again
● After You've Gone
● If You Could Care for me

BORN
South Africa: Struggle leader-statesman Nelson Rolihlahla Mandela.

SOUTH AFRICA in the 20th CENTURY

Nineteen Tens

Louis Botha and family.

Versailles delegates debate a League of Nations.

1919

BOTHA DIES, SMUTS TAKES OVER

South African prime minister Louis Botha, who has been the country's political and war leader since 1910, dies of pneumonia shortly after returning from the Versailles peace conference.

Born of Voortrekker parents, Botha showed both brilliance and ruthlessness on the field of battle during the Anglo-Boer War, penetrating deep into Natal and holding the line of the Tugela River against a numerically superior Imperial army. In 1900, just before the fall of Pretoria, he was appointed commandant general of the Boer forces, his commandos waging a bitter and for the most part effective campaign which ended only with the Peace of Vereeniging in May 1902.

A staunch advocate of reconciliation, Botha was the driving force of reconciliation between Afrikaners and English-speaking South Africans. At Versailles, he and his colleague (and former comrade in arms) Jan Smuts were dismayed by the harsh peace terms imposed on the Germans. Drawing on his experiences of conflict in his own country, he urged the victorious Allies to show leniency towards their former enemy, but his pleas were ignored – as were those of the American delegates, who eventually withdrew from the conference. He is succeeded as premier by Jan Smuts.

LEAGUE PROMISES WORLD PEACE

Delegates of 17 nations at the Versailles peace conference vote to create a League of Nations, an international body that will keep the world free of conflict. Its basic aims, enshrined in its covenant, are to settle disputes, to restrict the production of and trade in arms, and to take collective action against any attack on a member state. Among the League's chief architects is South Africa's Jan Smuts. Notable absentees from the membership list are the United States and, of course, a humiliated and angry Germany.

REACHING FOR THE SKIES

14 June. British pilot John Alcock and his American navigator, Arthur Brown, take off from Newfoundland in their Vickers Vimy biplane to attempt the first ever transantlantic flight, a distance of 1,900 miles. Their odyssey ends when the plane nosedives into an Irish bog just over 16 hours later. Neither man is hurt; both receive knighthoods.

Other aviation news: Britons Ross and Smith complete a 135-hour flight from Britain to Australia; American pilot Roland Rohifs attains a record altitude of 34,610 feet; Holland's KLM becomes the world's first international airline company; the first wireless telephones are installed in aircraft; American Robert Goddard

> 'There are a lot of hard-faced men who look as if they have done rather well out of the war.'
> *Economist John Maynard Keynes*

SOUTH AFRICA in the 20th CENTURY 1910s

The Vickers Vimy, nose buried in an Irish bog, completes the first transatlantic flight.

designs high-altitude rockets, but the scientific world scoffs at his dreams of space travel. In South Africa, Major Allister Miller's SA Aerial Transports, the country's first commercial airline, begins operating between Johannesburg and Durban.

WAR HERO DISMISSED FROM ARMY

South African John Sherwood-Kelly, who won the Victoria Cross in 1917, faces a court martial and is retired from the British army. His offence: as an officer in the North Russian Relief Force he refuses to send his men into action against the Bolsheviks and, worse, he reveals his reasons to the British press.

Stern's The Eternal Child.

LOCAL ARTIST MAKES WAVES

South African artist Irma Stern exhibits her unconventional paintings to critical acclaim in Berlin – the first of more than 100 one-person shows she will hold in Europe. On her return to South Africa in 1920, though, her work, strongly influenced by German expressionism, will be dismissed as 'revolutionary' and 'immoral'. It will also be investigated by police. Although Stern's international reputation continues to grow, she will not sell a single painting in her home country until 1931.

WHAT'S NEW IN 1919

- **Cambridge:** Ernest Rutherford, a New Zealand-born physicist, splits the atom (in theory).
- **Hollywood:** United Artists formed by the celebrated quartet of Douglas Fairbanks, D.W. Griffith, Charlie Chaplin and Mary Pickford. Says the president of rival Metro Pictures: 'So the lunatics have taken charge of the asylum.'
- **South Africa:** Clements Kadalie founds the powerful Industrial and Commercial Workers' Union (ICU).

Unionist Kadalie.

NEW IN THE HOME

In the kitchen: All-Bran high-fibre cereal, processed cheese (manufactured by Kraft), Pyrex glassware, pop-toaster, electric clock.
In the garden: Electric lawnmower.
On the road: Traffic lights, trailer caravans.

BORN
International: Authors J.D. Salinger, Iris Murdoch and Doris Lessing.
Southern Africa: Human rights campaigner Albertina Sisulu; Rhodesian leader Ian Smith.

DIED
International: US President Theodore Roosevelt; French artist Auguste Renoir.

1920s

SIGNED
1920: The Treaty of Versailles; League of Nations formally constituted.

GRANTED
1926: To the Dominions: equal status with Britain (Balfour Declaration).

ESTABLISHED
1922: University of the Witwatersrand. Fascist government in Italy, after Mussolini's 'Blackshirts' march on and occupy Rome.
1925: Afrikaans, as SA's second official language.
1926: Kruger National Park.
1927: The SA Iron and Steel Corporation (Iscor).

FLOWN
1927: The SA national flag, for the first time.

VOTED
1922: White Southern Rhodesians, for responsible government under Britain rather than union with SA.

OCCUPIED
1923: Germany's Ruhr industrial area, by French troops.

COLLECTIVIZED
1928: Soviet agriculture, on orders of Stalin; millions of peasant farmers (*kulaks*) are liquidated.

FIRST
1920: Broadcasting station (in Pittsburgh, USA). Trans-Africa flight (London to Cape Town). Planned 'Garden City' (Pinelands, Cape Town).
1921: Rugby series between Springboks and All Blacks (in New Zealand). Comrades Marathon run.
1922: SA Reserve Bank banknotes issued. *Reader's Digest* magazine appears, in the US.
1923: Radio broadcast in SA. British FA Cup competition.
1924: Mechanically driven petrol pumps in SA (Cape Town); car assembly plant (Port Elizabeth).
1925: Electric railway line in SA (Natal).
1926: Motor-driven liner to arrive in Cape Town (*Carnarvon Castle*). Television demonstrated (UK).
1927: 'Talkies' shown on SA movie screens.

DISCOVERED
1922: Pharaoh Tutankhamen's tomb, at Luxor, Egypt.
1923: Plutonium in the Waterberg, Transvaal.
1924: The million-year-old skull of a hominid, at Taung in the northern Cape; identified by Raymond Dart.
1925: Alluvial diamonds on west coast of South Africa.
1926: Alluvial diamonds near Lichtenburg, Transvaal.

LAUNCHED
1927: Investigation into the 'poor white' problem, funded by Carnegie Commission.

SENTENCED
1922: Mohandas Gandhi, to six years' imprisonment, in India.

POLITICS AND PROTEST
1920: Smuts forms cabinet. Transvaal Native Congress launches anti-pass campaign.
1922: White miners and other workers stage 'Red Revolt' on Witwatersrand.
1924: Barry Hertzog forms government after his National Party enters into pact with Labour Party.
1928: ANC organizes Cape rural workers.

PASSED
1920: Native Affairs Act, establishing separate councils to represent blacks.
1923: Natives (Urban Areas) Act, enforcing racial segregation in towns.
1924: Industrial Conciliation Act and an amended Mines and Works Act, entrenching job reservation.
1927: Native Administration Act, setting up an all-powerful Native Affairs Department. Immorality Act, prohibiting sexual relations between whites and blacks.

FAILED
1923: The Munich *putsch*: Adolf Hitler's bid for power in Bavaria. Hitler is arrested and imprisoned.

CRASHED
1929: The New York stock market, triggering worldwide economic depression.

SOUTH AFRICA in the 20th CENTURY

1920

PIONEER SOUTH AFRICAN PILOTS MAKE AVIATION HISTORY

4 February. The *Silver Queen*, a Vickers-Vimy bomber piloted by South Africans Pierre van Ryneveld and Quintin Brand, takes off from Brooklands airfield near London. Six weeks, a hundred hazards and two aircraft later the two men touch down at Youngsfield, just outside Cape Town, to complete the first ever trans-Africa flight.

Both pilots served with distinction in the First World War. Van Ryneveld, a Free-Stater, is later to become chief of staff of the Union forces; Brand commands the Royal Air Force's No.10 Fighter Group during the Battle of Britain (1940); both will be knighted.

The epic flight is part of a race sponsored by the London *Daily Mail*, which puts up a prize of £10,000; other competitors include crews entered by the Royal Air Force (also a Vickers Vimy), *The Times* of London (Vickers Vimy), the *Daily Telegraph* (Handley Page 0/400) and a private team in a De Havilland D.H.14A.

The *Silver Queen* crashes on the Cairo-Khartoum stretch; its replacement, also a Vimy, comes to grief near Bulawayo in Southern Rhodesia. The third aircraft, a De Havilland D.H.9 supplied by the Union Air Force and christened *Voortrekker*, successfully completes the final 2,300-kilometre run to Cape Town's Youngsfield aerodrome to be welcomed by a jubilant crowd.

Pierre van Ryneveld (right) and Quintin Brand pose in front of the Silver Queen *before their epic trans-Africa flight.*

AMERICA BANS BOOZE

January. Prohibition comes to all America with the passage of the 18th Amendment to the Constitution. More than 30 states are already 'dry', but the law (the Volstead Act) places a country-wide embargo on the manufacture, sale and consumption of alcohol – the 'demon drink' which prohibitionists blame for much of the poverty and hunger afflicting millions of American families. However, the ban soon creates its own evils: the proliferation of 'speakeasies' (illegal bars) that serve everything from moonshine to the finest of Scotch whisky, violent competition for the bootleg trade, corruption of public officials, gang warfare and the rise of Al Capone and other monstrous Mafia overlords. The Roaring Twenties have arrived.

Bootleg bunnies: women 'runners' adapt their garments for smuggling illicit alcohol.

POIROT STEPS IN

Agatha Christie's novel, *The Mysterious Affair at Styles*, appears on the bookshelves – the first of many detective stories about Hercule Poirot, the tubby little Belgian sleuth who always gets his man. Christie is to write more than 70 brain-teasing books, some of them featuring Poirot's female counterpart, the inquisitive village lady Miss Marple.

WIRELESS COMES OF AGE

Australian opera soprano Nellie Melba breaks new ground when she becomes the first professional singer to be paid for a live performance on the wireless. She gets a handsome £1,000 for a recital of songs (including 'Home Sweet Home') broadcast from the Marconi studios in Chelmsford, England. In a technological breakthrough across the Atlantic, KDKA radio station gives live coverage to Warren Harding's election as 29th US president.

Melba on air.

OLIVE SCHREINER DIES

Recent deaths include that of South African writer and feminist Olive Schreiner, perhaps best known for her novel *The Story of an African Farm*. The book was published, in 1883, under the pen-name Ralph Iron in order

51

SOUTH AFRICA in the 20th CENTURY
The Twenties

Olive Schreiner: icon of the early feminists.

Sarah Gertrude Millin: racist writer.

Charles Winslow.

Bevil Rudd.

Clarence Walker.

to sidestep prejudice against women, and received instant international recognition as the first novel of quality with a South African setting. It also contained controversial ideas about marriage and religion. Schreiner's *Women and Labour* (1911) has become a landmark in the women's movement.

HIT SONGS
- Avalon
- Margie
- Whispering

WEDDING OF THE YEAR
Mary Pickford, 'America's sweetheart' and the innocent heroine of scores of silent features, marries swashbuckling actor Douglas Fairbanks. Last year Fairbanks and Pickford (born Gladys Smith), a Canadian girl who made her screen debut in 1913, co-founded United Artists Corporation.

FIRST BOOK FROM 'THE BRILLIANT BIGOT'
Among the year's more notable literary debutantes is Sarah Gertrude Millin, who publishes the first of her more than 30 novels. *The Dark River* paints an unglamorous view of the Kimberley diamond diggings. Millin will become the country's most widely read South African author during the between-war years but her talent is corrupted by prejudice: she is obsessed with race, believing that love across the colour line leads to 'degeneration'. Much later, Nobel laureate Nadine Gordimer will call her 'the brilliant bigot'.

SOUTH AFRICANS STRIKE GOLD
Among gold medallists at the 1920 Olympic Games, held in Antwerp, are South Africa's Bevil Rudd (athletics; 400 metres), Clarence Walker (boxing; bantamweight), and Charles Winslow (tennis; men's singles).

SOUTH AFRICA in the 20th CENTURY — 1920s

WHAT'S NEW IN 1920

- **South West Africa:** This former German colony, occupied by Union forces in 1915, comes under South African administrative control in terms of a League of Nations mandate. Much later, it becomes the independent republic of Namibia.
- **In the home:** The recently developed electric iron goes on general sale.
- **John T. Thompson** patents the **Tommy-gun**.
- **Psychiatry:** Hermann Rorschach introduces psychiatrists to the 'inkblot test' – a method of gauging a patient's inner disturbance by his spontaneous reaction to random patterns on paper.
- **Bloody Mary** cocktails and the **icecream-on-a-stick** are introduced to the public.
- The word **deadline** becomes part of everyday language.

Early electric iron.

1921

ISRAELITES FALL TO POLICE BULLETS

21 May. Police kill 183 members of the Israelite religious sect and wound another 129 after a stand-off in the Bulhoek area near Queenstown, eastern Cape.

Earlier, the prophet Enoch Mgijima, leader of the Israelites, led a large group of his followers into the area in quest of land and in an attempt to create a 'refuge from oppression'. Talks fail to persuade the newcomers to leave, and in due course a large police detachment, armed with artillery, machine-guns and rifles, deploy on the surrounding hills. Their commanding officer issues an ultimatum, which is rejected: 'If it is to be a fight,' say the Israelites, 'Jehovah will fight with us and for us'. They then charge the police lines, and are mown down in their scores. The Israelites are one of more than a hundred independent churches born after Union in 1910, a time when black political hopes are steadily eroded by new race laws.

Prophet and protester Enoch Mgijima (top); interrogation of prisoners (above).

SMUTS TAKES OVER

General Jan Smuts, leader of the South African Party in succession to the late General Louis Botha, formally takes office as prime minister of the Union. Smuts, an outstanding guerrilla commander during the Anglo-Boer War (1899–1902), was largely responsible for drafting the Union constitution; served as minister of defence and the interior in the first Union cabinet, and, during the 1914–18 war, as field general and member of the Imperial War Cabinet. He played a crucial part in the creation of the Royal Air Force and of the League of Nations, and persuaded the British government to grant South Africa dominion status and, last year, to abandon the word 'Empire'.

ALL BLACKS BATTLE TO A DRAW

This year sees the first of the great rugby confrontations between Springbok and All Black. Battle is joined in New Zealand; the South Africans share the test series and remain unbeaten in the other matches. The Springbok line-up includes five members of the legendary Morkel family, ten of whom gain Springbok honours between 1903 and 1928.

YOUNG POLITICIAN FORMS NEW GERMAN PARTY

Adolf Hitler, a 31-year-old German war veteran, renames his small political group the National Socialist German Workers'

> 'Puritanism – the haunting fear that someone, somewhere, may be happy.'
> Writer H.L. Mencken, commenting on Prohibition in the United States

SONGS OF THE DAY
- The Fishermen of England
- Kitten on the Keys
- Wyoming Lullaby

SOUTH AFRICA in the 20th CENTURY
The Twenties

BORN
International: John Glenn, first American in space; Peter Ustinov, playwright and actor; author Norman Mailer; Russian scientist and dissident Andrei Sakharov; Prince Philip, Duke of Edinburgh. *South Africa:* Writer and sangoma Credo Mutwa.

DIED
International: Enrico Caruso, one of the greatest operatic tenors of all time, and the first performer to achieve worldwide fame through electronic recordings. The musical world also lost German composer Engelbert Humperdinck and French composer Camille Saint-Saëns. *South Africa:* Newspaperman, educationist and human rights campaigner John Tengo Jabavu.

John Tengo Jabavu (front centre): newsman and educator.

WHAT'S NEW IN 1921

- **Medical:** French researchers develop a successful vaccine for tuberculosis; insulin is isolated; the first birth control clinic founded, in London, by Marie Stopes.
- The **polygraph** or lie detector, invented by a Californian medical student, is used for the first time.

Birth-control pioneer Stopes.

- **Coco Chanel** unveils Chanel No.5 (on the fifth day of the fifth month, hence the name).
- **Miss America** beauty contest held for the first time, with eight entrants.
- First **drive-in restaurant** opens, in Dallas, Texas.
- Johnson and Johnson introduce the **Band-aid**.

Party (later to be shortened to Nazi Party). Hitler, born in Braunau, Upper Austria the son of a minor customs official – the original family name was Schicklgruber – studied art in Linz, Steyr and Munich, but failed to gain entry to the Vienna Academy. During the world war he served in a Bavarian regiment. He was wounded – temporarily blinded – on the Western Front in 1918.

NOT-SO-FUNNY COMEDIAN FACES ACCUSATIONS
One of Hollywood's most popular comedians, Roscoe 'Fatty' Arbuckle, is accused of debauchery, rape and assault after a 26-year-old female guest at one of his parties, held in a luxurious San Francisco hotel, dies of her injuries. Arbuckle is acquitted, but the allegations bring his screen career to an abrupt end.

'Fatty' Arbuckle: scandal in 'Frisco.

SOUTH AFRICA in the 20th CENTURY **1920s**

1922

RAND REVOLT TAKES HEAVY TOLL

Johannesburg, 10 March. Angry white workers, on strike since 28 December, storm and occupy police stations, railway installations and mines. They also attack the city's main post office and power station in a mass protest that has, in a few short hours, turned into open rebellion against the state.

As the violence escalates, prime minister Smuts calls in burgher commandos to help local police restore order, and instructs planes of the South African Air Force to strafe the rebels, who are especially strongly entrenched in the Fordsburg area. Within four days the revolt is crushed. A total of 153 people, including 72 of the state forces, lie dead, 534 are injured.

The so-called 'Red Revolt' was triggered by a mine-owners' threat to replace some 2,000 semi-skilled men with cheap black labour. By 10 January the mining industry had come to a virtual standstill as engineering, power-station and foundry workers joined the miners. They formed themselves into paramilitary units controlled by the extremist Federation of Labour; on 6 March William Andrews, leader of the Communist Party, called for a general strike.

How Andrews and his colleagues can reconcile Marxist principles with what has been essentially a racist campaign remains a mystery. However that may be, the Smuts government deals harshly with the rebels: most of their leaders are deported, several executed. About 15,000 whites later lose their jobs.

SOUTH AFRICANS GET NEW MONEY

The South African Reserve Bank issues its first banknotes, in denominations identical to those of British sterling. Up to now, commercial banks and some of the bigger commercial houses have supplied the country's paper currency.

The 'Red Revolt': whites protest (top); blacks leave Fordsburg (above).

Debut banknote and coin.

SONGS OF THE DAY
- Limehouse Blues
- Chicago
- Along the Road to Gundagai

WHAT'S NEW IN 1922

♦ The world's first suburban **shopping mall** opens for business, in the US.
♦ Synthetic **insulin**, developed in Canada, becomes available to diabetics.
♦ Signs of the times: the words **broadcast**, **bimbo** and **gigolo** are added to the English language.

Fashion in the Twenties

tubular, flat-chested, boyish, the curves hidden, and there is more than enough bare skin on show to shock her elders. The corset is in terminal decline – at least among the fashionable young. Hemlines begin to rise in 1922; bobbed hair disappears beneath the cloche hat; waistlines go up and then came down again, almost to the hip; young fingers are tipped with blood-red nails, young faces – and especially young eyes – painted with the new cosmetics. The Flapper, child of a revolution in mores and morals, has emerged.

The 20s Western woman, newly liberated by the cataclysm of war and her proven value in the workplace (she probably held down a man's job while her brothers were away fighting), is a very different creature from her Edwardian mother. She demands freedom – to speak her mind, to vote, to challenge the stuffy conventions of her over-formalized, over-dressed childhood, to smoke and drink in public, party all night, enjoy jazz, sex and travel, and wear simpler, smarter, more revealing clothes.

The new look, which quickly catches on in middle-class South Africa, is casual, slender, bright,

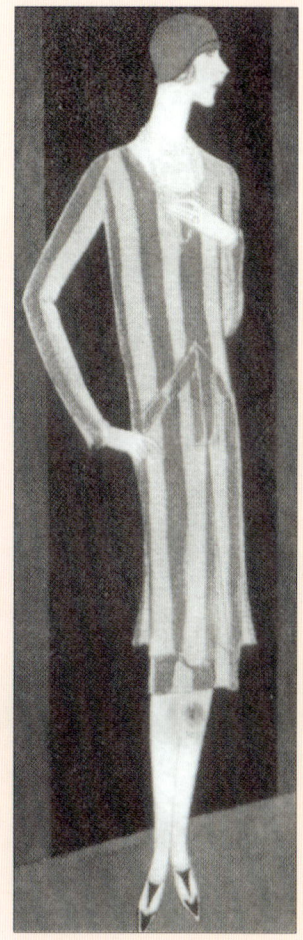

SOUTH AFRICA in the 20th CENTURY — 1920s

NEWTON BEGINS RECORD-BREAKING RUN

Forty-year-old Arthur Newton wins the second Comrades Marathon, keeping up such a pace that officials at the finish line are wholly unprepared for his arrival – despite his short break en route for a sustaining glass of brandy at the Star and Garter Hotel. This is the start of Newton's 15-year running career in which he will break every world distance record from the marathon to 100 miles. He wins the Comrades on four more occasions, and in 1928 completes the 5,472-kilometre transcontinental foot race across America. He is still running competitively at the age of 72.

RHODESIANS GO IT ALONE

Across the Limpopo River, a referendum held on 27 October gives Southern Rhodesians two choices: to become a self-governing colony, or to join the Union of South Africa as its fifth province. The all-white electorate opts for the former – by 8,774 votes to 5,989.

DEATH OF DE WET

One of South Africa's greatest military sons dies during the year. Christiaan de Wet, famed guerrilla leader during the Anglo-Boer War of 1899–1902, vigorously opposed Lord Milner's post-war assault on Afrikaner cultural identity; helped J.B.M. 'Barry' Hertzog form the Orangia-

Christiaan de Wet.

Unie Party, served as an Orange River Colony cabinet minister and, later, as a delegate to the National Convention that paved the way for Union. When war broke out in 1914, however, he led a 'peace commando' in the Boer rebellion, and was captured and imprisoned.

Although De Wet served only six months of his sentence, and continued to enjoy the respect of his countrymen, prison damaged him in both body and spirit. He spent his last years at his home in Klipfontein, gazing over the wide grassland plains from the stoep of his modest house. He died, in poverty, in February.

ANCIENT TREASURE-TROVE UNEARTHED

Luxor, Egypt. Egyptologist Howard Carter and his patron, Lord Carnarvon, reveal the greatest of all archaeological discoveries – the intact and unblemished tomb of the boy-king Tutankhamen, who died in 1322 BC. The tomb, among the very few ancient treasures to have escaped the attentions of grave-robbers, lies beneath a pile of rubble in the Valley of the Kings, sacred burial place of the pharaohs. It contains a gilded sarcophagus, furniture inlaid with gems, vases and other ornaments and a fabulous array of jewellery.

ARTS AND LEISURE

♦ Among literary works published during the year are *The Outline of History* by English writer H.G. Wells (previously noted for his science fiction), and poet T.S. Eliot's *The Wasteland*. James Joyce's new work, the 'dirty' stream-of-consciousness novel *Ulysses*, is banned.

♦ The first issue of *The Reader's Digest* appears on the shelves, breaking new publishing ground: its unique mix of sensible advice, homespun philosophy, hard information and

Howard Carter examines Tutankhamen's golden sarcophagus.

SOUTH AFRICA in the 20th CENTURY
The Twenties

The new magazine: a landmark in publishing history.

humour, packed into 30 or 31 articles (one for each day of the month), comes in pocket-sized format. The magazine is an instant success.
◆ Breaking all theatre conventions, dancer Isadora Duncan appears naked on the stage.

SPORT
Swimmer Johnny Weismuller, later to star as the silver screen's first film Tarzan, breaks the world 100-metres record, lowering the mark below 60 seconds for the first time. He goes on to become an Olympic champion.

BORN
International: Judy Garland (née Frances Gumm), who will leap to stardom in The Wizard of Oz; author Kingsley Amis. *South Africa:* Composer Stefan Grove; singer Eve Boswell; medical pioneer Christiaan Barnard; musician Todd Matshikiza.

DIED
International: Inventor Alexander Graham Bell, inventor of the telephone; Irish patriots Michael Collins (assassinated) and popular novelist Erskine Childers (executed for treason); French author Marcel Proust; polar explorer Sir Ernest Shackleton. *South Africa:* Casperus Hoogenhout, writer and prominent in the Afrikaans language movement.

Hitler and henchmen.

1923
NAZIS IN COUP FIASCO
Munich, Germany. In a forlorn and foolhardy bid for power Adolf Hitler, firebrand leader of the small National Socialist German Workers' (Nazi) party, attempts a *putsch* against the Bavarian government. On 11 November he places himself at the head of 3,000 armed Nazi stormtroopers and marches on the city centre. At his side are war hero General Erich von Ludendorff, and Hermann Goering, wartime successor to Manfred von Richtofen as commander of the 'Death Squadron'.

Children play with worthless German banknotes.

SOUTH AFRICA in the 20th CENTURY

BORN
International: Opera diva Maria Callas; actor Charlton Heston; film-makers Franco Zeffirelli and Richard Attenborough; astronaut Alan Shepard, first American in space; mime artist Marcel Marceau; statesman Henry Kissinger. *South Africa:* Writer Nadine Gordimer; poet Roy MacNab; actor, poet, writer William 'Bloke' Modisane.

The march is a fiasco: police open fire on the column; Hitler is wounded slightly in the shoulder, Goering seriously in the groin, and their followers scatter. The incident, though, gives the Nazis invaluable publicity.

Germany at this time – the fragile Weimar Republic – is fertile ground for political troublemakers. The economy is reeling under the burden of reparation payments for war damage; money is worthless: the new German paper mark has tumbled to 4.2 billion to the dollar; half a kilo of meat costs 3 billion marks and continues to rise in a wild spiral of hyper-inflation: the price of a house one day is the price of a loaf of bread the next. And millions of people are out of work, hungry, frightened – and angry.

SONGS OF THE DAY
- Who's Sorry Now?
- Farewell Blues
- Somebody Stole My Girl

RACE DIVIDE WIDENS
One of the most far-reaching race laws to date is passed by South Africa's parliament. The Natives (Urban Areas) Act gives white councils the right to exclude blacks from 'white' areas, and even from locations themselves – when, for example, a black person is deemed to be a vagrant or 'surplus to labour requirements'. The measure paves the way for the much later Group Areas Act, for mass forced removals and for increasingly harsh pass laws.

KLAN GROWS TO MONSTER SIZE
The racist Ku Klux Klan, among the fastest growing societies in America, claims its membership has breached the one-million mark for the first time. The Klan, which feeds on hatred – of outsiders in general and black people in particular – was founded in Georgia in 1915 by

One of the first automatic washing machines on the SA market.

Klansmen on the march.

PASTIMES
Games: Mah Jong, Contract Bridge, ping-pong.

Mah Jong.

Serious fun: Inventing and mixing (and drinking) cocktails.
Way-out: Flagpole sitting; seances (with ouija board).

Sitting pretty.

SOUTH AFRICA in the 20th CENTURY

The Twenties

WHAT'S NEW IN 1923

- **Interpol** *is founded.*
- **Aviation:** *A French pilot sets a new air speed record of 217 mph.*
- **US:** *The first issue of* Time *magazine appears.*
- **Inventions:** *American-led technological advances include Jacob Schick's electric shaver and Kodak's 16 mm Model A home movie camera.*
- **Cinema** *breaks new technological ground with the première of Sergei Eisenstein's* Battleship Potemkin.
- *Among words added to the English language are* hijack *and* aerosol.

Lenglen: queen of the courts.

William J. Simmons, an ex-preacher who assumed the rank of Imperial Wizard of the Invisible Empire. Amusing as the title might sound, the organization's activities evoke little laughter: klansmen, solid citizens by day, white-hooded angels of death by night, systematically assault, tar-and-feather and, increasingly, lynch those they perceive as enemies. On 15 September, in desperate response, the governor of Oklahoma declares martial law.

HUBBLE PROBES OUTER LIMITS

Astronomer Edwin Hubble, star-gazing through the giant telescope at Mount Wilson Observatory, California, proves that there are galaxies beyond our Milky Way – a discovery that fundamentally changes our ideas about the universe, its nature and limits.

Star-gazer Hubble.

Conclusive evidence of Hubble's greater, perhaps infinite, cosmos emerges from his observations of the Andromeda nebula.

SPORTING BRIEFS

- The first Le Mans 24-hour race is won by a French team driving a Chenard et Walcker.
- Cricket: Surrey and England batsman Jack Hobbs scores his 100th first-class century.

'Every day, in every way, I am getting better and better.'
French psychologist Emile Coué's suggested mantra for boosting personal self-confidence

- Tennis: Suzanne Lenglen wins the Wimbledon Ladies' Singles for fifth time in a row.

The Divine Sarah.

SARAH TAKES HER LAST BOW

Sarah Bernhardt, inarguably the Western world's most celebrated actress, dies at the age of 73. Known as 'the Divine Sarah', she made her international debut, with the Comédie-Française, in 1879 and went on to captivate audiences around the world, most notably in flamboyant, lavishly staged plays written for her by Victorien Sardou.

1924

WIRELESS STATIONS TAKE TO THE AIR

Hundreds of South Africans, many with home-made 'cat's-whisker' crystal sets, tune in to their first regular wireless programme when station JB takes to the air at 9 p.m.

Announcer Anne Manthey.

SONGS OF THE DAY
- Fascinating Rhythm
- It Had To Be You
- Parisian Pierrot

SOUTH AFRICA in the 20th CENTURY 1920s

on 1 July. Anne Manthey, the inaugural announcer, introduces the formal speeches and music from studios on the first floor of Stuttafords Building in Johannesburg. Towards the end of next year the Cape and Peninsula Broadcasting Association will begin its regular service from Greenmarket Square; Durban follows suit in December, all three independent companies providing a mix of music, talk, news and reports on the weather, the stock market and sport. The first rugby commentary goes over the air (from Newlands) in 1925.

But these pioneer stations struggle to survive. Three years down the line only 15,500 listeners have paid for licences, pirate broadcasters are clogging the ether, and in 1927 the newly formed national African Broadcasting Association, forerunner of the SABC, is granted a monopoly of the airwaves.

Dart and his famous find.

AFRICA THE 'CRADLE OF MANKIND' SAYS DART

Wits professor Raymond Dart identifies a fossilized skull found at Taung, in the Transvaal, as that of a man-ape who lived more than a million years ago. At first he takes the remains to be those of a baboon, but closer inspection and further specimens, from the limeworks in which the skull was found, reveal an entirely new type of primate. He names species *Australopithecus africanus*. Dart's discovery, and his assertion that Africa, not the northern hemisphere, was the 'cradle of mankind', sparks a controversy that will divide the scientific world for decades. He is eventually proved correct.

TOP MARRIAGE

Acclaimed actress Marda Vanne (born Margaretha van Hulsteyn) marries Nylstroom lawyer J.G. Strijdom. Vanne has already appeared on the London stage in leading roles, and will go on to enjoy further success in both London and on Broadway. Strijdom enters politics, eventually (in 1954) to become South African prime minister. The marriage will end in divorce.

BARRY HERTZOG TAKES OVER

General J.B.M. 'Barry' Hertzog, former Boer guerrilla commander, passionate Afrikaner patriot and leader of the National Party, becomes prime minister after reaching a pact with Colonel Frederick Cresswell's Labour Party. He will retain the premiership for the next 15 years – until the Second World War – during which time racial segregation and the erosion of the black people's rights will intensify.

Listening in to the first broadcast through a 'cats-whisker' receiver.

Hertzog and Cresswell dwarf Smuts in this Boonzaier cartoon.

SOUTH AFRICA in the 20th CENTURY
The Twenties

Aviatrixes – the heroines of the decade – help sell petrol.

PROGRESS FOR MOTORISTS

For the first time, Capetonian drivers can fill up at mechanically driven petrol pumps (until now, garages stocked four-gallon tins of fuel). Brands on offer include Shell, Pegasus and Atlantic.

In another motoring breakthrough, a French expedition led by Captain Delingette starts out from Algiers in a customized, 12-tyre Renault. It will arrive at Cape Town in July next year to complete the first trans-Africa overland journey. Delingette is accompanied on the journey by his wife, a mechanic and a manservant.

During the year, too, the Ford Motor Company opens its first South African assembly plant, in Grahamstown Road, Port Elizabeth. It employs 70 people and manages to turn out 12 'Tin Lizzies' – Model Ts – a day.

MAKING ENDS MEET

Most South Africans face hard times. Jobs are scarce, especially for the unskilled, wages abysmal outside the mining industry. Miners – timbermen, blasters, shift-bosses – are relatively well paid, but black men cannot rise above the lowly status of labourer.

A factory worker in the rag trade takes in just over £2 a month, a postman £15, a male shop assistant £20; teachers and cabinet makers £23. A pound will buy roughly half a kilo each of butter, jam, sugar, tea, rice, beef, mutton and bacon, two kilos of potatoes, 12 kilos of flour, a dozen eggs and three litres of milk.

At the other end of the wage scale, the commissioner of police earns £2,000 a year in 1924, the prime minister £3,500, the governor-general £10,000.

DEATH OF A LOSER

Practically nobody notices the death of 71-year-old pensioner George Walker. But he will always hold a special place in the annals of mining: in 1886 he and fellow-prospector George Harrison stumbled across the world's richest repository of gold – the 'ridge of white waters' on which Johannesburg has been built. Harrison sold his claim for £10, made his way to the Barberton goldfields and was never heard of again. Walker struck a slightly harder

BORN
International: US actor Marlon Brando; actress Lauren Bacall; politician Jimmy Carter; author Truman Capote. **South Africa:** *Jazzman Kippie Moeketsi; political leader Robert Sobukwe; actress Moira Lister.*

DIED
International: Italian composer Giacomo Puccini (his opera Turandot *premieres during the year); author Franz Kafka; George Mallory, in an attempt on still-to-be-conquered Mount Everest; Vladimir Ilyich Ulyanov, better known as Lenin, architect of the Russian revolution (Petrograd, formerly St Petersburg, is renamed Leningrad in his honour).* **South Africa:** *Political leader Alfred Mangena.*

Mountaineer Mallory.

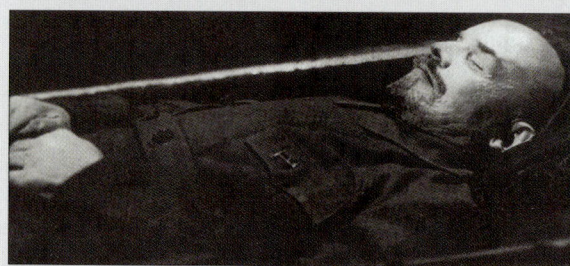

Lenin in death.

SOUTH AFRICA in the 20th CENTURY

WHAT'S NEW IN 1924

◆ **On sale** for the first time: spin-dryer for the home laundry; Kleenex tissues.

◆ **Motoring:** The Ford Motor Company produces its 10-millionth car, in the US.
◆ **US business:** Metro-Goldwyn-Meyer (MGM), Columbia Pictures and International Business Machines (IBM) are founded.
◆ **US:** The first gas-chamber execution takes place.
◆ **US:** American Indians are granted full citizenship.

Liddell, the Flying Scotsman, breasts the Olympic tape.

bargain: his claim fetched £350, after which he went to work on the new diggings, slipped into poverty and was eventually granted a modest allowance. Earlier this year the Chamber of Mines awarded him a pension.

LIDDELL RIDES FIERY CHARIOT TO VICTORY

Paris Olympics. Devout Scot Eric Liddell denies his British team possible victory in the 100 metres relay because the event is held on a Sunday. Instead he enters the 400 metres – and breaks the record. Much later his achievement, and those of his teammates (notably Harold Abrahams, who triumphs in the 100 metres), will be immortalized in the film *Chariots of Fire*.

For all that, though, the Games belongs to the 'Flying Finn',

Paavo Nurmi, who gains five golds in the distance events – even though two of them, the 1,500 and 5,000 metres, have to be run within little more than

Bantomweight medallist Willie Smith.

an hour of each other. At these Games, too, American swimmer Johnny Weismuller, destined to become Hollywood's first and most famous Tarzan, scoops three gold medals. The small South African squad manages just one gold: boxer Willie Smith wins the bantomweight division.

WORDS AND MUSIC

◆ Natal poet Roy Campbell's *The Flaming Terrapin* makes him an instant international literary celebrity.
◆ Other notable new works include E.M. Forster's *A Passage to India* and A.A. Milne's *When We Were Very Young*.
◆ Among musical events of the year is the première of George Gershwin's 'symphonic jazz' suite *Rhapsody in Blue*. His musical *Lady Be Good* also features on the year's sparkling arts-and-entertainment calendar.

SOUTH AFRICA in the 20th CENTURY

The Twenties

Edward, Prince of Wales.

1925

PRINCE CHARMING CAPTURES HEARTS

1 May. Edward, Prince of Wales, the world's most eligible bachelor and later to be crowned King Edward VIII, arrives at Cape Town to a tumultuous welcome before setting out on an exhausting round of receptions, speeches, luncheons, garden parties, banquets, ceremonies and meet-the-people forays. Four days later he embarks on an extensive tour of South Africa, Basutoland (now Lesotho), Bechuanaland (Botswana), Southern Rhodesia (Zimbabwe) and Northern Rhodesia (Zambia). Throughout his punishing three-month visit the young prince endears himself to all with his good looks, cheerful informality, sense of humour – and stoicism. He has, he says, taken excellent advice from an experienced Court official: 'Only two rules really count. Never miss an opportunity to relieve yourself; never miss a chance to sit down and rest your feet.'

DIAMONDS DISCOVERED ON WEST COAST

Captain Jack Carstens, a young Indian Army soldier on home leave in Namaqualand, stumbles across a large diamond in the desert sands near Port Nolloth, triggering one of the biggest rushes of the century. Prospectors pour into the 80-kilometre coastal strip to the south of the Orange River; a few become instant millionaires – precious stones lie everywhere in and on the alluvial gravels. One man, the noted geologist Hans Merensky, finds 487 diamonds beneath a single flat rock.

FINALE FOR 'THE GUV'NOR'

Leonard Rayne, the country's foremost stage personality, dies at the age of 55. The great actor-manager, who brought top-class drama to early South African theatre, took the male lead in his many productions both at Cape Town's Opera House and on tour, maintaining a remarkable standard of excellence, never playing down to what were often unsophisticated audiences. He invariably moved the ladies to tears with his performances, most notably in his best-known role as Napoleon in *The Royal Divorce*. It was Rayne, known to his company as 'the Guv'nor', who in 1910 recruited Freda Godfrey, the 'Mary Pickford of South Africa', after spotting her on a London stage. She has remained with him to the end.

PAVLOVA DELIGHTS LOCAL BALLET FANS

Legendary Russian ballerina Anna Pavlova overwhelms South African audiences with her brilliance during her season – which started on 29 December – at Cape Town's Opera House and later at the Standard Theatre, Johannesburg. For her final two performances in the Mother City

Godfrey: 'SA's Mary Pickford'.

Merensky: instant fortune.

Pavlova's Dying Swan.

SOUTH AFRICA in the 20th CENTURY

1920s

WHAT'S NEW IN 1925

- The **Charleston** is danced for the first time, in the South Carolina town of that name. Conservatives condemn it as 'immoral'; the young (and, soon enough, the not-so-young) take to it with enthusiasm.
- **Afrikaans** becomes South Africa's second official language.
- **Motoring**: Chrysler founds motor company, in the US.
- **Germany**: Hitler founds the SS (Schutzstaffel).
- **Britain**: Double-decker buses appear on city routes.
- **US**: The Frisbee is invented by students (the name is taken from the Frisbee company's pie-plates).

she choreographs a special dance to complement the magnificent ostrich-feather fan presented to her by local teachers. And it isn't the usually pale, withdrawn, coldly perfectionist professional who puts on the special show but, according to an enraptured *Argus* reviewer, 'a Pavlova in a gauzy, filmy mauve with golden wig, a living, breathing, happy woman delighted to display a present which has delighted her'.

SONGS OF THE DAY
- Show Me the Way to Go Home
- Always
- Manhattan

FIRST FAREWELL TO OLD LOCOS

The first signs that steam locomotives, those grand workhorses of South Africa's transport network, are on their way out appear in 1925. In January, five electric trains a day begin to ply their fast, smoke-free way along the 70-kilometre track between Estcourt and Ladysmith in Natal.

AMERICAN COURT REJECTS DARWIN

Dayton, Tennessee. Christian fundamentalists heave a sigh of relief when the court finds John Scopes guilty of teaching Darwin's theory of evolution to schoolchildren.

Scopes (centre) with Darrow (right) after the watershed trial.

However, Scopes's defence lawyer, the celebrated Clarence Darrow, steals the show – a trial that is followed closely throughout the Christian world – by leading the prosecutor (William Jennings Bryan) to admit, reluctantly, that the act of Creation 'might have continued for millions of years'.

LEISURE ROUND-UP

- Among the high points on the year's arts-and-leisure scene are the premières of two films destined to become classics: *The Phantom of the Opera*, and Charlie Chaplin's *The Gold Rush*.
- New books include Scott Fitzgerald's *The Great Gatsby*, Franz Kafka's *The Trial*, and Adolf Hitler's *Mein Kampf*.
- Design and decor displays at the Paris Exhibition launch the Art Deco movement.

George Bernard Shaw.

- Irish playwright George Bernard Shaw is awarded but rejects the Nobel prize for literature.

SPORT

A New Zealander becomes the first rugby player to be sent off for foul play in an international match. The All Blacks beat England 17-11.

65

SOUTH AFRICA in the 20th CENTURY

The Twenties

The Charleston, with variations, is all the rage in the mid-twenties.

TOP YOUNG MAGAZINES
- Gem
- Magnet
- Boy's Own Paper
- Jungle Jinks
- Tiger Tim's
- Playbox
- Peg's Paper

1926

DIGGERS DASH FOR DIAMONDS

Lichtenburg, western Transvaal. One of the world's last and greatest diamond rushes takes place on the farm Elandsputte, near this dusty little country town. News of the first find breaks in March and spreads like the proverbial bushfire, and within months more than 100,000 diggers are working the alluvial ground. At one point 30,000 hopefuls take part in an official claim-pegging race across the flat, dun-coloured veld – a single, frenzied mass scramble for instant wealth. Some are lucky, especially those whose claims lie over potholes in the ancient riverbed – natural repositories in which fabulous treasure had accumulated. Other diggers, perhaps just a few metres away, find nothing.

> 'What is good enough for the white man is good enough for you. Our aim is to be one with the white race.'
> *Clements Kadalie, founder of the Industrial and Commercial Workers' Union, speaking at a rally*

'SKUKUZA' TAKES OVER THE PRINCE OF PARKS

The eastern Transvaal's Sabie and Shingwedzi game reserves are combined to create the Kruger, South Africa's first national park. Appointed warden of this immense tract of Lowveld countryside is James Stevenson-Hamilton, an army colonel and Scottish laird who pioneered conservation in the region after taking over the fledgling Sabie a quarter of a century ago. To those who have worked with him he is known as Skukuza, which means 'he

Fortune-seekers race across the veld to stake their claims.

SOUTH AFRICA in the 20th CENTURY 1920s

Death of a heart-throb: Leading silent-screen lover Rudolph Valentino dies suddenly in New York, breaking a million women's hearts. Valentino, who emigrated from Italy in 1913, worked as a humble gardener before taking to the stage (as a dancer). He made his Hollywood debut in 1919 in The Four Horsemen of the Apocalypse *and went on to star in* The Sheik *(1921), which catapulted him to screen-idol status,* Blood and Sand *(1922) and other romantic features. His funeral, attended by thousands, resembles a state occasion; a number of female fans commit suicide.*

WHAT'S NEW IN 1926

♦ The **first motor-powered mailship**, Carnarvon Castle, joins the Union-Castle fleet. She is also the first of the line's vessels to weigh more than 20,000 tons.

♦ **Medicine:** An anti-tetanus serum is developed by the Pasteur Institute in Paris.
♦ **Women swimmers:** American Gertrude Ederle is the first woman to swim the English Channel, in a time of 14 hours 31 minutes. In South Africa, nurse Florrie Berndt swims the treacherous Atlantic Oceans waters from Robben Island to Cape Town.
♦ British aviation pioneer Alan Cobham completes a **round-the-world flight** via Australia in his red-and-white De Havilland DH 50, establishing routes for newly formed Imperial Airways.

Florrie Berndt.

who scrapes clean' – a reference to his intolerance of hunting and ruthless persecution of poachers.

PICTURES TRANSMITTED BY WIRELESS

January. Scottish electrical engineer John Logie Baird demonstrates, to a small London audience of scientists, a device that transmits half-tone pictures through wireless signals. Vague images appear on a flickering screen that measures just 5 by 3 cm. This follows experiments with silhouettes, conducted in collaboration with the American C.F. Jenkins, in 1923. Baird predicts that his 'television' machine will eventually be perfected to become

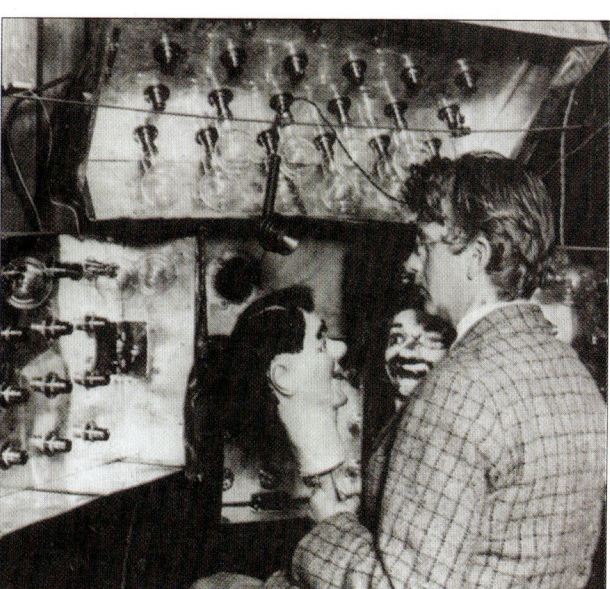

Television pioneer John Logie Baird.

67

SOUTH AFRICA in the 20th CENTURY

The Twenties

Monet, last of the great Impressionists.

BORN
International: Elizabeth, daughter to the Duke and Duchess of York; rock musician Chuck Berry; Norma Jean Baker (Marilyn Monroe); poet Alan Ginsburg. **South Africa:** Actress Yvonne Bryceland; revolutionary and politician Joe Slovo.

DIED
International: French Impressionist painter Claude Monet; master escape-artist Harry Houdini. **South Africa:** Pacifist campaigner Emily Hobhouse.

SONGS OF THE DAY
- Bye Bye Blackbird
- Some of These Days
- Black Bottom

a standard addition to the ordinary home. Most observers, however, remain sceptical.

DOMINION STATUS CONFIRMED
South Africa's status as an independent dominion is formally confirmed by a resolution adopted at the Imperial Conference. This states that the dominions are 'autonomous communities within the British Empire, equal in status, in no way subordinate to one to another in any respect of their domestic or external affairs, though united by a common allegiance to the Crown, and freely associated as members of the British Commonwealth of Nations'.

FAREWELL TO EMILY
South Africans, and especially the Afrikaner community, mourn the death of Emily Hobhouse, the feisty British pacifist who campaigned so vigorously on behalf of displaced Boers during the 1899–1902 war. Hobhouse proved such a thorn in the side of the British military that, on her second visit, she was denied access to the notorious concentration camps (General Kitchener referred to her as 'that bloody woman' and had her deported). Poor and in ill health, she eventually retired to a cottage in Cornwall, bought largely with donated funds collected in the Orange Free State. Her ashes will later be brought to South Africa and interred at Bloemfontein's National Women's Monument.

> 'For God's sake go down to reception and get rid of a lunatic who's down there. He says he's got a machine for seeing by wireless!'
> *A British businessman's response when approached by television inventor John Logie Baird*

Emily Hobhouse – 'that bloody woman' – in middle age.

SOUTH AFRICA in the 20th CENTURY **1920s**

ON THE BOOKSHELF

◆ Readers are beguiled by A.A. Milne's just-published *Winnie-the-Pooh*. Milne wrote the stories – about a fat and friendly bear and his assorted friends – for his son Christopher Robin.

◆ Also published is *The Seven Pillars of Wisdom*, a personal account of the Arab revolt by T.E. Lawrence (Lawrence of Arabia).

◆ Two notable new titles will grace South African bookshelves. C.J. Langenhoven, the versatile Afrikaans writer (of lyrical poetry, science fiction, detective, ghost and children's stories) and editor (of the Oudtshoorn newspaper *Het Zuid-Westen*) has published his *Die Krismiskinders*. Pauline Smith, another author from the sleepy little farming town of Oudtshoorn, produces *The Beadle*, which will be rated internationally as one of the best literary creations to emerge from South Africa.

THE SILVER SCREEN

◆ British (later Hollywood) director Alfred Hitchcock makes his first feature film, *The Lodger*.

◆ Other Hollywood highlights: Ramon Navarro stars in *Ben Hur*; Stan Laurel and Oliver Hardy make their first film, a short piece entitled *Putting Pants on Philip*. Laurel, an Englishman, once understudied Charlie Chaplin.

1927
NEW LAWS FURTHER SEPARATE THE RACES

Two far-reaching, race-driven parliamentary statutes are enacted during the year. The Immorality Act criminalizes sexual relations between black and white people, though for the time being marriages across the colour line will remain legal. Less dramatic but perhaps even more significant to the country's future is the Native Administration Act, which for the first time vests unquestioned authority, in matters affecting black South Africans, in a central Native Affairs Department. This will in due course become an all-powerful, largely unaccountable 'state within a state'.

REINS OF RADIO GATHERED TOGETHER

The giant Schlesinger Organization's African Broadcasting Corporation takes over the country's ailing radio transmission services, which have hitherto been provided by poorly run regional companies and their pirate or 'ham' competitors. Over the next decade the licenced listeners will increase from 20,000 to 125,000.

WHAT'S NEW IN 1927

◆ Plans for a **Soccer World Cup** are revealed by Frenchman Jules Rimet.

◆ **UK:** The British Broadcasting Corporation (BBC) is incorporated as a public utility.

◆ **US:** Pan-American Airways is founded, and advertises the world's first international flights.

◆ First **transatlantic telephone call**, at a cost of $75.

◆ The **iron lung** is invented, giving hope to victims of infantile paralysis (polio) and others.

◆ The word **nappy** is added to the English language.

Tycoon Schlesinger.

FIRST 'TALKIE' FILM SCREENED

Johannesburg cinema-goers are surprised and delighted by Sydney Haydon's presentation, at his Kinemas auditorium, of 'talking films'. The sound – the first to be produced on celluloid by means of a photo-electric cell – is well synchronized with the images on screen, though it is tinny, even harsh in quality.

Shortly afterwards African Consolidated Films imports *The Jazz Singer*, filmdom's first full-length 'talkie'. It features Al Jolson, his rendering of 'Mammy', other songs and fragments of speech. Jolson's first, trite but momentous words are 'Wait a minute! You ain't heard nothin' yet'. South African audiences seem less impressed – the sound has been created with the gramophone-like

SONGS OF THE DAY

● Ain't She Sweet
● My Blue Heaven
● Among My Souvenirs
● Sometimes I'm Happy

The year's 'bob' hairstyle becomes the butt of cartoonists; this drawing is entitled 'Miss 1927'.

SOUTH AFRICA in the 20th CENTURY
The Twenties

BORN
International: Cuban revolutionary Fidel Castro.
South Africa: Dancer Nadia Nerina; dancer and choreographer John Cranko; singer Gé Korsten.

DIED
Italian left-wing radicals Nicola Sacco and Bartolomeo Vanzetti, executed in the US after a controversial murder trial with heavy political undertones.

Sacco and Vanzetti: a political execution.

Panatrope system – but new and exciting ground has been broken: after *The Jazz Singer*, silent movies quickly become a mere memory.

> 'You two don't do nothing but smoke cigarettes all day long and crack jokes. You'll get yourselves in serious trouble if the Governor finds out you keep the whole prison awake night after night, romping about and laughing...'
> *Prison warder to writer Herman Charles Bosman and a fellow inmate of the condemned cells*

OK BAZAARS OPENS ITS DOORS
25 June. Enterprising traders Sam Cohen and Michael Miller open their first OK Bazaars, on downmarket Eloff Street, Johannesburg, and taste immediate, almost overwhelming success. The store breaks several long-standing retail conventions: everything the careful housewife may need, or want, is displayed on walk-around island counters; sales are conducted on a cash-and-carry basis; the range is wide, the quality high, the prices remarkably low. For a shilling, you can get a glass decanter or a lady's handbag; sixpence will buy you a bottle of Eau de Cologne. The multitudes pour in.

LINDBERGH CONQUERS THE ATLANTIC
Young American aviator Charles Lindbergh flies his specially adapted, 237-horsepower Ryan aeroplane, *The Spirit of St Louis*, non-stop from New York to Le Bourget airfield, Paris, to set a new solo record. The challenging 5,800-kilometre flight takes 33 hours 30 minutes.

STAGE AND SCREEN
The Academy of Motion Picture Arts and Sciences is founded in Hollywood; its first Oscars will be presented (by Douglas Fairbanks) in 1929. Premières include Cecil B. DeMille's epic film *King of Kings*; George Gershwin's stage musical *Funny Face*; and Florenz Ziegfeld's *Show Boat*, created by Jerome Kern and Oscar Hammerstein II.

OK Bazaars' first emporium.

SOUTH AFRICA in the 20th CENTURY **1920s**

1928
LADY MARY BREAKS AIR RECORD ...

Lady Mary Bailey, intrepid wife of South African financier Sir Abe Bailey, makes aviation history when she flies solo from London to Cape Town and back – the first time such a feat has been attempted. Her tiny De Havilland Moth is forced down by a desert sandstorm in the Sudan and by engine failure in Tanganyika, but she arrives safely at Pretoria's Swartkops air force base after a 44-day outward flight. For the return journey she takes the still largely uncharted west coast route.

Already a famed aviatrix, Lady Mary broke the world altitude record for a light plane in 1927 (18,000 feet) and, earlier this year, became the first woman to fly across the Irish Sea. Her achievements, however, are somewhat overshadowed by the American Amelia Earhart who, in June, became the first woman to fly the Atlantic.

Amelia Earhart: a legend in and beyond her own time.

Lady Mary: London to Cape Town and back.

BORN
International: South American revolutionary Ernesto 'Che' Guevara, in Rosario, Argentine; child actress Shirley Temple; artist Andy Warhol. *South Africa:* Human rights lawyer George Bizos (in Greece); traditional leader and politician Mangosuthu Buthelezi; writer, poet and publisher Lionel Abrahams.

... AND GERRY BOUWER CONQUERS THE VELD

During the year the time taken to negotiate the formidable overland route from Cape Town to Cairo is reduced even further. South African racing personality Gerry Bouwer and newspaper motoring editor Emil Mullin, driving a Chrysler, cover the distance in 93 days. Still not satisfied, Bouwer makes the return trip (with his wife as passenger) in a remarkable 40 days.

Bouwer is an adventurous soul, already well known to the public for his ground-breaking exploits. In 1922 he walked from Cairo to Johannesburg; two years later he raced his Chrysler Six against the Union Express from Cape Town to Johannesburg – and won by four hours. The time: 26 hours, 13 minutes.

NEW NATIONAL FLAG ADOPTED

The South African flag is flown for the first time – alongside the Union Jack – at ceremonies attended by the governor-general, the Earl of Athlone (in Cape Town) and his wife, Princess Alice (in Pretoria). Over the months there

71

SOUTH AFRICA in the 20th CENTURY

The Twenties

has been bitter and sometimes violent controversy over the design of a new emblem: royalists, especially Natalians, have been fierce in their support of the British standard; the anti-British faction has campaigned to cut the colonial connection completely; scores of ideas, some wonderful in their extravagance, have been produced. In the end the two sides settled on a compromise: the original orange, white and blue *Prinsenvlag* – which Jan van Riebeeck hoisted over the Cape in 1652 – with a central shield incorporating the Union Jack and the flags of the Boer republics.

MIRACLE FUNGUS FOUND

In what could be a dramatic breakthrough in the war against disease, Scottish scientist Alexander Fleming reports his discovery that a humble mould, a type of *Penicillium*, appears to attack a wide variety of harmful bacteria. The fungus is similar in its properties to that which grows on bread, so a drug devel-

> 'Ladies might become more intelligent, as in the past their brains have run to their hair.'
> *Editorial in* Outspan *magazine, commenting on the shingle hairstyles.*

Fleming at work.

oped from it should be safe to use in the treatment of human infections. The initial discovery was accidental: Fleming noticed that the green mould had appeared on, and destroyed, part of a *Staphylococcus* bacterial culture carelessly left exposed in his rather disorganized London laboratory.

LITERARY EYEBROWS RAISED

♦ D.H. Lawrence's sexually explicit *Lady Chatterley's Lover*, published privately in Florence, Italy, shocks some and titillates others of its limited readership. Lawrence is no stranger to dispute: he achieved fame with his *Sons and Lovers* in

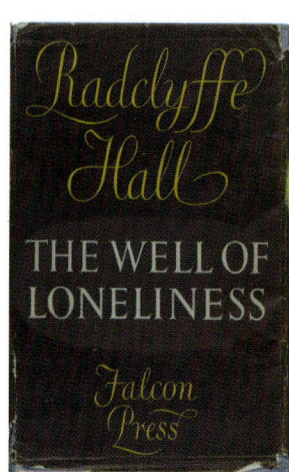
The book that shocks.

1913, but two years later faced prosecution for obscenity after publication of *The Rainbow*.
♦ Even less conventional is Radclyffe Hall's *The Well of Loneliness*, the first overtly lesbian novel. The book has been banned.
♦ Seventy years in the making, *The Oxford English Dictionary* finally appears on the bookshelves.

WHAT'S NEW IN 1928

♦ **US:** Herbert Hoover is elected President.
♦ **Enthroned:** Long-reigning emperors Hirohito in Japan; Ras Tafari in Ethiopia.
♦ **UK:** The voting age for women is lowered from 30 to a more sensible 21.
♦ **US:** The New York Stock Exchange enjoys record trade; the world's financial gurus are optimistic.
♦ **Debut products in the US:** Television sets (at $75 apiece); bubble gum.
♦ **Medicine:** Vitamin F discovered, smear test for cervical and uterine cancer developed, both in America.
♦ **Australia:** A flying doctor service is introduced.
♦ **Motor cars:** Ford's Model A replaces Model T; the Morris Minor car is launched in Britain.
♦ The words **media** and **cocktail** become part of the English language.

OLYMPICS HIGHLIGHTS

The Olympic Games, held in Amsterdam this year, takes a giant step forward when women compete on the athletics track for first time, in five events. The 'Flying Finn' Paavo Nurmi, though plagued by rheumatism and injury, wins the men's 10,000 metres to add to his triumphs of 1924.

Nurmi winning Olympic gold.

SOUTH AFRICA in the 20th CENTURY

MICKEY TAKES HIS FIRST BOW

The young commercial and animation artist Walt Disney introduces Mickey Mouse to cinema-goers. The rodent plays his first role in a short piece entitled *Steamboat Willie*; Disney himself provides the voice.

Disney and his mouse.

ELYSIAN FIELDS RECALLED

Author Juliet Marais Louw, who begins writing for the *Rand Daily Mail* in the later 1920s, will remember the simple pleasures of her youth in her book *Wagon Tracks and Orchards*. A typical passage: 'Someone would wind the gramophone and put on record after record, turning each one over to the other side, winding the handle – over and over again – for hours on end. I never hear 'Side by Side' or 'You Are My Honeysuckle' ... without smelling again the dust and heat and stuffiness, feeling the scrape of the work-hardened hands in mine, the swing of bodies under moist shirts, the exhilaration and the lightheartedness of the little lamplit rooms. Sometimes too we went out into the garden, sweet with the scent of night, and walked under orchard trees amid flowering blossoms. It was spring and we were young.'

1929 WALL STREET CRASHES

24 October – 'Black Thursday'. The boom on the New York stock market comes to a sudden and dramatic end as shares plunge, wiping out billions of dollars of investments.

SOUNDS OF THE 20S
- **Songs:** A Room with a View; I Can't Give You Anything But Love, Baby; Ol' Man River
- **Top jazz:** Louis Armstrong; Duke Ellington; Bessie Smith; Jelly Roll Morton; Pee Wee Russell

> 'The industrial condition of the United States is perfectly sound.'
> Charles Mitchell, chairman of National City Bank, just before the Wall Street crash

Wall Street: epicentre of financial disaster.

Panic-stricken speculators, who had cashed in on an unprecedented 18-month bull run to make massive profits, try frantically to offload their holdings.

A group of American banks seeks to stabilize the situation but, after a temporary respite, prices resume a downward spiral on 28 October, some of the leading stocks losing more than 60 percent of their value. Thousands of American families watch helplessly as their life savings disappear. European and other investors also lose heavily. The financial disaster threatens to trigger a world-wide depression.

BRAVE ATTEMPT ON SPEED RECORD

Ace British driver Malcolm Campbell chooses the flat, salt-encrusted Verneukpan, in South Africa's arid northern Cape, for his latest assault on the world land speed record. His odyssey has been plagued from the beginning by setbacks: he was involved in two air crashes on his way to the site; the tyres of his Napier-powered car, *Bluebird*, were torn to shreds in practice runs and, worst of all, he learnt at the last moment that rival

SOUTH AFRICA in the 20th CENTURY

The Twenties

Malcolm Campbell and Bluebird *prepare for the record run across Verneukpan, northern Cape.*

Henry Segrave had in the meantime pushed the mark up to 373.2 km/h – an impossible target at Verneukpan's altitude. So Campbell decides instead to attempt the 5-mile and 5-kilometre world records – which he duly breaks (with speeds of 339.6 km/h and 347.6 km/h respectively) even though the car's tyres are reduced to canvas during the run.

ANC LINKS UP WITH COMMUNISTS

Josiah Gumede, leader of the African National Congress, agrees to become president of the newly formed Marxist organization, the African League of Rights (ALR). This is a major coup for South Africa's communists: the league gains immediate popular support, enough to launch a vigorous campaign against racial discrimination. However, the movement collapses when its Soviet masters, convinced that economic depression will soon destroy capitalism, prohibits all alliances with non-communist bodies.

UNION AIRWAYS TAKES TO THE SKIES

26 August. Aviation pioneer and member of parliament Major Allister Miller inaugurates his new Union Airways, the country's first airline, by flying one of his tiny aircraft from Maitland aerodrome, near Johannesburg, to Port Elizabeth to deliver five bags of mail. The company's debut fleet comprises five open Gypsy Moths; the wind-blown passengers wear flying helmets and

ANC leader Josiah Gumede.

BORN
International: US civil rights campaigner Martin Luther King; actresses Audrey Hepburn and Grace Kelly; Anne Frank, whose wartime diary would touch millions of hearts around the world; playwright John Osborne. **South Africa:** *Activist and politician Joe Modise; test cricketer Jackie McGlew; actor Lawrence Harvey (born Mischa Skikne, in Lithuania); operatic singer Nellie du Toit.*

DIED
Lillie Langtry (the 'Jersey Lily'), British beauty, actress and one-time mistress of King Edward VII; French war leader Marshal Ferdinand Foch; Wild West lawman Wyatt Earp.

SOUTH AFRICA in the 20th CENTURY

WHAT'S NEW IN 1929

- ◆ **Germany:** Hitler's Nazi Party holds the first Nuremburg rally.
- ◆ **Hollywood:** Inaugural Academy Awards (Oscars) are presented, by Douglas Fairbanks.
- ◆ **Newspapers:** First Popeye cartoon appears.
- ◆ The **US motor industry** produces the first front-wheel drive (in a Cord), first synchro-mesh gearbox (Cadillac), and first car radio.
- ◆ **US:** The first colour television pictures are demonstrated.
- ◆ The **Vatican City** becomes an independent state.

A later Nuremburg rally; the first was held in 1929.

goggles for protection. In January next year Union Airways, based in Port Elizabeth, will invest in a more comfortable six-seater Fokker Universal but the airline is destined to be dogged by tragedy: in 1931 one of its planes (a Puss Moth) crashes with the loss of three lives just to the east of Cape Town, the Fokker comes to grief near East London, and disaster strikes again in 1933 when a pilot and four passengers are killed in the Eshowe area of Natal.

Finally, in 1934, the government takes over the ailing airline, renaming it South African Airways (which it will be called for the rest of the century).

CAPONE WINS CHICAGO TURF WAR

Chicago. Seven members of 'Bugsy' Moran's gang are shot to death on St Valentine's Day (14 February) by gunmen loyal to rival mobster boss Al Capone. This is the latest and most dramatic incident in a gangland war – for control of the illegal alcohol trade, protection rackets and gambling – that has already claimed hundreds of lives. Capone emerges the victor, though soon afterwards he is jailed, for a year, for carrying a concealed weapon.

FIRST EDITIONS

Books published this year include:
- ◆ Ernest Hemingway's *A Farewell to Arms*;
- ◆ Erich Maria Remarque's *All Quiet on the Western Front*;
- ◆ Denys Reitz's best-selling *Commando*, a moving account of the author's experiences during the Anglo-Boer War.

HITS OF THE DAY
- Tip-toe through the Tulips
- Sonny Boy
- Stardust

Corpses litter the floor after the St Valentine's Day massacre.

1930s

THE GREAT DEPRESSION
1930: Savage drought in SA; maize exports slump.
1932: 188,000 whites register for employment; no reliable statistics are produced for blacks. SA abandons the gold standard. Carnegie Commission reports on the status of 'poor whites'.
1933: Drought temporarily broken.

RESTRICTED
1930: Immigration to SA, especially of Jewish people, by the Quota Act.

ENFRANCHIZED
1930: White women over the age of 30.

DISCOVERED
1930: The planet Pluto (US).
1934: The Jonker Diamond, world's fourth largest, on the farm Elandsfontein.
1936: First australopithecines ('southern ape-men') at the Sterkfontein caves near Pretoria, by Robert Broom.

FIRST
1931: Wireless telephone link between UK and SA. Music recordings in SA (by Singer Gramophone Co, Johannesburg).'Talkies' produced in SA (by African Film Productions).
1932: Airmail and passenger services between UK and SA. Appearance of *Bantu World* newspaper. Atom split, by Cockcroft and Walton (UK); Chadwick discovers neutron at Cambridge (UK).
1933: Afrikaans Bible.
1934: Trolley-buses in Cape Town. International motor-racing event in SA (Border Hundred, East London).
1935: Springbok cricket series victory in England.
1936: Penguin books on sale, at sixpence a copy (UK). Television broadcasting service (by the BBC, London).
1938: Volkswagen cars assembled in Germany.
1939: Cricket 'Timeless Test', played in Durban.

PROCLAIMED
1931: Kalahari Gemsbok National Park, on Bechuanaland border. Pretoria as a city.
1932: University of Pretoria.
1939: Cape of Good Hope Nature Reserve.

CELEBRATED
1938: Voortrekker centenary.

POLITICS AND PROTEST
1930: ANC president Josiah Gumede and fellow radicals ousted in favour of moderates led by Pixley ka Isaka Seme. Radicals launch pass-burning campaign.
1931: Statute of Westminster gives SA full legislative independence.
1934: Smuts and Hertzog form United Party; 'Fusion' government takes office.
1935: All-Africa Convention founded.
1936: Representation of Natives Act passed (remaining blacks removed from common roll).
1938: Afrikaner nationalist (pro-German) Ossewabrandwag founded.

WORLD STAGE
1931: Japan invades Manchuria, launching the prolonged and brutal Sino-Japanese war.
1933: Hitler installed as German chancellor; Roosevelt as US president. Roosevelt launches 'New Deal'.
1934: Stalin launches massive four-year purge of Soviet Communist Party, armed forces and intelligentsia; millions imprisoned and executed.
1935: Mussolini invades Abyssinia. Nazi regime begins legal persecution of German Jews; sexual intercourse between 'Aryans' and Jews becomes capital offence.
1936: King Edward VIII abdicates; is succeeded by George VI. Spanish civil war begins. Germany reoccupies the Rhineland. Rome-Berlin 'Axis' pact signed.
1937: Japanese forces invade China, provoking worldwide reaction. Neville Chamberlain becomes British premier.
1938: Germany occupies Austria 'by invitation' (*Anschluss*). British and French sign Munich agreement approving German occupation of Sudetenland portion of Czechoslovakia; Chamberlain returns convinced of 'peace for our time'. Hitler and Stalin sign Non-Aggression Pact.
1939: German armies invade Poland. Britain and France declare war on Germany. SA follows suit after Smuts replaces Hertzog as premier.

1939: South Africa's politicians split on the war issue.

76 The Thirties

SOUTH AFRICA in the 20th CENTURY

1930

HARD TIMES AFTER WALL STREET CRASH

The Great Depression – and, in South Africa, a series of savage droughts – blight the world of the 1930s. Mines, factories, shops and businesses close down, maize exports decline by more than 80 percent, once-productive farmlands lie idle, the army of the unemployed grows, the soup-kitchen queues lengthen. And those lucky enough to have jobs see their wages plunge. Hunger stalks the streets.

The misery transcends racial barriers; all but a privileged few suffer. But nowhere is deprivation more visible than among the urban 'poor whites', most of them Afrikaans speaking with roots in the countryside. Events since the 1890s – the ravages of the Anglo-Boer War, poor rains, cattle disease, locust plagues among them – have impoverished much of the farming community and driven tens of thousands of rural whites into the cities, where they have to compete with cheap black labour. Many cannot do so, and sink into apathy. Others stay on the land as *bywoners* (subsistence tenant farmers) and squatters.

By the early 1930s the problem has become a crisis. A Carnegie commission report reveals that more than 300,000 out of a total white population of 1.8 million can be classed as 'very poor' – and the number grows as the depression deepens. One commissioner visits 600 homes and finds that fewer than a quarter of them are fit for human habitation.

Poor whites: the land can no longer support them; lack of skills, and competition from black labour, denies them city jobs.

ANC RADICALS OUSTED

January. The entire executive of the African National Congress resign in protest against ANC president Josiah Gumede's close links with the Communists. In a showdown in April, Gumede and his fellow militants are replaced by moderates led by Pixley ka Isaka Seme, a graduate of Columbia and Oxford universities and founder of South Africa's first black newspaper. Seme attempts to remain on good terms with the white establishment.

Children of the depression. Suffering among black South Africans goes unrecorded.

77

The Thirties

SOUTH AFRICA in the 20th CENTURY

Trolley-buses on Cape Town's Adderley Street.

QUIETER RIDES FOR CITY TRAVELLERS

The first of the new 'trackless trams', or trolley-buses, arrive in Cape Town on 25 August, and will in due course ply the thoroughfares of Pretoria and Durban as well as those of the Mother City. Special legislation will be introduced to allow both single- and double-deckers on the streets. Like the electric trams that have served city dwellers so honourably for close on half a century, they are confined to a fixed route but, powered by overhead lines, they enjoy a five-metre play on either side and are more manoeuvrable – and a great deal quieter – than what one Capetonian termed 'those monstrous masses of rowdy tin'. Trolley-buses will remain a familiar city feature until the end of the 1950s.

WHAT'S NEW IN 1930

- *In the kitchen:* Pre-packed sliced bread, frozen peas and the electric kettle appear on the US market.
- *Astronomy:* The planet Pluto discovered, by amateur American astronomer Clyde Tombaugh.
- *Motor industry:* Italian carmaker launches the Bugatti Royale, the largest production model ever built.
- *Dagwood and Blondie* make their comic-strip debut.

AIRSHIP BECOMES FIREBALL

Disaster strikes British aviation when the 777-foot-long, hydrogen-filled airship R.101 crashes and explodes near Beauvais, France, on its maiden flight. Flames engulf the craft, destroying it within minutes. A total of 44 crew and passengers, including British secretary for air Lord Thomson, die in the inferno; eight survive. It is thought that the airship lost height, and became difficult to handle, during a sudden rain squall.

NAZIS GRAB THE VOTES

15 September. Against all predictions Adolf Hitler's National Socialist (Nazi) party gains the second most votes in the German general election, increasing its representation in the Reichstag from 12 to 107 deputies. The Socialists top the polls, the Communists come in third.

Hitler is regarded by many as a nine-day wonder.

THE PASSING OF A GENIUS

Among deaths recorded is that of Thomas Edison, one-time newsboy and candy-seller (on the US's Grand Trunk Railway) and arguably the greatest of modern inventors and scientific developers. Edison patented more than 1,000 inventions, among them those for the automatic telegraph, the modern typewriter, the microphone, the phonograph, the electric light bulb, the carbon telephone transmitter, and the incandescent electric lamp. At school, he was adjudged an 'addled' pupil who would 'never amount to anything'.

Inventor Edison.

But some folk speculate that President Hindenburg may appoint him German chancellor, second highest office in the land, if only to show him up as the ignorant amateur his opponents believe him to be. Meanwhile, there are ugly scenes in the streets as Nazi thugs continue to harass Jews and smash Jewish shops.

SOUTH AFRICA in the 20th CENTURY 1930s

SPORTING HIGHLIGHTS

The young Australian batsman Donald Bradman sets new cricketing records when he goes on a run spree, scoring a mammoth 334 in the Leeds Test against England. A phenomenal 309 of these come in one day, and not a whole day at that: he arrives at the crease after the first wicket falls. Earlier in the year, in Australia, Bradman notched up 452 in a single innings. Uruguay, smallest by far of the competing nations, wins soccer's inaugural World Cup when it defeats Argentina 4-2 in front of a 90,000-strong home crowd.

Bradman strides to the crease.

ON THE SILVER SCREEN
- Bela Lugosi in *Dracula*
- Boris Karloff in *Frankenstein*
- Charlie Chaplin in *City Lights*

Record-breaker Amy Johnson accepts congratulations.

Aviatrix Amy Johnson, 27, becomes the first woman to fly solo from Britain to Australia when she lands her Gypsy Moth at Darwin early in April. Her departure from Croydon aerodrome goes largely unnoticed, but her well publicized trials en route – sandstorms and forced landings among them – soon capture the headlines.

American golfer Bobby Jones wins both the US and British amateur and open titles – the grand slam – and immediately announces his retirement, at the age of 28.

FILM STARS FACE VOICE TEST

♦ Some silent-movie stars are taking well to the new 'talking pictures', others apparently can't say a word for themselves. Swedish actress Greta Garbo's throatily sensual

Dietrich: silent no more.

voice perfectly matches her looks in *Anna Christie*; her first line: 'Gimme a whisky with ginger ale on the side – and don't be stingy, baby'. Sultry German rival Marlene Dietrich also scores a hit in *The Blue Angel*. Others are embarrassingly exposed, among them erstwhile heart-throb John Gilbert, whose appearance in *His Glorious Night* has audiences in stitches as he kisses a girl's arm and squeaks 'I love you, I love you, I love you'.

♦ The year's premieres also include *Blackmail*, Alfred Hitchcock's first sound film; *All Quiet on the Western Front*, and the Marx Brothers' *Animal Crackers*.

BORN
International: Actors Sean Connery, Clint Eastwood; astronaut Neil Armstrong; playwright Harold Pinter. *South Africa:* Actor Ken Gampu, photographer David Goldblatt; soldier and politician Magnus Malan.

DIED
International: Authors Sir Arthur Conan Doyle, D.H. Lawrence. *South Africa:* Cricketer Aubrey Faulkner.

Died: cricketing great Faulkner.

79

SOUTH AFRICA in the 20th CENTURY

The Thirties

1931

BOKS STEAMROLLER THEIR WAY TO VICTORY

The South African rugby team wins 23 out of 26 matches, including all four internationals, on their tour of the British Isles, scoring a total of 406 points while conceding just 124. They draw twice and lose once. Much of the credit goes to captain and fly-half Bennie Osler, a master tactician whose win-at-all-costs approach may make for dull, ten-man rugby but puts the required points on the board. The essence of the Osler game – which is to set the pattern of future Springbok dominance – is powerful forward play, possession and touch-kicks until the opponents' try-line is within striking distance.

Bennie Osler (right) and brother.

IN FASHION

- Femininity reasserts itself after the aggressively boyish Twenties; busts are back; waistlines rise; the ideal figure is tall, shapely, gracious.
- Wider shoulders, emphasized by the tailored suits and trench coats popularized by film stars Greta Garbo and Marlene Dietrich.
- Fox furs and tilted fedora hats.

Illustration of a 1931 Schiaparelli evening gown; the bird adds a Surrealistic touch.

WHAT'S NEW IN 1931

- **US:** New York's 102-storey Empire State Building, the world's tallest, is officially opened.
- **Records:** Swiss balloonist Auguste Picard becomes first man to reach the stratosphere; Malcolm Campbell breaks land speed record in the car Bluebird, averaging 295 mph at Daytona Beach, USA.
- **New products:** The pickup truck, the electron microscope, the electronic flash camera, the electric guitar, and Alka Seltzer.
- **Introductions:** Mrs Wallis Simpson meets the Prince of Wales, beginning a highly charged affair; Indian nationalist Mohandas Gandhi takes tea with King George and Queen Mary (the King wears a frock coat, Gandhi his usual loincloth and shawl).

MABEL FILLS TOP OFFICE

Mabel Malherbe, a leading light in various women's movements and founder of the magazine *Die Boerevrou*, becomes South Africa's inaugural lady mayor when she is elected first citizen of Pretoria. She later (in 1934) enters the national parliament – only the second woman to do so.

CHICAGO MOB LEADER IN DOCK

Elusive Mafia mobster Al Capone, boss of Chicago's notorious underworld since the St Valentine's Day massacre of 1929, is finally arrested – on charges of income tax evasion – after months of careful investigation by Elliot Ness and his 'Untouchables'. He is sentenced to 11 years' imprisonment, which effectively ends his criminal career.

Mob leader Capone.

BORN

International: Actor James Dean; media magnate Rupert Murdoch; writer John Le Carré.
South Africa: Retail king Raymond Ackerman; opera singer Joyce Barker; cricketers Basil D'Oliviera and Trevor Goddard; politician Mac Maharaj; cleric and campaigner Desmond Tutu.

DIED

International: Russian-born ballerina Anna Pavlova; Australian singer Dame Nellie Melba.
South Africa: Author (of Jock of the Bushveldt) Sir Percy FitzPatrick; Alfred Aloysius Smith, better known as 'Trader Horn'.

SOUTH AFRICA in the 20th CENTURY

1932

DEPRESSION BITES DEEP

Thousands of hunger marchers converge on London's Hyde Park from all parts of the country as the world-wide Great Depression deepens. Trade in commodities has been reduced to a trickle, bringing many countries – including South Africa – to the verge of bankruptcy; unemployment is at an all-time high: the numbers of the jobless grow to 6 million in Germany, 3 million in Britain. In the US a full quarter of the population depends for survival on charity, begging and pitiful welfare handouts, and drought is turning much of the central grain-belt into a giant dust bowl.

Franklin D. Roosevelt, the inspiring mayor of New York, promises 'a new deal for the American people' and wins the presidential election by a landslide. Despite Roosevelt's paralysis (he was stricken with polio ten years ago) he travels the length and breadth of the country, speaking directly to millions of ordinary folk. His recipe for recovery: a balanced budget, cuts in spending and government work schemes. He also promises an end to prohibition.

New Yorkers welcome the New Deal, Roosevelt's cure for depression.

Roosevelt heads for the White House. His stunning victory gives Americans new hope for the future.

WHAT'S NEW 1932

- **Britain:** Imperial Airways begins regular passenger service between London and Cape Town. The journey takes just over 10 days.
- **US:** Sweet manufacturer Forrest Mars markets the Mars Bar ®.
- **Science:** Vitamin C isolated by American scientists; Cambridge physicist James Chadwick discovers the neutron.
- **Australia:** Sydney Harbour bridge completed.

LEADING CAMPAIGNER DIES

One of South Africa's most admired black sons dies during the year. Solomon Plaatje, first secretary of the African National Congress, was educated only to primary level but had a gift for languages (he was fluent in eight) and, as a young man, worked as court interpreter during the siege of Kimberley. During this time he founded a Tswana-English newspaper, later becoming a vocal campaigner for human rights and, specifically, against the Native Land Act of 1913, a statute that allowed blacks to own land in just 7 percent of the country. Among Plaatje's books were Life in South Africa (published in 1916); and The Mote and the Beam, which was subtitled 'An epic of sex-relationship 'twixt white and black'.

Sol Plaatje.

GOOD YEAR FOR BOOKS

- Among notable titles published in 1932 are Ernest Hemingway's *Death in the Afternoon*, Damon Runyon's *Guys and Dolls*, Aldous Huxley's prophetic *Brave New World*, Stella Gibbons' *Cold Comfort Farm*, James Thurber's *The Secret Life of Walter Mitty* and, heralding a glittering literary career, Nancy Mitford's *Christmas Pudding*.
- John Galsworthy, author of the acclaimed *The Forsythe Saga*, wins the Nobel Prize for literature.
- Pearl Buck is awarded a Pulitzer Prize for *The Good Earth*.

HIT SONGS
- On the Sunny Side of the Street
- Falling in Love Again
- Ain't Misbehavin'
- Night and Day
- 42nd Street

SOUTH AFRICA in the 20th CENTURY

The Thirties

BORN
International: Actress Elizabeth Taylor. **South Africa:** Politician Pik Botha; singers Mimi Coertze and Miriam Makeba; playwright Athol Fugard; photographer Peter Magubane; actor Patrick Mynhardt.

DIED
South Africa: Daisy de Melker, convicted murderess and the first white woman to be executed in South Africa; writer C.J. Langenhoven; medical pioneer Jane Waterston.

Langenhoven (right) and some of his children's stories.

AIR ACE'S SON ABDUCTED, MURDERED

Celebrated aviator Charles Lindbergh, first to fly solo across the Atlantic (in 1927), suffers shattering personal tragedy when his baby son is kidnapped from the family home in New Jersey. The Lindberghs pay $50,000 in ransom money, but to no avail: the infant's dead body is found two months later, after a manhunt involving 100,000 officers and a host of volunteers.

1933

NAZIS TAKE OVER REICH

Berlin. Adolf Hitler, the toothbrush-moustached ex-Army corporal and fanatical leader of the Nazi party, becomes chancellor of the German Reich at the end of January, and moves quickly to consolidate his power. Immediately after the swearing-in ceremony, conducted by the ageing (and some say senile) President Paul von Hindenburg, a huge torch-light procession of his uniformed followers makes its way along the capital's main thoroughfare. Within a week he announces measures to control the press, ban public meetings, and intensify the persecution of Germany's Jews. Shortly afterwards he outlaws all other political parties and dissolves the trade unions. In March the first concentration camp, designed for opponents of the new regime, is established at Dachau.

On the night of 27 February the Reichstag building burns to the ground, an individual act of arson which Hitler blames on the Communists. Widespread fear of the 'Red Terror', skilfully manipulated by the Nazi propaganda machine, gains him massive voter support in the ensuing elections.

Flavour of the year.

BORN
International: Film director Roman Polanski; Australian novelist Bryce Courtenay (in South Africa). **South Africa:** Parliamentary speaker Frene Ginwala; pioneer of 'black' theatre Gibson Kente; novelist Wilbur Smith (in Northern Rhodesia, now Zambia).

President Hindenburg leads Hitler and his jackbooted henchmen to supreme power.

SOUTH AFRICA in the 20th CENTURY 1930s

TICKEY ENTERS THE ARENA

A new star on the circus firmament appears when 16-year-old trampolinist Eric Hoyland joins Boswell's on a six-month contract. Syd Boswell, loath to lose the services of the diminutive performer, persuades Hoyland to stay on as a clown, renaming him 'Tickey' after the threepenny bit, smallest of South African coins. Tickey will remain with Boswell's to entertain generations of children – and their parents.

Tickey the clown.

WHITE WOMEN'S RIGHTS: BERTHA LEADS THE WAY

The feminist movement in South Africa takes a giant step forward when 41-year-old Bertha Solomon claims her seat in the national parliament – the first woman to do so. Russian-born Bertha, a pint-sized bundle of energy and a gifted lawyer, arrived in the country when she was four years old and, after qualifying, fought fiercely for the women's vote. The struggle against male prejudice has been long and hard: members of the

Pathfinder Solomon.

Senate were told of the 'scientific fact' that women's brains were less developed than men's; even the enlightened writer C.J. Langenhoven condemned the campaign as part of 'a world-wide movement against authority and discipline'. The franchise was eventually (in 1930) extended to include white women over 30.

'BODYLINE' THREATENS EMPIRE

The gentle game of cricket proves anything but gentlemanly during the Ashes Tests in Australia. In a bid to neutralize the remarkable talents of young Aussie Donald Bradman, English pacemen Harold Larwood and Bill Voce are ordered by their captain, Douglas Jardine, to bowl 'bodyline' – at the batsman's head and body – to force him into evasive action and error. This they do, very effectively, and England wins the series. Furious Australian cricket lovers condemn the dangerous tactic. So too does their government, and at one point the very unity of the Empire is threatened.

Douglas Jardine's strike bowlers – Larwood and Voce – intimidate the Australian batsmen.

1934

WHITE LEADERS GET TOGETHER; MALAN BREAKS AWAY

Last year the country's two major political groups – Barry Hertzog's governing National Party and Jan Smuts' South African Party – entered into a coalition, a marriage of convenience forced on them by economic pressures. They now merge to create the United Party and the so-called 'fusion government'. More ominously, some of Hertzog's more uncompromising supporters, led by the hardliner Daniël Malan, one-time editor of *Die Burger*, depart to form the Herenigde Nasionale Party (Reunited National Party).

The 'fusion' cabinet: Barry Hertzog sits at centre; Jan Smuts at far right.

SOUTH AFRICA in the 20th CENTURY

GRAND PRIX TAKES OFF IN SA
Some 42,000 people flock to East London's hazardous new motor racing circuit – it takes in built-up areas and a twisting coastal road – to watch South Africa's first Grand Prix. The race, run on a handicap basis, is won by international driver Whitney Straight in a Maserati at an average speed of 152 km/h; second past the post is South Africa's J.H. Case in a Ford Special; Michael Straight, driving a Railton-Terraplane, comes in third.

BORN
International: Actresses Brigitte Bardot and Sophia Loren; fashion trend-setter Mary Quant.
South Africa: Activists and politicians Winnie Madikizela-Mandela and Abdul Kadar Asmal; politician and lawyer Dullah Omar; jazz pianist Abdullah Ibrahim (Dollar Brand).

NATIONAL AIRLINE LAUNCHED
After several disaster-ridden years, the privately run Union Airways finally relinquishes control to the government, who renames the airline South African Airways. Three years later it will invest in three 14-passenger Junkers JU52 aircraft. These ungainly, luxuriously fitted (they have adjustable, genuine leather seating) 'corrugated iron' machines, the first in South Africa to have radio communications, will fly between major centres within the country and, externally, as far as Kisumu in Kenya.

LEGENDARY CROOKS MEET STICKY END
Shreveport, USA. On 23 May armed robbers Bonnie Parker and Clyde Barrow, romanticized as Bonnie and Clyde, die in a hail of police bullets near this small Louisiana town. The lethal couple, both in their mid-twenties, left a trail of death and destruction during their four-year partnership in crime.

Two months later John Dillinger, the FBI's 'Public Enemy No.1', master of disguise and wanted on 16 murder charges, is shot to death outside a Chicago cinema. Among his other crimes were numerous bank hold-ups and ingenious escapes from prison.

Passengers alight from the new 14-seat Junkers.

To elude detectives while on the run, he erased his fingerprints with acid.

SONGS OF THE DAY
- Smoke Gets in Your Eyes
- Stormy Weather
- I Only Have Eyes for You
- The Isle of Capri

Bonnie and Clyde perform for the camera.

Dillinger under arrest.

SOUTH AFRICA in the 20th CENTURY 1930s

Shirley Temple.

King Kong terrifies New York.

WHAT'S NEW IN 1934

♦ **UK:** Women wear shorts at Wimbledon, to the dismay of traditionalists.
♦ **UK:** First 'cat's eyes' installed on British roads.
♦ **Cinema:** Donald Duck makes his debut, in The Little Wise Men.
♦ San Francisco's **Alcatraz island** is bought by US government for conversion to a maximum security prison.
♦ **US:** First laundrette opens, in Texas.
♦ The phrase **call girl** – a prostitute contactable by telephone – enters the English language.
♦ **US:** The cheeseburger is invented, in Louisville, Kentucky.

SCREEN NEWS

The enchanting, curly-haired, dimpled Shirley Temple receives a special Oscar award. King Kong, the gigantic ape, terrifies movie audiences as he tramples New York and sets new standards in special movie effects. Premier dancing duet Fred Astaire and Ginger Rogers get together for the first time, in The Gay Divorcée (they will soon be a Hollywood institution). A movie agent's report prior to this success says of Astaire: 'Can't act. Can't sing. Balding. Can dance a little.

ON THE BOOKSHELVES

♦ Henry Miller's *Tropic of Cancer*
♦ Agatha Christie's *Murder on the Orient Express*
♦ Robert Graves's *I Claudius*
♦ Pamela Travers' *Mary Poppins*
♦ George Orwell's *Down and Out in Paris and London*
♦ Mikhail Sholokhov's *And Quiet Flows the Don*
♦ James Hilton's *Goodbye Mr Chips.*

Astaire and Rogers: new standards in dance.

SOUTH AFRICA in the 20th CENTURY

1935

MUSSOLINI'S ARMIES INVADE ABYSSINIA

October. Italian troops cross the Eritrean border into Abyssinia to unleash all the weapons of modern warfare – tanks, planes, machine guns, poison gas – on Emperor Haile Selassie's poorly armed tribesmen. By the end of the year the invaders, numbering some 650,000 men, are in control of the whole country. Abyssinia (later Ethiopia) is one of only two fully independent African states, and an obvious target for Benito Mussolini's colonial ambitions. The League of Nations, despite widespread protest and a personal appeal from the Emperor, remains on the sidelines: the most that member states can agree on is a limited (and ineffective) range of sanctions.

BORN
International: Rock star Elvis Presley; comic actor Dudley Moore; film-maker Woody Allen; operatic tenor Luciano Pavarotti. **South Africa:** Writer André Brink; rugby player Frik du Preez; entrepreneur Sol Kerzner; golfer Gary Player.

DIED
International: T.E. Lawrence ('Lawrence of Arabia'), in a motorcycle accident. **South Africa:** Mining magnate Sir George Albu; cricketer Jock Cameron, suddenly, on the boat home after the 1935 tour of England; political activist Jeremiah Dunjwa.

RACE LAWS: PEACEFUL PROTEST FAILS

Opposition to the Hertzog government's race policy – segregation – hardens when 400 delegates meet at Bloemfontein to form the All Africa Convention (AAC). Among measures they find especially offensive are the new and harsher pass laws, the removal of Africans from the Cape franchise, and the proposed Native Trust and Land Act. The AAC is composed mainly of moderate reformists representing the African National Congress, the Communist Party of SA, the South African Indian Congress and the African People's Organisation. Its polite protestations are ignored by the government.

WHAT'S NEW IN 1935

- **Nylon**, first artificial silk-type fabric, developed by the US's DuPont chemical company.
- **Radio:** South Africans listen to their first commercial radio programmes, beamed from Lourenço Marques in Portuguese East Africa (Mozambique).
- **Publishing:** The Bodley Head publishing company begins marketing its Penguin range of cheap (but good) paperbacks. The reading public's response is overwhelming.
- **Motor industry:** The first Jaguar car, produced by the Sidecar Company in England. Price: £385.

PORTRAIT OF RHODES UPSETS LOCALS

May. The new Gaumont-British epic film, *Rhodes of Africa*, released in Britain last year, causes public uproar when it eventually appears on local screens. Walter Huston, who takes the lead, refused to travel out to South Africa; local actor Paul de Groot stood in for him in the location scenes, and the script is riddled with inaccuracies. Rhodes himself comes across as a colonial roughneck, Paul Kruger as an over-the-top caricature of Boer ruggedness.

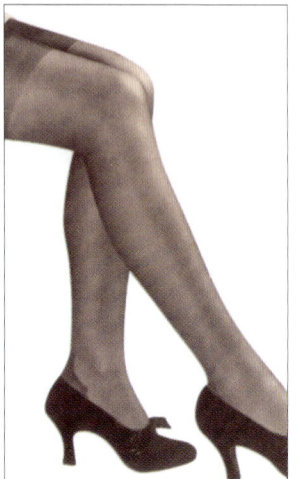

Damsel's delight: Nylon, developed in the US, is soon to yield the sheerest of stockings, though these will become readily available only after the Second World War.

Leaders of the early African National Congress.

SOUTH AFRICA in the 20th CENTURY

1936

KING EDWARD RENOUNCES THRONE

London, 10 December. People in Britain and throughout the Empire are stunned when King Edward VIII renounces the throne after a reign of less than a year. He has not yet been crowned.

In a dramatic broadcast from Windsor Castle, Edward tells his subjects at home and abroad that he has 'found it impossible to carry the heavy burden of my responsibility and to discharge my duties as King as I would wish to do without the help and support of the woman I love…'.

The woman in question is the American socialite and divorcée Wallis Simpson, whom Edward met while still Prince of Wales, and whom he is determined to marry.

The abdication puts a dramatic end to a constitutional crisis that has been debated (but largely unreported) in Britain's inner circles for months. The Church of England, which the king heads and whose faith he is sworn to defend, disapproves of divorce. So too do the Dominion premiers.

After the broadcast, Edward slips quietly away to France aboard a Royal Navy destroyer. He is succeeded by his younger brother, the Duke of York, who becomes King George VI.

The Duke and Duchess of Windsor in exile.

Athlete supreme: Jesse Owens wins four golds.

BERLIN OLYMPICS: JESSE SPOILS HITLER'S PARTY

August. More than 5,000 contestants from 53 nations compete in what Adolf Hitler announced was the Olympic Games that would demonstrate, once and for all, the superiority of the 'Aryan' race.

Germany's Nordic athletes perform superbly and her highly trained rowers, riders and weight-lifters sweep the board, raising the host country to the top of the medals table, but Hitler's party is well and truly spoilt by the young African-American Jesse Owens, whom Goebbels and his racist press dismissed as a 'black mercenary'. Owens wins four gold medals: for the 100 and 200 metres, the long jump and as lead member of the victorious 4 x 100 metres relay. Hitler refuses to meet Owens, storming from the stadium even as the crowd rises to applaud his victory in the 200-metre dash.

BORN
International: Fashion guru Yves Saint-Laurent. *South Africa:* Activist Philip Kgosana; politician F.W. de Klerk; sculptors Sydney Kumalo and Mashego Segogela; writer, playwright, musician Lewis Nkosi.

DIED
International: Russian behavioural scientist Ivan Pavlov. *South Africa:* Writer and mystic Eugène Marais; politician and human rights campaigner Walter Rubasana; veterinary scientist Sir Arnold Theiler; diamond magnate Sir Thomas Cullinan.

Mystic Marais.

> 'After I am dead, the boy will ruin himself in twelve months.'
> King George V, speaking of his son, the Prince of Wales, later King Edward VIII.

SOUTH AFRICA in the 20th CENTURY

SPAIN PLUNGES INTO CIVIL WAR

July. Spain's new left-wing Republican government comes under immediate threat when General Francisco Franco, the Nationalist leader, arrives from Morocco with an armed party to challenge its legitimacy, triggering a civil war that will devastate the country. Franco is supported by Fascist Italy and Nazi Germany, who promise military backing. France and Britain stand on the sidelines.

FASHION IN FERMENT

For the fashion conscious, mid-decade is a confusing time, with styles replacing one another in quick succession. Indeed different styles are in vogue at the same time. The *South African Lady's Pictorial* probably sums things up when it says: 'Paris has decreed that we need not all be alike, and there are three distinct trends'. These are 'the military idea' inspired by King George V's Jubilee celebrations in January, the 'Chinese note', and 'pleats,

Picasso's Guernica *conveys the mindless savagery of civil war.*

Spain's Franco (right).

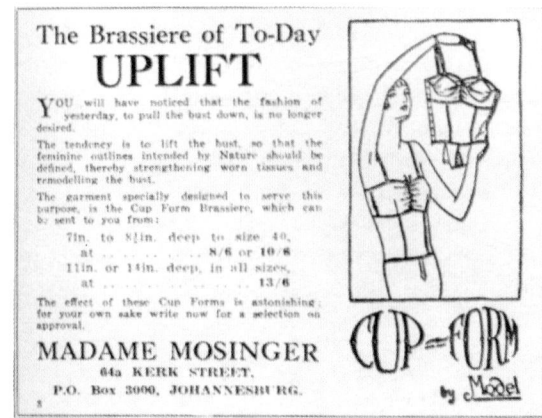
The new-look foundation garment.

pleats and yet more pleats.... In fact you must pleat everything – your scarf, your jabot, your collars and cuffs'. Undergarments have improved beyond measure since the days, not too long ago, when whalebone dispensed discomfort. The 'uplift' brassiere, of lace, net or satin, is now *de rigueur*. Swimwear has also advanced; costumes are still one-piece but backless, with halter neck and built-in bra. One popular model, a Jantzen advertised in the *Pictorial* in 1936, has a novel zip front.

SONGS OF THE DAY
- Blue Moon
- Red Sails in the Sunset
- The Way You Look Tonight

WHAT'S NEW IN 1936

- **Motor industry:** Hitler's brainchild, the Volkswagen or 'people's car', is unveiled. Its beetle shape will remain unchanged for half a century.
- **US:** The first automatic food-vending machines are installed.
- **Publishing:** Margaret Mitchell publishes her best-seller Gone With The Wind.
- **US:** Billboard *magazine's 'hit parade' of songs.*

The original 'Beetle' for the people.

SOUTH AFRICA in the 20th CENTURY

1930s

1937

CRAVEN'S 'DIVING PASS' HELPS SPRINGBOKS TO VICTORY

Philip Nel's Springbok rugby squad virtually sweeps the board on its tour of Australia and New Zealand, piling up 855 points in 28 matches (average 31 per match) – a remarkable feat in an era when games tend to be low-scoring. In the process it defeats the Australian national side 2-0 and the All Blacks 2-1, the first time the latter has tasted the bitterness of a home series loss against their long-standing rivals. In the Springbok line-up is 27-year-old scrumhalf Danie Craven, whose 'diving pass' produces a satisfyingly unsettling effect on opponents (though it seems to have little practical value). The South Africans will go on to defeat the British Isles – known for the first time as The Lions – in 1938.

WHAT'S NEW IN 1937

- **Boxing:** 'Brown Bomber' Joe Louis defeats James Bradock to capture the world heavyweight crown.
- **Walt Disney** produces his first animated feature film, Snow White and the Seven Dwarfs.
- **US:** San Francisco's Golden Gate bridge is opened.
- **Food:** Tinned spam – pork and ham – is marketed for the first time.

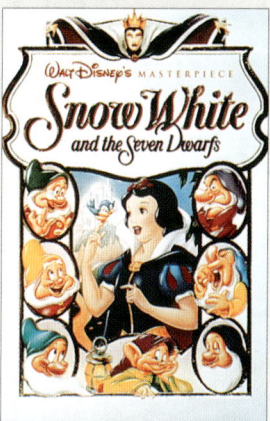
Disney's Snow White.

Craven in action: more show than substance.

Spam: new on the market.

ON THE BOOKSHELF

- Among the year's more notable titles are J.R.R. Tolkien's *The Hobbit*; John Steinbeck's novella *Of Mice and Men*; George Orwell's *The Road to Wigan Pier*.
- On the local scene, Eugène Marais' *The Soul of the White Ant*, in which the author likens a termite colony to a single organism, stirs international interest when it is published, posthumously, in an English edition; the author died last year. Stuart Cloete's *Turning Wheels* provokes controversy for its perceived criticism of the Voortrekkers.

BORN
South Africa: Singer Bobby Angel; writer Bessie Head.

DIED
International: Composers George Gershwin (at age 38, of a brain tumour) and Maurice Ravel; Hollywood 'sex goddess' Jean Harlow, of kidney disease; blues singer Bessie Smith; atomic scientist Ernest Rutherford; British politician Ramsay MacDonald.

Movie siren Harlow.

SOUTH AFRICA in the 20th CENTURY

The Thirties

1938

MUNICH: CHAMBERLAIN PROMISES 'PEACE FOR OUR TIME'

September. Neville Chamberlain, the British prime minister, flies home from his Munich meeting with Herr Hitler in euphoric mood, telling wellwishers at Hendon aerodrome that the pact reached with Nazi Germany guarantees 'peace for our time'. Shortly afterwards he appears before a huge, cheering crowd outside Buckingham Palace.

France's Monsieur Daladier and Italy's Signor Mussolini also attend the Munich conference, called to settle the mounting crisis over the Sudetenland area of neighbouring Czechoslovakia. The accord signed by the four leaders recognizes German claims to the area; Czech representatives are not present at the meeting.

Earlier, German troops massed along the Czech border, threatening all-out war. The accord ensures a peaceful solution, at least for the time being, but many doubt that the Nazi dictator's appetite for conquest will be satisfied for long: as maverick British politician Winston Churchill warns, the security of Europe cannot be achieved 'by throwing a small state to the wolves'.

Neville Chamberlain gives false hope.

The Munich agreement is the latest and most humiliating demonstration of 'appeasement' by Britain and France. In March the two countries, militarily far stronger than Germany, stood by as Hitler's troops streamed into Austria. The political union of Germany and Austria, known as the Anschluss and plainly illegal in terms of the Treaty of Versailles, was Hitler's first major step on the road to establishing his 'Thousand-Year Reich'.

'MARTIAN INVADERS' SPREAD PANIC

USA, November. Thousands of panic-stricken American radio listeners mill around city streets, crowd into churches or drive wildly into the countryside in the belief that giant and hostile Martians have invaded Earth. The cause of the hysteria: a CBS dramatization, with 'on-the-spot reports', of H.G. Wells' *War of the Worlds*, presented at Halloween by the up-and-coming young actor Orson Welles.

Hitler and Mussolini: on the way to forming their 'pact of steel'.

SOUTH AFRICA in the 20th CENTURY — 1930s

BORN
South Africa: Jurist Richard Goldstone; singer Margaret Singana; activist and politician Steve Tshwete; artist Ephraim Ngatane.

Professor J.L.B. Smith examines the 'living fossil', the coelacanth.

ANCIENT FISH DISCOVERED
A large, strange, grey-blue fish caught off the South African coast near East London has been identified as a coelacanth, a species that flourished in the seas of the Mesozoic era some 250 million years ago and was thought to have been extinct for at least 60 million years. Professor J.L.B. Smith, of Rhodes University, describes the specimen as a 'living fossil'.

VOORTREKKERS ARE REMEMBERED
The centenary of the Battle of Blood River is celebrated by Afrikaners throughout the country, many of them dressing up for the occasion in traditional Voortrekker garb. There is also renewed interest in *Volkspele*, a style of dance imported (in 1914) from Sweden but which was adopted, and adapted to local folk music, by sections of the Afrikaans speaking community. The foundation stones of the Voortrekker monument in Pretoria, and of a laager-type memorial on the battlefield itself, are laid as part of the celebrations.

SPORTING BRIEFS
♦ Italy's footballers retain the World Cup when they beat the more fancied Hungarians 4-2.
♦ American Helen Wills Moody snaps up Wimbledon's Ladies' Singles title for the eighth time.
♦ Don Budge is the first tennis player to win the Grand Slam (Australian, French, Wimbledon and US Men's Singles).
♦ England beats Australia by a massive innings and 579 runs in the final cricket Test, at the Oval, to level the series; Len Hutton scores a record 364.

ON THE BOOKSHELF
● Daphne du Maurier's *Rebecca*
● Graham Greene's *Brighton Rock*
● George Orwell's *Homage to Catalonia*
● First issues: *Picture Post* magazine, children's comic *Beano*

Voortrekker descendants celebrate centenary of Battle of Blood River.

WHAT'S NEW IN 1938
♦ *Shopping:* An Oklahoma supermarket introduces shopping trolleys.
♦ *In the kitchen:* Nestlé (Switzerland) introduces the first commercially successful instant coffee.
♦ *In the office:* Xerography (photocopying) invented; businessmen show little interest.
♦ *Shipping:* The Queen Elizabeth, world's largest passenger liner, is launched.

SOUTH AFRICA in the 20th CENTURY

1939

HITLER INVADES POLAND; ALLIES DECLARE WAR

1 September. Six swift-moving armoured and eight motorized German divisions, accompanied by swarms of bombers and fighters, roll across the Polish frontiers at dawn to trigger the second of the century's great wars.

The Polish defenders, courageous but poorly organized and ill-armed (many are still equipped as cavalry), prove powerless in face of the massive *blitzkrieg*. Within three days the invaders have cut the Corridor linking Poland's heartland with the Baltic port of Danzig. By 8 September the panzers are at the gates of Warsaw. Just over a week later Russian forces, their hands freed by the German-Soviet Non-Aggression Pact signed in August, invade Poland from the east.

Britain enters the fray on 3 September. In a broadcast to the nation a solemn Neville Chamberlain, the prime minister, announces that during the morning the British ambassador in Berlin 'handed the German government a final note stating that, unless we heard from them by 11 o'clock that they were prepared at once to withdraw their troops from Poland, a state of war would exist between us. I have to tell you that no such undertaking has been received, and that consequently this country is at war with Germany'. France follows suit a few days later.

WHAT'S NEW IN 1939

- German physicist Otto Hahn discovers **nuclear fission**. Scientists Albert Einstein, Edward Teller and Alexander Sacks warn US president Roosevelt that Germany could be developing an atomic bomb.
- **Spain:** Civil war ends; Franco takes over.
- **US:** First air-conditioned car, a Nash, takes to the road.
- **France:** Three-times murderer Eugen Weidmann is the last person to be executed publicly by guillotine.

A Polish family surveys what's left of their home.

The Holocaust begins: Polish Jews are marched through the streets of Warsaw.

SOUTH AFRICA in the 20th CENTURY 1930s

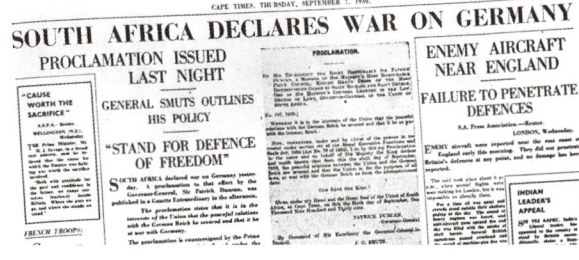

Smuts and Hertzog: parting of ways.

SOUTH AFRICA JOINS THE FRAY

The Union's duty (or otherwise) to declare war against Nazi Germany triggers a bitter dispute between prime minister Barry Hertzog and his deputy Jan Smuts. Smuts wins the day: following a heated parliamentary debate on 4 September, 80 members vote in favour of joining Britain and the other dominions in the coming struggle; 67 vote against the motion. Smuts takes over the premiership; the ageing Hertzog resigns from the United Party to patch up his quarrel with Nationalist D.F. Malan and to become Leader of the Opposition.

ON SCREEN

Two films, both destined to become cinema classics, premiere during 1939:

- *Gone with the Wind*, the dramatization of Margaret Mitchell's best-selling book about the American civil war, breaks all box office records. British actress Vivien Leigh and Hollywood heart-throb Clark Gable play the leads. Gable marries longtime lover Carole Lombard during the year.
- A new star, 17-year-old Judy Garland, shines in *The Wizard of Oz*, a charming fantasy about the other-world adventures of young farm-girl Dorothy and her friends the Scarecrow, the Tin Man and the Cowardly Lion.

BORN

South Africa: Poet Breyten Breytenbach; musician Hugh Masekela; actress Janet Suzman.

THE MUSIC SCENE

- The smooth, seductive big-band sound of the Glenn Miller orchestra holds a whole generation in thrall with such numbers as 'In the Mood' and 'Chattanooga Choo-Choo'.
- Other hits of the time include 'Over the Rainbow' (from *The Wizard of Oz*) and, as the war clouds gather and the storm breaks, 'We're Gonna Hang Out the Washing on the Siegfried Line' (popularized by stand-up comics Flanagan and Allen) and the sentimental (German) song 'Lili Marlene'.

'Frankly, my dear, I don't give a damn.'
Rhett Butler (Clark Gable) to Scarlett O'Hara (Vivien Leigh) in *Gone With the Wind*; the word 'damn' broke Hollywood's taboo against bad language on the screen

93

1940s

DIED
1945: US president Franklin D. Roosevelt; German dictator Adolf Hitler; Italian dictator Benito Mussolini.

WORLD AT WAR
1940: Germans occupy Denmark, Norway, the Low Countries and France. Luftwaffe fails to destroy RAF, and Hitler postpones planned invasion of Britain. SA volunteer force, with SAAF support, begins East Africa campaign.
1941: East Africa: SA troops capture Addis Ababa; main Italian force surrenders. North Africa: SA 1st Division arrives in Egypt, takes part in Eighth Army's Cyrenaica offensive. Eastern Front: Hitler invades Russia (June). Pacific: Japan attacks US naval base at Pearl Harbor, invades Philippines, Hong Kong, Malaya, Dutch East Indies. US enters war against Germany.
1942: North Africa: Tobruk surrenders to Rommel; 11,000 South Africans are among prisoners taken. Eighth Army defeats German and Italian forces at El Alamein (November); Allies land in Morocco and Algeria. Indian Ocean: British, SA and colonial troops invade Madagascar. Pacific: Singapore falls to Japanese (February); US carrier fleet defeats Japanese at battles of Midway and Coral Sea.
1943: Germans surrender in North Africa (May); Anglo-American forces go on to invade Sicily and Italy; Mussolini deposed; Germans establish defensive lines south of Rome. Eastern Front: German 6th Army surrenders at Stalingrad (February). Pacific: US forces defeat Japanese on Guadalcanal (January), invade New Guinea, Solomons, Gilberts.
1944: Pacific: US forces continue advance by 'island hopping'; Japanese suffer heavy defeat at Leyte Gulf. British 14th Army advances in Burma, Russians on Eastern front. Europe: Germans launch VI rockets ('flying bombs') at London. SA 6th (Armoured) Division arrives in Italy (April); Allies capture Rome (June); 6th Division enters Florence (August). Allies land in Normandy (June), capture Paris (August).
1945: Europe: Germany surrenders (May). Far East: US Air Force drops atomic bombs on Hiroshima and Nagasaki (August). Japan surrenders (September).

INTERNED
1942: Leading members of the Ossewa-brandwag, including future SA premier B.J. Vorster.

LAUNCHED
1947: US Marshall Plan, to rescue European economies.

FOUNDED
1945: United Nations; SA's Jan Smuts is among the principal architects; first session held in London.
1948: The independent states of India and Pakistan.

FIRST
1942: Golden Record ('Chattanooga Choo Choo') presented, to US bandleader Glenn Miller.
1943: Teenage idol (generally recognized as such): Frank Sinatra.
1944: Jet aircraft (German Me262) goes into production.
1947: Commercially produced microwave oven. Kalashnikov assault rifle (AK47) produced.

DISCOVERED
1947: The Dead Sea Scrolls.

MARRIED
1947: Britain's Princess Elizabeth, to Philip Mountbatten, newly created Duke of Edinburgh.

WELCOMED
1940: Nylon stockings.
1946: Two-piece bikini swimsuit.
1947: Dior's New Look.
1948: Transistor radio.

INVESTIGATED
1946: 'Native policy', by the Fagan Commission Report, released in 1948, discounts complete racial segregation as 'totally impractical'. However, rival Sauer report recommends exclusive white vote, a halt to integration at all levels, job reservation for whites.

LAUNCHED
1947: Mau Mau terror campaign in Kenya.

VISITORS TO SA
1947: The British Royal family.

POLITICS AND PROTEST
1940: Alfred Xuma becomes ANC president.
1943: ANC Youth League founded.
1946: Asiatic Land Tenure Act and Indian representation Act passed.
1948: D.F. Malan forms all-Afrikaner National Party (HNP) government, launches the era of institutionalized apartheid.
1949: James Moroka becomes ANC president.

SOUTH AFRICA in the 20th CENTURY **1940s**

German conquerors march through Paris.

1940

HITLER'S HORDES ROLL WESTWARDS

11 May. The deceptive calm of the six-month 'Phoney War' or 'Sitzkrieg' is shattered when German panzers smash into the Low Countries, sweeping all before them. Earlier in the year Hitler's armies occupy Denmark and, after a brief but bloody confrontation with a hurriedly put-together, poorly equipped Anglo-French expedition, Norway. It is now the turn of Luxembourg, Holland, Belgium – and of France, long held to be the strongest and best-armed European power.

But France has failed to modernize its military capability, its armed forces are demoralized, and its leaders have put their faith in the chain of defensive border fortifications known as the Maginot Line – which the Germans simply bypass by pouring a mass of tanks and mechanized infantry through the 'impenetrable' Ardennes forest. They then fan out to the south, where the French-held front rapidly crumbles, and to the west, towards Dunkirk on the coast, in pursuit of the retreating British Expeditionary Force and its French and Belgian comrades in arms.

The swastika rises above the streets of Paris on 14 June. A week later France capitulates. The armistice is signed in the depths of the Compiègne forest, at the very spot and in the same railway coach used for the humiliating German surrender of 1918. Adolf Hitler makes a brief appearance at the ceremony.

> 'We shall defend our island, whatever the cost may be. We shall fight on the beaches, we shall fight on the landing grounds, we shall fight in the fields and in the streets, we shall fight in the hills. We shall never surrender.'
> *Winston Churchill, 4 June*

Allied soldiers embark from Dunkirk for England.

THE MIRACLE OF DUNKIRK

Northern France, 4 June. Nearly 340,000 exhausted French, Belgian and, mostly, British troops are taken off the beaches of Dunkirk to complete one of the greatest rescue missions in the annals of warfare.

The operation began a week ago when the Allied forces, boxed into the Dunkirk enclave, face total annihilation and, in desperation, the Royal Navy dispatches a vast, makeshift evacuation fleet of destroyers, coastal vessels, ferries, river cruisers, fishing boats and small private craft. That they succeed against all the odds is due to a splendid rearguard action fought by the Allies, and to German inaction – inexplicably, the German armoured thrust is halted at the height of the battle.

By the end of June the Germans are in control of all Europe from the Baltic to the Pyrenees, with only Britain

SOUTH AFRICA in the 20th CENTURY

Long lines of troops wait for rescue on the beaches of Dunkirk.

standing alone. On the 18th Winston Churchill, the new British premier (he succeeded Chamberlain on 10 May) makes the first of his stirring speeches. 'Let us now brace ourselves to our duty', he tells a packed parliament, 'and so bear ourselves that, if the British Commonwealth and Empire lasts a thousand years, men will still say, "This was their finest hour." '

St Paul's Cathedral survives the London blitz.

HITLER'S FIRST DEFEAT: BRITISH WIN THE AIR WAR

Hermann Goering's boast that his Luftwaffe will bring Britain to her knees (and open the way for invasion) by knocking out the Royal Air Force proves vastly optimistic.

Throughout July and August waves of German bombers, escorted by Messerschmit fighters (Me109s) and fighter-bombers (Me110s), attack RAF airfields, drawing the Spitfire and Hurricane squadrons into fierce battles over the gentle countryside of southeast England.

The relentless assault brings the RAF close to exhaustion, despite the superb radar and ground observer early warning network the British have perfected (and, it is later revealed, the Ultra device that translates German military codes). But suddenly, on 7 September, Goering switches the attack to the cities, allowing the RAF time to recover.

On 15 September the Luftwaffe mounts its last and biggest daylight raid, and loses more than 60 aircraft. Hitler postpones the planned invasion; the Battle of Britain has been won, and Churchill pays tribute to victors: 'Never in the field of human conflict', he says, 'was so much owed by so many to so few'.

Henceforth it is the ordinary Briton who will face the brunt of battle. Savage air attacks are launched on major centres – among them Southampton, Bristol, Liverpool, Coventry, Glasgow and, above all, London – in a sustained attempt to destroy British industry and demoralize the civilian population.

UNION FORCES ADVANCE IN EAST AFRICA

'A strong contingent of South African troops has arrived in East Africa,' reports the *Cape Argus* in July. 'The troops, cheerful and fit, were given an enthusiastic send-off at their port of embarkation, and there were groups of cheering people at every station and siding...'

SOUTH AFRICA in the 20th CENTURY 1940s

General Brink plans the attack.

These are the first Union soldiers to be sent to the battlefront, drawn there by Italy's entry into the war a month earlier, and by the threat posed by Mussolini's African empire to the vital Suez seaway. They form a major component of the General Alan Cunningham's East Africa Force, and record their first victory on 16 December when, well supported by artillery and squadrons of the South African Air Force, they overrun the Italian garrison at El Wak, close to the Kenyan border. Major-General George Brink's two South African brigades then sweep into Italian Somaliland and Abyssinia.

NEW LEADER FOR ANC

Dr Alfred Xuma, generally regarded as a moderate, is elected president of the African National Congress, a post he is to hold until ousted by radicals in 1949. Xuma trained as a teacher but later switched to medicine, qualifying as a physician in the USA. He is the first African to gain a Ph.D. from the London School of Tropical Medicine.

Alfred Xuma.

ARTS AND ENTERTAINMENT

The year's novels include:
- Graham Greene's *The Power and the Glory*;
- Ernest Hemingway's *For Whom the Bell Tolls*.

On the film scene:
- Alexander Korda's *The Thief of Baghdad*;
- Walt Disney's magnificent animated feature, *Fantasia* (a box office failure) and his more commercial *Pinocchio*;
- Charlie Chaplin's *The Great Dictator*, which lampoons Adolf Hitler and (to a lesser extent) his partner in crime, Benito Mussolini;
- Bugs Bunny, the cartoon rabbit, makes his debut;
- Mickey Rooney and Bette Davis are voted 'King and Queen of the Movies' by American newspaper readers.
- The first ever colour television is broadcast, by CBS.

WHAT'S NEW IN 1940

Sheer pleasure.

- **Stone Age paintings:** Four youngsters stumble upon the Lascaux cave complex in southwestern France, revealing a stunning gallery of Stone Age paintings.
- **Nylon stockings** on sale nationwide for first time, in the USA.
- The US Army develops the **Jeep** (named from GP, acronym for 'general purpose' vehicle); Japan develops the advanced Zero fighter aircraft.
- **Rhesus factor** in blood is discovered.
- Hattie McDonald becomes **first black woman** to win an Oscar, for her performance in *Gone With the Wind*.
- Colonel Sanders' recipe for **Kentucky Fried Chicken** advertised for first time.
- The **Channel islands** become the first (and only) part of Britain to be occupied when German forces land on 1 July.

BORN
International: Singers John Lennon, Cliff Richard, Tina Turner; Brazilian footballer Pele. *South Africa:* Activist and revolutionary Johnson Mlambo; cricketer Eddie Barlow; writer J.M. Coetzee; politician Frederick van Zyl Slabbert; newspaperman Aggrey Klaaste; Azapo leader and playwright Strinivasa Moodley; musician Joseph Shabalala; poet Oswald Mtshali.

DIED
International: Exiled Russian revolutionary Leon Trotsky, murdered in Mexico City. *South Africa:* Mining magnate Sir Abe Bailey; political leader Abdullah Abdurahman.

A South African convoy on one of the few good East African roads.

SOUTH AFRICA in the 20th CENTURY

The Forties

The 1st South African Infantry Brigade parades through liberated Addis Ababa.

Rugby star Bennie Osler on his way to the front.

1941

SA TROOPS DO THEIR BIT 'UP NORTH'

Success follows success in East Africa as Major-General George Brink's 1st Division, brilliantly backed by the South African Air Force, spearhead the assault against Mussolini's armies in Abyssinia, and Dan Pienaar's brigade, supported by British colonial troops, sweep into Italian Somaliland. South African units occupy Addis Ababa on 6 April, restoring Emperor Haile Selassie to his ancient throne; the Duke of Aosta, Italian viceroy and commander-in-chief, surrenders the main body of his force on 19 May, and on 22 July the 22,000-strong Italian garrison of Gondar, an almost impregnable mountain fortress, capitulates.

Shortly afterwards the 1st and 2nd South African divisions are sent north to join the Eighth Army in its campaign, codenamed 'Crusader', for control of the Western Desert. Great tank battles rage for days on end before the Axis forces, commanded by General Erwin Rommel, begin their retreat to El Agheila. South African armoured cars take part in the Eighth Army's advance, their crews celebrating Christmas in the streets of Benghazi.

Altogether, some 160,000 South Africans of all races are serving in North Africa and the Middle East, all of them volunteers.

SURPRISE ATTACKS BRING USA, RUSSIA INTO THE WAR

Two treacherous assaults on powerful but hitherto neutral nations totally change the global balance of power, bringing the United States and Russia (Germany's erstwhile ally) into the war. Britain and her dominions no longer stand alone.

On 30 June Hitler launches 'Operation Barbarossa', sending 100 German divisions, together with their Finnish and Romanian allies, eastwards across an 1,800-mile frontier stretching

Carnage at Pearl Harbor.

SOUTH AFRICA in the 20th CENTURY 1940s

from the Black Sea to the Baltic. However, after shattering initial reverses, in which whole armies are encircled and captured, the Soviets regroup and, helped by the early onset of a bitter Russian winter, manage to hold out. At the end of the year the panzers are still short of their primary objective: Moscow.

At dawn on Sunday 7 December, 360 Japanese carrier-borne warplanes attack the US Pacific Fleet in Pearl Harbor, on the Hawaiian island of Oahu. The assault catches both Washington and the local US commanders by surprise, although it shouldn't: the Japanese diplomatic and naval codes were broken months ago. The warnings they contained, however, seemed to indicate Thailand, Malaya or the Philippines as the main target.

The Ossewa-Brandwag goes through its paces.

Robey Leibbrandt.

ROBEY LEIBBRANDT CAPTURED
During these dark days of war the Ossewa-Brandwag ('ox-wagon sentinel'), a pro-German South African underground movement, is highly active, its paramilitary 'soldiers' waging a sustained campaign of sabotage. Among its more notable recruits is Sydney Robey Leibbrandt, a heavyweight boxer who represented South Africa at the 1936 Berlin Olympics and became a fervent disciple of Adolf Hitler. The Germans train their protégé as a paratrooper and saboteur and, in 1941, send him back to take command of the movement and to topple the pro-Allied government of Jan Smuts.

Leibbrandt makes a secret landfall on the lonely Namaqualand coast, goes into hiding in the Soutpansberg mountains close to the Limpopo River and is eventually captured, tried for treason and sentenced to death (this is later commuted).

Also prominent in the movement is B.J. Vorster, a future prime minister and president of South Africa. Vorster, like many of his fellow activists, is interned for the duration.

HIT SONGS
- A Nightingale Sang in Berkeley Square
- When You Wish Upon a Star
- The White Cliffs of Dover
- You Are My Sunshine

ATLANTIC CHARTER CATCHES WHITE GOVERNMENT OFF BALANCE
August. Prime Minister Winston Churchill and President Franklin D. Roosevelt, meeting aboard a battleship off the Newfoundland coast, devise a 'blueprint for future peace and security' which comes to be known as the Atlantic Charter. Among its major clauses is an undertaking that 'the great nations of the world would do what they could to afford assurance that all men in all lands may live out their lives in freedom from fear and want'.

In South Africa, black nationalists adopt the charter, calling on the Smuts administration to do the same. The government remains largely silent on the matter.

STAGE, SCREEN AND AIR
◆ **Radio:** comedian Tommy Handley does his bit to lift and sustain British morale with his ITMA (*It's That Man Again*) show; popular partners in lunacy include Colonel Chinstrap and Mrs Mopp. Dorothy Sayers' classic radio play *The Man Born to be King* is aired for the first time.

99

SOUTH AFRICA in the 20th CENTURY

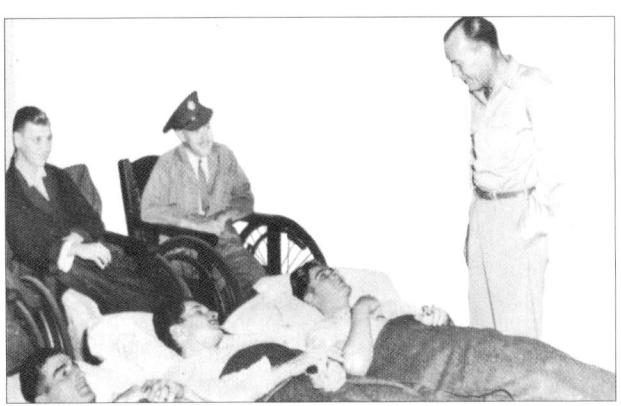

Multi-talented British entertainer Noël Coward, one of the luminaries to tour Commonwealth countries, chats to South African war casualties.

BORN
International: Singers Joan Baez and Bob Dylan; actor Bruce Lee; American politician Jesse Jackson. *South Africa:* Singer Patience Afrika; poet and novelist Stephen Gray; actor and writer Welcome Msomi; demagogue Eugene Terre'Blanche.

DIED
International: Writers James Joyce and Virginia Woolf, who commits suicide by drowning; aviatrix Amy Johnson, killed while ferrying military aircraft; pianist 'Jelly Roll' Morton. *South Africa:* Author and adventuress Princess Radziwill, whose unwelcome attentions had driven the misogynistic Cecil Rhodes to distraction half a century earlier. John Henderson Soga, the black South African missionary and writer living in retirement in Britain, is killed, along with his wife and son, in a German air raid on Southampton.

The BBC uses the first bar of Beethoven's Fifth Symphony – the Morse code for 'V' (for Victory) – as its signature in broadcasts to occupied Europe.
♦ **Stage:** Noël Coward's frothy play *Blithe Spirit* opens in London.
♦ **Screen:** Film of the year is *Citizen Kane*, written and directed by the young genius Orson Welles (he also takes the lead). The film, employing powerful new cinematic techniques, is a barely disguised profile of the autocratic newspaper magnate William Randolf Hearst. Gary Cooper wins an Oscar for his part in *Sergeant York*.

Rommel (centre) and staff.

1942

TOBRUK SURRENDERS

Western Desert, 21 June. General H. B. Klopper, South African commander of the port and fortress of Tobruk on the Libyan seaboard, surrenders the garrison to Rommel's Afrika Korps and two Italian armoured divisions. Some 35,000 troops, among them more than 10,000 South Africans, are taken prisoner.

The capitulation stuns the Allies, and deeply embarrasses Winston Churchill, British prime minister and war leader, who is meeting with President Franklin D. Roosevelt in Washington at the time.

During the earlier phases of the desert battle Tobruk served as the symbol of gritty resistance, holding out against repeated enemy onslaughts, but since then the Eighth Army has apparently changed its priorities and allowed the defences to deteriorate.

ALAMEIN BREAKTHROUGH

Western Desert, 23 October. The eccentric General Bernard Montgomery, affectionately known to his troops as 'Monty', begins the long-awaited Eighth Army attack on the 100,000-strong Axis forces dug in at El Alamein, west of Cairo. Battle commences with a 1,000-gun rolling barrage; infantry, backed by engineers and heavy tanks, advance cautiously through minefields in their head-on attempt to penetrate Rommel's five-mile-deep defensive line. This they finally do 12 days later, to record a stunning (and much-needed) victory for British and Commonwealth arms.

Rommel himself is not present in the early stages of the battle but, when his stand-in (General Stumme) dies of a heart attack on the field, rushes back from his sickbed in Germany to take charge. By this time his Afrika Korps has lost much of its armour and is desperately short of petrol. He orders the general retreat towards Tunisia on 4 November.

Defending Tobruk: South African gunners relax during a lull.

SOUTH AFRICA in the 20th CENTURY — 1940s

BLACK HERO DESTROYS ENEMY SHIP

Western Desert, July. Lance-Corporal Job Mosego, a black South African soldier serving in the Western Desert, wins the Military Medal – among the highest of decorations – for his audacious destruction of an enemy freighter in Tobruk harbour. Under guard as a prisoner of war, he manages to creep aboard the ship, places a tin filled with gunpowder (extracted from live ammunition found in the sand of his prison compound) among the drums of petrol in the hold, and lights the fuse, and up goes the ship. In the words of the citation, he displays 'ingenuity, determination and complete disregard for personal safety, punishment by the enemy, or the ensuing explosion ...'.

HIT SONGS
- White Christmas (Bing Crosby)
- We'll Meet Again (Vera Lynn)
- This is the Army, Mr Jones

ON THE WARTIME SCREEN

The year brings forth a rash of sentimental films, most with a war setting, some of which will achieve classic status. Among the latter are:
- *Casablanca* starring Humphrey Bogart and Ingrid Bergman, whose 'Play it, Sam' is to be misquoted over the decades. The producers regard the movie as something of a cheap throwaway and are astonished, and delighted, when it takes off.
- The charming actress Greer Garson stars in both *Mrs Miniver* and *Random Harvest*;
- *Holiday Inn*, an otherwise forgettable feature in which Bing Crosby sings the all-time hit 'White Christmas'.

Gung-ho actor Errol Flynn is rejected by the military on health grounds.

WHAT'S NEW IN 1942

- Frosted sugar **corn-flakes**, marketed by Kellogg.
- **Physics**: Enrico Fermi achieves a controlled nuclear chain reaction, at the university of Chicago.
- The word **freebie** enters the English language.

BORN
International: Boxer Muhammad Ali (born Cassius Clay); guitarist Jimi Hendrix, singer Aretha Franklin; actress Barbara Streisand; musician Paul McCartney. **South Africa**: Future president Thabo Mbeki; activist and politician Jacob Zuma; cricketer Ali Bacher; sculptor Mslaba Dumile; artist Lucky Sibaya.

DIED
International: The Duke of Kent, brother to King George VI, in an air accident; Lord Baden-Powell, hero of Mafeking (in 1900) and founder of the Boy Scouts; actor John Barrymore. **South Africa**: Former prime minister Barry Hertzog; architect Rex Martienssen.

ON THE AIRWAVES

- Darling of British forces world-wide is songstress Vera Lynn, whose weepy 'We'll Meet Again' introduces her radio programme *Sincerely Yours*.
- Glenn Miller is awarded musical history's first Gold Disc (one million sales) for *Chattanooga Choo-Choo*.

1943 THE TURN OF THE TIDE

The balance of power tilts dramatically as the Allies gird themselves for an assault on Hitler's Fortress Europe, and the US, gathering its immense strength, first halts and then reverses Japanese incursions in the Pacific. Major developments: North Africa: In November 1942 an Anglo-American invasion force under General Dwight Eisenhower lands in Morocco and Algeria in the west, while Montgomery's Eighth Army continues its advance from El Alamein, squeezing the greatly reinforced German army in a massive pincer movement. The Germans surrender in May 1943.

Glenn Miller's band produces its golden sound.

SOUTH AFRICA in the 20th CENTURY

The Forties

A black South African soldier, one of many, in his desert bunker.

Germans on the retreat in North Africa.

Europe: In July 1943, a 3,000-ship armada carries an Allied army to the shores of Sicily. After a short, sharp campaign, they gain control of the island and, in September, invade southern Italy. Naples falls later that month.
Russia: On 31 January Von Paulus's starving Sixth Army, trapped at ice-bound Stalingrad, surrenders; 600,000 men march into captivity, few survive. The Russians then mount a massive attack, capturing Kursk after the greatest tank battle of the war.
The Pacific theatre: In mid-1942 US carrier-borne aircraft shatter the Japanese navy at the battles of the Coral Sea and Midway; American seaborne forces invade Guadalcanal in the Solomons. In January 1943 the Japanese relief force, after suicidal attempts to dislodge the GIs, retreat from the island. In November, the Americans begin 'island hopping', capturing Bougainville (in the Solomons) and Makin (in the Gilberts).

BLACK MOVEMENTS LAUNCHED

Anton Lembede, a 29-year-old lawyer, Africanist and anti-Communist intellectual, is elected first leader of the African National Congress Youth League. Other prominent members are Nelson Mandela and Oliver Tambo, partners in South Africa's first black legal practice, and the young trade unionist Walter Sisulu.

Also launched during the year is the Non-European Unity League, a militant body influenced by Trotskyist ideas, and whose Ten Point Programme urges non-collaboration and boycott as weapons in the working man's fight against the white establishment.

STAGE, SCREEN AND DANCE

♦ Rodgers and Hammerstein's new musical *Oklahoma* is staged in New York.
♦ Movies include *Jane Eyre*, with Orson Welles, Joan Fontaine and the young Elizabeth Taylor; the tear-jerking *Lassie Come Home*; the screen version of Hemingway's *For Whom the Bell Tolls*,

Trade unionist Sisulu.

IN FASHION

♦ **The line:** Severe; shoulders are square, skirts short. The tailored suit is favoured.
♦ **Materials:** Practical and hard-wearing. Artificial silk is in demand and there is always a lively trade in parachute silk.
♦ **The legs:** America stops manufacturing silk stockings in 1942 so most women have to make do with everyday flesh-coloured lisle.
♦ **The feet:** Practical, no-nonsense shoes with low, sometimes wedge-shaped heels and rounded toes.
♦ **The head:** Hats are small, cute, angled over the eye; hair shortish, swept up in front and kept in place with combs or long, languorous and falling down over one cheek.

Wartime utility.

Cute headwear.

SOUTH AFRICA in the 20th CENTURY 1940s

Jitterbug frenzy.

American GIs land on 'bloody Omaha' beach, Normandy.

with Gary Cooper and Ingrid Bergman, and *The Outlaw*, which stars big-busted Jane Russell.
- The jerkily frenzied Jitterbug sweeps the free world's dance floors.

BORN
International: British politician John Major; fashion guru Mary Quant; Polish politician Lech Walesa. *South Africa:* Equestrienne Gonda Beatrix; activist Chris Hani; actor John Kani; politician Pallo Jordan.

Sex symbol Russell.

WHAT'S NEW IN 1943

- *Aviation:* Lockheed's super-fast (550 mph) P-80 jet warplane goes into production in California.
- The *aqualung*, invented by French engineer and naval officer Jacques Cousteau.
- *Irish Coffee* is served for the first time, to weary passengers at Shannon airport, Ireland.

1944

D-DAY: ANGLO-AMERICANS LAND IN NORMANDY

6 June. US, British and Canadian forces, under the overall command of General Dwight Eisenhower, land on the beaches of Normandy to open up the long-awaited second front.

The greatest armada of all time – close to 5,000 war-ships and transports – carry 180,000 men through choppy seas to their five landfalls, codenamed Omaha, Utah, Gold, Sword and Juno.

During the weeks leading up to D-Day, Allied air forces mount a relentless assault on the enemy's communications network, bombing and strafing roads, bridges and railway installations. British and US airborne divisions are dropped behind the invasion area during the night of 5/6 June to cause further chaos.

The Germans have constructed a formidable coastal defence system, including strongpoints, protected gun emplacements and a variety of beach and underwater obstacles (known as 'Rommel's asparagus'), and Allied planners have anticipated a high casualty rate. Some 60 enemy divisions, several of them armoured,

British Bren-gunners in action.

103

SOUTH AFRICA in the 20th CENTURY

The Forties

Liberated French villagers welcome Canadian troops.

stand poised to repel any seaborne landing in the general area. In the event, only those US units assaulting Omaha suffer severe losses, the others making good headway. By the evening of the D-Day they have established a bridgehead five miles deep in places.

The weather and uncertainty work in favour of the Allies. German intelligence has discounted an invasion during the stormy conditions prevailing and, in any event, believes the main landings will take place farther north, in the Pas de Calais – a belief reinforced by clever British deception tactics. German frontline commanders are unprepared; indeed some of the generals are away at the time, on a war games exercise. Nor do the mobile reserves intervene effectively: only the panzer (armoured) units can throw the invaders back into the sea, but the tanks stand idle – Hitler personally has to give the order for their release, and the dictator, filled with medicinal drugs and surrounded by fearful advisers, is allowed to sleep through the crisis.

ITALY: ALLIES ADVANCE; SA TROOPS TAKE FLORENCE

On 4 June, two days before the D-Day landings and after a long, hard slog up the rugged 'spine' of Italy, the Allies finally enter Rome to the cheers of thousands of jubilant citizens.

Two months earlier the 6th South African (armoured) division, commanded by General Everard Poole, joined the fray, passing through Rome on 6 June and going on to engage a stubborn German enemy, with success, in a number of engagements. Following some tough fighting, it enters Florence on 4 August.

ON SCREEN
♦ Betty Grable and Rita Hayworth are the universal pin-ups
Top films include:
♦ Lawrence Olivier's version of Shakespeare's *Henry V*, an exuberant (and timely) portrayal of British grit
♦ *National Velvet*, in which youthful Elizabeth Taylor and Mickey Rooney take their gift horse all the way to the top.

HIT SONGS
● You'll Never Know
● On the Sunny Side of the Street
● Don't Fence Me In
● Swinging on a Star

BORN
International: Singer Diana Ross. **South Africa:** Poet Mongane Wally Serote; cricketer Graeme Pollock.

DIED
International: British 'Chindit' commander Orde Wingate; bandleader Glenn Miller. **South Africa:** Soldier, author, politician Denys Reitz.

Allied forces probe into Holland; townsfolk give thanks for liberation.

Elizabeth Taylor stuns in National Velvet.

SOUTH AFRICA in the 20th CENTURY 1940s

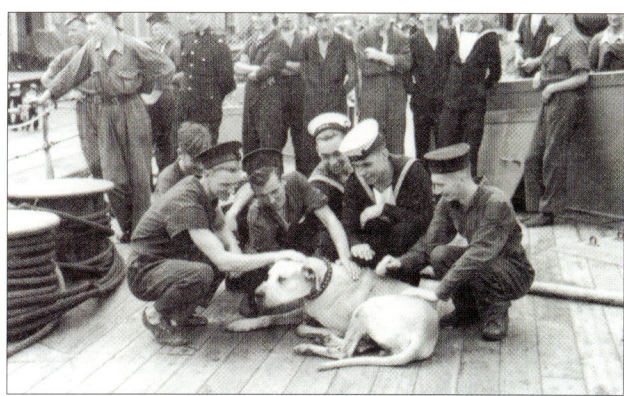

A familiar presence in and around Simonstown is Just Nuisance, a Great Dane adopted and much loved by British sailors during the war years. The dog was formally attested into the Royal Navy, given the rank of Able Seaman, and on his death was buried with full military honours: 200 officers and men stood with bowed heads as the Last Post sounded, the honour guard fired the farewell volley and the flag-draped coffin was lowered into its grave on Red Hill.

1945
VICTORY IN EUROPE: SOUTH AFRICA CELEBRATES

The Star covers VE ('Victory in Europe) Day.

8 May. South Africans join the free world in celebrating the end of the war in Europe. Streets and buildings are ablaze with flags, bunting and oceans of ticker-tape, the men 'bright with nosegays in their lapels, and city typists with colourful favours pinned to their frocks'. *The Star* newspaper reports: 'By 3 p.m. the City Square was packed with 10,000 people.... All listened to Mr Churchill's speech and at the closing words, "God Save the King", the trumpets rang out and the crowd took up the anthem with full hearts.

'As the last notes died away the sirens blared again. Motorists sounded their hooters. Tram-drivers rang their gongs. People cheered, shouted and sang. Young men started dancing like Dervishes on the lawns and threw fire-crackers into the air. Others ran like monkeys along the ledges of the City hall. It was a mad, merry unforgettable moment into which the people tried to compress all the relief they felt from the suspense, anxiety and strain of five years of terrible war.'

Home is the soldier: Corporal Zinn arrives back in Johannesburg.

HOLOCAUST REVEALED

The full horrors of the Holocaust – Hitler's 'Final Solution' of the 'Jewish problem' – are exposed as Allied occupation forces enter dozens of Nazi death camps. Millions have died in their gas chambers; thousands of pitiful survivors, many barely-living skeletons, listlessly await their liberators.

The great majority of victims – an unimaginable six million of them – were Jews, but huge numbers of slave labourers, Gypsies, religious dissidents, homosexuals and the mentally retarded have also been exterminated.

The names of the camps – among them Buchenwald, Dachau, Bergen-Belsen, Treblinka and, above all, Auschwitz – will be inscribed in the halls of infamy for as long as human conscience persists.

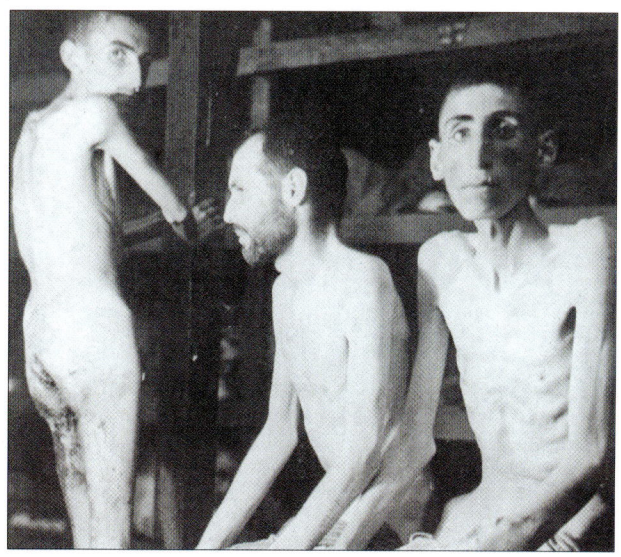

Death-camp survivors.

SOUTH AFRICA in the 20th CENTURY

The Forties

> 'In spite of the joy you can't help reflecting that our larders are bare, everyone's house needs painting, our clothes are shabby and you can't buy a sheet or blanket unless you're bombed out or newlywed.'
> *British housewife*

Mussolini (centre) and mistress in death.

TWO DICTATORS DIE
Onetime Italian dictator Benito Mussolini and his mistress, Clara Petacci, are captured and shot by partisans on 29 April. Their corpses are hung by the heels, and publicly reviled, in Milan's Piazza Loretto. Two days later Adolf Hitler, his 'Thousand Year Reich' in ruins around him, shoots himself in his Berlin bunker. The end comes minutes after Eva Braun, his long-time mistress and new wife (they married the day before), takes poison.

CHANGING OF THE GUARD
US president Franklin Delano Roosevelt dies on 12 April, just days before the Allied armies finish their job in Europe. He is succeeded by Harry S. Truman. Two months later, in an astonishing about-face, the British people vote Winston Churchill out of office – Clement Attlee's Labour Party wins the election by a landslide. General Charles de Gaulle, charismatic leader of the wartime Free French forces, becomes president of France.

New British premier Clement Attlee, left, in joyful mood.

WHAT'S NEW IN 1945
- **Microwave oven** invented, in Massachusetts, USA.
- **Ebony** magazine launched, in Chicago.
- London's **Heathrow airport** opens for business.
- The word **genocide** enters the English language.

ARTS AND LEISURE
- **New books:** *Animal Farm* (George Orwell); *Brideshead Revisited* (Evelyn Waugh); *Cannery Row* (John Steinbeck).
- **Films:** Billy Wilder's *The Lost Weekend*, with Ray Milland; David Lean's *Brief Encounter*, with Trevor Howard and Celia Johnson; Alfred Hitchcock's aptly titled *Spellbound*, with Gregory Peck and Ingrid Bergman.

BORN
International: Comic actor Steve Martin; musician Bob Marley.
South Africa: Playwright and satirist Pieter-Dirk Uys; cricketer Barry Richards; composer Peter Klatzow.

DIED
International: British politician David Lloyd George; Nazi leaders Heinrich Himmler and Joseph Goebbels; brilliant US general George S. Patton.
South Africa: Sculptor Anton van Wouw; poet Samuel Mqhayi.

Anton van Wouw.

THE BOMB

A deadly mushroom cloud heralds the atomic age.

The General Assembly of the United Nations meets for the first time. The 51-state organization was founded in San Francisco in April 1945; here Jan Smuts, one of the principal architects, signs the Charter on behalf of South Africa.

The war in the east comes to an abrupt, sensationally dramatic and awesomely decisive conclusion with nuclear explosions that destroy two major Japanese cities. Shortly after American B-29 aircraft drop the atom bomb – the most powerful weapon ever devised by man – on Hiroshima (6 August) and Nagasaki (9 August), Japanese emperor Hirohito announces a cessation of hostilities.

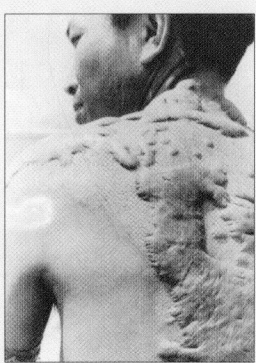

Scarred for life.

Thousands of people in the two cities have been instantly vaporized by the explosions; many more die slower deaths; still others will bear the scars for life. Some 60,000 of Hiroshima's 90,000 homes are either incinerated or levelled by the blast.

The two bombs are the product of a secret research and development mission, led by Dr Julius Robert Oppenheimer and codenamed the Manhattan Project, conducted at the remote Los Alamos site in New Mexico, USA.

1946

FEW POST-WAR BLUES FOR SA

White South Africans live the good life while Britons suffer shortages – 'austerity' is the key word in the post-war period; food, clothing, sweets, cigarettes, spirits continue to be tightly rationed. British bread becomes even darker than the wartime 'victory loaf', its wheat content reduced to the 1942 level; the weekly allowance of butter, margarine and cooking fat has been cut from eight to seven ounces; shoppers are allowed only minuscule portions of meat, bacon and poultry; the year begins in grim fashion; Christmas has been a cheerless affair, the rations pitiful, the shelves bare of nuts, raisins, candied fruits. And turkey, at 15 shillings a pound in London, was seven times more expensive than in Cape Town.

South Africa on the other hand enjoys abundant supplies of just about everything – including eggs, which are limited to one per person per week in the UK. Oddly enough, though, South African drinkers face a shortage of beer.

MINERS STRIKE, TWELVE DIE

12 August. Some 60,000 black mineworkers go on strike in a bid for better working conditions and a minimum daily wage of 10 shillings. Premier Smuts responds sharply, even brutally: next day police arrest John Marks, the workers' leader, raid union offices and, at Nigel on the East Rand, clash head-on with strikers. Six workers are shot dead, another six trampled to death in the ensuing panic. Over 1,000 more are injured in other incidents.

SOUTH AFRICA in the 20th CENTURY

The Forties

CHURCHILL WARNS THE WORLD

5 March. British war leader Winston Churchill, on a visit to the United States, paints a sombre picture of the future when he warns of a Soviet menace still ill perceived by the largely complacent free world. 'From Stettin in the Baltic to Trieste in the Adriatic,' he tells a packed audience in Fulton, Missouri, 'an Iron Curtain has descended across the Continent. The dark ages may return on the gleaming wings of science. Beware, I say. Time may be short.'

The bikini, the swimsuit that shocked.

SIGNS OF THE TIMES

The year opens new horizons for boffins, city travellers, sunbathers and young mothers. In Philadelphia, scientists unveil a giant, remarkably advanced calculator, grandfather of the ever more sophisticated computers that are to come. ENIAC (an acronym for Electronic Numerical Integrator and Calculator) weighs 30 tons, 'thinks' with its 18,000 electronic valves and can perform 5,000 additions and subtractions each minute. In Italy, the first mass-produced scooter, the Vespa, hits the streets. In Paris, Micheline Bernardini models a shockingly revealing swimsuit nicknamed 'the Bikini' (after the Pacific atoll on which the US has just tested a nuclear device) and immediately receives 50,000 fan letters; beach-lovers in Calvinist South Africa are slow to take the plunge. In the US, Dr Benjamin Spock turns domestic conventions upside down with liberal, spare-the-rod advice in his *The Common Sense Book of Baby and Child Care*.

BORN
International: US politician Bill Clinton. *South Africa:* Activists Steve Biko and Alan Boesak; musician Lemmy 'Special' Mabaso; golfer Hugh Biocchi; cricketer Mike Proctor.

DIED
International: Nazi war criminal Hermann Goering, in prison, by his own hand; British television pioneer John Logie Baird; authors H.G. Wells and Gertrude Stein; comic actor W.C. Fields. *South Africa:* Architect Sir Herbert Baker; artist Charles Bell; aviation pioneer Evelyn Driver; African nationalist John Dube; musician William Bell.

1947

ROYALS TOUR SOUTH AFRICA

If there are any doubts about the affection in which South Africans – at least most of them, of all races and both white language groups – hold the British monarchy, they are dispelled during the two-month-long Royal visit.

On 17 February King George VI, Queen Elizabeth and their two daughters, Elizabeth and Margaret, arrive at Cape Town harbour aboard HMS *Vanguard* to a tumultuous welcome. The King opens parliament, and he and his family, escorted by General Smuts, ascend Table Mountain before setting out on an exhausting tour of South Africa, Bechuanaland and Southern Rhodesia. On one occasion, the Royal Family listen to a 15-year-old singer's first solo; the child's name: Miriam Makeba. Later in the year Princess Elizabeth marries Philip Mountbatten in what is widely regarded as the wedding of the century.

SOUTH AFRICA'S 'FIRST LADY' UNEARTHED

Dr Robert Broom's relentless search for the origins of humankind is rewarded

> 'The government is like a man who has a corn-field which is invaded by birds. He chases the birds from one part of the field and they alight in another part. We shall see whether it is the farmer or the birds who gets tired first....'
> *Pimville (Soweto) squatter leader Oriel Monongoaha*

The Royal family on tour; from left to right: Princess Elizabeth, SA premier Jan Smuts, King George VI, Queen Elizabeth, Princess Margaret.

SOUTH AFRICA in the 20th CENTURY 1940s

Broom (right) sweeps Sterkfontein for man's ancestors.

Preparing for partition: Muslims march in London.

by his discovery, in the Sterkfontein caves west of Pretoria, of a million-year-old female skull. This he names *Plesianthropus transvaalensis*, popularly known as 'Mrs Ples'.

DEAD SEA SCROLLS DISCOVERED

A remarkable collection of leather and papyrus manuscripts dating from the first century AD are unearthed, by accident, when a desert shepherd enters a hidden cave near the Dead Sea in search of lost sheep. The scrolls promise to throw new light on the life and beliefs of Christ and the very early Christians.

FIRST 'FLYING SAUCERS' REPORTED

Reports of Unidentified Flying Objects – UFOs – come in from all parts of the world during the year. The first is recorded by American pilot Kenneth Arnold, who claims he saw nine brightly lit craft, collectively shaped like a saucer, skimming at speed near the Cascade Mountains in the state of Washington.

INDIA, PAKISTAN GAIN FREEDOM

Political leaders agree, with the reluctant consent of Mohandas Gandhi, on the partition of the Indian subcontinent into separate Hindu and Muslim states. The separation of India and Pakistan, both which gain their independence of Britain in August, triggers an unprecedented mass migration and massacres in which an estimated half-million men, women and children of both faiths lose their lives. Gandhi, the Mahatma (which means 'Great Soul') and father of modern India, does not have long to live: he will be assassinated, by a Hindu extremist, next year.

WHAT'S NEW IN 1947

- *Polaroid* camera hits the market.
- Mikhail Kalashnikov invents the *AK-47* assault rifle.
- First *duty-free shop* opens, at Shannon airport, Ireland.
- *Aviation:* American pilot Chuck Yeager breaks the sound barrier.
- *Music:* First solid-body electric guitar developed, by American musician Les Paul.
- *Cricket:* 'Brylcreem Boy' Dennis Compton scores a record 3,816 runs, including 18 centuries, during the English county season.
- The phrase *cold war* enters the English language.

HIT SONGS
- Cruising Down the River
- Maybe It's Because I'm a Londoner
- Almost like being in love
- Zip-a-dee-doo-dah

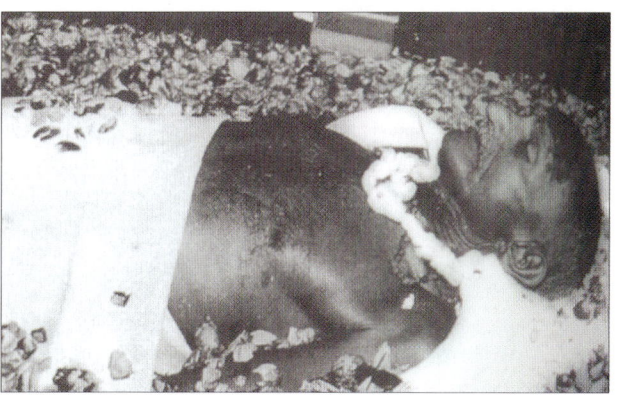
Gandhi: struck down, early in 1948, at the defining moment.

SOUTH AFRICA in the 20th CENTURY

The Forties

BORN
South Africa: Academic and human rights campaigner Mamphela Ramphele; singer Bles Bridges.

DIED
International: Chicago Mob leader Al Capone; industrialist Henry Ford. *South Africa:* Political leader Josiah Gumede; writer C. Louis Leipoldt; ANC idealogue Anton Lembede.

Daniël Malan (centre): harbinger of a grim future.

1948

NAT VICTORY HERALDS ERA OF APARTHEID

28 May. The dark clouds of institutionalized apartheid finally descend on South Africa with the victory of Daniël Malan's Herenigde Nasionale Party (Reunited National Party) in the all-white general election. The HNP, with the crucial support of Nicolaas Havenga's Afrikaner Party, squeeze in to win a parliamentary majority of just five seats.

Field Marshall Jan Smuts, one-time Boer guerrilla hero, war leader and prime minister since 1939, loses his seat to a Nationalist candidate.

The outcome is a victory for Afrikanerdom. The 'poor white' problem has largely been solved, but the old anxieties are still there. The war years boosted local industry and the demand for black labour; job reservation is under threat; post-war immigration has increased competition in the workplace, and Smuts's recent liberal statements on race add to the climate of insecurity among white wage-earners. Fear tips the balance at the polls.

Malan's Nationalists have focused sharply on race, promising to keep the white vote intact, to halt integration at all levels, and to safeguard white jobs and white privilege within the framework of a supremacist master-plan.

ISRAEL FOUNDED; WAR ERUPTS

14 May. Jews throughout the world celebrate as the nation of Israel is born. Joy, though, turns to anxiety as Arab armies – from Egypt, Syria, Iraq, Lebanon and Jordon – invade the tiny new state. They capture some territory, including part of Jerusalem, but elsewhere Israeli forces hold the line. Fighting continues, inconclusively, for the rest of the year.

NEW LOOK BRIGHTENS THE FASHION SCENE

Young Christian Dior's 1947 'New Look' summer collection brings a bright light to the darkness of austerity. Gone are the square shoulders and practical, hard-wearing fabrics of the war years; in are long, full ballerina skirts in soft materials underlayed by rustling taffeta petticoats; waists are small, tightly belted, coats tent-like with high collars. Heels are high and so are busts; hats tiny and about to disappear altogether. Glamour and femininity, missing from the fashion scene since 1940, are back with a vengeance.

A Dior ensemble.

SPORTING HIGHLIGHTS

◆ **Cricket:** The MCC tour of South Africa starts dramatically. Captain Dudley Nourse has some fine players in his team – the Rowan brothers, Bruce Mitchell, Tufty Mann, Lindsay Tucket, strike bowler Cuan McCarthy among others. The visitors, though, win the first Test, played at Kingsmead, by the proverbial hair's-breadth. England's last-wicket pair (Alec Bedser and Cliff Gladwin) need eight runs off the last over; the winning single, a leg-bye, comes off the last ball.

Israeli civilians flee the fighting.

SOUTH AFRICA in the 20th CENTURY 1940s

Sturgess in action.

Police battle with rioters in and around the Cato Manor informal settlement; 106 die.

- **Tennis:** South Africans Eric Sturgess and Sheila Summers chalk up a notable victory when they win the mixed doubles at both the French Open and Wimbledon. Sturgess also reaches the semi-finals of the Wimbledon Singles and Men's Doubles.
- **Boxing:** Eight South African boxers compete at the first post-war Olympics, held in London. Five of them reach the semi-finals; Gerald Dreyer and George Hunter go on to win gold for SA.

WHAT'S NEW IN 1948

- **Car models** on show include the first of the beetle-shaped Morris Minors and the Land Rover, Britain's answer to the all-purpose Jeep. British Daimler introduces the first electrically operated car windows.
- **Literature:** Alan Paton earns an international reputation with his novel *Cry, the Beloved Country*.
- South Africa annexes **Marion** and **Prince Edward** islands.
- First **LP** (long-playing) records on sale.

BORN
South Africa: Politician Patrick Lekota; Zulu monarch Goodwill Zwelithini; playwright, writer, painter Zakes Mda.

1949
RIOTS TAKE HEAVY TOLL

15 January. Some of the worst race riots in South Africa's history claim an estimated 106 lives as residents of the Cato Manor squatter camps, on the fringes of Durban, attack members of the local Indian community. Roving gangs, armed with clubs, single out small traders for 'punishment' following the reported murder, by an Indian, of an African boy. Indian property owners retaliate with vigour. The missing boy is eventually found unharmed.

PEOPLE'S REPUBLIC PROCLAIMED AT THE HEAVENLY GATE

China, 1 October. After years of bitter internal warfare Mao Tse-tung's armies finally roll back their Nationalist enemies to create the world's most populous Communist state. Speaking to cheering crowds at the Gate of Heavenly Peace Square, Peking (later to be known as Beijing), Mao proclaims that China 'will no longer be a nation subject to insult and humiliation'.

Most countries, including the Soviet Union and Great Britain, formally recognize the People's Republic of China. A Soviet statement declares that the Communist victory 'dealt a cruel blow to the aggressive plans of Imperialists in the Pacific region'. The United States withholds recognition.

HIT PARADE
- Buttons and Bows (originally sung by Bob Hope)
- Rudolph the Red-nosed Reindeer (Gene Autrey)
- Galway Bay (Bing Crosby)
- Riders in the Sky (Vaughan Monroe)

ON SCREEN
Laurence Olivier's stunning production of *Hamlet* wins five Oscars; the screen version of Graham Greene's *The Third Man*, starring Orson Welles, attracts critical acclaim. Britain's Ealing Studios comes up with a trio of charming comedies: *Passport to Pimlico*, *Kind Hearts and Coronets* (Alec Guinness in several different roles) and *Whisky Galore*.

BORN
South Africa: Muslim poet Shabbir Banoobhai; politician Nkosazana Zuma; rugby player Morné du Plessis; cricketer Clive Rice.

1950s

DIED
1950: Jan Christiaan Smuts.
1952: King George VI.

AT WAR
1950: United Nations and Communist North Korea (later joined by China); SAAF squadrons take part.

INAUGURATED
1950: Springbok Radio. University of the Orange Free State.
1952: Defiance Campaign (by the ANC). Congress of Democrats. Coloured People's Organisation.
1953: Federation of the Rhodesias and Nyasaland. SA Liberal Party. Jan Smuts Airport, Johannesburg.
1954: The Black Sash movement. Sasolburg (oil from coal plant).
1955: Four-year Treason Trial, after police crackdown.
1957: Angolan freedom movements.
1959: Pan-Africanist Congress, by Robert Sobukwe.

DISBANDED
1950: Communist Party of SA; soon reconstituted as SA Communist Party.

INSTALLED
1952: Kwame Nkrumah, as premier of Gold Coast.
1953: Elizabeth II, as queen of England.
1954: J.G. Strijdom, as SA premier.
1958: Hendrik Verwoerd, as SA premier.

1959: Fidel Castro, as revolutionary leader of Cuba.

ON THE MARCH
1951: War Veterans Torch Commando.

CELEBRATED
1952: Van Riebeeck tercentenary.

ADOPTED
1955: The Freedom Charter, by Congress of the People, at Kliptown.

FIRST
1950: Afrikaans feature movie: Jamie Uys's *Daar Doer in die Bosveld*.
1951: 'Duzi' river canoe marathon.
1952: SA uranium plant, on West Rand.
1953: James Bond novel.
1954: Polio vaccine developed, by Jonas Salk.
1957: Space satellite, the Soviet *Sputnik* 1, launched; tracked from SA. Parking meters installed (in London).

RECORD
1951: SA gold output. Giant Orange Free State mines begin production.

CLOSED (TEMPORARILY)
1956: Suez Canal, after Anglo-French and Israeli forces attack Egypt; SA ports benefit from round-the-Cape traffic.

REVERTED
1957: Simon's Town base, from Britain to SA Navy.

ACTS PASSED
1950: Population Registration. Group Areas. Suppression of Communism.
1951: Bantu Authorities. Abolition of Passes (replaced by all-purpose reference book). Riots lead to Public Safety and Criminal Law Amendment acts.
1952: Native Laws Amendment (influx control). Prevention of Illegal Squatting.
1953: Reservation of Separate Amenities. Bantu Education.
1954: Native Resettlement.
1959: Promotion of Black Self-Government.

REMOVED
1954: Black people, from the western Cape (a continuing process for the next few years).
1956: Coloured voters, from the common roll.

CHAMPIONS
1950: Boxer Vic Toweel, world bantomweight title.
1951: SA's rugby Springboks, on tour of Britain.
1959: Golfer Gary Player, victor at British Open.

Drum, launched in 1951 for a black readership, became Africa's most popular magazine.

SOUTH AFRICA in the 20th CENTURY 1950s

The race divide: public buildings have separate facilities.

1950

LAW-MAKING BLITZ ENTRENCHES APARTHEID

Daniël Malan's Nationalist government launches a massive onslaught on civil liberties with the passage of a number far-reaching race laws, each designed to entrench segregation deeper in the country's social fabric.

Racially mixed marriages were banned last year; now the Immorality Act places a total embargo on close relations between black and white people.

But the new regime first has to define race – and this it tries to do with its Population Registration Act. The Act establishes a crude formula which holds that physical appearance (colour), 'customary association' and 'repute' will distinguish one kind of South African from another.

From this measure flows much else, including a racially based identity document and, most notably, the Group Areas Act, which brings together all the previous laws into one all-embracing legal code confining each of the race groups to its own residential and trading areas. Straightaway the Act forces thousands of urban folk, most of them Indians and coloureds, out of their homes and business premises.

Meanwhile the process of 'Afrikanerization' continues apace. The government has been insisting that all public employees must be bilingual – on the face of it, a quite reasonable requirement, but one which prompts the wholesale replacement of English-speakers by Afrikaners. Before long, senior and middle-echelon positions in every branch of the civil service, police and armed forces are filled by those loyal to the *volk* and the National Party.

LOCAL BOY WINS WORLD TITLE

Johannesburg, 31 May. Vic Toweel, the 24-year-old former wood-carver from Benoni, becomes the first South African to fight for, and win, a world boxing title when he defeats veteran bantamweight champion Manuel Ortiz at the city's Wembley stadium in front of a partisan crowd of 30,000. For most of the fight the challenger takes heavy punishment, but he later recalls: 'When the bell ended the ninth round I was numb with pain, but my head cleared, and for the first time I knew I was going to win.'

RADIO SERVICES EXPAND

Local broadcasting takes a giant step forward with the launch of Springbok Radio, a light, bright, bilingual commercial service that focuses largely on romantic serials, audience participation shows and pop music. Springbok's signature tune is 'Vat Jou Goed en Trek Ferreira', the first song to be aired; the first advertiser is Edblo; the first voice that of Eric Egan.

Programmes include what are to prove long-running *Radio Juke Box*, *Hospital Time*, *Lux Radio Theatre* and, most popular show of all in the years to come, *Pick-a-Box*.

Meanwhile, the SABC relays its last BBC news broadcast. The BBC service is replaced by bulletins prepared by the newly formed SABC News Department.

Egan: first voice on radio.

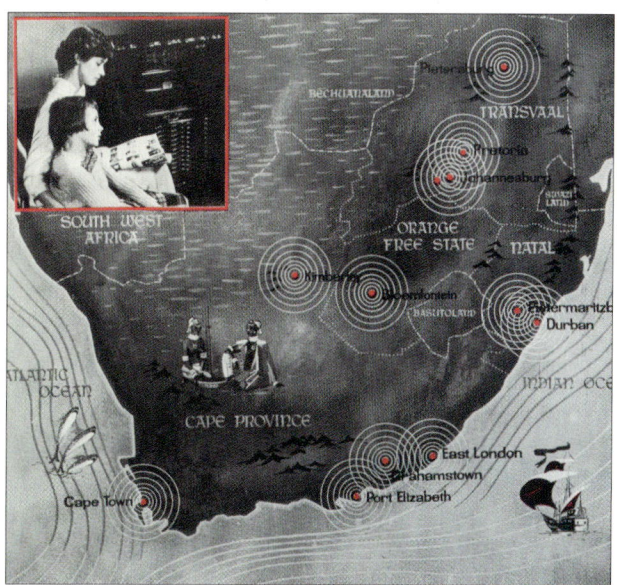
Springbok Radio leaps into the future.

113

SOUTH AFRICA in the 20th CENTURY

The Fifties

A Mustang of the 'Flying Cheetahs' squadron during the Korean war.

LEADING CIRCUS FOLDS ITS TENT
Pagel's Circus, which has entertained three generations of South Africans, is up for sale. The asking price is £10,000; assets include three camels, two elephants, five Shetland ponies, five horses, nine lionesses and two seals.

NO PUBLIC HANGINGS IN SA
The Minister of Justice, Mr C.R. Swart, announces that he is not prepared to reintroduce public hangings. Europeans were sometimes hanged but, however bad they were, 'they had dear ones and it would be terrible for them if Natives and Coloured people were allowed to laugh and make jokes at a European execution'.

WAR BREAKS OUT IN KOREA
June. Communist North Korean troops cross the 38th parallel that divides North and South Korea, threatening a major confrontation between the Western Allies and the Soviet bloc. US president Harry Truman immediately orders American naval and air forces to go to the aid of its southern ally. Next day the UN Security Council instructs all UN member nations to 'furnish such assistance to the Republic of Korea as may be necessary to meet the armed attack'. In due course South Africa answers the call, sending a token squadron of fighters – the 'Flying Cheetahs' – to the battle zone.

The Korean war escalates rapidly. Northern forces advance to capture Seoul, the southern capital, before the US 10th Corps lands at Inchon to link up with General Douglas MacArthur's UN Army, and, on 1 October, to cross into North Korea, pushing quickly on to the Chinese border. By the end of November, however, they have turned tail and are reeling back before a massive assault by Communist Chinese troops.

THE 'OUBAAS' GOES TO HIS LONG HOME
11 September. Jan Christiaan Smuts, former Anglo-Boer War guerrilla hero, war leader and prime minister, dies at the

Korea is plunged into war; as always, it is ordinary folk who suffer.

Smuts on Table Mountain.

SOUTH AFRICA in the 20th CENTURY

WHAT'S NEW IN 1950

- A new breed of young American female music-lover, the **bobbysoxer**, makes her appearance. She is noisy, enthusiastic, wears knee-length stockings, loves Frank Sinatra and dates at the soda fountain.
- **On the road:** Figures released show that South Africa's road accident death rate, at 17.7 per 10,000 vehicles, is twice that of the US.
- **Package holidays** and **holiday villages** (notably in Majorca and Corsica) become features of the European tourism scene.
- Charles Schultz's **Peanuts** introduces a new type of cartoon strip.
- The first **credit cards** are issued, by Diners Club.
- **Medicine:** First kidney transplant (in Chicago); first sex-change operation (in Denmark).
- First **lifts** with automatic doors, installed by Otis Elevators in Dallas, Texas.

The drive-in movie: social mecca of the fifties.

age of 80. Known with affection – among people of colour as well as by whites – as the 'Oubaas', he stood tall on both the world and the South African stages for close on half a century, counting among his friends such great and diverse men as Mohandas Gandhi and Winston Churchill.

For all his political stature, though, Smuts remained remarkably unassuming, humble in lifestyle, modest in his tastes, a quiet and brilliant thinker who had impressed the scientific fraternity with his theories relating human history to climate and geology.

He was also one of the leading naturalists of his time, with a profound knowledge of, and love for, the natural world in all its forms.

Fifties heart-throb Frank Sinatra, beloved of the bobbysoxers.

BESTSELLER TO BE FILMED

London, 12 June. Among those selected for parts in the film version of Alan Paton's *Cry the Beloved Country* are the African-Americans Canada Lee and talented newcomer Sidney Poitier, with Clive Brook and several local actors. Lee, who will play Kumalo, featured in the New York production of *Othello* and in a number of films, including *Body and Soul* and *Lifeboat*. Zoltan Korda will direct the movie.

BORN
International: Britain's Princess Anne; singers Karen Carpenter and Stevie Wonder. **South Africa:** Racing driver Jody Scheckter.

DIED
International: American entertainer Al Jolson; literary figures George Bernard Shaw, George Orwell and Edgar Rice Burroughs; Russian ballet dancer Vaslav Nijinsky. **South Africa:** Statesman 'Onze' Jan Christiaan Smuts; cartoonist Daniël Boonzaier; aviation pioneer John Weston.

LOCAL STARGAZER LAUDED

Amateur astronomer and semi-invalid R.P. de Kock, of Cape Town, is honoured for his work: last year he made a remarkable 5,769 observations of 157 variable stars with the use of a six-inch refractor. In 1941 he discovered the comet that now bears his name.

> 'Nicky and I are one for ever and ever'
> Movie star Elizabeth Taylor, at the first of her eight weddings

1951

NATS WIDEN WEDGE BETWEEN BLACK AND WHITE

The Nationalist government powers ahead in its drive to split the races with its Prevention of Illegal Squatting Act, aimed at getting rid of 'black spots' within 'white' areas. From now on, no black South Africans can live on either private or public land without official permission. Thousands of householders are soon being 'endorsed out' of the country's major centres. Many of those who lose their homes have nowhere else to go.

The year also sees the beginnings of the 'homelands' system – the Bantustans that will finally and forever (for four decades, as it turns out) exclude Africans from the political mainstream. 'The fundamental idea', explains Minister of Native Affairs Hendrik Verwoerd, 'is Bantu control over Bantu areas as and when it becomes possible for them to exercise control efficiently and properly for the benefit of their own people.' The Bantu Authorities Act establishes tribal authorities run by the Native Affairs Department but which, the minister promises, pave the way for black self-government in the reserves.

There are moves, too, against the coloured community. Most far-reaching of these is the Separate Registration of Voters Act, designed to remove coloured people from the common roll. Here, though, the government itself comes up against the law: these voting rights have been written into the constitution, and any changes will require a two-thirds majority approval by both houses of parliament. The Act is immediately challenged in the streets (by the low-key Franchise Action Committee and, more energetically, by the largely white War Veterans' Torch Commando) and in the Appellate Division of the Supreme Court. The issue will drag on for years; in the end, the Nats will pack both the Senate and the court with party faithfuls and push the measure through.

Native Affairs minister Verwoerd, third from left, plans the future.

Whites, en route to Durban's City Hall, march against apartheid.

TORCHLIGHT RALLIES PROTEST APARTHEID

Adolph Malan's Torch Commando, a 250,000-strong movement made up largely of white ex-servicemen, takes to the streets in massive numbers during the year. Its torchlight processions – in protest against the government's apartheid policy generally and in particular its attempts to remove coloured people from the voters' roll – illuminate the thoroughfares of Cape Town, Port Elizabeth, Johannesburg and, later, Durban.

Malan – known as 'Sailor Malan' – has impeccable credentials: he is a war hero who flew with the Royal Air Force, took part in the battles of Dunkirk and Britain, and was promoted group captain – one of the RAF's youngest. He was highly decorated both for his leadership qualities and for the 35 enemy 'kills' he made.

SOUTH AFRICA in the 20th CENTURY 1950s

NOURSE CHALKS UP DOUBLE TON

In his last year at Test level the great South African cricketer and team captain Dudley Nourse scores a gritty 208 against England at Trent Bridge. The marathon innings lasts a painful 9½ hours – literally painful, since he makes it despite the agony of a broken left thumb. He is shortly to retire, having represented his country in 32 consecutive Tests since 1935 (34 in all).

Altogether, he has scored 2,960 runs at international level, including nine centuries, at an average of 53.82 – and all by a man who was virtually self-taught.

Dudley Nourse.

BRITISH FESTIVAL SIGNALS END OF POST-WAR GLOOM

Both Londoners and visitors flock in their thousands to the Festival of Britain, opened on a reclaimed 27-acre bomb-site at Battersea, on the city's south bank, by the King and Queen at the beginning of May. The only South African invited to perform at the celebrations is the theatrical pioneer and actor André Huguenet, who appears in James Elroy Flecker's *Hassan*.

The Festival, held just 100 years after Queen Victoria's Great Exhibition showcased Britain's industrial and commercial might, signals the hoped-for end of post-war austerity and is described by Herbert Morrison as 'the people giving themselves a pat on the back' (meanwhile, 53,000 horses are being slaughtered to make up for Britain's beef shortage). Among the imaginatively designed structures are the Royal Festival Hall, the sweeping Dome of Discovery and, symbolizing the spirit of the future, the Skylon – a glowing, needle-shaped aluminium feature which (like Britain itself, says one humorist) has no visible means of support.

London's Skylon: spirit of the future, at the Festival of Britain.

KOREAN PEACE CLOSER AFTER NUKE THREAT

Politicians on both sides begin to look for ways to end the thankless Korean war after UN forces halt the joint Chinese-North Korean army's southward advance near the 38th parallel. Moves towards peace take on a new urgency when UN commander Douglas MacArthur, who has already urged the use of nuclear bombs, threatens to invade China. He is dismissed in April because, in President Truman's words, 'he wouldn't respect the authority of the President. I didn't fire him because he was a dumb son of a bitch, although he was, but that's not against the law for generals'.

BRITISH AGENTS DEFECT

Red-faced British Intelligence officials admit that two of their diplomats have deserted, and that they may have been

WHAT'S NEW IN 1951

- The first commercially available **computer**, the Univac 1, is unveiled by Remington Rand.
- **Politics:** Winston Churchill is voted back as Britain's prime minister.
- Mountaineer Eric Shipton produces what is alleged to be photographic evidence of the **Abominable Snowman**, a mysterious denizen of the Himalayas.
- Miss Sweden wins the first **Miss World** contest, held in London.
- **Medicine:** The influential mass-circulation Reader's Digest *magazine* is among the first to point out the link between smoking and cancer.
- **Cable television** is launched, in Chicago.

SOUTH AFRICA in the 20th CENTURY

The Fifties

Guy Burgess.

Donald MacLean.

working as double agents for years. Guy Burgess, 40, and Donald Maclean, 38, both Cambridge graduates, are last seen on 25 May when they board a cross-channel ferry en route to Paris. They eventually re-emerge in Moscow. Their defection intensifies speculation that a 'third man', an even more influential mole within the establishment, is involved.

ARTS AND ENTERTAINMENT

◆ British composer, songwriter and dramatist Ivor Novello dies. He was acclaimed for such hit musicals as *The Dancing Years* and *King's Rhapsody*, and for his songs 'Keep the Home Fires Burning' (written when he was just 21) and 'We'll Gather Lilacs in the Spring Again'. Among the year's hit shows are *South Pacific* and *Kiss Me Kate*.

◆ Movie blockbusters include *Quo Vadis* and *An American in Paris*, starring dancers Gene Kelly and Leslie Caron. Newcomer Marlon Brando causes a sensation with his performance, opposite Vivien Leigh, in *A Streetcar Named Desire*.

◆ The young South African actor Lawrence Harvey (born Mischa Skikne) makes his stage debut in London's West End.

Lawrence Harvey.

◆ Among best-selling books are Nicholas Monsarrat's *The Cruel Sea*, the intimate story of two wartime ships and their crews (Monsarrat wrote it while living in Johannesburg); Herman Wouk's *The Caine Mutiny*; James Jones's *From Here to Eternity*; the reclusive J.D. Salinger's *Catcher in the Rye*, which elevates an adolescent drop-out to cult status; and John Wyndham's *The Day of the Triffids*, a creepy sci-fi story of global near-extinction.

◆ South African poet Roy Campbell publishes his second autobiographical work, *Light on a Dark Horse*.

◆ Muddy Waters records 'Rolling Stone', which will eventually inspire an American magazine and a British rock band.

Scene from the film version of The Cruel Sea.

Poet Roy Campbell.

BORN
International: Chess master Anatoly Karpov; footballer Kevin Keegan. *South Africa:* Churchman and politician Frank Chikane; musicians David Kramer and Taliep Petersen; rugby star Errol Tobias.

DIED
International: British politician Ernest Bevin; French war hero turned collaborator Marshal Philippe Petain; literary figures Sinclair Lewis and André Gide. *South Africa:* Political leader Pixley ka Isaka Seme; composer and conductor Theo Wendt; writer Herman Charles Bosman; naturalist Frederick William FitzSimons; trade unionist Clements Kadalie; aviation pioneer Allister Miller; palaeontologist Robert Broom.

SOUTH AFRICA in the 20th CENTURY **1950s**

1952

DEFIANCE CAMPAIGN LAUNCHED

Nelson Mandela plans strategy with Nana Sita, president of the Transvaal Indian Congress.

As white South Africans celebrate the 300th anniversary of Van Riebeeck's landing, the ANC and its communist allies call for a 'national day of pledge and prayer'. Addressing a 50,000-strong rally in Freedom Square, Fordsburg, ANC president James Moroka says that whites 'cannot escape the fact that whatever page they turn in the history of South Africa they find it red with the blood of the fallen, with ill-will and insecurity...'.

The rally is a prelude to the Defiance Campaign, which begins on 26 June with mass protests in major centres. These continue in the weeks that follow, many of them drawing inspiration from Mahatma Gandhi's 'passive resistance' movement. Protesters deliberately breach the law, entering 'forbidden' areas without passes, joining 'Europeans-only' queues, walking through 'Europeans-only' entrances.

Police react sharply: hundreds of homes are raided, 35 protest leaders are charged with promoting communism; by October, 6,000 people are under arrest.

ANC president and leader of the Defiance Campaign James Moroka (top centre, with arms raised) addresses supporters.

WHAT'S NEW IN 1952

◆ *Aviation:* First scheduled passenger jet flight, by Britain's Comet, between London and Johannesburg.
◆ *In the home:* Survey reveals that one British household in three lacks a bath.
◆ *US:* Dwight (Ike) Eisenhower, borne along on the 'I Like Ike' slogan, wins the presidential election by a landslide.

Ike in victory mode.

◆ *Africa:* The young visionary Kwame Nkrumah becomes first African prime minister of a colony in transition when he is elected premier of the Gold Coast, later to be renamed Ghana.
◆ *Motor cars:* The first safety belts are fitted in motor cars in the US.

Death march: the royal coffin is borne through London's streets.

KING GEORGE DIES

Britain and the Commonwealth mourn the passing of King George VI, who dies in the early hours of 6 February of heart failure. A heavy smoker, he was in frail health since his operation for lung cancer last year. The king ascended the throne after his brother, Edward, abdicated in 1936, and served as the dignified symbol of British fortitude through the grim war years. He is succeeded by his elder daughter Elizabeth, who hears the news from husband Philip as they stroll in the grounds of the Kenya's luxurious safari-type

SOUTH AFRICA in the 20th CENTURY

BORN
International: Actor Christopher Reeve; tennis player Jimmy Connors. *South Africa:* Musician Sipho 'Hotstix' Mabuse; playwright Maishe Maponya; politician and poet Mathews Phosa; activist and politician Popo Molefe; swimmer Karen Muir; politician Matamela Cyril Ramaphosa; film-maker Leon Schuster.

Theatre personality Hendrik Hanekom.

DIED
International: Argentine's first lady Eva Perón; British speed ace John Cobb, who is killed when his boat disintegrates on Loch Ness, Scotland; Israeli statesman Chaim Weizmann. South Africa: Theatrical pioneer Hendrik Hanekom.

Treetops Hotel. On her return to London as Britain's new sovereign, she is met at the airport by a solemn Winston Churchill, the prime minister, and opposition leader Clement Attlee.

MAU MAU KILLINGS WRACK KENYA
21 October. British troops fly into Nairobi, capital of Kenya colony, as tension mounts over killings committed by the sinister underground movement known as Mau Mau. A state of emergency is declared. Around 40 people, many of them white settlers, have been murdered during the past few weeks. Mau Mau terrorists, who belong to the Kikuyu tribe, operate only at night, their weapons the panga and, increasingly, firearms of one sort or another. The taking of oaths is central to their campaign; one such pledges that 'if I leave a European farm without killing the European owner, may this oath kill me'.

Witchdoctors are used in the fight against Mau Mau.

ZATOPEK BURNS UP THE TRACK
Star of the Helsinki Olympics is the 29-year-old Czech runner Emil Zatopek, who wins both the 5,000 and 10,000 metres and then makes his first-ever attempt on the gruelling marathon – which he also wins. All three of his times are Games records. His wife Dana breaks the women's Olympic javelin mark.

YOUNG GIRL'S DIARY PUBLISHED
Hearts the world over are stirred by *The Diary of Anne Frank*, a slim volume written by a young Jewish girl in hiding from the Nazis in wartime Amsterdam. Anne was just 13 in 1942, when her family and four Jewish friends moved into a secret annexe to Otto Frank's office. Two years later they were betrayed and sent to Auschwitz concentration camp. Anne was later moved to Bergen-Belsen, where she died – just a few weeks before the war ended. Of the eight hideaways, only Otto survived.

STAGE AND SCREEN
◆ Agatha Christie's new play, *The Mousetrap*, opens at London's Ambassador theatre. The classic who-dunnit, which features Richard Attenborough as the detective, receives modest reviews, but its run is destined to continue unbroken until (at least) the end of the millennium.
◆ Charlie Chaplin's film *Limelight* entrances some, bores others with its sentimentality; Chaplin plays an ageing comedian in decline, the young Claire Bloom his protégée. Gene Kelly captivates in *Singin' in the Rain*. A delicious newcomer, the blonde and busty Marilyn Monroe, is introduced to filmgoers in *Niagara*. Monroe, born Norma Jean Baker, is destined for stardom; studio publicity managers are already hard at work.
◆ Among books published are John Steinbeck's *East of Eden*; Evelyn Waugh's *Men at Arms*; and South African author Nadine Gordimer's *The Soft Voice of the Serpent*.

Anne Frank and part of her diary.

SOUTH AFRICA in the 20th CENTURY

1950s

1953

CENTRAL AFRICAN FEDERATION LAUNCHED

Britain's master plan to bring together her three Central African territories bears fruit with the creation of the Federation of the Rhodesias and Nyasaland. Optimists believe the three different components will complement each other to the benefit of all the region's people, black and white. Northern Rhodesia is rich in minerals; Southern Rhodesia provides agricultural wealth and skills; backward Nyasaland will serve as a reservoir of labour.

However, whites remain in control in the two Rhodesias, and the arrangement is condemned by African nationalists, notably Joshua Nkomo in the south, Kenneth Kaunda in the north and, from London (where he is practising as a physician), Nyasaland's Dr Hastings Banda. Sir Godfrey Huggins is the Federation's first premier; he will later be succeeded by the tough and charismatic Sir Roy Welensky.

QUEEN ELIZABETH IS CROWNED

London, 2 June. For the first time, millions of television viewers throughout the world bear witness to the pageantry of a coronation as Queen Elizabeth is enthroned. The young

Federal leader Welensky.

Queen rides from Buckingham Palace to Westminster Abbey in a golden coach flanked by outriders. By her side is her husband, Prince Philip, Duke of Edinburgh; following in procession are the British and Commonwealth premiers in their separate coaches – some of whose drivers are aristocratic volunteers in disguise (professional coachmen are in short supply in 1950s' Britain).

HILLARY, TENSING ON TOP OF THE WORLD

Nepal, 29 May. With perfect timing, a British-led expedition conquers Mount Everest, the world's highest peak – just four days before Britons celebrate the coronation of their new queen. At 11.30 a.m. New Zealander Edmund Hillary and his Sherpa guide Tensing Norgay clamber to the 29,002-foot summit to plant the flags of the United Kingdom, Nepal and the United Nations.

> 'We done the bugger.'
> *Sherpa Tensing, after the conquest of Mount Everest*

Edmund Hillary.

The coronation of the young Queen Elizabeth II.

SOUTH AFRICA in the 20th CENTURY

The Fifties

Verwoerd's victims: a bleak future.

BLACK SCHOOLING FACES DISASTER

Parliament passes the Bantu Education Act, which brings all black education under state control, effectively destroying the fairly progressive mission schools where, according to a government spokesman, 'dangerous, liberal ideas are fed by outsiders into untrained minds'. Hendrik Verwoerd, minister of Native Affairs, explains that the Act will 'train and teach people in accordance with their opportunities in life'. These are, of course, largely limited to unskilled and menial jobs.

CHURCH ACCUSED OF HYPOCRISY

The Anglican Church in South Africa, which does not allow non-white children to attend its schools, rejects criticisms of hypocrisy. 'In a country where there is as much colour prejudice as there is in South Africa,' it says, 'it is probable that a non-European boy or girl would not be happy in a European school. Inevitably the child would be self-conscious. It would be impossible for the school authorities to ensure that he would be accepted by other children.'

BORN

South Africa: Musician Johnny Clegg; activists Gabriel 'Tokyo' Sexwale and Jeff Radebe.

WHAT'S NEW IN 1953

◆ **DNA**, the key genetic molecule, is defined by Cambridge University scientists James Watson and Francis Crick.
◆ **Playboy** magazine hits the streets, with Marilyn Monroe occupying the centrefold.
◆ **Cricket:** England win the Ashes for the first time since the 'bodyline' debacle of 1932–33.
◆ **Wedding:** John F. Kennedy, Senator for Massachusetts, marries Jacqueline Bouvier.
◆ Cheap **Bic** ballpoint pens go on sale in France.

John and Jackie Kennedy.

DEATH OF A TYRANT

5 March. Josef Stalin, the tyrant who has ruled the Soviet Union for close on three decades, dies of a cerebral haemorrhage. He will go down in the annals as both a resolute war leader and a psychotic butcher, responsible for the death of millions. He is succeeded by Georgi Malenkov, but this is a stop-gap appointment: in the wings is the 59-year-old Nikita Kruschev, a tough peasant-politician who masterminded the great Ukrainian purge.

EXECUTIONS

British mass-murderer Reginald Christie is hanged at Pentonville prison, London – which raises questions about

The sick society: apartheid in action.

SOUTH AFRICA in the 20th CENTURY

1950s

> 'Mam, I didn't do it. Christie done it.'
> Timothy Evans, shortly to be hanged for the murder of his wife and baby at London's 10 Rillington Place. Later, more bodies are found, and serial killer Reginald Christie is also hanged. Evans eventually receives a posthumous pardon.

the execution, four years earlier, of Timothy Evans. Evans was a mentally retarded young man convicted of murdering his wife and baby in the same house in which some of Christie's victims were found.

Convicted American spies Julius and Ethel Rosenberg die, in the electric chair, amid accusations of judicial bias: they were brought to trial at the height of the infamous anti-communist witch-hunts engineered by Senator McCarthy.

SCREEN HITS
- *Roman Holiday*, with Gregory Peck and Audrey Hepburn;
- *Gentlemen Prefer Blondes*, with Marilyn Monroe;
- *From Here to Eternity*, with Burt Lancaster, Deborah Kerr and Frank Sinatra, wins eight Oscars.

Ducktails gather round for a jukebox jam session.

1954

FAST FORWARD FOR FASHION

As the decade rolls on, so the emphasis shifts firmly to youth – and rebellious youth at that. Young men lead the fashions, though the smarter (or more pretentious) set cling to their cavalry twills, hacking jackets, corduroy shooting caps and duffel coats. British Teddy Boys, making up for the long bleak years of war and austerity, don their Edwardian finery, to be followed by the blue-jeaned, leather-jacketed 'ducktails', their folk heroes the young (and still slim) Marlon Brando of *The Wild One* and *On the Waterfront*, and James Dean, the rebel

Marilyn Monroe gets the wind-up in The Seven Year Itch.

A Dior printed chiffon.

123

SOUTH AFRICA in the 20th CENTURY

Sex-kitten Bardot: striking a chord.

The full-skirted fifties dress.

without a cause. Then come the sideburned Elvis lookalikes and, as the Sixties approach, the scooter generation of Mods in their bell bottoms and their rivals for attention, the Rockers.

The scene changes even more kaleidoscopically for the girls, though tight sweaters, wide belts, full skirts – sometimes absurdly full, the petticoats almost 18th-century in their extravagance – and flat shoes are the style for quite a while. Brigitte Bardot's tumbling locks strike a chord with the more adventurous; the monstrously absurd 'beehive' hairstyle makes its appearance towards the end of the decade; other girls stick to the safer pony-tail (plus white ankle-socks and, back at home, Pat Boone on the record player). Waists rise and fall with the A-line, the Trapeze and the H-line before disappearing altogether with the balloon-like sack dress.

BILL SEEKS TO REMOVE BLACKS

Cape Town, 2 March. Dr Hendrik Verwoerd, Minister of Native Affairs, introduces the Native Resettlement Bill, which provides for the forced removal of blacks – including those with freehold title to their land – from the magisterial district of Johannesburg. The African National Congress (ANC) condemns the measure.

Albert Luthuli, president-general of the ANC, is banned from attending public gatherings and is restricted to the magisterial district of Lower Tugela, Natal, for two years.

Verwoerd: forced removals.

BREAKTHROUGH IN WAR AGAINST POLIO

A new vaccine against infantile paralysis, or polio, has been developed by Dr Jonas Salk, an American virologist. Thousands of children around the world have fallen victim to the virus, which attacks the motor neurone cells in the spinal cord. At some periods in some places – in Britain at the end of the forties, for example – it has reached epidemic proportions. Dr Salk himself, however, is opposed to the clinical trials now being held: he cautions against infecting children, even though his vaccine contains only 'dead' viral properties.

UK RATIONING ENDS; LET THE GOOD TIMES ROLL

London, 3 July. Britons can finally throw away their ration books – which thousands do, jubilantly, in Trafalgar Square and around the country; crowds besiege London's Smithfield meat market. After 14 years of dreary eating, the good times are back again.

ARTS AND LEISURE

◆ **Films:** British-born Alfred Hitchcock's chilling film *Rear Window*, with James Stuart and Grace Kelly; MGM's frenetic musical *Seven Brides for Seven Brothers*; Elia Kazan's *On the Waterfront*, with Marlon Brando. The gentle 1953 comedy *Genevieve*, about a vintage car, is still packing the cinemas.

BORN
South Africa: Trade unionist and politician Jay Naidoo.

SOUTH AFRICA in the 20th CENTURY 

◆ **Radio:** British situation comedy reaches its high point during the decade with such shows as *The Goons* (Harry Secombe, Peter Sellers, Spike Milligan and Michael Bentine); *Take It From Here* (with Dick Bentley, June Whitfield and Jimmy Edwards in *The Glums*); and *Educating Archie*, featuring a ventriloquist's dummy and a new radio character in Tony Hancock, a self-opinionated busybody with deeply held prejudices. Dylan Thomas' *Under Milk Wood*, narrated by Richard Burton, is broadcast (by the BBC) to acclaim. A young unknown named Elvis Presley releases his first seven-single, 'That's All Right, Momma'. The year's hit: 'Fly me to the Moon'.

◆ **Books:** William Golding's *Lord of the Flies*; Kingsley Amis' *Lucky Jim*; Bloemfontein born J.R. Tolkien's *Lord of the Rings* (first volume). Ernest Hemingway wins the Nobel Prize for Literature for *The Old Man and the Sea*.

◆ **Sport:** Briton Roger Bannister becomes the first man to run the mile in under four minutes, at Oxford on 6 May. West Germany beats Hungary 3-2 (after being 2-0 down) in soccer's World Cup, in Switzerland. Lester Piggot, at 18, becomes the youngest ever jockey to win the Derby.

South Africans rally for freedom at Kliptown.

1955
HISTORIC CHARTER DEFINES THE FUTURE

Johannesburg. 26 June. More than 3,000 delegates of all races crowd onto the athletics track at Kliptown, the site chosen for the Congress of the People. The congress is convened to approve the historic Freedom Charter.

A British newspaper records the scene, describing 'African grandmothers, wearing Congress skirts, Congress blouses or Congress doeks.... Young Indian wives, with glistening saris and shawls embroidered in Congress colours; grey old African men, with walking sticks and Congress armbands; young city workers with broad hats, bright American ties and narrow trousers; smooth Indian lawyers and businessmen, moving confidently among the crowds in well-cut suits; and a backcloth of anonymous African faces, listening impassively to the hours of speeches...'.

The Charter, heavily socialist in tone but seen by many here and abroad as a blueprint for a future, free South Africa, states that the country belongs to all its inhabitants regardless of race, and that no government can justly exercise authority except by the will of the people. It goes on to urge, among other things, the creation of a non-racial democracy, equal rights and protection before the law, equal job and education opportunities, a redistribution of the land, and the nationalization of mines, banks and heavy industries.

Bannister breaks the tape.

SOUTH AFRICA in the 20th CENTURY

The Fifties

WHAT'S NEW IN 1955

- **Warsaw Pact** signed, bringing USSR and Eastern Bloc countries together into military alliance.
- The first **Disneyland** opens, in Anaheim, California.
- **Blue jeans** become the biggest selling item in women's clothing.
- The name **Beatnik** enters the English language.
- **Football:** First floodlit international football match, between England and Spain, at Wembley, in the UK.

Beatniks lead the assault on formality.

LIONS ROAR TO VICTORY

The British Lions' tour of South Africa opens the eyes of local rugby chiefs to the wonders of the free-flowing game. The visitors, led by Robin Thompson, display a backline brilliance rarely seen before as they sweep all before them, scoring 94 tries in their 24 matches.

Nearly 100,000 spectators cram into Johannesburg's Ellis Park stadium for the final Test – a nail-biting affair in which the Springboks trail 19-13 until the dying minutes. Then, with just 30 seconds of injury time remaining, Western Province wing Theunis Briers goes over midway between posts and corner flag, and the conversion will give South Africa victory. But kicker Jack van der Schyff, finding the moment too much for him, fails with the attempt.

The memory of a great match is to be stained by the 'punishment' meted out to Van der Schyff: he is consigned to rugby's wilderness.

ROSA TRIGGERS CIVIL RIGHTS PROTEST

Montgomery, Alabama, 2 December. Mrs Rosa Parks, a black woman, makes history when she sits at the front of a bus in defiance of the state's race laws. She is arrested, triggering a boycott of the city's transport system. The boycott is led by a young Baptist pastor, Dr Martin Luther King.

ARTS AND LEISURE

- **Pop music:** Bill Haley and the Comets usher in the era of rock 'n roll when their lively number, 'Rock Around the Clock', provides the soundtrack for the film *The Blackboard Jungle* and shoots to the top of the charts. Chuck Berry and Petula Clark make their first recordings: 'Maybelline' and 'Majorca' respectively. The Platters release 'The Great Pretender'. Other hits: 'Rosemarie', 'Give Me Your Word', and 'Cherry Pink and Apple Blossom Blue'.
- **Films:** *Rebel Without A Cause* elevates James Dean to teenage cult status when it goes on circuit – four weeks after the moody

Chuck Berry.

Cult actor James Dean speaks for a whole generation.

> '... a priggish schoolgirl captain of the hockey team.'
> Lord Altrincham's impression of the young Queen Elizabeth

DEATH OF A TOWN

In a massive show of strength nearly 3,000 police, armed with rifles and Sten guns, surround the 'black spot' suburb of Sophiatown as officials move the first of its residents – 110 families – for resettlement.

Sophiatown is a dilapidated, crime-ridden area but, for all its problems, has a deep sense of community and a character very much its own, a vibrant bohemian home to artists, writers and musicians as well as to some 60,000 ordinary folk.

Writer Can Themba (left) holds court in Sophiatown's 'House of Truth'.

Sign of the times.

A later evacuee will recall the callous way in which the removals are carried out: 'We had to take everything and throw it outside.... I felt such pity for my husband, because he had built that house with his bare hands. That house was our one and only little kingdom...'.

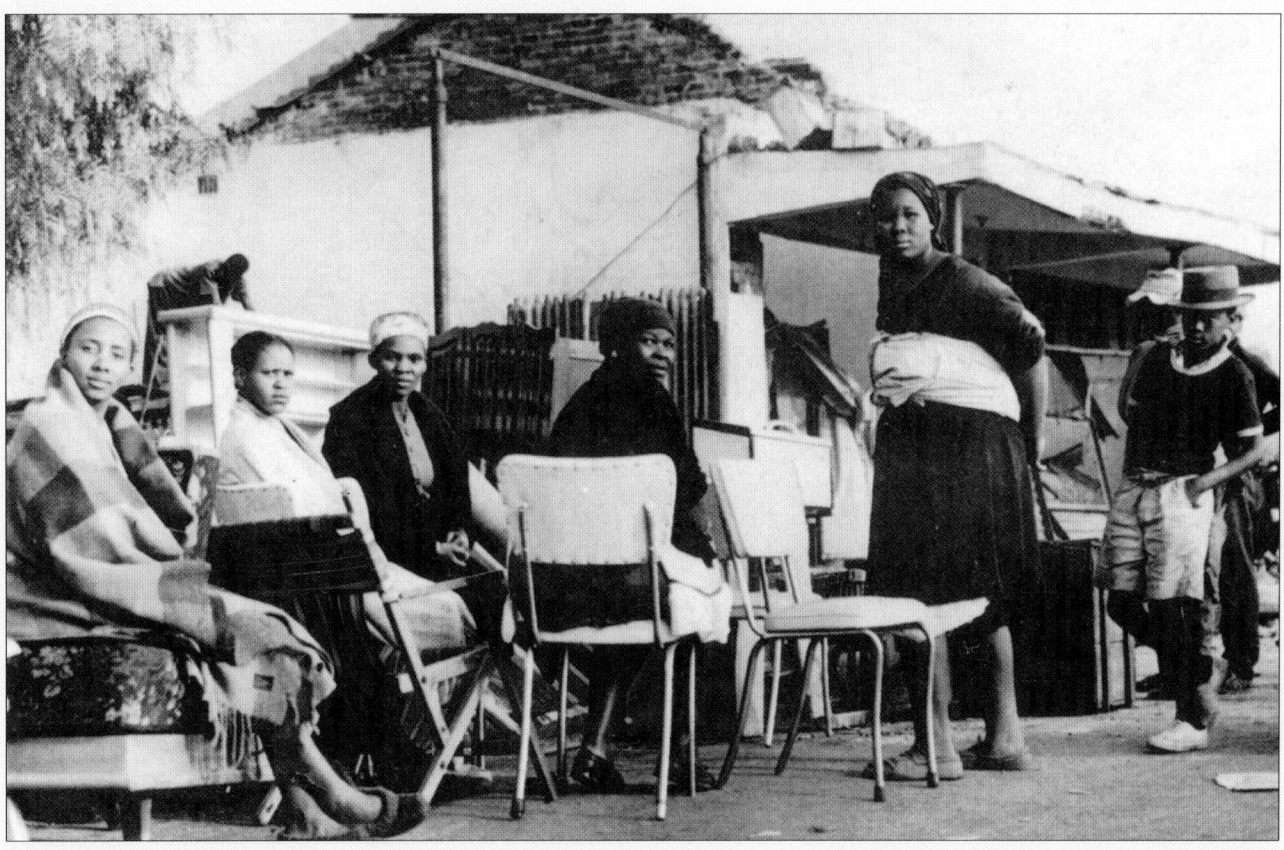

Women wait for their 'one and only little kingdom' to be destroyed.

SOUTH AFRICA in the 20th CENTURY

BORN
South Africa: Road-runner Bruce Fordyce; politician Bantu Holomisa; artist William Kentridge; playwright and musician Mbongeni Ngema; cricketers Peter Kirsten and Garth le Roux; actress Alice Krige.

The scene at Le Mans: 80 die.

DIED
International: Physicist Albert Einstein; writer Thomas Mann; actor James Dean; Ruth Ellis, last British woman to be executed; 80 spectators die when three cars crash on the Le Mans racetrack. South Africa: Pathologist and anti-malaria pioneer David Annecke.

young star's death in a road smash. Marilyn Monroe entrenches herself as Hollywood's premier sex symbol with her performance in *The Seven Year Itch*.
* **Books:** J.P. Donleavy's *The Ginger Man*; Vladimir Nabokov's *Lolita*; Ian Fleming's *Moonraker*; Joy Packer's *Valley of the Vines*; the first edition of *The Guinness Book of Records*.
* **Plays:** Samuel Beckett's *Waiting for Godot*; Tennessee Williams' *Cat on a Hot Tin Roof*.
* **Cricket:** South Africa lose the Test series against England 3-2, but only after a magnificent fight-back from 2-0 down. The third match, at Manchester's Old Trafford, is memorable for centuries by stand-in captain Jackie McGlew and Rhodesian Paul Winslow, the latter a whirlwind innings that breached the century mark with a towering six.

HIT PARADE
* I'll Be Home: Pat Boone
* Heartbreak Hotel: Elvis Presley
* Rock Island Line: Lonnie Donegan
* Que Sera Sera: Doris Day
* It's Almost Tomorrow: The Dream
* Memories Are Made of This: Dean Martin
* Why Do Fools Fall in Love: Teenagers

19**56**

COLOUREDS KICKED OFF THE VOTERS' ROLL

Coloured voters are finally removed from the common roll to bring to an end a sad political saga that began in 1951.

In that year the Separate Registration of Voters Act was passed by a simple instead of the two-thirds parliamentary majority required by the constitution, and was thrown out by the Appellate Division of the Supreme Court. So too was a later Bill declaring parliament to be the supreme law-making authority.

Prime Minister J.G. Strijdom then abandoned all scruples and packed both the upper house of parliament (the Senate) and the Appellate Division with National party loyalists. Now, after five years of bitter controversy, the Act has legality and one more piece of apartheid 'social engineering' is firmly in place.

CARS TAKE THE HIGH ROAD

The trauma and impoverishment of world war are fast becoming a distant memory. America and the other industrialized countries are now well on the way to wealth creation – a heady era of prosperity gleefully celebrated by the US auto industry.

ACTIVISTS CHARGED WITH TREASON

5 December. SA police arrest 156 people – among them Nelson Mandela, Walter Sisulu, Helen Joseph and Lilian Ngoyi – for treason. The charges relate to their involvement in the adoption of the Freedom Charter which, it is alleged, is a communist document.

American cars are big, fast and flashy, adorned with fins, bright with chromium and colour. This is a 1956 Buick Riviera.

SOUTH AFRICA in the 20th CENTURY 1950s

From left: Lilian Ngoyi, Helen Joseph, Rahima Moosa and Sophie Williams on their way to present petitions to Prime Minister Strijdom.

WHAT'S NEW IN 1956

- First **VCR** demonstrated, in Chicago, US.
- First transatlantic automatic **telephone exchange**.
- The first **Eurovision song contest** is held, and is won by the Swiss entry.
- The terms **pop group** and **wheeler dealer** enter the English language.

PM IGNORES BIG MARCH

Thousands of women gather in the grounds of Pretoria's Union Building to protest against regulations that force women to carry passes. Led by Lilian Ngoyi and Helen Joseph, they present 7,000 petitions. The premier, Mr Strijdom, refuses to see them.

BLACK LAWYER FROZEN OUT

Philemon Nokwe, who was the first black person to be called to the Transvaal Bar, is told he cannot take up chambers in His Majesty's Buildings, Johannesburg. The decision is regarded as a victory for the small group of white advocates who complain that they would not have been able to handle the library's law books after Mr Nokwe had touched them, and that, once installed, he would have been able to take tea in the common-room.

SUEZ DEBACLE; HUNGARIAN REVOLT CRUSHED

In a surprise attack, British and French troops invade the Suez area, capturing Port Said before advancing south to bombard the town of Suez. The move is a reaction to President Nasser's earlier seizure of the Suez Canal. Washington has been kept in the dark and is both embarrassed and furious. Moreover, the State Department suspects the Anglo-French have made a secret deal with the Israelis, who have swept into the Gaza Strip and Sinai Peninsula. Relations between the US and its European partners plunge to an all-time low.

Meanwhile, the Soviet Union has taken advantage of the international crisis to crush the pro-democracy rebellion in Hungary. Tanks and infantry move into Budapest in a massive show of force; the rebels, mostly students, are armed with little more than courage and Molotov cocktails, and the

> 'We are not at war with Egypt. We are in armed conflict.'
> *British premier Anthony Eden*

Hungarian freedom fighter.

Suez: part of the Anglo-French task force.

129

SOUTH AFRICA in the 20th CENTURY

The Fifties

BORN
International: Tennis players Bjorn Borg and Martina Navratilova. *South Africa:* Politicians Tony Leon and Trevor Manuel.

DIED
International: Film-maker Alexander Korda; authors A.A. Milne and Bertolt Brecht; big-band leader Tommy Dorsey; American sociologist and sex expert Alfred Kinsey; horror actor Bela Lugosi; cricketer C.B. Fry. *South Africa:* Writer and poet Herbert Dhlomo.

streets are soon cleared. The rebel leader, prime minister Imre Nagy, is arrested and, later, executed.

SPORTING HIGHLIGHTS
♦ English and Surrey off-spin bowler Jim Laker sets a new record when he takes all but one of the wickets in the Old Trafford Test against the visiting Australians. His 19 dismissals cost just 90 runs.
♦ Iron man Rocky Marciano retires as world heavyweight champion at the age of 33. He has never been defeated in a professional fight.

WHAT'S NEW IN 1957
♦ The first **atomic power plant** comes on stream, in Pennsylvania, US.
♦ The link between **smoking** and **lung cancer** is revealed, by the British Medical Research Council.
♦ London gets its first **parking meters**.
♦ **Politics:** Harold Macmillan replaces Anthony Eden as British prime minister.
♦ **Sports:** Althea Gibson becomes the first black tennis player to win a Wimbledon title; Juan Fangio wins a record fifth Grand Prix championship.

Lady champion Althea Gibson.

Fr. Trevor Huddleston, who has campaigned long, hard and, in the end, without success to save Sophiatown from the bulldozers of the 'social engineers', finally calls it a day. His best-selling book, Naught For Your Comfort, *stirs the world's conscience. He leaves South Africa for Britain, where he is consecrated Bishop of Stepney, later taking office as Archbishop of the Indian Ocean. He eventually serves as chairman of the Anti-Apartheid Movement.*

♦ Australian swimmers and Hungarian middle-distance runners are stars of the Melbourne Olympics.

SHOWBUSINESS
♦ **Top films:** *High Society*, with Grace Kelly, Bing Crosby, Frank Sinatra, Louis Armstrong; *The King and I*, with Yul Brynner and Deborah Kerr; David Niven in *Around the World in 80 Days*; the biblical extravaganza *The Ten Commandments*; *War and Peace*, with Henry Fonda and Audrey Hepburn; Marilyn Monroe in *Bus Stop*.

♦ **First nights:** *My Fair Lady* on Broadway, with Julie Andrews and Rex Harrison; John Osborne's powerful *Look Back in Anger* in London; Brendan Behan's *The Quare Fellow* at Stratford-upon-Avon.
♦ **Music:** Ex-truck driver Elvis 'the Pelvis' Presley, 21, appears on US television's *Ed Sullivan Show* to sing 'Hound Dog' and 'Love Me Tender' to captivate teenage America. His 'Heartbreak Hotel' has been on the charts for months.
♦ **Weddings of the year:** Prince Rainier of Monaco

SOUTH AFRICA in the 20th CENTURY

1950s

Actress Grace Kelly marries into the 700-year-old Grimaldi dynasty.

> 'Space travel is utter bilge'
> Richard Wooley, British Astronomer Royal

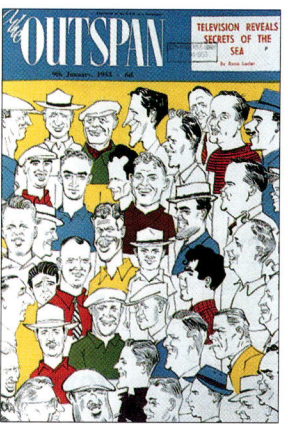

and actress Grace Kelly; acclaimed playwright Arthur Miller and actress Marilyn Monroe.

1957
SOVIETS LAUNCH MAN-MADE SATELLITE

The Russians are the first to breach the earth's gravitational pull when they launch their man-made moon, which they name *Sputnik-I*, into a 500-mile high orbit. The satellite is 22 inches in diameter and weighs 185 pounds (83.6 kilograms). Apparently the Sputnik programme was completed in record time: Soviet premier Nikita Kruschev, in need of a propaganda coup, gave its chief designer – one-time political prisoner Serghei Korolyev – just six weeks to complete the job. American pride is severely dented, although the Pentagon has so far refused to comment. The space race is on.

BRITONS, AMERICANS PROTEST

The Africa Bureau, based in London, reports wide support among British entertainment and sporting personalities for a manifesto deploring racial discrimination in South Africa. This follows the refusal of African Consolidated Theatres to make arrangements for non-whites to see *The Pajama Game*. Among those who sign the manifesto are John Gielgud, Peggy Ashcroft, Michael Redgrave, Peter Ustinov, Flora Robson and Dr Julian Huxley. A month later Mrs Eleanor Roosevelt, widow of the late president, heads a list of 123 prominent Americans who sign a 'declaration of conscience' protesting apartheid. The declaration calls for a day of international protest on 10 December – Human Rights Day.

SA'S BEST-LOVED MAGAZINE DIES

Outspan, South Africa's most popular English medium magazine and regarded by many as a national institution, finally closes down. Aimed mainly at women, its first issue appeared in 1927 and over the 30 years since it has attracted an enormous following – 100,000 readers at one stage, of which nearly half have been men. It is replaced with a slicker, more modern periodical called *Personality*.

LITTLE ROCK KIDS BREAK RACE BARRIER

Little Rock, Arkansas, 25 September. Segregation in the Deep South ends when President Eisenhower, finally acting on the US Supreme Court's ruling made three years ago, sends in 1,000 fully armed federal paratroopers to guard nine black children as they enter the town's Central High School. An angry crowd of jeering whites yells 'Go home, niggers' as the six girls and three boys make their way through the lines of soldiers. Seven demonstrators are arrested.

TOP FILMS
- *Twelve Angry Men*, with Henry Fonda
- *The Incredible Shrinking Man*, with Grant Williams; notable for its advanced special effects
- *And God Created Woman*, with Brigitte Bardot, whose nude scenes shock the prudes

SOUTH AFRICA in the 20th CENTURY

'THE VON' SPEARHEADS ST HELENS TRIUMPH

Tom van Vollenhoven, South African rugby star turned professional, takes his club St Helens to victory against Hunslett in the British League championship with a stunning 80-yard break. He evades 11 tackles before scoring.

MUSICIANS HONOURED

Pianist Elsie Hall celebrates her 80th birthday by performing with the Cape Town Symphony Orchestra. Australian-born Hall, once an infant prodigy whose talents were recognized by such luminaries as Johannes Brahms and the playwright G.B. Shaw, settled in South Africa in 1919. Local musician Erik Chisholm, despite his residence in an apartheid society, is invited to the Soviet Union to conduct the state orchestra in two performances.

GHANA GAINS INDEPENDENCE

Accra. Dr Kwame Nkrumah, soon to be known as The Redeemer, becomes premier of the first of the British African colonies – the Gold Coast and British Togoland, now amalgamated – to gain full independence. The Union Jack is lowered over the city's parliament buildings at midnight on 6 March, to be replaced by the flag of Ghana, a name taken from an ancient Islamic state in present-day Sudan, far to the east.

In his younger days Nkrumah, who was educated in the USA, almost joined the Roman Catholic priesthood, but then fell under the spell of the black nationalist Marcus Garvey. His favourite maxim is 'Seek ye first the political kingdom.'

BORN
South Africa: Activist and politician Mohammed Valli Moosa; boxer Sugarboy Malinga; rugby personality Nick Mallett; cricketer Kepler Wessels.

DIED
International: Actor Humphrey Bogart; composer Jan Sibelius; fashion king Christian Dior.
South Africa: Archbishop Geoffrey Clayton; financier Ernest Oppenheimer; artist Jacob Pierneef; poet Roy Campbell.

Jacob Pierneef.

'Sputnik doesn't worry me one iota. Apparently from what they [the Russians] say, they have put one small ball into the air.'
US president Dwight D. Eisenhower

1958

NEW PREMIER TAKES OFFICE

Hendrik French Verwoerd becomes prime minister of South Africa following the death of J.G. Strijdom. As Minister of Native Affairs the new premier, regarded as a ruthless visionary who will dedicate himself to the separation of the races, masterminded the 'grand apartheid' measures that created the Bantustans. He is also largely responsible for the current harsh laws relating to influx control and the much-hated 'pass', or personal reference, book.

MOVEMENT GOES UNDERGROUND

The ANC leadership, plagued by bannings and arrests, gives urgent orders to its branches to implement the 'M-Plan' – which means the organization is about to go underground. The plan, drawn up in 1952 during the Defiance Campaign, has as its declared aim 'To reorganize the ANC into house and block "cells", and to enable it to work by word of mouth...'.

RACE PLAY DEFIES APARTHEID

New playwright Athol Fugard thumbs his nose at the politicians when, at the high tide of apartheid, he includes black actors in the stage production of *No Good Friday*. The play will go on to be staged and televised overseas.

Tom van Vollenhoven scores his momentous try.

SOUTH AFRICA in the 20th CENTURY

1950s

'BUSBY'S BABES' DIE IN AIR DISASTER

Eight members of the Manchester United football team – affectionately known as 'Busby's Babes' after manager Matt Busby – are killed when their aircraft crashes at icy Munich airport. They include team captain Roger Byrne, centre-forward Tommy Taylor, David Pegg and Bill Whelan. Eight journalists (among them former England goalkeeper Frank Swift) and five substitute players also lose their lives in the disaster. Other players and staff, including Busby himself, are seriously injured. The squad were on their way home, from Belgrade in Yugoslavia, after qualifying for the European Cup semifinals.

DRUG CRIPPLES THOUSANDS OF NEWBORN

About 7,000 babies have been born with hideous physical abnormalities – deformed or missing limbs for the most part – in Germany and, to a lesser extent, other parts of Europe. The cause is thought to be Thalidomide, a drug prescribed for morning sickness in pregnant mothers.

ON THE BOOKSHELF

Laurens van der Post's love of the desert and its people is beautifully expressed in his *Lost World of the Kalahari*. Nadine Gordimer's second novel, *A World of Strangers*, establishes her as a major literary figure.

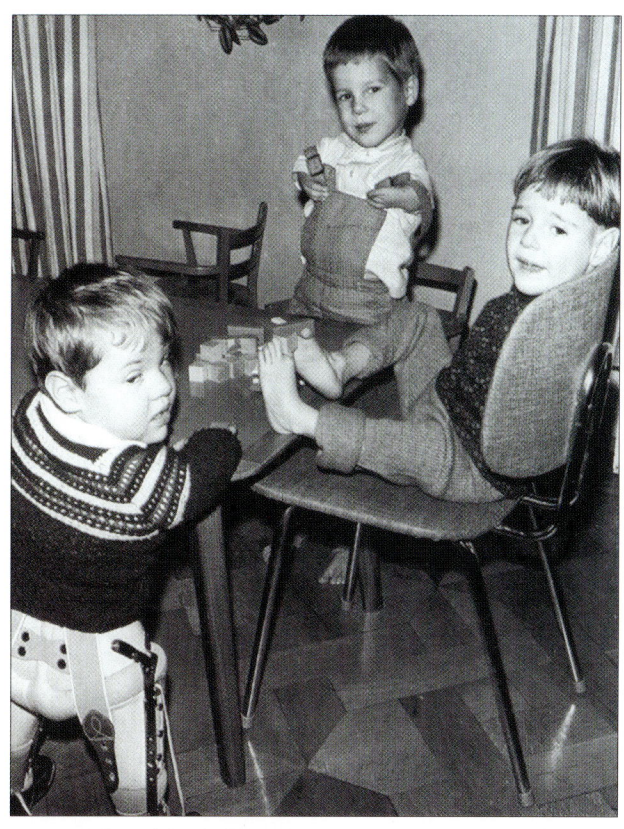

Young victims of the Thalidomide tragedy.

Jazz king Miles Davis.

FLAVOURS OF THE YEAR

♦ Buddy Holly and the Crickets; Newcomer Cliff Richard; Elvis Presley, who releases his 'Jailhouse Rock'; Connie Francis ('Who's Sorry Now?'); the Everley Brothers ('All I have to do is Dream')
♦ Free-style ('progressive') jazz, as played by Miles Davis and Thelonius Monk. But Armstrong and Ellington hold their own, and trad jazz is alive and well in London, where ex-Etonian Humphrey Lyttleton, Chris Barber, Ken Colyer and Mr Acker Bilk are producing great sounds.
♦ Angry Young Men, personified by British playwright John Osborne and novelist John Braine, whose best-selling *Room at the Top* is filmed. It stars South African Laurence Harvey and French actress Simone Signoret.
♦ The hula hoop: 25 million are sold worldwide before the brief craze passes.
♦ Fashion styles (notably the trapeze line) by 23-year-old designer Yves Saint Laurent, who holds his first show, in Paris.

The hula hoop: craze of the moment.

SOUTH AFRICA in the 20th CENTURY

The Fifties

WHAT'S NEW IN 1958

- *Integrated circuits* developed by two American engineers – working separately.
- Up-and-coming *fashion* designer Yves Saint Laurent holds his first show, in Paris.
- US launches its first space *satellite*.
- *Lego* makes its debut on the toy market.
- The *skateboard* is invented, in California.
- The *Campaign for Nuclear Disarmament* (CND) is founded, in Britain.
- The word *hi-fi* enters the English language.

BORN
International: Entertainers Prince, Madonna and Michael Jackson; athlete Daley Thompson. **South Africa:** Politician and banker Tito Mboweni; footballer Gary Bailey; rugby players Naas Botha and Danie Gerber; musician Steve Kekana; politician Peter Mokaba; author Dorothy L. Sayers.

DIED
International: Suffragette Cristabel Pankhurst; birth-control pioneer Marie Stopes; actors Tyrone Power and Robert Donat; composer Ralph Vaughan Williams. **South Africa:** Politician J.G. Strijdom.

The PAC's Robert Sobukwe.

1959
POLITICAL GROUPS SPLIT

Robert Sobukwe and some of the more radical members of the ANC have resigned from the organization to form the Pan-Africanist Congress. Sobukwe, 34, a former secretary of the ANC Youth League and editor of the periodical *The Africanist*, has long been opposed to the ANC's moderate stance, its commitment to peaceful change and its non-racial character. He and his supporters reject the Freedom Charter, adopted in 1955, for its concessions to whites and Indians.

The white political opposition, the United Party, has also split with the defection of its liberal element. The new grouping, to be known as the Progressive Party, is led by Dr Jan Steytler and includes Helen Suzman among its number. Mrs Suzman is its only sitting member of parliament.

Castro: successful revolutionary.

CUBA FALLS TO CASTRO

2 January. Fidel Castro, the young rebel leader, has led his rag-tag guerrilla army to victory against Cuban dictator Fulgencio Batista's government forces, proclaiming the new revolutionary regime to a cheering crowd from his headquarters in the town of Santiago de Cuba. Batista and his entourage have fled to the Dominican Republic; rebel troops, led by Camilo Cienfuegos and Argentinian radical Ché Guevara, have taken over the presidential palace and the Camp Columbia army base near the Cuban capital Havana. In an attempt to retain much-needed US friendship, Castro later assures Congressional leaders that 'we are not communists'.

The Progressive Party's Helen Suzman speaks her mind.

SOUTH AFRICA in the 20th CENTURY

> 'On the Beach is about the end of the world, and Melbourne sure is the right place to film it.'
> Movie actress Ava Gardner

ARTS AND LEISURE
◆ **Films:** *On the Beach*, with Gregory Peck, Ava Gardner and Frank Sinatra; Alfred Hitchcock's *North by North West*, with Cary Grant and Eve Marie Saint; Billy Wilder's *Some Like It Hot*, with Marilyn Monroe, Tony Curtis and Jack Lemmon. Wilder's *Ben Hur*, with Charlton Heston, wins a record 11 Oscars.
◆ Hit singles: 'Livin' Doll': Cliff Richard; 'It Doesn't Matter Any More': Buddy Holly.
◆ Golfer Gary Player wins his first British Open title – after trailing eight strokes behind the leader going into the final round.

BORN
South Africa: Trade unionist and politician Sam Shilowa; actor, playwright, producer Percy Mtwa; golfer David Frost.

DIED
International: Racing driver Mike Hawthorn, in a car smash; singer Buddy Holly and two fellow musicians, in a light-plane accident; gung-ho actor Errol Flynn; architect Frank Lloyd Wright; blues singer Billie Holliday; film-maker Cecil B. de Mille. *South Africa:* Former premier Daniël F. Malan; writers Davidson Jabavu and Pauline Smith.

Frank Lloyd Wright.

Davidson Jabavu.

His finest hour: Gary Player, victor at the British Open.

WHAT'S NEW IN 1959

◆ **Apartheid** is formally condemned by the United Nations.
◆ The **Dalai Lama** flees to India.
◆ The **Barbie doll** makes her debut.
◆ **Motoring:** Britain's Morris Mini is launched, displacing the Morris Minor. Also introduced is BMW's Isetta 'bubble car'.
◆ First touch-button **copier** (Xerox 914).
◆ **State of emergency** declared in Southern Rhodesia.

The beloved Morris Minor: on the way out.

Township Talent:

In February 1959 African musical theatre leaps into an exciting new era with the première of *King Kong* at the university of the Witwatersrand's Great Hall. The jazz opera, an exuberant celebration of township life, revolves around the legendary Sophiatown boxer and gangster hero Ezekiel Dhlamini, who drowned himself rather than face the prospect of life in prison.

The moving spirits behind the sparkling extravaganza are musician Todd Matshikiza, novelist Harry Bloom, lyricist Pat Williams and producer Leon Gluckman. It has an all-black cast; Dorothy Radebe fills the female role as queen of a shebeen called Back of the Moon, but she is pregnant and is soon replaced by a rising young singing star, Miriam Makeba. The show is acclaimed by critics and theatre-goers alike, and will eventually (two decades later) be staged at the Shaftesbury theatre in London's West End.

King Kong is at the crest of an artistic surge that is sweeping through the black townships of the north. Music, in its several forms, leads the way. The pre-war pace – set by *marabi*, a bouncy, anything-goes sound that borrowed increasingly from American jazz and the big-band music of Armstrong, Basie and Ellington – becomes ever more

A scene from the new jazz opera King Kong.

sophisticated and eventually produces its own stars. Most popular are Kippie Moeketsi, who plays clarinet and sax with the Shantytown Sextet and the Jazz Pioneers; trumpeter Hugh Masekela, and the innovative Cape jazz pianist Dollar Brand (who will take the name Abdullah Ibrahim after his conversion to Islam in the late 1960s).

Meanwhile other kinds of music also charm the air. The penny-whistles and home-made guitars of *kwela* are heard in the streets of Alexandra and Sophiatown and, popularized by such artists as Spokes Mashiyane and Lemmy 'Special' Mabasa, attract a countrywide audience in the 1950s and 1960s. Then there is the 'soul music' of the 1970s, which produces such notable groups as Harari and the Soul Brothers; the Afro-rock of the 1980s and, always, the traditional, seductive rhythms of *mbube*, the voice-only, rural sounds of the Zulu 'choral band'. *Mbube* was the earliest musical form to be recorded, but makes its first major impact with the song 'Wimoweh', written by Solomon Linda and sung by Miriam Makeba. Much later, the *mbube* group Ladysmith Black Mambazo gets together with Paul Simon to produce the acclaimed *Graceland* album.

Joie de vivre *on stage: music and dance reach stunning heights in the fifties.*

the Golden Years

No staged musical of the time quite matches the vibrant splendour of *King Kong*. *Ipi Tombi* draws bigger and perhaps more appreciative audiences, both locally and overseas, but, though lively, tuneful, graced by some memorable numbers and a lead singer of stature (Margaret Singana), it's a hybrid show contrived with non-African theatre-goers in mind. More authentic is Mbongeni Ngema's *Sarafina*, set in the Soweto of the 1980s and presented with flair, and to resounding applause, both at home and abroad (it is also filmed, but with rather less success).

Straight drama, too, begins to flourish in fresh and exciting guise. Welcome Msomi breaks new ground in the 1970s with *uMubatha*, a Zulu play based on Shakespeare's *Macbeth*. Msomi takes the production to New York, where he settles with his family and launches the Zulu Dance Theatre. Special, too, is *Woza Albert!*, created by Percy Mtwa, Gibson Kente and Mbongeni Ngema, also presented in New York - and in London, where it is adjudged the 1983 Play of the Year by the periodical *City Limits*.

Music: an integral part of any celebration.

Johannesburg's Jazzolomos: Jacob Lepers (bass), Ben Mrwebi (alto sax), Sol Klaaste (piano).

Much thespian energy is expended within what has become known as 'black theatre', in which productions – often a rich mix of words, music, song and dance – are written by black South Africans for black audiences. A striking feature is its sparkling spontaneity, which is in part rooted in African tradition: performers share in the creation of the work rather than follow a script. Athol Fugard's highly rated *Sizwe Bansi is Dead* (like *Woza Albert!*, voted 1974 Play of the Year, by London's theatre critics) is for instance largely 'workshopped' by actors John Kani and Winston Ntshona, both of whom win Tony awards.

137

1960s

DIED
1961: UN secretary-general Dag Hammerskjöld, in an air crash near Ndola, Northern Rhodesia.
1963: US president John F. Kennedy: assassinated.
1965: British statesman Winston Churchill.
1966: SA premier Hendrik Verwoerd: assassinated.
1968: US civil rights leader Martin Luther King: assassinated. US presidential contender Robert Kennedy: assassinated.

AT WAR
1960: Rival factions in newly independent Congo.
1964: US forces and Vietcong guerrillas in Vietnam; ongoing. Portuguese forces and guerrillas in Mozambique and Angola; ongoing.
1967: Arabs and Israelis, for six days.
1968: Nigerian government forces and Biafran secessionists. Czech dissidents and invading Soviet 'peacekeepers'.

Beatles memorabilia.

INVADED
1962: Cuba, by US-sponsored Cuban exile force. The invasion fails.

BUILT
1961: The Berlin Wall.

HONOURED
1960: SA's Albert Luthuli, with the Nobel Peace prize.

ADOPTED
1960: The blue crane, as SA's national bird.

INAUGURATED
1960: Independent Congo republic (formerly Belgian Congo).
1962: Independent Tanganyika, Uganda and Algeria (after bloody civil war). South West African Peoples' Organisation (Swapo).
1963: Independent Kenya. Organisation of African Unity.
1964: Independent Malawi. Independent Zambia.
1965: The rebel white state of Rhodesia, following Ian Smith's Unilateral Declaration of Independence (UDI).
1966: Independent Botswana. Independent Lesotho. Jonas Savimbi's Unita movement in Angola. Mao Tse-tung's Chinese 'cultural revolution'.
1968: Independent Swaziland.
1969: SA Students' Organisation, formed by Steve Biko.

LAST APPEARANCE
1960: Of SA, at the Olympic Games (until 1992).

TERMINATED
1963: Federation of the Rhodesias and Nyasaland.
1966: Cape Town's District Six (residents are gradually moved out).
1967: SA's mandate over South West Africa, by the UN. Cricket Tests between SA and England, after the 'D'Oliviera affair'.

DESTROYED
1969: Part of Tulbagh in the Cape, by an earthquake.

POLITICS AND PROTEST
1960: British premier Harold Macmillan delivers 'wind of change' speech. Anti-pass law campaign culminates in Sharpeville massacre; state of emergency declared; ANC and PAC banned. Whites-only referendum approves move to republic.
1961: SA leaves Commonwealth; becomes republic. Liberation movement goes underground; Umkhonto we Sizwe ('Spear of the Nation') formed.
1962: Sabotage Act passed.
1963: ANC activists arrested in Rivonia area. Nelson Mandela is among those committed for trial.
1964: Mandela and others sentenced to life imprisonment.
1966: B.J. Vorster succeeds H.F. Verwoerd as prime minister.

INTRODUCED
1961: Decimal coinage in SA.
1965: The mini-skirt.

STAGED
1960: Lionel Bart's *Oliver*, in London.
1961: SA musical *King Kong*, in London.
1963: SA playwright Athol Fugard's *Blood Knot*, in London and New York.
1969: Woodstock music festival, near New York.

FIRST
1961: Man in space: Soviet cosmonaut Yuri Gagarin.
1963: Big Beatles success: 'I Want to Hold Your Hand'.
1964: Wilbur Smith novel: *When the Lion Feeds*.
1965: Photographs of Mars: transmitted by US spacecraft *Mariner* IV.
1966: Soccer World Cup won by England.
1967: Heart transplant, at Groote Schuur hospital, Cape Town. Krugerrands issued.
1969: Moon walk, by US astronaut Neil Armstrong.

The Sixties

SOUTH AFRICA in the 20th CENTURY

1960
MASSACRE AT SHARPEVILLE

21 March. At 1.15 p.m. police fire into an unarmed crowd in the township of Sharpeville, near Vereeniging in the Transvaal, killing 69 people and wounding 186.

Earlier, some 20,000 demonstrators, organized by the Pan-Africanist Congress (PAC) and protesting against the pass laws, gather outside the local police station. Police reinforcements, including four armoured cars, are brought in and, when stones are thrown and scuffles break out, they open fire with .303 rifles and Sten guns. They carry on shooting at the retreating crowd.

The carnage makes world headlines. There are calls for UN sanctions (vetoed by Britain and the US); the South African economy suffers a massive flight of capital, stemmed only by new strict currency controls.

A wave of strikes and stayaways sweeps the country. Verwoerd's government arrests the PAC's Robert Sobukwe and others, declares a state of emergency, and bans both the PAC and the African National Congress (ANC).

The massacre is a watershed in the struggle for freedom: peaceful resistance is clearly seen to have failed; the liberation movement, many of its leaders either in prison or in exile, goes underground.

South African police mop up after the killings at Sharpeville. Sixty-nine people are shot to death, many of them in the back.

Dead and wounded litter the dusty ground outside Sharpeville police station.

SOUTH AFRICA in the 20th CENTURY

HUNDREDS DIE IN MINE COLLAPSE
21 January. In the worst disaster in South Africa's mining history, the Clydesdale colliery's Coalbrook north shaft collapses, killing 435 underground workers. Round-the-clock rescue efforts continue for several weeks, without success.

IRONIC TWIST TO TV BAN
South Africa's long wait for television continues: the medium, it seems, will corrupt local viewers. Says Prime Minister Hendrik Verwoerd: 'When a new discovery holds dangers, a government must be careful not to import it before they know how to ward off any dangers there might be.' A few weeks later, in an ironic twist, he himself appears on small screens around the world when David Pratt, a disturbed white farmer present at the opening of the Union Exposition near Johannesburg, tries to assassinate him. Two pistol shots are fired, one hitting the South African premier in the cheek, the other nicking his ear.

Macmillan and Verwoerd: a harsh wind of change.

MACMILLAN HERALDS END OF COLONIALISM
3 February. Visiting British premier addresses a joint sitting of the houses of parliament in Cape Town, and stuns them by warning whites that a 'wind of change' is blowing through the continent. 'Whether we like it or not,' he continues, 'this growth of national consciousness is a political fact.' His speech clearly signals the end of the colonial era in Africa.

YOUNG CRICKETER BREAKS RECORD
Schoolboy batsman Graeme Pollock, 16, becomes the youngest South African to score a century in first class cricket when he hammers 102 for Eastern Province against Transvaal B at the Wanderers. 'If [his] burning ambition is to win a Springbok cap,' says Geoff Summerton in his match report, 'then, like the giant with seven-league boots, he took a mighty stride towards his goal...'.

ON SCREEN
◆ British-born Hollywood director Alfred Hitchcock breaks new cinematic ground with his mystery-horror film *Psycho*, featuring Anthony Perkins as insane motel-keeper Norman Bates and Janet Leigh as his victim. Her grisly death, while taking a shower, will become a celebrated fragment of movie lore.
◆ Among other acclaimed films are Federico Fellini's *La Dolce Vita*, which directs a harsh spotlight on Italian high society; and *Exodus*, the inspiring story of the state of Israel's birth and early years.

WHAT'S NEW IN 1960

◆ **Africa:** Six states gain their independence: Central African Republic, Chad, Congo (Brazzaville), Congo (Kinshasa), Nigeria and Togo.
◆ **Kariba Dam**, on the Zambezi, is opened by the Queen Mother. It will create the world's largest man-made lake.
◆ **Royal wedding:** Princess Margaret marries top fashion photographer Anthony Armstrong-Jones.
◆ **Theatre:** Royal Shakespeare Company founded.
◆ New words added to the English language include **sit-in**, **dropout** and **mouse** (computer attachment).

Princess Margaret and husband.

Pollock the mature batsman.

SOUTH AFRICA in the 20th CENTURY — 1960s

THE COMING OF CAMELOT

A new dawn in American and world politics breaks when the stylish, 43-year-old John Kennedy is elected president of the United States. His assets: boyish good looks, charisma, a beautiful wife, Afro-American support, the Catholic vote and the promise of a 'new frontier'. Kennedy's victory margin over his rival, republican candidate Richard Nixon, is a minuscule 0.1 percent, but wide enough to carry him into the White House.

> 'Ask not what your country can do for you. Ask what you can do for your country.'
> *President John Kennedy, in his inauguration speech*

Kennedy: new dawn.

THE LAST GAMES

South Africa enters the Olympic arena for the last time for three decades, sending a squad of 58 to Rome. It wins just three medals (one silver, for boxing; two bronzes); hurdler Gert Potgieter, considered a favourite for gold, was injured in a road smash in West Germany a few weeks before. The Soviet Union finishes top of the log, gaining 103 medals against the US's 71, but it is black American athlete Wilma Rudolph who steals the show. Rudolph, the twentieth child of a dirt-poor Tennessee family, was crippled by polio in infancy, wore leg-irons until she was six and orthopaedic shoes until age 11, but talent and sheer guts have propelled her to the pinnacle of achievement: she wins the 100 and 200 metres events and gains a third gold in the 4 x 100 metres relay.

MAGIC BEAM

The world's first laser device, successfully concentrating light to produce a powerful beam, is demonstrated by the US's Hughes Research Laboratories. The word is an acronym for 'light amplification by the stimulated emission of radiation'.

Laser breakthrough.

CONGO SLIDES INTO CHAOS

Civil war breaks out in the Congo (formerly Belgian Congo) when regional leader Moise Tshombe declares the independence of copper-rich Katanga province. Looting and killing continues in other parts of the country after soldiers of the Force Publique mutiny. UN troops are flown in. Army commander Joseph-Désiré Mobutu, 31, ousts national premier Patrice Lumumba in September. Shortly afterwards Lumumba is murdered, perhaps on Tshombe's orders.

Congolese soldiers make wholesale arrests.

ARTS AND ENTERTAINMENT

- Play of the year: Robert Bolt's *A Man for All Seasons*.
- Books: Harper Lee's *To Kill a Mockingbird* tops the best-seller lists. A British court rules that D.H. Lawrence's *Lady Chatterley's Lover* is not obscene; all 200,000 copies of the book are sold out on the first day.
- Musicals: Lionel Bart's *Oliver!* Top singles: Elvis Presley's 'It's Now Or Never'; Cliff Richard's 'Please Don't Tease'; Rolf Harris's 'Tie Me Kangaroo Down, Sport'.
- Dance craze: the Twist, triggered by Chubby Checker's hit 'Let's Twist Again'.

BORN

South Africa: Rugby player Carel du Plessis.

DIED

International: Actor Clark Gable; writers Boris Pasternak, Albert Camus and Neville Shute; filmmaker Mack Sennett; UK politician Aneurin 'Nye' Bevan. **South Africa:** Aviatrix Lady Mary Bailey.

SOUTH AFRICA in the 20th CENTURY

The Sixties

1961

SA BECOMES A REPUBLIC, LEAVES COMMONWEALTH

31 May. A rainsoaked but stoic crowd gathers in Pretoria's Church Square to hear premier Hendrik Verwoerd introduce C.R. Swart, the country's first republican state president. Mr Swart resigned as governor-general of the Union at the end of April.

In the referendum held last October, 850,458 whites voted in favour of republican status, 775,878 against. Dr Verwoerd carried this mandate with him to the Commonwealth prime ministers' conference in London in March, but with little confidence. It had been clear to him for some time – indeed since well before the referendum – that his fellow premiers regarded the apartheid state as a pariah, and that the country's expulsion was inevitable. He therefore pre-empted the decision, telling the conference that he 'thought it better for South Africa and the Commonwealth to withdraw [the] application for re-admission to membership'.

Many of those who voted for a republic – a status they believed could be maintained while remaining within the Commonwealth – feel betrayed.

'Hats off to the past, but jackets off to the future.'
C.R. 'Blackie' Swart, SA's first State President

TREASON TRIALISTS ACQUITTED

Pretoria, 29 March. All the remaining accused in the protracted treason trial are found not guilty by a special court. The judgement ends a saga that began before dawn on 5 December 1956, when police arrested 140 people of all races in sweeping raids throughout the country. An additional 16 were later taken into custody, but the total number has, over the past half-decade, been whittled down to 28 over the years. Among those acquitted are Ahmed Kathrada, Helen Joseph, Lilian Ngoyi, Walter Sisulu and Nelson Mandela.

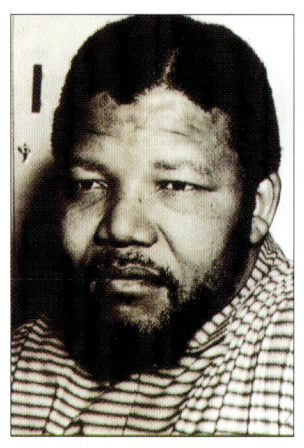
Mandela: the 'Black Pimpernel'.

BLACK STRUGGLE GOES UNDERGROUND

24 May. In an attempt to avoid the nation-wide strike, called for by the black leadership, to protest the imminent proclamation of a republic, police round up more activists to bring the number of those detained to almost 10,000.

Among key figures sought by the authorities is Nelson Mandela, who evades arrest: he is not at his Orlando home when police arrive. His wife Winnie refuses them entry when they fail to produce a search warrant, but they return later with the document and rummage through the house.

Meanwhile, Mandela and Oliver Tambo have been busy reorganizing the underground opposition on a cell basis. Mandela goes on to help found Umkhonto we Sizwe, which means 'spear of the nation', as an independent paramilitary unit dedicated to sabotage and disruption.

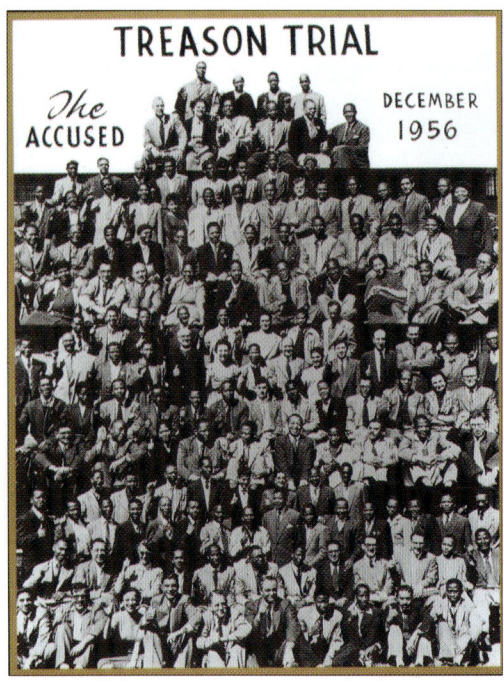
The treason trialists; Mandela is at the centre of the third row.

SOUTH AFRICA in the 20th CENTURY 1960s

Albert Luthuli (centre): Nobel Peace prizewinner.

LUTHULI WINS NOBEL HONOUR

Chief Albert Luthuli, who was elected president of the ANC in 1952 and led mass protests against the Sharpeville shootings last year, is awarded the Nobel Prize for Peace. Although an advocate of non-violence, he was arrested and imprisoned for his role in the protest movement, and is currently restricted to his home town of Stanger in Natal.

BAY OF PIGS DEBACLE EMBARRASSES KENNEDY

17 April. An invasion force of some 1,500 Cuban exiles, backed by the US Central Intelligence Agency, makes an ill-planned landing at the Bay of Pigs in a chaotic attempt to overthrow Fidel Castro. They are quickly defeated and rounded up by disciplined Cuban troops backed by tanks and Russian-made MiG fighter aircraft. Many are executed, the remainder imprisoned. US President John F. Kennedy is deeply embarrassed by the fiasco.

KENYAN LEADER RELEASED

Nairobi, 21 August. Kenya's Jomo Kenyatta is released and returns to public life. The nationalist leader was imprisoned nine years ago for his alleged part in the Mau Mau uprising.

Cosmonaut Yuri Gagarin.

RUSSIANS WIN SPACE RACE

The Soviet Union is the first country to put a man in space when Major Yuri Gagarin orbits the earth in the space capsule *Vostok*. The flight, from blast-off to safe recovery, takes 108 minutes. Just over a month later naval commander Alan Shepard becomes the first American to breach the space barrier as his craft, *Freedom 7*, completes a 190-kilometre, 15-minute non-orbiting flight.

WHAT'S NEW IN 1961

- **Metric:** South Africa converts to decimal currency.
- **The Pill**, an oral contraceptive, is widely available.
- **The office:** IBM develops the adjustable 'golf ball' typewriter.
- **UK:** satirical magazine Private Eye launched.
- **Founded:** Amnesty International, US Peace Corps, World Wildlife Fund and Weight Watchers.

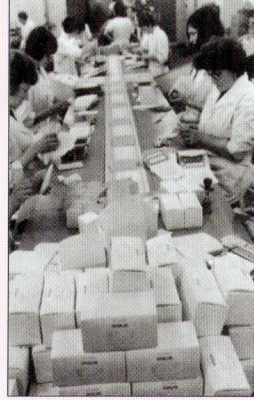
Packing the Pill.

BERLIN WALL GOES UP

The flood of East Germans fleeing into West Berlin has been halted, abruptly, by the erection of a massive wall between the Communist and Western sectors. Crowds of West Berliners gather at the famed Brandenburg Gate to jeer at East German workmen and their armed guards.

West Berliners manoeuvre parcels over the wall to loved ones.

SOUTH AFRICA in the 20th CENTURY

The Sixties

1962

'BLACK PIMPERNEL' IS JAILED

Nelson Mandela, commander-in-chief of Umkhonto we Sizwe (the ANC's military wing) and known as the 'Black Pimpernel' for his elusiveness, is arrested for incitement and illegally leaving the country. He is sentenced to serve five years in prison.

Earlier in the year, shortly after the start of the sabotage campaign, Mandela was smuggled out of South Africa to address African leaders in Addis Ababa, went on to Algeria for military training and travelled to London to meet British parliamentarians.

Meanwhile a young student activist, Thabo Mbeki, secretly leaves the country and is detained in Bulawayo. The British Labour Party intervenes to keep him from being sent back, and he is granted political asylum by Tanzanian president Julius Nyerere. In due course he leaves Africa to study in Britain.

After a run on Broadway, **West Side Story** *makes it to the big screen.*

Mandela (far left) in Algeria for military training.

THE MUSIC SCENE
◆ Hits: 'Are You Lonesome Tonight' and 'Wooden Heart': Elvis Presley; 'Runaway': Del Shannon; 'Take Five': Dave Brubeck Quartet.
◆ New talent: 20-year-old Bob Dylan. In Britain, a pop group called The Beatles emerges from Merseyside; says local music-shop owner Brian Epstein: 'I want to manage these four boys. It wouldn't take more than two half-days a week.'
◆ Top screen musical: *West Side Story.*

BORN
South Africa: Singer Jonathan Butler; boxer Brian Mitchell; rugby player Uli Schmidt.

DIED
International: Dag Hammarskjöld, in a plane smash; psychologist Carl Jung; Congo political leader Patrice Lumumba, killed while 'escaping' from custody in Katanga province; writer Ernest Hemingway, by his own hand. *South Africa:* Actor André Huguenet.

SOUTHERN RHODESIAN NATIONALISTS BANNED

Tensions are heightened in Southern Rhodesia as the premier, Sir Edgar Whitehead, bans Joshua Nkomo's Zimbabwe African People's Union (ZAPU). He condemns the organization as a terrorist movement, and orders the arrest of dozens of its leaders. The banning is the culmination of months of largely black-on-black violence, triggered by ZAPU's bid to marshal grassroots support for its opposition to the white regime. Rural chiefs have been the main victims of the violence.

'Political power grows out of the barrel of a gun.'
Mao Tse-tung

SOUTH AFRICA in the 20th CENTURY — 1960s

MARILYN DIES FROM DRUG OVERDOSE

5 August. Sex symbol Marilyn Monroe dies from an overdose of sleeping tablets. Early this morning she was found lying naked in bed, with the telephone receiver clutched in her hand, by her doctor and housekeeper.

Ms Monroe, who is thought to have been a close associate of US President John F. Kennedy and his brother Robert, suffered from sleeplessness and depression. She made 23 films, her last entitled *The Misfits*. Lately, however, her career has been plagued by her personal problems, and two months ago she was dropped from the cast of *Something's Got To Give*.

Marilyn Monroe, born Norma Jean Baker, spent most of her childhood in foster homes before becoming a photographer's model and bit-part player. She then scaled filmdom's heights as a sexy 'dumb blonde' comedienne and, on occasion, she showed true talent as a serious actress: her roles in *Bus Stop* and *The Prince and the Showgirl* (with Laurence Olivier) won critical acclaim. She was married three times, first to an aircraft worker at the age of 16, briefly to baseball star Joe di Maggio and latterly to leading playwright Arthur Miller.

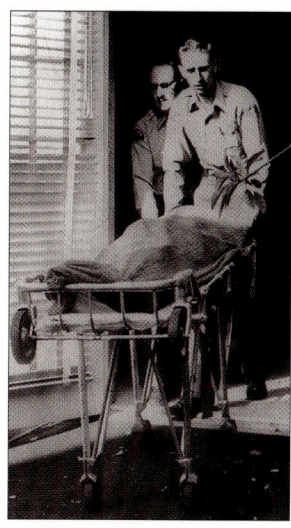

Monroe's last journey.

CUBAN MISSILE CRISIS: SOVIETS BLINK FIRST

28 October. A global nuclear war is averted at the last moment when Soviet premier Nikita Kruschev backs down and agrees to remove Russian missiles supplied to and installed in Fidel Castro's Cuba. More nuclear weapons were aboard Soviet vessels heading for the Caribbean.

The supply of missiles, which pose a direct threat to American cities, provoked a head-to-head confrontation between Kruschev and US President John F. Kennedy, who ordered a naval blockade of the island a week ago. Since then the world has held its breath as the two superpowers headed for high noon. The Soviets are the first to blink.

Kennedy's stature as world leader is enhanced; Kruschev is humiliated – but not as badly as he could have been. Kennedy is at pains to soften the blow, describing the Russian premier's decision as 'statesmanlike'. Moreover, it appears that they have made a secret deal involving the dismantling of US missile sites in Turkey.

Kennedy and Kruschev: averting the third world war.

ARTS AND ENTERTAINMENT

- The Beatles, a new British group, are turned down by Decca in favour of the Tremeloes (says Decca manager Dick Rowe: 'I'm sorry, Mr Epstein, but groups with guitars are definitely on the way out.'). The mop-topped quartet – John, Paul, George and Ringo, who replaces Pete Best – go on to record with Parlophone; their first single is 'Love Me Do', first LP *Please Please Me*. The year's other hits include 'The Young Ones': Cliff Richard; 'Telstar': the Tornados; 'I Remember You': Frank Ifield, and 'Stranger on the Shore': Mr Acker Bilk.
- Films: Ruggedly handsome Scotsman Sean Connery is cast as the lead in *Dr No*, the first of the Bond films. Most acclaimed feature film is David Lean's epic *Lawrence of Arabia* (with Peter O'Toole); notables also include *The Loneliness of the Long-distance Runner* (with Tom Courtenay) and *Lolita* (with James Mason).
- Books: Alexander Solzhenitsyn's *One Day in the Life of Ivan Denisovich*; Ken Kelsey's *One Flew Over the Cuckoo's Nest*; Anthony Burgess's *A Clockwork Orange*; Anne Porter's *Ship of Fools*.

WHAT'S NEW IN 1962

- **Space:** Astronaut John Glenn becomes the first American to be placed in orbit.
- **Africa:** Algeria and Uganda gain independence.
- **On the shelf:** First tab-opened cans appear in supermarkets.
- First passenger **hovercraft** enters service, across Britain's River Dee estuary.

BORN
South Africa: Boxer Baby Jake Mathlala.

DIED
International: Scientist Auguste Piccard; Mafia boss 'Lucky' Luciano; Nazi war criminal Adolf Eichmann, executed by Israelis following his abduction by Israeli agents from Argentina, and trial; writer William Faulkner. **South Africa:** Political leader Alfred Xuma; rugby player Bennie Osler.

SOUTH AFRICA in the 20th CENTURY

1963
POLICE SWOOP NETS ACTIVISTS

Johannesburg, 12 July. Seventeen people, including 10 members of Umkhonto we Sizwe, military wing of the banned African National Congress, are arrested in a police raid on the Liliesleaf farmhouse, in the suburb of Rivonia. They include Walter Sisulu (former ANC secretary-general), Govan Mbeki, Raymond Mhlaba, Frank Mogothlana, Philip Mokolo, and Ahmed Kathrada of the Transvaal Indian Congress. Also taken into custody are Dennis Goldberg, a civil engineer from Cape Town; Lionel Bernstein, a listed Communist; Arthur Goldreich, an industrial designer and well-known artist; Goldreich's wife Hazel; and Dr Hillard Festenstein, head of the South Rand Laboratories of the Institute of Medical Research. All are being held under the recently introduced 90-day clause of the General Laws Amendment Act.

Detectives searching the premises find, among other things, a diary belonging to Nelson Mandela, together with notes on his recent African tour and on guerrilla warfare. Mr Mandela is currently serving a five-year prison sentence.

The face of despair: forced removals begin in earnest.

'GRAND APARTHEID' PLANNED

The Nationalist government shows it is serious about what is coming to be known as 'grand apartheid' – separate states, separate administration of urban areas, the removal of communities, tightened border controls. Signposts to the future include the Transkei Bill, which will create a semi-independent 'Native' country with its own cabinet, civil service and flag; a full-scale drive to repatriate one million 'foreign workers'; the sealing of South Africa's borders with neighbouring territories, and a ten-year plan to clear the Western Cape of black people.

KING DREAMS OF BROTHERHOOD

Washington, 28 August. President John Kennedy and civil rights leader Martin Luther King address nearly half a million people, mostly black, at the Lincoln Memorial. King's speech will long be remembered. 'I still have a dream', he says. 'It is a dream chiefly rooted in the American dream. I have a dream that one day this nation will rise up and live out the true meaning of its creed: "We hold these truths to be self-evident, that all men are created equal". I have a dream that the sons of former slaves and the sons of former slave owners would sit together at the table of brotherhood.'

King: a message for all.

Rivonia gallery: trialists include (from left, top row) Nelson Mandela, Walter Sisulu, Govan Mbeki and Raymond Mhlaba; (bottom row) Elias Motsoaledi, Andrew Mlangeni, Ahmed Kathrada and Dennis Goldberg.

Winnie Mandela (centre) in traditional dress during the Rivonia Trial.

SOUTH AFRICA in the 20th CENTURY **1960s**

PRESIDENT KENNEDY ASSASSINATED

22 November. Dallas, Texas. President John Kennedy is shot in the head by a lone gunman as he rides through this city in an open limousine, his wife Jacqueline by his side. He is rushed to Parkland Memorial Hospital, but is pronounced dead 25 minutes after admission.

An hour later Vice-President Lyndon Johnson, his wife Lady Byrd, Mrs Kennedy and White House staff hurry aboard Air Force One for the flight back to Washington. Mr Johnson is sworn in as the 38th president of the US during the flight.

Lee Harvey Oswald, a 24-year-old one-time marine, is arrested for the murder of a Dallas patrolman, Officer J.D. Tippett, and is questioned in connection with the Kennedy assassination.

Jacqueline Kennedy, her husband shot to death, scrambles towards presidential bodyguards.

> 'If anybody really wanted to kill the president of the United States, it's not a very hard job. All one has to do is get on a high building some day with a telescopic rifle ....'
>
> *US President John F. Kennedy, just before his trip to Dallas*

The bloody climax: Ruby shoots Oswald, Kennedy's assassin.

24 November: Oswald, now the prime suspect in the presidential killing, is shot to death by Jack Ruby, a local nightclub owner, while police are moving him from Dallas police headquarters to a safer place of security. The shooting is witnessed by the full complement of journalists and television cameramen, and by millions of viewers worldwide.

In due course the Warren commission of inquiry will conclude that there was no evidence to support allegations of a conspiracy, and that both Oswald and Ruby acted entirely on their own.

CENTRAL AFRICAN FEDERATION BREAKS UP

The Federation of the Rhodesias and Nyasaland, launched with such high hopes just 10 years ago, is being rapidly dismantled. The two northern territories are marching quickly towards full independence; Southern Rhodesia, still firmly controlled by the country's white minority, is likely to press for the same status but will have a much more difficult path to tread – especially now that it is run by Winston Field's hard-line Rhodesian Front, which ousted the relatively progressive Whitehead government in January.

FUGARD ENTERS WORLD THEATRE

Port Elizabeth playwright Athol Fugard establishes his international reputation with *The Blood Knot*. Its central theme is South Africa's race classification system. The first of Fugard's 'family trilogy', it is staged in London and New York to critical acclaim.

147

SOUTH AFRICA in the 20th CENTURY

The Sixties

Elizabeth Taylor: biggest hit.

ARTS AND LEISURE

◆ **Film:** Biggest box-office success is *Cleopatra*, with Elizabeth Taylor and Richard Burton. Also notable are *Tom Jones* and *The Sword in the Stone*. Ursula Andress makes Hollywood history when she lands the lead in *Four For Texas*: she and other aspirants pose nude for the screen test.
◆ **Television:** The BBC lifts its ban on references to religion, sex, politics and royalty in its comedy shows. American audiences are bewildered by the first-ever TV instant replay (of the Army-Navy game of US football).
◆ **Hit parade:** 'She Loves You', 'I Want To Hold Your Hand', 'From Me To You' (all from the Beatles). Also Gerry and the Pacemakers: 'You'll Never Walk Alone'. Dylan releases *The Freewheelin' Bob Dylan*; his 'Blowin' in the Wind' and 'Don't Think Twice, It's All Right' go straight to the top. So does 'Puff the Magic Dragon' by Peter, Paul and Mary, and Dusty Springfield's 'I Only Want to be with You'.
◆ **Books:** Rachel Carson's ground-breaking *The Silent Spring*; Betty Friedan's *The Feminine Mystique*; John Le Carré's *The Spy Who Came in from the Cold*; *The Ochre People*, by South African expatriate Helen 'Noni' Jabavu, editor of London's prestigious *New Strand* magazine.

BORN
South Africa: Musician Lucky Dube.

DIED
International: British politician Hugh Gaitskell; poet, playwright, film director Jean Cocteau; singer Edith Piaf, the 'Little Sparrow' of Paris streets; novelist Aldous Huxley.
South Africa: Human rights activist Cissie Gool; war hero and activist Adolf 'Sailor' Malan.

'Little Sparrow' Edith Piaf.

WHAT'S NEW IN 1963

◆ **Kenya** gains its independence on 12 December – the 29th African country to do so since 1960. The sole remaining British colony north of the Congo River is Gambia.
◆ Britain's **Great Train Robbery** nets thieves more than £2 million – a record.
◆ **Medicine:** First successful kidney transplant, in Leeds, UK.
◆ **Product debuts:** Push-button telephones; the tranquilizer Valium; the hologram;
◆ **Space:** Soviet cosmonaut Valentina Tereshkova is the first woman to be launched into orbit.

Freewheeler Bob Dylan: straight to the top (pictured later in life).

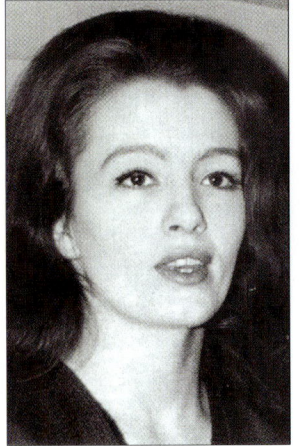

The centre of a scandal that eventually brings down Britain's Tory government is London call-girl Christine Keeler: she shares her favours between war minister John Profumo and Soviet naval attaché Captain Eugene Ivanov. In the ongoing witch-hunt, society doctor Stephen Ward is charged with living off Keeler's immoral earnings, and commits suicide.

148

SOUTH AFRICA in the 20th CENTURY **1960s**

1964

LIFE SENTENCES FOR RIVONIA TRIALISTS

The highly publicized 'Rivonia trial' drags on for seven months. At its conclusion, Nelson Mandela and other leading ANC members are convicted of armed incursion, guerrilla warfare and more than 200 acts of sabotage. Mandela, Walter Sisulu, Govan Mbeki, Dennis Goldberg, Ahmed Kathrada, Raymond Mhlaba, Andrew Mlangeni and Elias Motsoaledi are sentenced to life imprisonment.

Speaking from the dock, Mandela declares: 'During my lifetime, I have dedicated myself to this struggle of the African people. I have fought against white domination, and I have fought against black domination. I have cherished the ideal of a democratic and free society in which all persons live together in harmony and with equal opportunities. It is an ideal which I hope to live for and to achieve. But if needs be, it is an ideal for which I am prepared to die.'

WILBUR'S FIRST BOOK PUBLISHED

Wilbur Smith makes his debut as best-selling writer with *When the Lion Feeds*, a rip-roaring African adventure yarn with a smattering of healthy sex thrown in – but local censors ban it. Even the author's copies, sent out by the London publishers for his private collection in Cape Town, are confiscated at Customs. By the time the ban is lifted, 11 years in the future, more than three million copies of the book will have been sold.

SPORT AND LEISURE

◆ Boxer Cassius Clay (later to be known as Muhammad Ali and, less formally, as the 'Louisville Lip'), the talkative 21-year-old challenger, surprises everyone when he defeats Sonny Liston to become world heavyweight champion.
◆ The year's hit movie is Disney's *Mary Poppins*, which introduces Briton Julie Andrews to the big screen and will win her an Oscar for best actress next year. *My Fair Lady*, with Rex Harrison and Audrey Hepburn (two more Britons), collects eight Oscars. Other box-office draws are *Goldfinger* (Sean Connery as Bond); *Zorba the Greek* (Anthony Quinn); Stanley Kubrick's *Dr Strangelove* (Peter Sellers in several parts); *The Carpetbaggers*; *A Fistful of Dollars*, one of the first and best of the spaghetti westerns; and *A Hard Day's Night*, the first Beatle film. Stanley Baker's epic *Zulu*, about the gritty defence of Rorke's Drift in 1879, stars Baker, the young Michael Caine, and Chief Mangosuthu Buthelezi as King Cetshwayo.
◆ Top of the pops: 'Oh, Pretty Woman': Roy Orbison; 'Can't Buy Me Love': The Beatles.

A triumphant Cassius Clay.

> 'No Viet Cong ever called me nigger'
> *Boxer Cassius Clay, on his refusal to fight in Vietnam.*

WHAT'S NEW IN 1964

Rhodesia's Ian Smith.

◆ Ian Smith becomes **Southern Rhodesian** premier; threatens to declare independence.
◆ **SA:** Johannesburg gets its first recorded snowfall.
◆ **Hollywood:** Sydney Poitier is the first black man to win an Oscar for best actor, in *Lilies of the Field*.
◆ The soldier doll **Action Man** makes his debut.

The Beatles: well on top.

BORN
South Africa: Rugby player André Joubert.

DIED
International: Indian statesman Jawaharlal Nehru; actors Alan Ladd, Peter Lorre, Eddie Cantor; playwright Brendan Behan; newspaper magnate Lord Beaverbrook; mute Harpo Marx, one of the three hilarious brothers; composer Cole Porter.

The Swinging Sixties

Young London fashion guru and ex-art student Mary Quant rides the revolutionary wave with her short skirts and bold geometric designs. She opens her first 'boutique', Bazaar, in Chelsea. Her creed: the young 'are tired of wearing the same as their mothers'; the style: simple, free, fun and cheap. Gone are hats, gloves, stockings, heels and waists. European men's styles are almost as adventurous; in South Africa, the tailored, practical (and oh-so-boring) safari suit, successor to the more rugged bush shirt, catches on as both business and leisure wear, and lasts well into the next decade.

Men's fashion: adventurous.

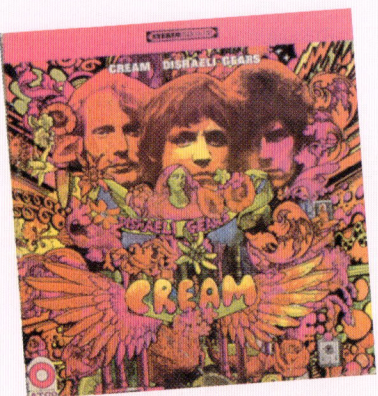

A Cream album cover.

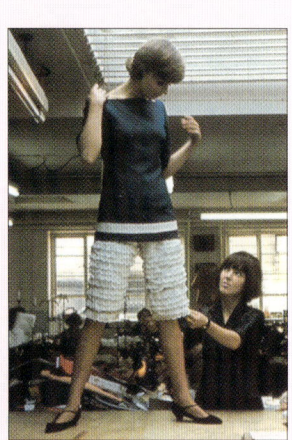

Mary Quant (right) and model.

Mick Jagger: on the way up.

Pop outfits.

Beatlemania: triggered by the mop-topped foursome.

Americans joyfully succumb to Beatlemania as the 'Fab Four' Liverpool superstars head stateside to appear on the *Ed Sullivan Show*, and to be mobbed by shrieking fans. They fill vast stadiums, give press conferences, wear longish hair and granny-glasses, project a carefree, rather cynical image that perfectly matches the mood of the sixties' young.

'I Want To Hold Your Hand' rockets to the top; 'Can't Buy Me Love' and 'Feel Fine' sell millions. The Rolling Stones, described as 'dishevelled and bizarre', are beginning to carve out their own constituency.

The conventional nightclub, that dimly lit, essentially middle-class, middle-aged institution, is on the way out. Taking over is the brash discotheque with its strobes, amplified pop, leggy lemon-haired go-go girls and boundless youthful energy.

SOUTH AFRICA in the 20th CENTURY — 1960s

1965

REBEL RHODESIA TAKES THE PLUNGE

Salisbury, 11 November. In a dramatic broadcast at 11.00 a.m. – the eleventh hour of the eleventh day of the eleventh month – Southern Rhodesian premier Ian Smith announces the colony's unilateral assumption of independence. The declaration, known as UDI, follows months of fruitless talks with the British Labour government.

The rebel regime, which represents Rhodesia's 250,000 whites (or just 5 percent of the total population), sacks the colonial governor, Sir Humphrey Gibbs, but confirms its continuing loyalty to the Queen. Sir Humphrey, in turn, sacks Ian Smith, a move that has little more than symbolic implication.

Mr Smith's government has assumed draconian powers to control the rebel state's finances, trade and press, and to impose rationing.

The British Lord Chancellor condemns the action as 'one of the most irresponsible in the history of the Commonwealth', and Prime Minister Harold Wilson announces a range of economic sanctions, including an embargo on the sale of oil to the breakaway territory. Non-aligned nations, particularly African 'frontline' states, urge Mr Wilson to send in troops. This, however, could be a difficult logistical exercise and, for the British government, a politically disastrous one: as Smith repeatedly points out, most white Rhodesians are of British stock, with 'kith and kin' in the old country.

Point of no return: Ian Smith signs the independence declaration.

'Tune in, turn on, drop out.'
Timothy Leary, guru of the 'psychedelic generation', promoting the hallucinogenic drug LSD

TEENAGER SETS NEW WORLD RECORD

South African swimmer Karen Muir, just 12 years old, captures the headlines when she breaks the world 110-yard (about 100 metres) backstroke record in Blackpool, England. She goes on to set 16 more world marks during the next four years.

TRENDS: THE YEAR OF TWIGGY AND 'THE SHRIMP'

Long-legged model Jean Shrimpton startles Australians when she appears at the Melbourne races in the mini-skirt, but bared knees become the rage and, soon enough, accepted fashion among the young and slim. Pencil-thin, waifish Lesley Hornby, universally known as Twiggy, who is 17 years old but looks much younger, leads the charge; London's humming Carnaby Street and King's Road displace Paris as the mecca of fashion, particularly men's fashion. Long hair (not a curl or wave in sight), pale faces, mascara-loaded eyes, shifts, lacy stockings and sling-back shoes are in. Men's hair also lengthens. London's new, young, trendy celebrities – designer Mary Quant, photographer David Bailey, decorator Terence Conran, hairdresser Vidal Sassoon, actor Terence Stamp, singer Adam Faith among others – are the role models for an entire generation.

London's Carnaby Street: fashion mecca.

SOUTH AFRICA in the 20th CENTURY

The Sixties

WHAT'S NEW IN 1965

- **Space:** First space walk successfully completed, by Soviet cosmonaut Alexei Leoniv; US astronaut Edward White follows shortly afterwards.
- **Vietnam:** US president Lyndon Johnson orders the bombing of targets in North Vietnam, sends 3,500 marines in to Da Nang to protect the airfield – the first US troops to be committed. By year's end there are 125,000 American servicemen in Vietnam.
- **SA:** Cape Town municipality lifts its ban on two-piece beachwear; the bikini, however, is still illegal in Durban.
- The words **psychedelic** and **flower power** become common usage.
- **Smoking:** US introduces health warnings on cigarette packets.

Flower child.

Julie Andrews in The Sound of Music: *too good to be true.*

TWO FINE ARTISTS PASS AWAY

Two of South Africa's leading creative spirits die. Ingrid Jonker, the Afrikaans writer and poet whose *Rook en Oker* (Smoke and Ochre) was published to acclaim two years ago, takes her own life by drowning.

The year also brings the death of Bertha Everard, doyenne of a remarkable family group of woman painters that has included her sister Edith, her daughters Ruth and Rosamund, and Ruth's daughter Leonora. The older members held their first group exhibition in 1931, each showing an individual style but all illuminating the pleasant countryside around their home in the small town of Carolina, eastern Transvaal. Edith died in 1962; Rosamund became

Artist Bertha Everard.

a pilot and was killed, shortly after the war, while serving with the British Air Transport Auxiliary.

ARTS AND LEISURE

- The year's biggest box-office success is *The Sound of Music*, a syrupy extravaganza featuring Julie Andrews as the cheerful novitiate in charge of Christopher Plummer's charming if too-good-to-be-true family. Andrews wins an Oscar for her role in *Mary Poppins*. Other top movies are David Lean's *Dr Zhivago* (with Omar Sharif and Julie Christie), *Darling* (with Dirk Bogarde and, again, Ms Christie), and *Thunderball* (yet another James Bond, with Sean Connery).
- Top of the charts: 'I Just Don't Know What To Do With Myself': Dusty Springfield; 'The Carnival Is Over' and 'I'll Never Find Another You': The Seekers; 'Help!': the Beatles; 'Downtown': Petula Clark. Each of the Beatles is awarded an MBE.
- Magazines: *Fair Lady* is launched in South Africa.

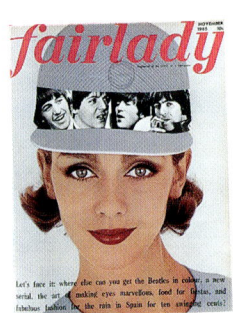

BORN
South Africa: Soccer player John 'Shoes' Mosheu.

DIED
International: Statesman and war leader Winston Churchill; poet T.S. Eliot; architect Charles Jeanneret,

Winston Churchill's funeral.

(Le Corbusier); missionary, musician and medical doctor Albert Schweitzer; black nationalist Malcolm X, assassinated in Harlem, New York; comic actor Stan Laurel; singer Nat 'King' Cole; the horse Trigger, Roy Rogers' constant screen companion. **South Africa:** Composer and conductor Erik Chisholm; schoolteacher Frederick Harris, former member of the outlawed African Resistance Movement and Chairman of the South African Non-Racial Olympic Committee, is executed for detonating a bomb at Johannesburg railway station.

SOUTH AFRICA in the 20th CENTURY **1960s**

1966

VERWOERD ASSASSINATED BY PARLIAMENTARY MESSENGER

South African prime minister Dr Hendrik Verwoerd is stabbed to death in parliament, Cape Town.

Shortly after two in the afternoon Dr Verwoerd enters the House, with his wife Betsie at his side, to address members for the first time since the general election. He has just taken his seat when a man dressed in the uniform of a parliamentary messenger approaches, his hand held high and gripping a knife.

He stabs the Prime Minister four times in the chest. The assassin is identified as Dimitri Tsafendas, illegitimate son of a Greek father and Mozambican mother. Tsafendas was educated locally but was shunned by the white community because of his dark complexion. He later travelled extensively, living in 10 different countries before returning to South Africa. He is adjudged mentally unfit to stand trial.

SOUND AND SCREEN
- Hit singles: 'Yellow Submarine', 'Eleanor Rigby' and 'Paperback Writer': all The Beatles; 'Strangers in the Night': Frank Sinatra; 'These Boots Are Made For Walking': Nancy Sinatra; 'California Dreamin': the Mamas and the Papas; 'The Green, Green Grass of Home': Tom Jones; 'Reach Out and I'll Be There': the Four Tops; 'Distant Drums': Jim Reeves.

> 'In a decade dominated by youth, London has burst into bloom. It swings; it is the scene.'
> Time Magazine

- Films: *A Man for All Seasons*, with Paul Scofield (Best Picture); *Who's Afraid of Virginia Woolf*, with Elizabeth Taylor and Richard Burton.
- Television: The *Star Trek* series makes its debut on America's NBC.
- Books: Truman Capote's *In Cold Blood*; Jacqueline Susann's *Valley of the Dolls*; South African author Credo Mutwa's *Ndaba My Children*.

THE DEATH OF DISTRICT SIX

Children play in Upper Ashley Street.

District Six, the suburb close to central Cape Town and home to about 60,000 mainly coloured people, is declared 'white' in terms of the Group Areas Act. Officialdom also regards it as a slum, and bulldozers move in to begin demolishing the houses. The residents, who are to be moved farther out onto the windblown Cape Flats, are understandably angry. Few deny that the suburb has its problems – it is ramshackle, crime-ridden and unsanitary – but it has personality, vitality and a powerful sense of community. It is also endowed with charm. Its streets are a pandemonium of people, cars, horse-drawn wagons, hawking carts; of traders who stock everything from banjos to beans, dimly lit little shops filled with spices and herbs and joss-sticks. District Six has a soul.

The bulldozers do their worst.

SOUTH AFRICA in the 20th CENTURY

The Sixties

WORLD CUP: ENGLAND TRIUMPH IN EXTRA TIME

Wembley; 30 July. Football comes full circle when England, inventor of the game and this year's host country, wins the World Cup. Led by midfielder Bobby Moore, they beat West Germany 4-2 after going 2-2 into extra time. Geoff Hurst scores the two goals that seal victory, both of them controversial: the first hits the crossbar and, according to the Germans, fails to cross the line; the second comes as a jubilant crowd, thinking the final whistle has gone, invades the field.

BORN
South Africa: Cricketer Alan Donald; singer Yvonne Chaka-Chaka; runners Elana Meyer and Zola Budd.

DIED
International: Nigerian Prime Minister Sir Abubakar Tafawa Balewa, with 50 politicians and army officers, in a coup; novelist Evelyn Waugh.
South Africa: One-time Ossewa-Brandwag leader Robey Leibbrandt; artist Irma Stern; ballerina Nadia Nerina.

On the way to the cup: one of England's four goals.

Ballet star Nadia Nerina.

1967

BARNARD'S CARDIAC TEAM FIRST TO TRANSPLANT HUMAN HEART

Cape Town, 4 December. Cardiac surgeon Christiaan Barnard makes medical history when he and his Groote Schuur team perform the first-ever human heart transplant. The organ, harvested from a 25-year-old female accident victim, is implanted into middle-aged Louis Washkansky. The operation is a surgical success but Washkansky dies 18 days later, of pneumonia, after anti-rejection drugs damage his immune system.

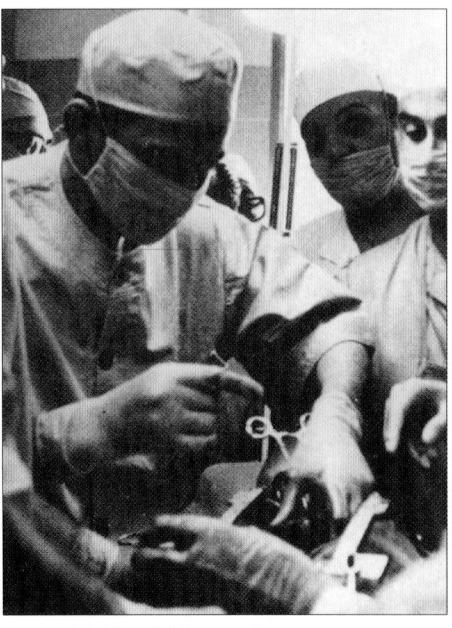
Barnard (left) with his transplant team.

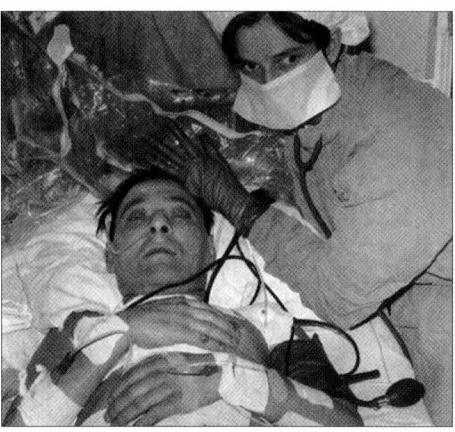
Pioneer heart patient Washkansky and nurse.

Dr Barnard is already known in medical circles for his pioneering work on intestinal atresia, a fatal condition arising from an insufficient blood supply from pregnant mother to foetus, and for his research into heart conditions. After studying advanced surgery in the United States, he returned to South Africa to develop an artificial heart valve, and to conduct transplant procedures on animals.

> 'This was the most exciting experience I have ever had. It was like watching a bullfight. There were the classical manoeuvres – beautifully executed – that always precede the grand finale.'
> *Groote Schuur intern, after the world's first heart transplant*

SOUTH AFRICA in the 20th CENTURY 1960s

An Israeli mobile column on the move.

ISRAELIS VICTORIOUS IN SIX-DAY WAR

10 June. It takes the Israeli armed forces just six days to defeat a coalition of Arab states, and to capture vast tracts of territory in the process.

The seeds of victory are sewn on 5 June, when Israeli warplanes launch a pre-emptive strike against Egypt, Syria, Jordan and Iraq, destroying hundreds of their aircraft on the ground. Troops capture East Jerusalem (after fierce hand-to-hand fighting with the Jordanians), the strategic Golan Heights and the West Bank of the Jordan River. Mobile columns of infantry with strong air, tank and artillery support then roll back the Arab armies to occupy the Sinai Peninsula and the Gaza Strip. Some Israeli units reach the Suez Canal, others penetrate 12 miles into Syria before the ceasefire comes into effect.

Guitar maestro Jimi Hendrix.

TOP OF THE CHARTS
- San Francisco: Scott McKenzie
- Whiter Shade of Pale: Procul Harum
- Release Me: Engelbert Humperdinck
- I'm a Believer: The Monkees
- There Goes My Everything: Engelbert Humperdinck
- Hello Goodbye: The Beatles
- The Last Waltz: Engelbert Humperdinck
- Penny Lane: The Beatles
- Georgy Girl: The Seekers
- Light My Fire: The Doors

HIPPIE REVOLUTION SWEEPS THROUGH YOUNG AMERICA

While London swings with brittle flair, a whole generation of young Americans is opting out of society to seek personal freedom, peace, gentleness, love, compassion and brotherhood – and to protest the horrors of the Vietnam war, which television brings into every home every night. They congregate in the Haight-Ashbury district of San Francisco, venue of the recent Monterey pop concert that featured Jimi Hendrix, the Grateful Dead and The Beatles. They are known as hippies, and as the 'flower children' for the blossoms that garland their hair. They wear headbands and beads; they listen to Hendrix, Janis Joplin, Bob Dylan, Joan Baez; they make love, openly and without shame; they take drugs (marijuana for the most part; LSD for the real trip); many live in communes; one of their favourite words is 'psychedelic', which describes the vivid colours, perceptions and sensations their hallucinogens create. Most are from white middle-class families; more than two-thirds are college educated.

Haight-Ashbury's 'summer of love' doesn't last long – the place turns into a tourist attraction and gawping visitors clog the area. But young people all over America catch on, and protest becomes a constant refrain on campuses and in the streets. Sometimes it turns ugly. On 21 October thousands gather in Washington in the biggest demonstration yet against the war in Vietnam; military police wield batons and fire teargas, a dozen protesters are injured, hundreds arrested.

Janis Joplin.

Hippie twosome.

> 'A hippie wears his hair long like Tarzan, walks like Jane, and smells like Cheetah.'
> *Actor Buster Crabbe*

155

The Sixties

SOUTH AFRICA in the 20th CENTURY

WHAT'S NEW IN 1967

- *Shopping:* Raymond Ackerman buys four small Cape Town stores – the first in what is to become the giant Pick 'n Pay chain.
- The first signs of the **greenhouse effect** – the warming of the Earth – are discerned.
- The musical show **Hair**, which exposes audiences to full-frontal nudity on stage, premieres in New York.
- **Megastar Elvis Presley** marries Priscilla Beaulieu in the pop wedding of the year.

The musical Hair: *life, laughter (and nudity) on stage.*

BORN
South Africa: Rugby players François Pienaar, Joel Stransky and Gary Teichmann; boxer Vuyani Bungu.

DIED
International: Three US astronauts, in a flash fire on the launch pad of their Apollo spacecraft; Soviet cosmonaut Vladimir Komarov; South American revolutionary Che Guevara, shot in the Bolivian jungle; nuclear scientist Robert Oppenheimer; British politician Clement Attlee; poet John Masefield; actor Spencer Tracy; actresses Vivien Leigh and Jane Mansfield.
South Africa: Nobel laureate Chief Albert Luthuli.

1968

D'OLIVIERA'S SELECTION TRIGGERS CRICKET CRISIS

South African sport takes a giant step towards international isolation when coloured cricketer Basil D'Oliviera, who plays for Worcestershire, is refused entry to the country of his birth. His long-held dream, of taking to the field at his beloved Newlands (Cape Town), is shattered – and so, within a year or two, are the dreams of many a future Springbok.

Basil D'Oliviera.

All-rounder D'Oliviera, who learnt his cricket in the narrow little streets of Cape Town's Signal Hill, earned his selection to the English national squad after making his mark in the Lancashire League and county circuit. He recently scored a fine century against Australia at the Oval and was an obvious choice for the MCC tour of South Africa, but was omitted from the initial selection list. This is generally held to be a 'diplomatic' decision, and it triggers massive public outrage.

D'Oliviera then agrees to accompany the MCC as correspondent for *The News of the World*, but is refused entry. South Africa, says Prime Minister John Vorster, 'cannot allow those organizations, individuals and newspapers to make political capital out of such relations or to use certain people or sportsmen as pawns in their game to bedevil relations, to create incidents and to undermine our way of life...'. Shortly afterwards one of the English cricketers (Tom Cartwright) drops out, and D'Oliviera is invited to join the squad. But Vorster refuses to accept the selection, claiming the touring party is 'no longer a cricket team, but a team of troublemakers for South Africa's separate development policies...'. The MCC cancel the tour.

FINE ARTIST SLIPS QUIETLY AWAY

The death of local artist Heidi Herzog, painter of exquisite floral canvases, passes unnoticed. In the years before the Second World War Swiss-born Herzog worked in Europe with Lemercier and Favory, and held a number of successful exhibitions, but war and the death of her husband and two children shattered her spirit. She eventually found her way to South Africa, where she lived in desperate poverty, much of the time in backyard domestic workers' quarters in Durban and Johannesburg. She continued to paint, but without recognition, and it is only in the years to come that she will be discovered, her talent known and valued.

> 'Until the shameful parts of women are covered, I am convinced God will not fill the Vaal Dam.'
>
> *Gert Yssel, campaigning – against the mini-skirt – on behalf of the National Association for Public Morality and Welfare*

SOUTH AFRICA in the 20th CENTURY — 1960s

Coretta King (centre) mourns her husband's death.

KING AND KENNEDY SHOT TO DEATH

In a year of high drama, of much tragedy and little honour, two of America's foremost public figures die by the hand of an assassin.

On 3 April civil rights leader Martin Luther King, the great preacher of peace, tells his Tennessee audience that he has 'seen the Promised Land. I may not get there with you, but I want you to know that we as a people will get to the Promised Land'. Next day he is gunned down by a sniper, later identified as one James Earl Ray.

Two months later Senator Robert Kennedy, brother of the late President John F. Kennedy, is shot to death in Los Angeles' Ambassador Hotel. On the campaign trail for the Democratic presidential nomination, Kennedy was celebrating his victory in the California primary and is on his way out through the hotel's kitchens when a young Palestinian immigrant, Sirhan Sirhan, shoots him five times with a .22 pistol.

ARTS AND ENTERTAINMENT

♦ Cinemagoers are treated to a feast of fantasy; notable offerings are *The Planet of the Apes*, *Rosemary's Baby* and, most memorably, Stanley Kubrick's mysterious, moving *2001: A Space Odyssey*. Other box-office giants are Zeffirelli's beautiful *Romeo and Juliet*; the screen version of *Oliver!*, and *Bullitt*, with Steve McQueen.

♦ Top of the charts: 'Hey Jude': The Beatles; 'Those Were The Days': Mary Hopkin; 'Cinderella Rockafella': Esther and Abi Ofarim; 'What A Wonderful World': Louis Armstrong; 'Lily the Pink': Scaffold; and 'Love is Blue': Paul Mauriat. Jimi Hendrix produces the album *Electric Ladyland*.

♦ Books: John Updike's *Couples* and Gore Vidal's *Myra Breckinridge*, both about America's preoccupation with sex. Alexander Solzhenitsyn's *Cancer Ward* and *The First Circle* are published in Europe. Solzhenitsyn will be expelled from the Soviet Members' Union and, in 1970, will win the Nobel Prize for Literature.

DIED

International: Cosmonaut Yuri Gagarin, in air crash; comedians Tony Hancock, by suicide, and Bud Flanagan; Film-maker Anthony Asquith; authors Upton Sinclair, John Steinbeck and Enid Blyton. **South Africa:** Authors Sarah Gertrude Millin and Can Themba; political activist Z.K. Matthews; musician Todd Mathshikiza.

> 'In the future, everybody will be world famous for fifteen minutes.'
> *Pop artist Andy Warhol*

WHAT'S NEW IN 1968

♦ **Space:** Apollo 8 takes pictures of Earth.
♦ First **abortion clinic** opened, in London.
♦ Kodak markets its **Instamatic camera** (right).
♦ The **Jacuzzi** bath is invented, in California.
♦ **Wimbledon** invites professional players to compete for the first time.
♦ Nuclear **Non-Proliferation Treaty** signed.
♦ **The Beatles** open their Apple boutique in London.
♦ The word **overkill**, spawned by the Vietnam war, enters the English language.

SOUTH AFRICA in the 20th CENTURY

The Sixties

1969
ARMSTRONG BECOMES FIRST MAN ON THE MOON

20 July. Millions of televiewers around the world watch as Neil Armstrong climbs down from his lunar capsule, *Eagle*, to tread the Moon's surface – and to launch an odyssey that will one day take us to the stars. As his feet touch the desolate moonscape he intones: 'That's one small step for man, one giant leap for mankind'.

Also in *Apollo* 11 are astronauts 'Buzz' Aldrin and Mike Collins. Aldrin and Armstrong explore the surface of the Moon's Sea of Tranquility, take photographs (one of them is of man's first extra-terrestrial footprint), position instruments, collect rocks and raise the American flag. Collins remains in the orbiting spacecraft.

CHURCH SHUTS OUT BLACK MOURNERS

East London, 3 April. The Dutch Reformed Church bars nine black people from attending the funeral of Dennis Hoft, a 35-year-old white man. Hoft is described by his workmates as 'very popular with everybody', and was especially well liked by his African staff, each of whom had contributed 50 cents for a wreath inscribed with the words 'God be with you till we meet again'.

WHAT'S NEW IN 1969

- **Aviation:** The Anglo-French supersonic Concorde and Boeing's giant 747 take off for the first time.
- **Politics:** Richard Nixon takes office as US president.
- **Middle East:** Yasser Arafat becomes leader of the Palestine Liberation Organization; Libya's Colonel Muammar Gadaffi ousts King Idris.
- **Vietnam:** US troops begin to pull out.
- **Fashion:** The mini-skirt loses ground to the ankle-length 'maxi' dress.

War in Vietnam: Americans have had enough.

STEVE BIKO LAUNCHES BLACK CONSCIOUSNESS MOVEMENT

The University of Natal activist Steve Biko forms the Black Students' Organisation, a movement which is committed to black consciousness and which rejects the second-class role that blacks have played within the multiracial National Union of Students (NUSAS). 'The integration they talk about is artificial', he says. 'A one-way course, with the whites doing all the talking and the blacks the listening.' The movement, influenced by African-American activism in the United States, seeks to instil ethnic pride in the black people of South Africa.

Activist Steve Biko.

DEMOS PLAGUE SPRINGBOK RUGBY TOUR

Dawie De Villiers' rugby Springboks are having a hard time of it on their tour of the British Isles as anti-apartheid demonstrators turn out in force. They besiege the stadiums, hurl smokebombs onto the

Neil Armstrong descends to take his 'first, small step'.

SOUTH AFRICA in the 20th CENTURY — 1960s

field at some matches, scatter tin-tacks at others and chant slogans. Against Midlands East at Leicester, the tourists avoid the mob by arriving two hours early, and more than a thousand police are deployed to keep the peace (the 'Boks nevertheless win 11-9 and run off to a standing ovation).

Most of the demonstrators feel genuine outrage that their country is playing host to sporting ambassadors of the apartheid regime, but they are surrounded, in one journalist's words, 'by as fine a rabble as you could wish to see, representing every breed of political and religious troublemaker – trade union agitators, Sinn Fein, Young Socialists, communists, Britain-haters, Maoists, anarchists...'.

The tourists win 15 of their 24 matches, with five defeats and four draws. But, for the first time in their history, they fail to beat any of the four Home Unions.

ARTS AND ENTERTAINMENT

◆ Nearly half a million young Americans gather in an open field near Woodstock, New York State, for a weekend of music, pot-smoking and togetherness. Summer rain and inadequate facilities fail to dampen their spirits;

Woodstock: the 'nicest bunch of kids'.

the local sheriff says: 'This is the nicest bunch of kids I've ever dealt with'. Performers during the nonstop 19-hour music-fest include Joan Baez, Jimi Hendrix, Janis Joplin, Jefferson Airplane, The Who, and Crosby, Stills, Nash and Young.

◆ Among the year's hit singles: 'Aquarius' and 'Let the Sunshine In': the Fifth Dimension; 'In the Year 2525': Zager and Evans; 'Proud Mary': Creedence Clearwater Revival.

Baring all at Woodstock.

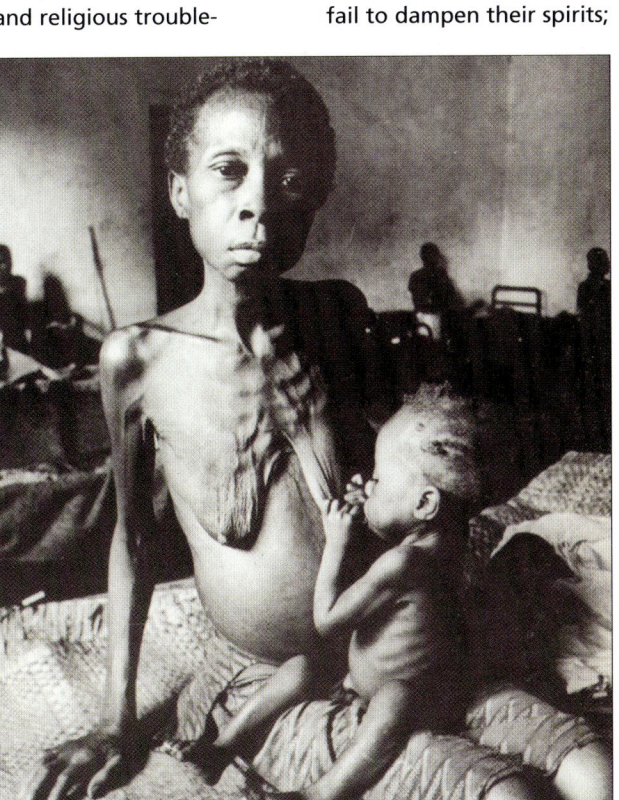

In 1967 the Ibo people of Nigeria's southeastern province, led by the charismatic Colonel Odumegwu Ojukwa, declared their independence, triggering a savage, three-year civil war. By 1969, 1.5 million have succumbed to hunger; 6,000 are dying each day.

BORN
South Africa: Sportsmen Lucas Radebe, Hansie Cronjé, Jonty Rhodes and Ernie Els.

DIED
International: American soldier and politician Dwight Eisenhower; Vietnamese leader Ho Chi Minh; Congolese leader Moise Tshombe; boxer Rocky Marciano; writer Jack Kerouac, voice of the 'beat generation'; sci-fi novelist John Wyndham; horror actor Boris Karloff; actress Judy Garland, from a drug overdose. **South Africa:** Second heart transplant patient Philip Blaiberg, who survived for 20 months; women's rights campaigner Bertha Solomon.

1970s

DIED
1970: Antonio Salazar, long-time dictator of Portugal. The installation of a new, more liberal regime has profound effects on Portuguese African territories (Angola and Mozambique). Egypt's President Nasser, succeeded by Anwar Sadat.
1976: Chinese leader Mao Tse-tung.
1977: SA Black Consciousness leader Steve Biko, in police custody.

CRISIS PRECIPITATED
1972: In US politics, by the arrest of five men for breaking into Democratic Party national headquarters in Washington's Watergate apartment complex.
1973: In world economy, as Opec closes ranks and the oil price rises. In the Middle East, as Egypt and Syria attack Israel at Yom Kippur (Jewish holy day).

RETREATED
1973: US troops, from Vietnam.

BUILDING BRIDGES
1971: SA premier B.J. Vorster launches era of 'détente', aimed at forging 'normal and friendly relations' with African nations.
1974: Vorster meets leaders of eight independent African states.

INVADED
1975: Angola, by SA forces.

REOPENED
1975: The Suez Canal, after eight years.

RESCUED
1976: 240-plus passengers and crew of hijacked Air France airliner, by an Israeli force, from Uganda's Entebbe airport.

INAUGURATED
1971: The state of Bangladesh (formerly East Pakistan). A reign of terror in Uganda, after Idi Amin ousts President Milton Obote.
1972: SA Black People's Convention, to co-ordinate Black Consciousness groups. SA's Hendrik Verwoerd dam.
1974: SA 1820 Settlers' Monument,

Township poverty: part of the legacy of apartheid.

in Grahamstown. Market Theatre, Johannesburg.
1975: The independent republics of Angola and Mozambique. SA Reform Party (renamed, twice in quick succession, Progressive Reform Party and Progressive Federal Party).
1976: SABC television service. The 'independent' republic of Transkei.
1977: The 'independent' republic of Bophuthatswana.
1979: Zimbabwe-Rhodesia, under Bishop Abel Muzorewa, as a stop-gap arrangement pending independence talks with Britain. The 'independent' republic of Venda.

RESIGNED
1974: US president Richard Nixon, after 'Watergate Affair' unravelled by *Washington Post* and others.
1978: SA premier B.J. Vorster, after 'Information scandal' uncovered by *Rand Daily Mail* and others. He is succeeded by P.W. Botha.

LANDED
1971: Soviet unmanned spacecraft, on Mars. US astronauts on Moon, which they explore by lunar vehicle.

POLITICS AND PROTEST
1974: Riotous Assemblies Amendment Act passed.
1976: Soweto students rise in revolt.
1977: Two SA newspapers and 17 organizations banned. United Party disbands.
1978: UN passes Resolution 435 demanding supervised elections in South West Africa (Namibia).
1979: P.W. Botha launches 'constellation of [African] states' initiative, and 12-point 'total strategy' to counter perceived 'total onslaught' against SA. Industrial Conciliation Act gives impetus to labour reform and black trade union movement.

FIRST
1971: Cape to Rio yacht race.
1974: Sextuplets born, at Groote Schuur hospital, Cape Town.
1977: UN sanctions imposed against SA (arms embargo).
1978: Test-tube baby, in England.

CHAMPIONS
1972: SA women bowls team, who win world title (in Australia).
1973: Boxer Arnold Taylor, who wins world bantamweight title.
1974: Anneline Kriel, who becomes Miss World. Golfers Bobby Cole and Dale Hayes, who win pairs World Cup.
1976: Black golfer Vincent Tshabalala, who wins the French Open.
1977: SA's Jody Scheckter, who wins world Formula 1 title. Surfer Shaun Thompson, who wins World Cup (in Hawaii).

SOUTH AFRICA in the 20th CENTURY

1970

THE LAST HURRAH: SPRINGBOKS TRIUMPH IN CLEAN SWEEP

South Africa's cricket team, captained by accomplished tactician Ali Bacher and including players that rank among the finest in the history of the game, sweep all before them in the series against Bill Lawry's visiting Australians.

The record speaks for itself: at Newlands, victory by 170 runs; at Kingsmead, by an innings and 129 runs; at the Wanderers, by 307 runs; at St George's Park, by 323 runs.

The South Africans outplay the visitors in every department, and highlights there are aplenty: Eddie Barlow's two centuries; Barry Richards' elegantly, even disdainfully, punishing batsmanship; the aggressive bowling of Peter Pollock and Mike Proctor (between them they take 41 of the 80 Australian wickets to fall), and above all the majesty of Graeme Pollock at the crease. The great left-hander chalks up 512 runs in the first three matches of the series, including what will be a long remembered 274-run onslaught in the first innings at Kingsmead – the biggest Test score in the country's cricketing history.

This is the great age of South African cricket – and the thrilling but also poignant end of an era. For by now, apartheid is very much an international issue and the Springboks are steadily being excluded from the world sporting arena.

Strike bowler Mike Proctor.

WHAT'S NEW IN 1970

- **SA politics:** The National Party is returned to power in the general election – but with a reduced majority for the first time since 1948.
- Rebel **Rhodesia** declares itself a republic.
- **Nigeria:** Civil war ends with the collapse of the breakaway Biafran state.
- **Britain:** Gay Liberation Front mounts its first demonstration.
- **Egypt:** The giant and environmentally controversial Aswan Dam project is finally completed.
- **Northern Ireland:** Rubber bullets are used for the first time, by British troops.

Winnie Mandela: arrest and imprisonment.

WINNIE UNDER HOUSE ARREST

Winnie Mandela, wife of jailed African National Congress leader Nelson Mandela, is placed under house arrest after serving 17 months of solitary confinement. Eight years ago she was banned under the Suppression of Communism Act and, last year, detained in terms of the Terrorism Act. She will soon be imprisoned again – for receiving guests at her Johannesburg home.

Mrs Mandela, a trained social worker, has been involved in extra-parliamentary activities since the early 1960s, when she served on the Natal executive of the ANC.

ZULU PLAY A SMASH HIT

Audiences thrill to the moody power of Welcome Msomi's production of *uMabatha*, a Zulu play based on Shakespeare's *Macbeth* but set during the tyrannical reign of King Shaka. *uMabatha*, initially created for Elizabeth Sneddon's Natal Theatre Workshop, is staged in major South African venues (including Cape Town's Maynardville open-air theatre) and, to acclaim, in New York and other overseas centres. Msomi will eventually – after years of harassment by the local security police – fulfill his talent in the Bedford-Stuyvesant ghetto area of New York, where he will launch his Zulu Dance Theatre.

NUCLEAR WEAPONS FOR SA?

South Africa is to join the United States, Britain and France as the Western world's only producers of enriched uranium, a crucial element in maintaining the West's nuclear arsenal. Prime Minister B.J. Vorster announces that local scientists have developed a cheaper process than that used by the other countries. The breakthrough means that, in theory, South Africa will be able to produce its own atomic weapons.

SOUTH AFRICA in the 20th CENTURY

The Seventies

SOUTH AFRICAN SKYWATCHER'S COMET SHINES

Bennet's Comet, bright enough to be seen with the naked eye, appears over the southern night sky. It is one of two comets named after the amateur astronomer Jack Bennet, who lives in Pretoria. Bennet is the world's only modern skywatcher to have made a visual discovery of a supernova.

LAW SHUTS OUT STAR GOLFER

Gary Player shakes his head in bewilderment when local Indian golfer Sewsunker 'Papwa' Sewgolum is refused permission to play in the South African Open. 'We are slowly putting our head in a noose', the maestro says.

Sewgolum, who has beaten Player on occasion and twice won the Natal Open, may have to give up the game he loves and, with it, any chance of earning a decent income. There are no local golfers of colour capable of giving him a good game, and he cannot make a living outside the 'white' circuit. Last year he averaged just R56 a month, or about R40 after expenses. This has to support his wife, five children and elderly mother.

BOKS BOUNCE BACK

Dawie de Villiers' rugby Springboks recover in spectacular style after their nightmare British tour last year to trounce the All Blacks 3–1 in the home series. The Newlands Test is an especially ferocious battle between the two traditional rivals: there are cuts and bruises aplenty; Piston van Wyk has to have seven stitches in his lip; Syd Nomis loses two teeth and the rest of his front teeth are loosened; Mannetjies Roux is hospitalized for kidney damage and suspected fractured vertebrae; De Villiers has a jaw injury.

SINGLES OF THE YEAR

- Bridge Over Troubled Water: Simon and Garfunkel
- Turn Up Your Radio: The Master's Apprentices
- Lookin' Out My Back Door: Creedence Clearwater Revival
- Venus: Shocking Blue
- The Wonder of You: Elvis Presley
- In the Summertime: Mungo Jerry
- Wanderin' Star: Lee Marvin
- I Hear You Knocking: Dave Edmunds
- All Right Now: Free

ASIANS ENDURE GRAVE INDIGNITIES

The government's refusal to grant a visa to a top Japanese jockey adds to the confusion surrounding Asiatic citizens of and visitors to South Africa. In theory they are 'honorary whites', but their status depends on circumstances: for entry into the country, they are classed as Asians; under the Group Areas Act, they are white; under the Population Registration Act they are 'Asiatic, other'; and they remain undefined under the Immorality and Mixed Marriages acts.

Meanwhile the Chinese community is suffering indignities. Patricia Tam, 13, is forced to withdraw from the finals of a junior tennis tournament, Miss Ava Junkin from Rhodes University's Rag Queen contest; Chinese residents of Port Elizabeth may no longer enjoy the miniature golf course or the Humewood skating rink; Mrs Weiyien Wong Noether, Taiwanese wife of a German-born businessman, is held at Jan Smuts airport and advised not to book into the same hotel as her husband.

Ferocious rugby: Piston van Wyk is helped from the field.

This Dave Marais cartoon lampoons bully-boy B.J. Vorster and his 'Chinese policy'. The caption reads: 'Game, set and match. Now go and play in your own group area'.

SOUTH AFRICA in the 20th CENTURY 1970s

WELCOME TO THE FLOPPY

Computer users are offered a valuable new tool: they can store data on IBM's new 'floppy disk' – a small, flat, easy-to-handle memory bank. It will quickly displace the punched cards and magnetic tapes in use for the past few years.

ARTS AND ENTERTAINMENT

◆ **Music:** The Beatles break up after years of tension between songwriters John Lennon and Paul McCartney. Cult blues singer Janis Joplin, 27, dies of a heroin overdose. Jimi Hendrix also dies.

BORN
South Africa: Rugby player Chester Williams.

DIED
International: French statesman Charles de Gaulle; Egyptian leader Gamal Abdel Nasser; philosopher Bertrand Russell; conductor Sir John Barbirolli; author E.M. Forster. Four students at Kent State University, Ohio, are shot by National Guardsman during campus demonstrations against the US invasion of Cambodia; eight Israeli children, in a school bus, in an attack by the Popular Front for the Liberation of Palestine. *South Africa:* Sculptor Elsa Dziomba; author N.P. van Wyk Louw; community leader James Mpanza, self-proclaimed 'king of Orlando'.

◆ **Stage and screen:** The film version of Arthur Hailey's *Airport* begins a rash of disaster movies. *Love Story* has the world weeping in the aisles. The year's ten top box-office drawcards are Paul Newman, Clint Eastwood, Steve McQueen, John Wayne, Elliott Gould, Dustin Hoffman, Lee Marvin, Jack Lemmon, Barbara Streisand, and Walter Matthau.

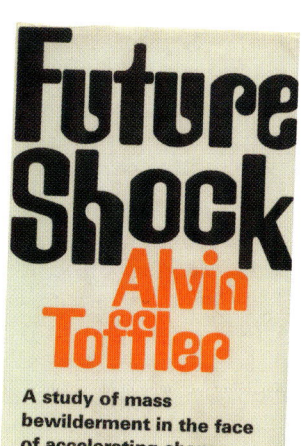

◆ **Books:** A million copies of *The New English Bible* are sold in the first week of publication. Australian author Germaine Greer, in *The Female Eunuch*, argues persuasively that modern society is 'castrating' women, and that there needs to be a fundamental change in the way the female gender perceives itself. Almost as influential but in quite a different way is Alvin Toffler's *Future Shock* (the trauma of technological change). John Fowles' *The French Lieutenant's Woman*; Irwin Shaw's *Rich Man, Poor Man*.

◆ **Sport:** Brazil win the Soccer World Cup for the third time, beating Italy 4-1 in Mexico City. South African teenager Sally Little wins the individual title in the World Golf Championships in Spain. Australian Margaret Court defeats America's Billie Jean King 14-12, 11-9 in a marathon Wimbledon ladies' final.

Swinging Sally Little.

> 'You can't reheat a soufflé.'
> *Beatle Paul McCartney, on speculation that the group will re-form*

1971

VORSTER LAUNCHES NEW ERA OF 'DETENTE'

International pressures mount against South Africa's racist government: cultural and sporting links with the outside world are steadily evaporating; the United Nations declares illegal South Africa's occupation of South West Africa (later Namibia); South Africa's friendship with white ruled rebel Rhodesia is helping marshal the forces of opposition to the apartheid regime. Prime Minister John Vorster clearly perceives the dangers of isolation and the need to establish 'normal and friendly relations' with African states and embarks on a policy of détente. He begins the process by inviting Malawi's Dr Hastings Kamuzu Banda to visit him in Cape Town. Banda accepts.

B.J. Vorster and Malawi's Banda: cosying up to black Africa.

SOUTH AFRICA in the 20th CENTURY

The Seventies

On course for Rio: the start of the yacht race.

FIRST CAPE-TO-RIO RACE A SUCCESS

16 January. Spectators crowd the seafront from the harbour to Sea Point, and the slopes of Signal Hill, and Table Bay is bright with the sails of leisure craft as the first Cape-to-Rio yacht race gets under way. The 5,900-kilometre race is well covered by press and radio; published charts plot the progress of each entrant, and the event is a huge success. Line honours go to *Ocean Spirit*; overall winner is John Goodwin's Knysna-built *Albatross* II.

SPORT BEDEVILLED BY RACE LAWS

Newspaper opinion polls in South Africa indicate that white players are 100 percent in favour of multiracial cricket.

Meanwhile 35-year-old Glen Popham, who captained the all-white Springbok karate squad against a British side, and who won a gold at the 'white' South African Games, reveals that he is classed as a coloured. Initially he posed as white to learn the sport, trained at a white gymnasium, and was entertained in white homes. 'I felt awful,' he says, 'because I could never return their hospitality.'

THE SILLY SIDE OF SEGREGATION

A survey of apartheid, conducted by *Tribune*, reveals a quite ludicrous state of affairs. Examples: coloured hospital nurses may not attend white patients – in a country where black nursemaids bath and feed white babies; an Indian cancer specialist is barred from lecturing white students; whites and blacks may not share the same party line; a Chinese married to a white person for the past 30 years is charged under the Immorality Act; Indian barmen may not serve in ladies' (cocktail) bars, but Indian waiters serve women in hotel bedrooms; a black nuclear physicist is offered a teaching post at a homeland high school – at R55 a month; white family life is considered sacred, while the wives and children of black workers are officially described as 'superfluous appendages'.

WHAT'S NEW IN 1971

- **Tennis:** The South African government refuses a visa application from African-American tennis player Arthur Ashe.
- **Cricket:** All-rounder Mike Proctor, playing for Rhodesia, equals the world record when he scores six consecutive first-class centuries.
- **Uganda:** Burly General Idi Amin ousts President Milton Obote in a military coup.
- **Space:** Two US astronauts, David Scott and James Irwin, drive a lunar vehicle on the Moon's surface; the unmanned Soviet spacecraft *Mars III* makes a soft landing on Mars.
- **Computers:** Intel's new microprocessor, built into a minuscule microchip, promises dramatic decreases in the size (and cost) of computers and massive increases in their capacity.
- The first home **VCR**s go on sale.
- **Britain** introduces decimal coinage.
- The **Greenpeace** environmental group is founded.

Arthur Ashe: refused entry to South Africa.

SOUTH AFRICA in the 20th CENTURY — 1970s

Louis 'Satchmo' Armstrong: will play no more.

1972

UGANDA'S ASIANS, ACCUSED OF 'SABOTAGE', FORCED INTO EXILE

President Idi Amin expels about 50,000 Asians from Uganda, claiming that they have been 'sabotaging the economy'. The Asian community has been a feature of the East African demographic scene for more than a century; most of its members hold British passports and are heading for Britain. Amin overthrew Milton Obote's corrupt socialist regime last year, a move that was generally welcomed by Western nations, but his 'reforms' have amounted to little more than a reign of terror, and international opinion is turning against him.

BORN
South Africa: Tennis player Amanda Coetzer; marathon runner Josiah Thugwane; rugby player Joost van der Westhuizen.

DIED
International: Former Soviet leader Nikita Kruschev; couturier 'Coco' Chanel; composer Igor Stravinsky; jazzman Louis Armstrong. **South Africa:** Novelist and editor Rolfes Dhlomo; Perla Seidle Gibson, the wartime 'Lady in White' who sang to troopships leaving and entering Durban harbour; ballet dancer and choreographer Frank Staff.

ARTS AND ENTERTAINMENT

◆ Top movies: Stanley Kubrick's *A Clockwork Orange*, a portrayal of adolescent savagery set to Beethoven's ninth symphony; Clint Eastwood's pscho-drama *Play Misty for Me*; Eastwood again in *Dirty Harry*. Gene Hackman starts the 70s car-chase vogue with his tearaway performance in *The French Connection*.
◆ Books: Frederick Forsyth's *The Day of the Jackal*; William Blatty's *The Exorcist*. South Africa: Oswald Mtshali's *Sounds of a Cowhide Drum*; Lawrence Green's *A Taste of South-easter*; Karel Schoeman's *Op 'n Eiland (On an Island)*.

Writer Lawrence Green.

Idi Amin: reign of terror.

LOCAL ACTRESS HONOURED

In a rare honour for a South African, Moira Lister is voted stage actress of the year by the Variety Club of Great Britain. Ms Lister, who trained in Johannesburg under Leontine Sagan, moved to London in 1943, appeared in Shakespearean theatre and then turned to less specialized, lighter stage, screen and television roles. She played a season with John Gielgud and Noël Coward in *Present Laughter*, with Rex Harrison in *The Yellow Rolls Royce*, with Vivien Leigh in *The Deep Blue Sea* and with Yul Brynner in *Double Man*. For two years, from 1967 to 1969, she ran her own television show, called *The Very Merry Widow*.

SOUNDS OF THE YEAR
- My Sweet Lord: George Harrison
- Maggie May: Rod Stewart
- It's Too Late: Carole King
- Joy to the World: Three Dog Night
- Ernie: Fastest Milkman in the West: Benny Hill
- Hugh Masekela releases *Union of South Africa*

ON SCREEN
- *The Godfather* (with Marlon Brando)
- *Cabaret* (with Liza Minnelli and Joel Gray)
- *Deliverance*
- *The Poseidon Adventure*

SOUTH AFRICA in the 20th CENTURY
The Seventies

HOSTAGE DRAMA AT OLYMPICS

Munich, 6 September. Eleven members of the Israeli Olympic squad die in a shoot-out at the Munich Games. Early in the morning Palestinian gunmen of the Black September group infiltrate the Israeli compound and kill two men, a weightlifter and the wrestling coach, before taking nine others hostage. West German chancellor Willie Brandt then offers them safe passage, but police open fire as they are boarding the plane. All the hostages, together with four Palestinians and one policeman, perish in the gun battle.

WHAT'S NEW IN 1972

- **Black Peoples' Convention**, an umbrella body for adherents of the loosely structured Black Consciousness Movement, is launched; Steve Biko forms the South African Students' Organization.

Steve Biko addresses students.

- **Apartheid:** The Pietermaritzburg Philharmonia Society loses its government grant because it insists on playing to multiracial audiences; famed American songstress Eartha Kitt is barred from performing in the Bloemfontein city hall.
- **US politics:** Five men, equipped with bugging devices, are arrested while breaking into the Democratic Party offices in Washington's Watergate complex; a major political scandal looms.
- **Germany:** Police round up the notorious Baader-Meinhoff gang of terrorists.
- **Guam:** Japanese soldier Shoichi Yokoi, hiding away for 27 years and unaware that the Second World War has ended, gives himself up.
- **Rhodesia:** Ian Smith's police arrest former premier Garfield Todd and his vocal daughter Judith. They are regarded as a threat to public order.
- **Products:** The pocket calculator; the throw-away plastic wristwatch; the car dashboard cassette player; a supermarket cash register with automatic scanning facility; Nike running shoes.

Hot pants: crude but revealing.

FASHION FOCUSES ON THE OBVIOUS

Calf-length and midi skirts, though elegant enough and hyped by the fashion industry as the ultimate in trendiness, haven't really caught on with the youthful masses: the young and slender want something more exciting. And they get it – hot pants. These tight shorts are unsubtle, crude even, but they do show off the backside and legs. Other popular newcomers are the platform shoe (shades of the 1940s look) and the sexy knee-length boot.

The late Sir Basil Schonland, South Africa's pioneer of radar and radio location of aircraft.

MUSIC SCENE

- This is the year of the teenybopper – the 10-, 11- and 12-year-old fan who idolizes David Cassidy, the too-good-to-be-true Osmonds and, most of all, the Jackson Five and its child star, Michael Jackson.
- Top of the charts: 'American Pie': Don Maclean; 'I'd Like to Teach the World to Sing': The New Seekers; 'Amazing Grace': Royal Scots Dragoon Guards Band; 'Long-haired Lover from Liverpool': Jimmy Osmond; 'Without You': Nilsson; 'Puppy Love': Donny Osmond; 'Heart of Gold': Neil Young.

BORN
South Africa: Cricketer Shaun Pollock.

DIED
International: The Duke of Windsor, formerly King Edward VIII; Kwame Nkrumah, first president of Ghana; poets Ezra Pound and Cecil Day Lewis; anthropologist Louis Leakey; character actress Margaret Rutherford; 400 Rhodesian miners in Wankie colliery explosion. *South Africa:* Trade unionist J.B. Marks; author Lawrence Green (his last book, *When the Journey's Over,* is published during the year); aviation pioneer Pierre van Ryneveld; physicist Sir Basil Schonland.

SOUTH AFRICA in the 20th CENTURY **1970s**

1973

ARABS STRIKE DURING YOM KIPPUR

6 October. Disciplined Egyptian and Syrian forces, backed by Palestinian soldiers, invade the Israeli-held Sinai Peninsula and Golan Heights without warning.

For once, Israeli military intelligence proves faulty: no-one expected an attack on the holiest of Jewish days – Yom Kippur, the Day of Atonement. The fighting is hard and unforgiving on two fronts. The Israelis advance but fail to take either Damascus or the Suez Canal, where their tanks are brought to a standstill. Nevertheless Israel manages, in the end, to keep all the territory captured during the 1967 war.

REMARKABLE WRITER DIES

Kathleen Lindsay, the world's most prolific novelist, dies at her home in Somerset West, Cape. This extraordinary woman wrote 906 books under a variety of pen-names, among them Elizabeth Fenton (stories with a South African setting), Margaret Cameron (historical romances), Mary Richard and June Darnley (modern love stories), Nigel MacKenzie (science fiction), Hugh Desmond (crime and thrillers), Betty Manvers (doctor-nurse romances), and Molly Waring (adventure and romance in exotic places). Ms Lindsay was married four times and widely travelled, but for all that was a true home-lover who ran her house, kept 30 cats and made her own clothes. She wrote only at night, typing with two fingers, and worked on several books at the same time.

Kathleen Lindsay.

> 'Television has brought the brutalities of war into the comfort of the living room. Vietnam was lost in the living rooms of America, not on the battlefields....'
> Journalist Marshall McLuhan

ARNIE GRABS WORLD TITLE

Sheer guts and determination – and a measure of luck – earn South African boxer Arnie Taylor the world bantamweight crown. Taylor is battered by his opponent, Mexican Romeo Anaya, in the early rounds of the fight at the Rand stadium, and is dropped in the eighth. But Anaya is slow to retire to a neutral corner and the bell saves Taylor, who recovers splendidly to win by a knockout in the 14th.

CEASEFIRE IN VIETNAM

Intense pressure from large sections of the American people, and especially from the youth, forces President Richard Nixon to abandon the war in Vietnam. A cease-fire, and a freeze on troop movements, is agreed at the Paris peace talks on 23 January and US troops pull out, leaving the South Vietnamese forces and their civilian supporters to face Ho Chi Minh's all-conquering North Vietnamese army and its Viet Cong allies.

Civilians bear the brunt of a nightmare war waged, since the early 1940s, for control of Vietnam.

SOUTH AFRICA in the 20th CENTURY
The Seventies

BUTHELEZI 'ABHORS' APARTHEID

Chief Gatsha (Mangosuthu) Buthelezi, speaking at Howard University, the US's best-known African-American academic institution, defends his decision to work within the 'degrading' apartheid system, saying he 'abhors' segregation but there's no other option open to him. He urges anti-apartheid activists to give American firms in South Africa a deadline to improve their workers' wages.

Back at home, four white mayors of Reef towns boycott a church service because the black mayor and mayoress of Soweto are due to attend; and four young coloured women are charged by railway police for using a 'white' exit at Cape Town's Salt River station.

ARTS AND LEISURE

- **Top films:** *The Sting*, with Paul Newman and Robert Redford (and a haunting Scott Joplin ragtime score); *The Exorcist*, with Linda Blair; *Sleeper*, with Woody Allen; *Paper Moon*, with Ryan O'Neal and daughter Tatum.
- **Hit singles:** 'Tie a Yellow Ribbon': Dawn; 'Welcome Home': Peters and Lee; 'Merry Christmas Everybody': Slade; 'I Love You Love Me Love': Gary Glitter; 'You're So Vain': Carly Simon; 'Goodbye Yellow Brick Road': Elton John.
- **Shows:** Des and Dawn Lindberg stage South Africa's first multi-racial musical production, *Godspell*.
- **Sport:** South Africa's colour bar is breached when African-American Bob Foster fights local boy Pierre Fourie. Golfer Hugh Biocchi wins the Swiss Open.

Apartheid at work: coloured people are arrested for using a 'white' exit.

> 'A lie can be half-way around the world before the truth has got its boots on.'
> British politician James Callaghan, on the media

WHAT'S NEW IN 1973

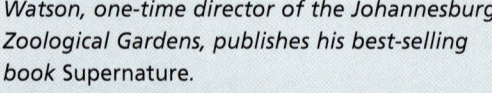

- **SA politics:** Eugène Terre'Blanche and six like-minded colleagues, meeting in a Heidelberg (Transvaal) garage, form the ultra right-wing Afrikaner Weerstandsbeweging (AWB). The Democratic Party is launched by Theo Gerdener.
- **Publishing:** South African naturalist and author Lyall Watson, one-time director of the Johannesburg Zoological Gardens, publishes his best-selling book *Supernature*.
- **OPEC:** The Organization of Petroleum-Exporting Countries closes ranks and hikes prices, provoking a world-wide energy crisis.
- **Products:** The first colour office copier is manufactured by Canon in Japan; the first disposable lighter, by Bic, in France.
- **Australia:** The aboriginal community gets the vote.
- The phrase **child abuse** enters the language.

DIED

International: Painter Pablo Picasso; Chilean leader Salvador Allende, after a CIA-inspired coup; former US president Lyndon B. Johnson; Israeli statesman David Ben-Gurion; playwright and entertainer Noël Coward; poet W.H. Auden; Kung Fu guru and movie star Bruce Lee; actors Bette Grable and Edward G. Robinson; writers Nancy Mitford, Pearl S. Buck and Bloemfontein-born J.R.R. Tolkien. *South Africa:* Expatriate poet and writer William Plomer; expatriate dancer John Cranko; artist Maggie Laubser; actor Lawrence Harvey; cricketer Herbie Taylor.

SOUTH AFRICA in the 20th CENTURY — 1970s

1974

LOCAL WOMAN PRODUCES SIX OF THE BEST

Cape Town, 11 January. Mrs Susan Rosenkowitz gives birth to six healthy babies – David, Nicky, Jason, Emma, Grant and Elizabeth – at the city's famed Groote Schuur hospital. Their combined weight is just 11.04 kilograms.

The Rosenkowitz children will remain the world's only living sextuplets until their sixth birthday – on the exact date of which, by an extraordinary coincidence, a woman gives birth to six babies in Florence, Italy.

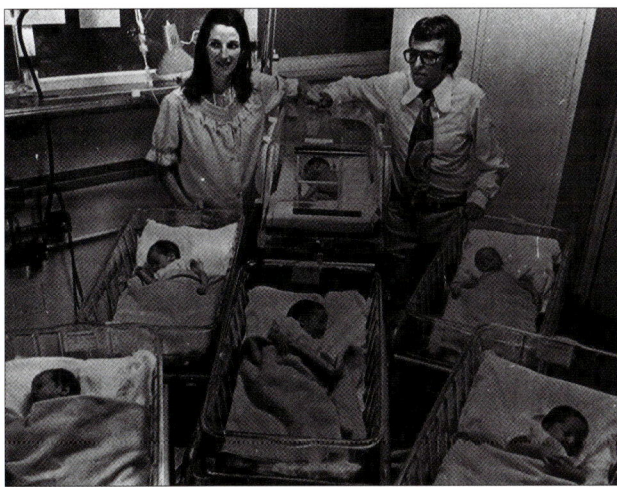

The Rosenkowitz six.

LIONS TEACH BOKS A LESSON

Willie-John McBride's British Lions give South Africans a sharp lesson in the art of 15-man running rugby and leave the country as only the third team in the game's annals to record a full-length unbeaten tour.

When the home side is defeated in the first Test, at Newlands, the selectors panic and field a total of 33 different players in the four remaining internationals, three of which the Lions win. The fourth, after a disputed South African try in the dying moments, is drawn.

Major elements of the Lions' success are imaginative generalship and brilliance at half-back. Writes a French correspondent: 'The price of a Springbok skin, once so highly prized, is of very little value at this time.... Who wants a goat's head above his mantelpiece?'

SPORTING HIGHLIGHTS

◆ Muhammad 'I'm the Greatest' Ali regains the world heavyweight boxing championship when he defeats George Foreman in the steamy heat of Zaïre (the fight becomes known as the 'rumble in the jungle') by knockout in the eighth.
◆ Top South African golfers Bobby Cole and Dale Hayes win the pairs World Cup.
◆ Germany defeat Holland to win the Soccer World Cup.

THE ARTS IN SA

◆ Cape Town-born pianist Abdullah Ibrahim, formerly known as Dollar Brand, returns from the US to record *Manenberg*, a fine mix of jazz, Eastern music and South African *marabi*. Ibrahim began his career with the Shantytown Sextet, later playing with the Jazz Epistles. He left the country in the mid-1960s, caught the attention of the great Duke Ellington, performed several times at the Newport Jazz Festival and toured to acclaim in the US and Europe.
◆ Acclaimed writer Nadine Gordimer follows her prize-winning novel *Guest of Honour* with *The Conservationist*, which wins the prestigious Booker McConnel award. Playwright Athol Fugard stages his semi-documentary *Statements after an Arrest under the Immorality Act*. Poet Mongane Wally Serote publishes his verse volume *Tsetlo*.

WHAT'S NEW IN 1974

Richard Nixon: resigns to avoid impeachment for 'high crimes'.

◆ **US politics:** Embattled US President Richard Nixon, in deep trouble over the Watergate affair, resigns in order to avoid impeachment for 'high crimes and misdemeanors'.
◆ **Opened in South Africa:** The 1820 Settlers' Memorial in Grahamstown; the Market Theatre, Johannesburg.
◆ **China:** An ancient 'army' of 6,000 terracotta soldiers is discovered in a burial mound.
◆ **US:** AT&T becomes the first large corporation to ban discrimination against gay people.
◆ **Ethiopia**'s Emperor Haile Selassie is deposed.

'There will be no whitewash at the White House.'
President Richard Nixon, as the Watergate scandal gathers momentum

SOUTH AFRICA in the 20th CENTURY

The Seventies

BORN
South Africa: Athlete Hezekiel Sepeng.

DIED
International: Argentinian politician Juan Peron; jazzman Duke Ellington; Hollywood mogul Sam Goldwyn; aviation pioneer Charles Lindbergh.
South Africa: Theatrical pioneer and producer Leontine Sagan.

Gorgeous Anneline Kriel, 19 years old, lifts white South African spirits when she wins the Miss World title.

TOP OF THE POPS
- You Won't Find Another Fool Like Me: The New Seekers
- The Lord's Prayer: Sister Janet Mead
- Gonna Make You a Star: David Essex
- Evie: Stevie Wright
- Tubular Bells: Mike Oldfield
- Lonely This Christmas: Mud
- Billy, Don't Be a Hero: Paper Lace

SA'S 'PEACE OFFENSIVE' GETS UNDER WAY

The South African government's policy of 'détente' – the quest for an understanding with, and acceptance by, African nations – gets into top gear with a flurry of diplomatic activity. Prime Minister John Vorster visits Liberia; delegations from the Ivory Coast and Central African Republic visit South Africa; and foreign minister Hilgard Muller meets his Zambian, Botswanan and Tanzanian counterparts in Lusaka. Vorster also meets Zambia's Kenneth Kaunda, in a railway carriage on the Victoria Falls bridge, in a determined effort to resolve the decade-long Rhodesian crisis that has been bedevilling relations between the countries of southern Africa. Rhodesian rebel leader Ian Smith, however, remains stubborn, and the attempt fails.

ARTS AND LEISURE

◆ Joan Brickhill, the South African actress, costume designer and producer, stages her *Meropa/KwaZulu* at the London Palladium as part of the Royal Command Performance – the first such honour extended to local artistes. Ms Brickhill and her husband, the impresario Louis Burke, are known for their spectacular musical extravaganzas.
◆ South African actor John Kani wins a Tony award

1975

SA FORCES ENTER ANGOLA

South African troops move into south-central Angola to protect the Unita stronghold of Huambo – three months before Angola formally assumes independence.

The incursion is part of a complex strategy in which Holden Roberto's FNLA and Jonas Savimbi's Unita, in collaboration with the United States, France and Kenneth Kaunda's Zambia, have been fighting to prevent the Marxist MPLA from coming to power in Luanda.

Initially, South Africa appears to be a reluctant party to the conspiracy but Washington's offer of helicopters, spotter aircraft and enriched uranium tips the balance. The South African government, however, seems unaware that it has been negotiating only with the US State Department and CIA, and that the US Congress, the ultimate authority, is unlikely to approve the deal.

France, which covets the oil of the Cabinda enclave, also weighs in with some bribes – Mirage fighter aircraft, submarines and the promise to build nuclear plants in the Republic – but withdraws the offers when it cannot match the American bid. In the event, South Africa's intervention ends in humiliating withdrawal – after an apparent reversal of US policy. The abandoned 'invasion' has international repercussions, among them condemnation by the OAU.

South African troops on the border: withdrawal under US pressure.

SOUTH AFRICA in the 20th CENTURY 1970s

for his role in the US production of Athol Fugard's *Sizwe Bansi is Dead*.

◆ Poet and author Breyten Breytenbach, who has spent the past few years in Europe, is arrested for re-entering South Africa on a false passport. He is convicted under the Terrorism Act and sentenced to seven years in prison.

◆ Films: The year's biggest box-office draw, and the young Steven Spielberg's first major success, is the shock-horror movie *Jaws*. Other features on circuit: *The Rocky Horror Picture Show*, and the award-winning *One Flew Over the Cuckoo's Nest*.

◆ Hit singles: 'Sailing': Rod Stewart; 'Bohemian Rhapsody': Queen; 'Bye Bye Baby': Bay City Rollers; 'Stand By Your Man': Tammy Wynette; 'I Can't Give You Anything but Love': Stylistics.

◆ Books: André Brink's *An Instant in the Wind*; James Clavell's *Shogun*; David Niven's *Bring on the Empty Horses*; Jack Higgins's *The Eagle Has Landed*. Miriam Tlali becomes the first black South African woman to have a novel published when her debut book, *Muriel at the Metropolitan*, goes on sale.

Novelist Miriam Tlali.

SOUTH AFRICANS GET READY FOR TELEVISION

The South African Broadcasting Corporation's new 35-storey complex at Auckland Park, Johannesburg, is complete and hour-long test patterns (later extended to two hours) are being beamed each day in preparation for South Africa's first television service. Crowds gather on the pavement outside city showrooms to stare at the screens; thousands of sets are sold; rooftops grow antennae, and newspaper columns are crammed with advice on everything from model sizes to television meals. The service is due to be inaugurated on 5 January next year – over two decades after TV came to the rest of the world.

DIED

International: Former Ethiopian emperor Haile Selassie; Spanish dictator Francisco Franco; Saudi Arabia's King Feisal; historian Arnold Toynbee; racing driver Graham Hill; scientist Sir Julian Huxley; composers Dmitri Shostakovich and Arthur Bliss; shipping tycoon Aristotle Onassis; author P.G. Wodehouse; singer Josephine Baker; actress Susan Hayward; actor James Robertson Justice. **South Africa:** Trade unionist George Champion (born Mhlongo); advocate and activist Bram Fischer; Black Consciousness revolutionary David Maphgumzana Sibeko; artist Alexis Preller.

Fugard's Sizwe Bansi is Dead*: a Tony for John Kani.*

WHAT'S NEW IN 1975

◆ **South Africa:** The Reform Party (later renamed the Progressive Reform Party) is formed by dissident members of the United Party.

◆ **Southern Africa:** Mozambique and Angola become independent nations.

◆ **Firsts for women:** Margaret Thatcher is elected leader of Britain's Conservative Party; Japan's Junko Tabei leads a 15-woman expedition to the top of Mount Everest.

◆ **Vietnam:** Saigon falls to Viet Cong forces; American citizens and a few chosen locals are evacuated from the US embassy as thousands scramble for places on the departing helicopters.

◆ The **'space race'** ends with a link-up between the Soviet Union's Soyuz 19 and the US's Apollo 18.

◆ **Office:** The first laser printer (IBM 3800) is unveiled.

◆ **Arthur Ashe**, who was banned in 1971 from playing tennis in South Africa because of his skin colour, becomes the first black man to win the Wimbledon Men's Singles.

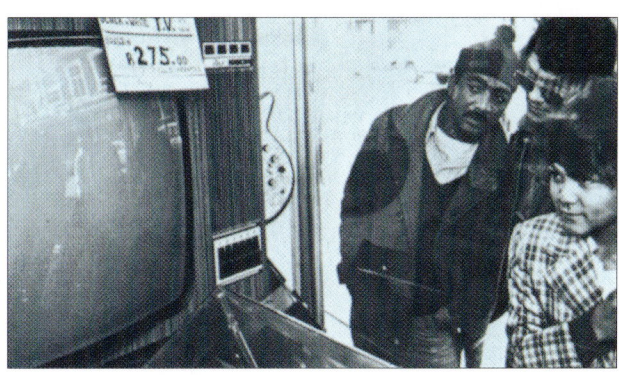

The small screen comes to South Africa – 20 years late.

SOUTH AFRICA in the 20th CENTURY

1976

TELEVISION COMES TO SOUTH AFRICA – AT LAST

5 January. South Africa finally enters the modern age when the first television programmes are beamed from Johannesburg's spanking new, technically advanced Auckland Park broadcasting complex. The service begins transmitting at 6.00 each evening (3.00 p.m. on Saturdays) and offers 37 hours of viewing a week. Half the programmes are in Afrikaans, half in English – and there are no commercials: licence fees, at R36 apiece, are the SABC's sole source of television revenue.

The country is enchanted by the novelty; presenter Mike Hobbs and newsreaders Nigel Kane and Michael de Morgan take on instant star quality; most popular of the early programmes are *The Villagers*, an ongoing story about the ordinary folk of a gold-mining community (the script, by John Cundill, is quite excellent), and *Willem*, which features a rather whimsical private eye.

Tennis star Bjorn Borg (left): youngest Wimbledon champion.

> 'Twenty years ago, when Bantu Education was introduced, our fathers said: "Half a loaf is better than no loaf". But we say: "Half a gram of poison is just as killing as a whole gram".'
> Soweto Students' Representative Council

WHAT'S NEW IN 1976

♦ **SA politics:** The Transkei 'homeland' is granted full independence.
♦ **Apartheid:** Cape Town's imposing Nico Malan theatre complex is opened to all races, but petty apartheid continues: black sun-lovers are ordered off Cape beaches, turned away from religious services (in Bellville); an Indian doctor is forbidden to help operate on a white child; a white barmaid is fined for serving a black journalist.
♦ **Pact:** SA signs an economic, scientific and industrial pact with Israel.
♦ **China:** A massive earthquake kills some 250,000 people.
♦ The **Apple** computer company is founded.
♦ The phrase **junk food** enters the language.

THE LEISURE SCENE

♦ **Sport:** Black South African golfer Vincent Tshabalala wins the French Open with a 69, 70, 66, 67. Back problems, however, will stunt his promising career. Blond Swedish hunk Bjorn Borg, 20, becomes the youngest tennis player to win the Wimbledon Men's Singles. The South African government eases sporting apartheid, permitting multiracial teams to represent the country; sporting clubs remain segregated.
♦ **Top films:** *Rocky*, with droopy-eyed newcomer Sylvester Stallone; *All the President's Men*, with Robert Redford and Dustin Hoffman; *Taxi Driver*, with Robert de Niro and child actress Jodie Foster.

CRAZES

♦ Macramé
♦ Pet rocks
♦ Skateboards
♦ Bean bags

♦ **Hit singles:** 'Mississippi': Pussycat; 'Don't Go Breaking My Heart': Elton John and Kiki Dee; 'Save Your Kisses For Me': Brotherhood of Man; 'When a Child is Born': Johnny Mathis; 'Under the Moon of Love': Shawaddywaddy; 'Fernando': Abba.

DIED

International: Chinese leader Mao Tse-tung; mystery novelist Agatha Christie; actresses Sybil Thorndike and Edith Evans; composer Benjamin Britten; singer and black activist Paul Robeson; tycoons John Paul Getty and Howard Hughes; British military commander Bernard Montgomery; film-maker Carol Reed. *South Africa:* Dancer Gary Burne; comic actor Sid James; Xhosa poet James Ranisi Jolobe; author Stuart Cloete; musician Elsie Hall.

STUDENTS RISE, SOWETO BURNS

16 June. Large parts of Soweto are in flames after students take to the streets en masse. Hundreds are killed, thousands injured, vehicles destroyed, buildings gutted in the worst riots since the apartheid regime came to power nearly three decades ago. What began this morning as a peaceful march to a planned rally, at the Orlando stadium, turns into a stampede when police lob teargas into the crowd. Shots are fired, stones thrown and, as news of trouble spreads, the barricades go up. 'My patience is at an end', police commissioner J.F. Visser announces. Prime Minister B.J. Vorster tells security force chiefs to restore order 'at all costs'. The Soweto uprising lasts three days, and spreads to other centres, continuing in varying degrees of intensity for eight months. The spark that ignites the trouble, a commission of inquiry will later find, is a Transvaal provincial education authority directive that Afrikaans – a language unfamiliar to thousands of blacks – be used as a medium of instruction in black secondary schools. For youngsters trying to make headway within an inferior schooling system, this was the last straw. Afrikaans, says a social worker, 'is the language of pass laws, permits and police'. A protester calls it a 'tribal language'. But of course the crisis has deeper roots: it goes to the heart of South Africa's sickness – to a 'Bantu' educational system deliberately designed to retard black advancement, to brutal segregation and the denial of fundamental civic and political rights.

Youngsters on the march: Afrikaans 'the last straw'.

'The most potent weapon in the hands of the aggressor is the mind of the oppressed.'
Steve Biko

Hector Petersen is carried from the fray – the picture that caught the world's eye.

Police vehicles move in to restore order.

173

SOUTH AFRICA in the 20th CENTURY

1977

STEVE BIKO DIES IN POLICE CUSTODY

Pretoria, 12 September. The young Black Consciousness activist Steve Biko, in police custody since 18 August, dies of head injuries.

Biko was arrested in Port Elizabeth 26 days ago and, according to justice minister Jimmy Kruger, proved troublesome, threatened a hunger strike and feigned illness. The district surgeon and other examining doctors 'could not find anything wrong'. The prisoner's death, added Mr Kruger, 'leaves me cold'.

The truth, however, appears to be much harsher. Biko was held under Section 6 of the Terrorism Act but never formally charged. Over a three-week period he was stripped, placed in leg-irons, interrogated and beaten. Just when and where the fatal blow was inflicted have not been established. Major Harold Snyman, in charge of the five-man interrogation team, later maintains that the prisoner had banged his head against a wall during a scuffle.

Biko's condition deteriorated to the point where doctors felt moved to recommend hospital treatment. Naked, shackled and unconscious, he was bundled into the back of a police Land Rover and driven the 1,500 kilometres to Pretoria. And there, in the words of Sydney Kentridge, counsel for the Biko family, he died 'a miserable and lonely death on a mat on a stone floor of a prison cell'.

Steve Biko: lonely death.

FAREWELL TO THE LAST OF THE LINE

Cape Town, 6 September. The military band strikes up 'Auld Lang Syne', and the dockside crowd takes up the poignant refrain, as the great ocean liner makes her stately way out to sea. She is *Windsor Castle*, flagship and sole surviving member of the Union-Castle passenger fleet, and she is making her last voyage. Reflects an old man with memories of happy days: 'It's like the end of a way of life.'

Union-Castle's mailships – *Athlone, Stirling Castle, Dunottar, Cape Town, Durban, Dunvegan, Pretoria, Arundel, Windsor, Carnarvon, Warwick, Winchester, Pendennis* and many others – are recalled with nostalgic affection by thousands of British and South African travellers.

The service was born in 1900, when Sir Donald Currie merged his Castle Mail Packets with the rival Union company, and for the next 77 years it carried more South Africans between England and southern Africa than all the other lines combined. Its vessels also served with honour in the Second World War: some of the biggest and best of them were lent to the British government as armed merchant cruisers and, later, as troopships. *Edinburgh Castle*, was converted into an auxiliary aircraft-carrier.

With peace, the liners returned to their family. Some of them became 'settler ships', bringing nearly 30,000 people to South Africa as new immigrants. But by the end of the 1960s the airlines, offering cheaper and faster services, had eroded all but a trickle of the sea-going passenger trade.

Grand lady of the sea: **Windsor Castle** *on her last voyage.*

SOUTH AFRICA in the 20th CENTURY — 1970s

THE KING IS DEAD

Memphis, Tennessee, 18 August. Millions of fans around the world mourn the death of country and rock superstar Elvis Presley. More than 80,000 visitors pay their last respects at Graceland, the singer's mansion home where the body lies in state (so great is the press of people that fewer than half are able to file past the coffin) and there are unprecedented scenes of mass grief at the funeral. Wreaths in the shape of guitars and hound-dogs decorate the cemetery.

The cause of death appears to have been a drug overdose: insiders say the singer was addicted to tranquillizers and barbiturates.

Presley burst onto the pop charts 21 years ago to hold his vast and growing audience spellbound with numbers such as 'Heartbreak Hotel', 'Hound Dog' and 'Jailhouse Rock'. His hip-thrusting stage performances, loaded with sexual innuendo, earned him the nickname 'Elvis the Pelvis'. He later changed his style, to that of balladeer, and his appearance: the clothes became extravagant, the body thickened, eventually to the point of grossness. But he remained the 'King'.

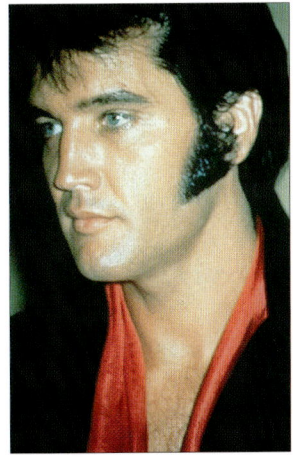

Elvis Presley: drug addiction.

> 'That was a great game of golf, fellas.'
> Crooner Bing Crosby's last words

WHITE POLITICS CHANGES FACE – BUT NOT COLOUR

The once-dominant but now ailing United Party (UP), wracked by internal dissension, finally disbands to become the short-lived South African Party, which changes its name to the New Republic Party. UP leader Sir De Villiers Graaff retires. The liberal Progressive Reform Party, which has been absorbing defectors from the waning UP, and whose most prominent member is parliamentarian Helen Suzman, becomes the Progressive Federal Party.

> Quote of the year: 'There is no reason for any individual to have a computer in their home'
> Ken Olsen, president of Digital Equipment Corporation

WHAT'S NEW IN 1977

- The first **mass-produced computer**, Apple 11, is launched.
- **Astronomy:** South African stargazers collaborate with US colleagues to discover rings around the planet Uranus.
- **Canary Islands:** Two Boeing 747s collide on the ground killing 574 – the worst disaster in aviation history.
- **Cricket:** Australian Kerry Packer signs up 35 top players, for a series of one-day internationals, to revolutionize the game.
- **Surfing:** South Africa's Shaun Thompson takes on the best (in Hawaii) to win the world surfing championship.

Shaun Thompson: riding high to take world championship.

The National Party is returned to office at the general election. A total of 17 extra-parliamentary organizations and two newspapers are banned. Bophuthatswana, a cluster of seven separate areas scattered over the western Transvaal, the northern Cape and southern Orange Free State, is granted the status of an independent republic. The UN Security Council imposes an embargo on the supply of arms to South Africa.

BORN
South Africa: Cricketers Makhaya Ntini and Paul Adams.

DIED
International: Stage and screen lose some of their finest during the year, including comic actors Charlie Chaplin and Groucho Marx; straight actor Peter Finch; actress Joan Crawford; director Roberto Rossellini; playwright Terence Rattigan; crooner Bing Crosby; diva Maria Callas; rock star Marc Bolan. Also politician Anthony Eden; rocket pioneer Wernher von Braun; writer Vladimir Nabokov. *South Africa:* Novelist Joy Packer; rugby player Hennie Muller.

SOUTH AFRICA in the 20th CENTURY

THE LEISURE SCENE

◆ Sci-fi and special effects pull in the cinema audiences, with *Star Wars* and Steven Spielberg's mystical *Close Encounters of the Third Kind* leading the way. Woody Allen's *Annie Hall* grabs two major Oscars; *Saturday Night Fever*, with young John Travolta in the lead, sets new standards of dance. Television's *The Waltons* and African-American saga *Roots* capture the heart of the home viewer.

◆ Hit singles: 'Mull of Kintyre': Wings; 'When I Need You': Leo Sayer; and three negatives: 'Don't Cry for Me, Argentina': Julie Covington; 'Don't Give Up on Us': David Soul, and 'Don't Leave Me This Way': Thelma Houston.

◆ Books: *A Hundred Years of Solitude* by Gabriel Garcia Marquez; *The Thorn Birds* by Colleen McCullough.

1978

VORSTER OUT, BOTHA IN AFTER 'INFO SCANDAL'

P.W. Botha replaces John Vorster as South African premier following revelations about large-scale misuse of State funds.

Senior members of the Department of Information are said to be involved in covert propaganda and other irregular projects. Vorster is appointed State President; Connie Mulder, the Minister of Information, resigns.

Earlier, relentless investigation by the *Rand Daily Mail* and other newspapers led to an official inquiry by Mr Justice Mostert, and then to the appointment of the Erasmus Commission. Vorster was cleared of direct responsibility for the 'Info Scandal', but it seems he had known of the irregularities. The affair damaged his standing in the National Party and in the country at large. He is also said to be in declining health.

Pieter Willem Botha, the former Minister of Defence, is reputed to be one of the government's leading hawks. His accession to the premiership coincides with serious internal and regional threats to the white regime: the newly independent status of Mozambique and Angola, guerrilla incursions into South West Africa (Namibia) and the disintegration of rebel Rhodesia have brought new impetus to the South African liberation struggle. 'We shall go forward in faith and humble obedience to God,' Botha says after his election by the NP parliamentary caucus. 'We will not bend our knees before Marxism or revolution.'

LUNG CANCER KILLS PAC LEADER

Robert Sobukwe, founder and first president of the Pan-Africanist Congress (PAC), succumbs to lung cancer at the age of 54.

A keen sportsman in his youth – he played rugby, and was Eastern Province (black) tennis champion – Sobukwe was Secretary of the ANC Youth League but later rejected the movement's moderate stance, its commitment to peaceful change and non-racial character. He became a militant Africanist who believed in the 'liberation of Africa within our lifetime' and, along with other radicals, resigned in 1958 to form the PAC. The new body rapidly gained support and was strong enough, by 1960, to mount massive anti-pass law protests – a campaign culminating in the Sharpeville massacre and the banning of extra-parliamentary organizations.

Sobukwe was imprisoned, and at one point found himself sewing mailbags with Nelson Mandela. While in prison, he also took an external degree in economics. On his conditional release in 1969 he was restricted to the Kimberley area and, in 1975, qualified in law.

P.W. Botha: new premier.

John Travolta in Saturday Night Fever: *new standards in dance.*

> 'Scornful of patient organization building, the PAC believed the people were ready to respond to a call to arms. "Show the light, and the masses will find the way".'
> *Robert Sobukwe, leader of the PAC*

SOUTH AFRICA in the 20th CENTURY — 1970s

WHAT'S NEW IN 1978

- **Apartheid:** The SA government gives the go-ahead for theatres, places of worship and, for serious cases, hospitals to open their doors to all races.
- The **Arab-Israeli peace accord** signed at Camp David, Maryland.
- **Beauty pageant:** South Africa's Margaret Gardiner wins the Miss Universe title, in Mexico City.
- **Jonestown, Guyana:** More than 900 men, women and children, followers of People's Temple cult leader the 'Reverend' Jim Jones, kill themselves in the biggest peacetime mass suicide of the modern era.
- **Oldham, England:** Louise Brown, the world's first 'test-tube' baby, is born.

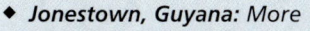

South Africa's Miss Universe, Margaret Gardiner.

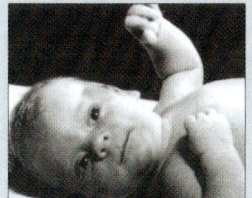

Baby Louise Brown.

The serried ranks of the Jonestown dead.

'PAPWA' DIES IN OBSCURITY

Sewsunker 'Papwa' Sewgolum, the first South African golfer to win international honours, dies at his home in Natal. Largely self-taught (though Gary Player became something of a mentor) and with a wildly unorthodox style, Sewgolum won the Dutch Open title on three occasions. He was also prominent on the local circuit – despite the apartheid barriers. On one occasion he was obliged to receive the victor's trophy in the pouring rain, while officials and other players sheltered in the clubhouse. He enjoyed few of the rewards of sporting success, and died a poor and largely forgotten man.

RHODESIA IN TURMOIL; PEACE PLAN CONDEMNED

Ian Smith's rebel Rhodesian regime reaches an understanding with moderate black politician Bishop Abel Muzorewa to bring about majority rule. Observers, including Andrew Young, the US ambassador to the United Nations, condemn the deal as unworkable: it excludes both Joshua Nkomo and Robert Mugabe, the two nationalist leaders who matter.

Meanwhile the six-year bush war assumes new dimensions of horror when 12 Britons – missionaries and their families – are massacred at the Elim Pentecostal mission station in the mountainous eastern part of the country. Five months later an Air Rhodesia Viscount is downed by a SAM-7 heat-seeking missile near Lake Kariba – the second such incident. Eighteen of those on board survive the impact, 10 of whom are shot to death by a unit of Nkomo's guerrillas on the ground.

Caretaker Abel Muzorewa.

Robert Mugabe.

Joshua Nkomo.

SOUTH AFRICA in the 20th CENTURY

The Seventies

WHITE WOMAN SEES THE DARKER SIDE

A 44-year-old white Sea Point woman is ordered off 'Whites-only' buses, treated as a maid, and has a broken marriage – because a brain tumour is making her skin turn dark. Mrs Rita Hoefling says: 'Now I know what apartheid is like. I cannot begin to count the times I've been thrown off buses. A travelling salesman once came to the door and asked if he could see the "Madam". When I told him I owned the house, he said he did not like sarcastic maids.' She has been shunned by society, her friends, her husband and son, and cannot find a job, because of her new skin colour.

Rita Hoefling (left).

SPORTING HIGHLIGHTS

♦ Motorcycling: South African Kork Ballington, riding for the Kawasaki works team, wins the world 250 cc and 350 championships.
♦ Cricket: Fast bowler Garth le Roux is adjudged Man of the Series in Kerry Packer's ground-breaking world tournament of one-day internationals in Australia.
♦ Soccer: Argentina wins the World Cup, in Brazil, defeating the Netherlands 3-1 in extra time.
♦ Tennis: Martina Navratilova defeats Chris Evert to win the Wimbledon Ladies' Singles. Bjorn Borg captures the Men's Singles title for the third year in a row.
♦ Endurance: South African granny Mavis Hutchinson walks from Los Angeles to New York, for charity.

BORN
South Africa: Footballer Benni McCarthy.

DIED
International: Israeli leader Golda Meir; Kenyan leader Jomo Kenyatta; anthropologist Margaret Mead; singer and songwriter Jacques Brel; cricketer Herbert Sutcliffe. *South Africa:* Activist Moses Kotane; political leader Robert Sobukwe.

TOP OF THE POPS
● Rivers of Babylon: Boney M
● Mary's Boy Child: Boney M
● You're the One I Want: John Travolta, Olivia Newton-John
● Stayin' Alive: Bee Gees
● You Light Up My Life: Debby Boone

1979

BREAKTHROUGH ON THE LABOUR FRONT

In perhaps the most progressive move of the apartheid era, the Nationalist government accepts most of the findings of the Wiehahn and Riekert commissions appointed to investigate the labour situation. The commissions recommend the maximum use of all available skills and the removal of almost every law that discriminates against black workers.

Job reservation has steadily been crumbling under the pressure of market forces. Now black South Africans are to be brought fully into the economy through better training, integration and the elimination of the wage gap through collective bargaining.

BOTHA PLANS THE FUTURE

Durban, August. Premier P.W. Botha outlines a 12-point plan – the key elements of what he calls a 'total strategy' for the security and gradual transformation of South Africa. The programme, he says, will counter the 'total onslaught' that has been mounted against South Africa. The plan includes the recognition of the rights of ethnic groups, the creation of a 'constellation of southern African states', the removal of 'unnecessary discrimination' and, most important, a new constitution.

YOUNGEST TO SWIM THE CHANNEL

A world mark is set by 12-year-old South African Kevin Anderson when he becomes the youngest person to swim the English Channel. The record is shattered the very next day by an even younger British boy.

LOCAL DRIVERS ARE CHAMPIONS

East London-born Jody Scheckter, driving for the Ferrari works team, wins at Monza to become South Africa's first world motor-racing champion. Remarkably Scheckter, 27, had never personally owned a car until earlier this year, when he bought a second-hand Rolls Royce.

Not to be outdone, South Africa's Désirée Wilson is the first woman ever to win a Formula 1 race when she passes the finishing line at Brand's Hatch, England. Shortly afterwards she wins the 1,000-kilometre Monza Endurance Classic.

World champion Jody Scheckter.

SOUTH AFRICA in the 20th CENTURY — 1970s

WHAT'S NEW IN 1979

♦ **World leaders:** B.J. Vorster resigns as South African state president; Bishop Abel Muzorewa becomes premier of interim Zimbabwe-Rhodesia; Margaret Thatcher becomes Britain's first woman prime minister.

Dennis and Maggie Thatcher.

♦ **Venda** is granted full independence.
♦ **Honours:** SA-born Alan Cormack shares a Nobel Prize (with Briton Godfrey Hounsfield) for the development of the CAT scanner; SA-born businessman Michael Edwardes is knighted for rescuing the ailing British Leyland company.
♦ **Uganda:** Tyrant Idi Amin is overthrown.
♦ **Products:** Sony launches the Walkman, the first personal stereo; Nike markets the first air-cushioned trainers.

HIT SINGLES
- YMCA: The Village People
- I Don't Like Mondays: Boomtown Rats
- My Sharona: The Knack
- Do Ya Think I'm Sexy: Rod Stewart
- Sunday Girl: Blondie
- Bright Eyes: Art Garfunkel

SUN CITY TAKES SHAPE

Work begins on Sol Kerzner's multi-million rand Sun City project north of Rustenburg, Transvaal. The vast complex, which grows to include three hotels, a casino, swimming pools, a large man-made lake, spacious grounds planted with an enormous variety of indigenous and exotic flora, and an international standard golf course, is set near the rugged Pilanesberg range in the 'independent' state of Bophuthatswana. Gambling is illegal in South Africa, but the 'independent' republics, creations of the apartheid regime and poverty stricken for the most part, have their own laws. Casinos are obvious money-spinners and more are likely to be built.

MIXED MESSAGES ON RACE

The government relaxes the Group Areas Act and will permit the races to mix at a wide range of venues, including drive-ins, hospitals, libraries, fêtes and restaurants. Meanwhile, six residents of upmarket Sandton are being prosecuted for allowing their domestic workers to have their children stay with them for the Christmas holidays.

ARTS AND LEISURE

♦ **Screen:** Biggest of the year's box-office draws are the space thriller *Alien* (with Sigourney Weaver) and three soul-searching movies about the Vietnam war: Francis Ford Coppola's moody *Apocalypse Now* (with Martin Sheen and Marlon Brando); *Coming Home* (with John Voight); and *The Deer Hunter* (with Robert de Niro).
♦ **Stage:** Play of the year is Peter Shaffer's *Amadeus*, a brilliant profile of the musical genius Mozart. South African playwright Zakes Mda publishes three works: *Dark Voices Ring*, *Dead End*, and the award-winning *The Hill*. Also staged is Maishe Maponya's *The Hungry Earth*.
♦ **Music:** British punk rocker Sid Vicious is found dead in his Greenwich Village, New York, apartment. Elton John is the first of the West's rock stars to perform in the Soviet Union.
♦ **Books:** Steven King's *The Dead Zone*; John le Carré's *Smiley's People*; André Brink's *A Dry White Season*; Etienne le Roux's *Magersfontein, O Magersfontein*; Nadine Gordimer's *Burger's Daughter*.

DIED

International: Former admiral and mentor to Prince Charles, Lord Mountbatten, killed by an IRA bomb; aviation engineer and inventor Barnes Wallis; actresses Mary Pickford and Jean Seberg; actor John Wayne; singer Gracie Fields; royal dressmaker Norman Hartnell; politician and financier Nelson Rockefeller.
South Africa: Artist and writer Gladys Mgudlandu.

Sun City: a leisure resort in the making.

1980s

Charles and Diana – engaged.

TAKING OFFICE
1980: Robert Mugabe, as premier of Zimbabwe (formerly Rhodesia).
1981: Veteran Hollywood actor Ronald Reagan, as US President.
1985: Mikhail Gorbachev, as Soviet leader.

TARGETED
1981: By lone gunmen: Pope John Paul II; US president Ronald Reagan; both are wounded but survive.

KILLED
1980: Beatle John Lennon, by a deranged fan.
1981: Egyptian leader Anwar Sadat, by Muslim extremists.
1982: Exiled SA liberation activist Ruth First, by a letter-bomb, in Maputo.
1984: Indian premier Indira Gandhi, by her Sikh bodyguards.
1985: Millions of Ethiopians, by famine.
1986: Mozambique president Samora Machel, in an air crash.
1987: All aboard the SAA jumbo jet *Helderberg*, which plunges into the ocean near Mauritius.
1989: Hundreds of pro-democracy protesters in Beijing's Tiananmen Square, by government troops.

ABOLISHED
1980: Restrictions on black workers in 'white' areas.
1981: Nearly 800 mostly obsolete apartheid laws.
1986: SA's pass laws; the Mixed Marriages Act, and the notorious Section 16 of the Immorality Act.

MARRIED
1981: Britain's Prince Charles and Lady Diana Spencer.

LAUNCHED
1981: Ciskei, as an 'independent' republic. *Columbia*, America's (and the world's) first space shuttle.
1982: US president Ronald Reagan's 'constructive engagement' policy on SA.
1985: Congress of SA Trade Unions (Cosatu); Koeberg nuclear power plant, near Cape Town.

DISRUPTED
1981: The Springbok rugby tour of New Zealand, by anti-apartheid demos.

INVADED
1980: Iran, by Saddam Hussein's Iraqi armies, triggering a brutal eight-year war.
1982: The Falkland islands, by Argentine troops, who are expelled by a hurriedly assembled British task force.

EXPLODED
1986: The US space shuttle *Challenger*, killing its crew of seven; a reactor fuel pile at the Chernobyl nuclear plant, in the Ukraine.
1988: Pan Am flight 103, over the small Scottish town of Lockerbie, killing all on board and 11 on the ground.

COLLAPSED
1987: Stock exchanges around the world, on 'Black Monday' (19 October).
1989: The Berlin Wall, beneath the hammer-blows of a jubilant citizenry.

IDENTIFIED
1983: The human immunodeficiency virus (HIV), catalyst of the now-rampant Acquired Immuno-Deficiency Syndrome (AIDS).

THE ECONOMY
1981: The gold price reaches an all-time high, breaching the $800 mark.
1983: Recession is compounded by savage drought.
1985: Economy in crisis; rand plunges; international disinvestment begins.
1987: Sanctions campaign intensifies.

POLITICS AND PROTEST
1982: Breakaway Nationalist MPs, led by Andries Treurnicht, form the right-wing Conservative Party.
1983: United Democratic Front launched to oppose P.W. Botha's proposed three-chamber racial constitution.
1984: New constitution implemented after elections; black people excluded. Serious unrest; army called in to patrol townships.
1985: State of emergency declared in 36 districts; 'street committees' formed in townships. Botha delivers his damp-squib 'Rubicon' speech.
1986: SA military mounts raids on alleged ANC bases in Botswana, Zimbabwe and Zambia; raids coincide with visit of Commonwealth Eminent Persons Group to SA.
1987: NP wins (white) general election, but Conservative Party emerges as a force. Institute for a Democratic SA (Idasa) orchestrates groundbreaking contact between representatives of the white establishment and the ANC, in Dakar, West Africa.
1989: F.W. de Klerk replaces P.W. Botha as State President; launches post-election reform initiative; peaceful mass protest marches take place in major centres.

SOUTH AFRICA in the 20th CENTURY 1980s

1980

ZIMBABWE CELEBRATES INDEPENDENCE

Salisbury, 17 April. Rhodesia dies at midnight with the birth of Zimbabwe, ending 90 years of colonial rule.

Some 30,000 people – including heads of state and prime ministers – gather at the city's Rufaro stadium to watch as the Union Jack is lowered, the new Zimbabwe flag is hoisted, and Prince Charles, heir to the British throne, hands over the reins of state. Zimbabwe's first President, the Rev. Canaan Banana, and the Prime Minister, Robert Mugabe, formally take office.

Earlier in the year Mugabe swept to victory in the country's first free election.

The nation-wide celebrations are a sequel to the bloody bush war that escalated after Ian Smith's unilateral declaration of independence in 1965. In his inaugural speech, Mugabe says: 'If yesterday you hated me, today you cannot avoid the love that binds you to me and me to you.'

A triumphant Robert Mugabe on Zimbabwe's independence day.

FREE MANDELA CAMPAIGN LAUNCHED

Johannesburg, 10 March. Bishop Desmond Tutu, General Secretary of the South African Council of Churches, launches a movement for the release of imprisoned ANC leader Nelson Mandela. Various black, coloured and Indian political groups immediately pledge their support for the campaign.

VISITING SPORTSMAN ATE HUMAN FLESH

Uruguayan rugby player Roberto Canessa is the man who first suggested eating the flesh of his dead companions after he and 26 others were marooned high in the Andes when their aircraft crashed in 1972, killing 29 passengers. He later led a two-man expedition to seek help. The 27-year-old wing three-quarter is a member of the South American squad currently on tour in South Africa.

REFORM PROCESS GETS UNDER WAY

The Botha administration launches its reform programme, part of the Prime Minister's 'total strategy', by abolishing the upper house of parliament, the Senate, and replacing it with a President's Council.

The dissolution of the Senate spells the end of the 70-year-old Westminster parliamentary system introduced with the Act of Union in 1910.

The Council comprises nominated white, coloured and Indian (but no black) members, and is charged with investigating a new form of government for the country. It will take two years to present its proposals.

GUERRILLAS SABOTAGE FUEL PLANTS

Sasolburg, 2 June. Explosions, massive fires and a pall of smoke reaching hundreds of metres into the sky mark the success of two synchronized guerrilla attacks on Sasol and Natref installations. Eight fuel storage tanks are destroyed. A third attack, on the Secunda plant, fails in its objective, although some damage is reported.

Pressure mounts for the release of Nelson Mandela, the world's best-known political prisoner.

SOUTH AFRICA in the 20th CENTURY
The Eighties

PETTY APARTHEID ALIVE AND WELL

Pretoria University breaks new ground by admitting two coloured veterinary students. But the City Council, which provides transport to Onderstepoort for practical studies, bans brown students from its 'whites-only' bus.

If you are a black foreign diplomat you can visit the Cango Caves with white fellow-visitors. But if you are a black South African you park in a separate area and are then shown around in a black tour group, which starts at a different time from the white group. The two groups may pass each other once inside the caves.

CRICKET GREATS FINALLY BOW OUT

Two of South Africa's greatest cricketers die during the year.

Arthur Dudley Nourse will long be remembered for the 208 he scored against England at Trent Bridge in 1951 – a 9½-hour innings he played with a broken thumb – and his century against the lethal attack of Australians Bill O'Reilly, Clarrie Grimmett and Ernie McCormick.

Jack Cheetham won his national colours as a batsman (and as a superb fielder) against the 1948–49 MCC tourists, and captained the Springboks from 1952 to 1955.

'I demand that you stick to apartheid. It was so dark in there I didn't realize they were black.' (Cartoon: Tony Grogan)

> 'The lady's not for turning.'
> *British premier Margaret Thatcher*

DIED

International: Yugoslav leader Josip Tito; singer and songwriter John Lennon, murdered in New York by a deranged fan; Botswana leader Seretse Khama; wartime German admiral Karl Doenitz; Soviet leader Alexei Kosygin; film director Alfred Hitchcock; actress Mae West; actors Peter Sellers, Steve McQueen, Jimmy Durante; legendary athlete Jesse Owens; playwright Arthur Miller; philosopher Jean-Paul Sartre; photographer and designer Cecil Beaton; naturalist and author (of Born Free) Joy Adamson, murdered in Kenya; British holiday king Billy Butlin. **South Africa:** American-born Capetonian author, playwright and naturalist Robert Ardrey; liberal politician Margaret Ballinger; musician and composer Gideon Fagan; actress Freda Godfrey, known in her heyday as 'the Mary Pickford of South Africa'; playwright, screenwriter and novelist Noël Langley; cricketer Herbert Wade, who captained the first South African side to win an overseas series (England, 1935).

ARTS AND ENTERTAINMENT

♦ Top films: *The Empire Strikes Back*, second in the *Star Wars* trilogy; *Raging Bull* (with Robert de Niro); *American Gigolo* (with Richard Gere).
♦ Music: Irish rock group U2 release their first album, *Boy*.
♦ Hit singles: 'Woman in Love': Barbra Streisand; 'Don't Stand so Close to Me': The Police; 'Starting Over': John Lennon.
♦ Plays: Athol Fugard's *A Lesson from Aloes* is staged to acclaim in London and New York.

John Lennon and Yoko.

Margaret Ballinger.

Right-wing rabble-rouser Eugène Terre'Blanche, leader of the Afrikaner Weerstandsbeweging (Afrikaner Resistance Movement) and a powerful orator with a penchant for uniforms, Nazi-type symbols and paramilitary ceremony, campaigns for a blanke volkstaat (white homeland).

SOUTH AFRICA in the 20th CENTURY — 1980s

WHAT'S NEW IN 1980

♦ **US politics:** Ronald Reagan charms his way to a landslide victory in the presidential elections. Incumbent 'nice guy' Jimmy Carter carries just six of the 50 states.

Ronald Reagan and wife Nancy.

♦ **Washington state, US:** Mount St Helen's erupts in a massive volcanic explosion that spews debris, and blights the countryside, for miles around.

♦ The first **compact disc** (CD) is developed by the Dutch company Philips; vinyl recordings are on their way out.

♦ **Rubik's Cube**, a kind of three-dimensional jigsaw puzzle of 26 pieces, teases the world's brains; 100 million are sold.

♦ South African scientist **Aaron Klug**, graduate of Wits and Cape Town universities, is awarded the Nobel chemistry prize for his work on molecular structures.

♦ **Solidarity**, the Polish workers' movement, is launched: the first major challenge to Soviet power in Eastern Europe.

♦ Televiewers around the world are asking: 'Who killed JR?', the senior and scheming Ewing brother (played by Larry Hagman) in the long-running Texas oil-industry drama *Dallas*.

♦ Published: J.M. Coetzee's *Waiting for the Barbarians*; Elsa Joubert's *The Long Journey of Poppie Nongena*, the moving story of a black South African woman's struggle to keep her family together.

1981

VIOLENT DEMOS THREATEN SA RUGBY PLAYERS

The Springbok rugby squad in New Zealand completes what will prove to be its last, and most troubled, tour before the curtain finally falls on South African sport.

The visitors lose the demo-plagued series by the narrowest of margins – in the last minute of the final Test – but come away with honour.

But much more is at stake: the New Zealand anti-apartheid movement and especially HART ('Halt All Racist Tours') are out to sabotage the series and deny South Africa a place in the world arena. Violence swirls around the Gisborne stadium, venue of the first game. The match against Wiakato, at Hamilton, is called off after a threat, by a man who is said to have terminal cancer, to crash his stolen aircraft, kamikaze-style, on the main grandstand. In Nelson, a powerful bomb is removed from the visitors' hotel, and on the day of the game 22 protesters are arrested, some armed with explosives, vicious four-pointed spikes and other offensive weaponry on them. The final Test is marred when a light aircraft mounts a sustained flour-bomb assault on the players.

New Zealand demonstrators go all out to wreck the Springbok rugby tour.

SOUTH AFRICA in the 20th CENTURY

The Eighties

WHAT'S NEW IN 1981

- **Athletics:** Coloured South African expatriate runner Sydney Maree wins the New York Mile.
- **Technology:** First in-car computer developed by BMW, in Germany.
- **Space:** *Shuttle* Columbia makes its maiden flight, from Cape Kennedy, US.
- **SA publishing:** *July's People*, by Nadine Gordimer; *A Ride in the Whirlwind*, by Sipho Sepamla.

Sydney Maree.

SANCTIONS NOOSE TIGHTENS

P.W. Botha's programme for reform is taken a step further when 790 obsolete, mostly discriminatory, laws are removed from the statute books. Nevertheless the international sanctions campaign intensifies.

Major Western nations reject a UN General Assembly demand for near comprehensive embargoes (including a ban on the supply of oil), but support the idea of a blacklist targeting 'collaborators'. Various lists are drawn up – of sportsmen, entertainers, film companies, businesses involved in military projects – that have maintained links with South Africa.

NEW DISEASE BAFFLES SCIENTISTS

US medical experts are puzzled by an outbreak of what appears to be a new kind of killer affliction that destroys the human immune system, causing weight loss, lung infections and skin cancers. The disease, later to be named AIDS, appears to attack homosexuals only, though one of the 152 cases reported so far has involved an intravenous drug user. San Francisco, Los Angeles and New York are the worst hit centres. There is widespread concern, initially in North America, soon elsewhere, as the incidence increases.

Public awareness mounts as the threat of AIDS grows.

A BUSY YEAR FOR KILLERS

This may well go down in the history books as the year of the assassins.

Egypt's President Anwar Sadat, watching an anniversary march-past, is shot by four uniformed men who emerge from an armoured vehicle wielding automatic weapons (the vehicle is part of the parade). He collapses in a pool of blood. Sadat shared the 1978 Nobel Peace Prize for his part in healing the Arab-Israeli rift.

Much luckier are the Roman Catholic pontiff and US President Ronald Reagan. Pope John Paul II is shot in the stomach while driving through Rome in his open-top 'popemobile'; a 23-year-old Turkish gunman is arrested. Reagan is hit in the left lung when John Warnock Hinckley, 25, fires six shots at him. Hinckley later explains that he was trying to impress his 'girlfriend', the movie actress Jodie Foster (whom he has never met).

'MAD MIKE' COMES A CROPPER

The art of the African coup descends to comic-opera levels when a band of 44 South African mercenaries, led by Colonel 'Mad Mike' Hoare, attempt to overthrow the socialist Seychelles government of President Albert René. Passing themselves off as members of a club called the 'Froth Blowers' intent on a golfing and

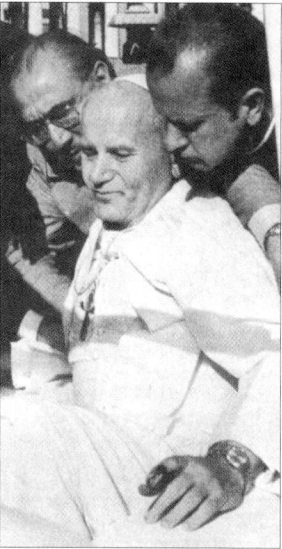

Pope John Paul: wounded.

drinking holiday on the Indian Ocean island, they are unmasked when local Customs find a gun in one of the golf-bags. They then shoot up the airport, hijack an Air India airliner and are arrested on their return. Hoare, notorious for his exploits as a mercenary commander in the Katanga province of the Congo (now Zaïre) in the 1960s, is sentenced to 10 years' imprisonment for kidnapping (a lesser charge than hijacking). Four others are also jailed; the rest are released.

DIED

Novelist A.J. Cronin; actor William Holden; actress Natalie Wood; pianist and composer Hoagy Carmichael; rock musician Bill Haley; motorcyclist Mike Hailwood; publisher De Witt Wallace, founder of Reader's Digest; Albert Speer, German architect and friend of Hitler.

SOUTH AFRICA in the 20th CENTURY — 1980s

Diana and Charles: wedding of the century.

BILLIONS WATCH ROYAL WEDDING

London; 29 July South African viewers join billions around the world to witness the marital vows of Prince Charles and the lovely Lady Diana Spencer in what has been billed the wedding of the century (as was his mother's, 34 years ago). Yesterday, Charles lit the first of 102 beacons strung out across the British Isles, and Londoners crammed into Hyde Park to watch a spectacular firework display. Today people in their tens of thousands line the route from Buckingham Palace to St Paul's cathedral. The bride is wearing an ivory silk taffeta dress with a 25-foot train; she is attended by five bridesmaids and two pages.

STAGE, SCREEN AND SONG

◆ Top films: *Chariots of Fire*, with Ben Cross, Ian Charleson and South African actress Alice Krige; Steven Spielberg's comic-book adventure *Raiders of the Lost Ark*, with Harrison Ford; *The French Lieutenant's Woman*, with Meryl Streep and Jeremy Irons; Roman Polanski's *Tess*, with Nastassja Kinski.
◆ Television: *Brideshead Revisited*, adapted from Evelyn Waugh's 1945 novel.
◆ Stage ballet-musical: Andrew Lloyd-Webber's hit *Cats*.
◆ Hit singles: 'Stand and Deliver': Adam and the Ants; 'Jesse's Girl': Rick Springfield; 'Don't You Want Me': Human League. Diana Ross (once one of The Supremes) and Lionel Ritchie (of The Commodores fame) get together to sing the song 'Endless Love'.

> '640K [of computer memory] ought to be enough for anybody'
> *Microsoft CEO Bill Gates.*

1982

LETTER BOMB KILLS SA ACTIVIST

Activist and author Ruth First is killed by a letter bomb, which almost certainly originates from the South African security establishment, in the Mozambican capital Maputo. Ms First was the wife of Joe Slovo, who has masterminded the operations of Umkhonto we Sizwe, the ANC's military wing. Ruth First, a dedicated Marxist, helped found the Congress of Democrats in 1953, edited its journal *Fighting Talk*, and was one of those arrested and tried for treason in the mid-1950s. In 1963 she was detained in solitary confinement under the notorious '90-day clause', attempted suicide, and on her release joined her husband in London, later lecturing at Durham University. Five years ago she was appointed professor at and research director of the Centre for African Studies at Maputo's Eduardo Mondlane University. The fatal letter was delivered shortly after the UNESCO conference at the Centre. She leaves a husband and three daughters, Gillian, Shawn and Robyn.

Marxist Ruth First: assassination victim.

NEW RIGHT-WING PARTY FORMED

20 March. More than 6,000 cheering supporters greet the founding of the Conservative Party in Pretoria today. The move follows the parliamentary walkout earlier this year by 16 rebel MPs, including NP ministers Dr Andries Treurnicht and Dr Ferdi Hartzenberg. The new party rejects P.W. Botha's power sharing proposals in favour of old-style apartheid.

SOUTH AFRICA in the 20th CENTURY
The Eighties

WHAT'S NEW IN 1982

- South Africa's **Atomic Energy Corporation** is established; **Sasol 3** (at Secunda) begins to produce marketable fuels.
- South African activist **Barbara Hogan** is convicted of treason and sentenced to 10 years in prison.
- Fifteen **rebel English cricketers**, who tour South Africa in defiance of sporting sanctions, are banned from representing their country for three years. Among them are Graham Gooch, John Embury, Geoff Boycott and Derek Underwood.
- **Soccer:** Italy wins the World Cup for the third time, beating West Germany 3-1 in the final (Madrid, Spain).
- **Diet Coke** is launched onto the soft-drinks market.
- **Computers:** The microchip revolution hits the office, the factory and, increasingly, the home. A computer game character, Pacman, is adjudged Time Magazine's Man of the Year.

Activist Hogan.

Falklands: British troops move into battle position.

HONOUR FOR ANC MARCHER
The African National Congress awards its highest honour to the late Lilian Ngoyi. Ms Ngoyi led the 20,000-woman march on the Union Building in 1956 in protest against the country's pass laws.

VOILENT DEATH OF A UNIONIST
Prominent labour leader Dr Neil Aggett, who tried to bring unity to the South African trade union movement and who was detained by security police last year, is found hanging in his cell. It is later revealed that Aggett was held in solitary confinement, deprived of sleep and subjected to 60 hours of non-stop interrogation before he died.

Aggett: torture and death.

BRITISH RECAPTURE FALKLANDS
After a short, sharp and bloody little war for control of the Falkland Islands in the South Atlantic, the 20,000-strong Argentinian army of occupation surrenders to British troops. The fighting begins when a British task force of some 70 ships, among them HMS *Hermes* and *Invincible* and the commandeered *QE2*, land an invasion force.

SA RAIDS LESOTHO
The SA Defence Force launches a lightning raid on 12 targets in

Admirers of civil rights activist Lilian Ngoyi pay their last respects.

SOUTH AFRICA in the 20th CENTURY — 1980s

Maseru, capital of Lesotho, killing 41 'political' refugees. Among the dead are women and children. Western countries, including Britain, have condemned the incursion as a 'flagrant violation' of Lesotho's sovereignty.

Rising star Michael Jackson.

WORDS AND MUSIC

◆ Michael Jackson, 24 years old and the fastest rising star on the pop scene, releases the LP *Thriller*, three years after his sensational *Off the Wall*, which sold ten million copies (plus millions more of the spin-off singles).
◆ Other hits of the year: 'Fame': Irene Cara; 'The Lion Sleeps Tonight': Tight Fit; 'Come On Eileen': Dexy's Midnight Runners; 'Physical': Olivia Newton-John; 'Eye of the Tiger': Survivor.
◆ A new kind of recording, called 'rap' (words spoken rhythmically over a beat), appears on the market. The first release: 'The Message' by Grandmaster Flash and the Furious Five.
◆ Top films: Drag captivates movie audiences with two major and surprisingly tasteful comedies: *Tootsie* (with Dustin Hoffman) and *Victor/Victoria* (with Julie Andrews). The year's biggest box-office draw, though, is Steven Spielberg's marvellously childish *ET: The Extra-Terrestrial*. *Chariots of Fire* wins the Oscar for best film of 1981. Italian actress Sophia Loren is jailed for tax evasion.
◆ Top television: *Fame* (dancing teens); *Cheers* (barflies); and, as always, the Ewings of *Dallas*.
◆ Stage: South African playwright Gibson Kente's *Now is the Time* is premiered.

DIED
International: Soviet leader Leonid Brezhnev; Princess Grace of Monaco (formerly filmdom's Grace Kelly), in a car smash; politician R.A. 'Rob' Butler; actor Henry Fonda; comedians Jacques Tati and Arthur Askey; actresses Ingrid Bergman and Romy Scheider; jazz pianist Thelonius Monk; concert pianist Artur Rubinstein; legless Second World War air ace Douglas Bader.
South Africa: Painter Walter Battiss; musician Anton Hartman.

1983

NEW CONSTITUTION GETS GO-AHEAD

A massive 'yes' vote in the referendum appears to be a mandate for far-reaching reform. A total of 1.36 million white, Asian and coloured people endorse P.W. Botha's proposed new constitution, 691,000 vote against. The proposals offer the coloured and Indian communities a role in the government of the country, though power will effectively reside in white hands. Black South Africans – the vast majority – remain outside the central political process: they are deemed to be citizens not of South Africa but of the various 'national states'.

The new arrangement is complex. It involves, first, an executive president presiding over a Cabinet that will handle 'general affairs' – matters affecting all three race groups. Second, there are three Ministers' councils dealing with 'own affairs' – that is, with each group's particular concerns. The legislature will comprise a three-chamber Parliament made up of a 178-seat House of Assembly for the whites, an 85-seat House of Representatives for the coloured people and a 45-seat House of Delegates for Indians.

RALLY LAUNCHES NEW DEMOCRATIC MOVEMENT

Cape Town, 20 August. A vast crowd attends the national launch of the United Democratic Front, an umbrella organization embracing a wide variety of bodies opposed to P.W. Botha's constitutional plan. The UDF promises to become the country's largest internal political movement in decades.

SLAUGHTER IN THE STREETS

Pretoria, 20 May. At least 16 people – nine whites

SOUTH AFRICA in the 20th CENTURY

The Eighties

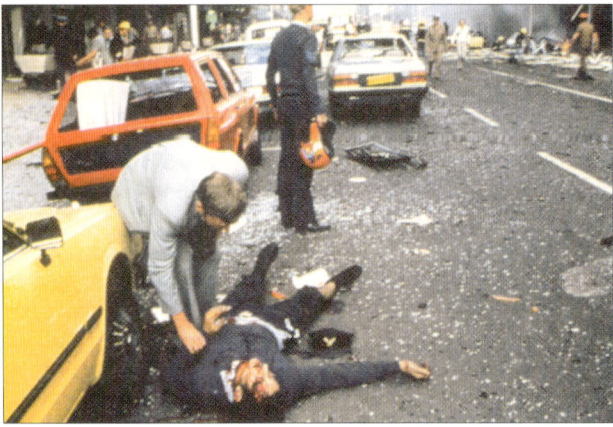

Carnage on the streets of Pretoria as a huge bomb explodes.

CRAZES

- Swatch watches: fun, fashionable timepieces in all sizes, shapes and colours;
- Cabbage Patch Kids: big, ugly, messy dolls with pudding faces;
- Computer hacking: mostly harmless home entertainment, with dangerous spin-off potential: a clever amateur breaks into the US's number one defence computer.

and seven blacks – are killed and 188 injured in a huge bomb-blast in what is, to date, South Africa's worst ever terror attack.

The bomb explodes at 4.28 p.m. in front of the South African Air Force headquarters in the city centre. Bodies, limbs, blood, clothing and debris litter the scene.

ARTS LOSE TALENTED QUARTET

Four notable figures of the South African arts world pass from the scene during the year:
- Jazz musician Kippie Moeketsi, whose talent was nurtured in Sophiatown and who later worked with the Shantytown Sextet, the Jazz Pioneers and Abdullah Ibrahim, blows his last note. Moeketsi, shining star of the 60s, was injured by gangsters in the latter part of that decade, an incident that triggered his slow decline.
- Marc Raubenheimer, the 31-year-old internationally respected South African concert pianist, perishes in an air disaster.
- London-born Capetonian Mary Renault, famed for novels that breathed life into classical history and myth, dies at the age of 78. Her published books, among them *The Last of the Wine* (1956), *The King Must Die* (1958) and *The Bull from the Sea* (1962), were well received by critics and the reading public, though they angered conservatives with their sympathetic treatment of homosexuality.
- Self-taught Willem Coetzer, who dies aged 83, was known for his meticulous paintings of Afrikaner subjects. His 'Dusty Shelf' is one of the Johannesburg Art Gallery's most popular exhibits.

ARTS AND ENTERTAINMENT

- New books by South African authors include J.M. Coetzee's *The Life and Times of Michael K*; Madge Swindell's blockbuster *Summer Harvest*; and Menan du Plessis' *A State of Fear*, which wins the Olive Schreiner prize.
- Television: The final episode of the record-breaking series M*A*S*H, which reveals the futility of war, is watched around the world by 125 million viewers.
- Movies: *Return of the Jedi*, third in the *Star Wars* trilogy; *Yentl*, with Barbra Streisand; *Terms of Endearment*, with Jack Nicholson and Shirley MacLaine.
- Oscars: Richard Attenborough's *Gandhi* (starring Ben Kingsley) sweeps the board, winning eight Oscars.

DIED
International: Actors Ralph Richardson and David Niven; actress Gloria Swanson; playwright Tennessee Williams; authors Rebecca West and Arthur Koestler; composer William Walton; singer Karen Carpenter; boxer Jack Dempsey.
South Africa: Politician John Vorster; activist Yusuf Dadoo.

John Vorster.

Abdullah Ibrahim, better known as a pianist, blows his sax.

SOUTH AFRICA in the 20th CENTURY — 1980s

- Chart-toppers: 'Red Red Wine': UB40; 'Total Eclipse of the Heart': Bonnie Tyler; 'Uptown Girl': Billy Joel; 'Karma Chameleon': Culture Club; 'Every Breath You Take': The Police; 'Beat It': Michael Jackson. Madonna, the uninhibited young pop star, releases her first album, whose cuts include 'Everybody', 'Borderline' and 'Holiday'.

SPORTING BRIEFS
- Boxer Gerrie Coetzee becomes the first South African to hold a world heavyweight title when he challenges, and beats, American Michael Dokes.
- Stanley Amos, believed to be the world's oldest professional jockey, finally retires at age 65. Two years ago he broke Tiger Wright's record for the highest number of winners (2,454) in the history of South African racing.

On track: Mary Decker (left) follows Zola Budd to disaster.

Nobel laureate Tutu (right): 'new hope for millions'.

1984

TOP AWARD FOR 'TURBULENT PRIEST'

Oslo, 11 December. Desmond Tutu, the 53-year-old General Secretary of the South African Council of Churches and Bishop-Elect of Johannesburg, is awarded the Nobel Peace Prize at a packed ceremony presided over by King Olaf of Norway. Afterwards, Tutu says that the award 'kindles new hope in the millions who are voiceless'. South Africa, he predicts, will remain in the grip of civil war until apartheid is dismantled. Tutu is a powerful advocate of economic sanctions. Fully aware of the hardship they are causing, he nevertheless believes the embargoes are the surest means of forcing political change.

GAMES FIASCO AS ZOLA TRIPS MARY

London, 6 April. Zola Budd, the waif-like 17-year-old barefoot prodigy from the Orange Free State, applies for a British passport – which will enable her to run for Britain at the Los Angeles Olympic Games. Four months ago, in January, she shattered Mary Decker's world 5,000 metres record.

The *Daily Mail* newspaper takes up Budd's cause, and she receives the precious document in less than two weeks. But disaster strikes at the Games: Decker plunges off the track after tripping over Budd's flying heels in the 3,000 metres. Budd limps home well down the field, and leaves the arena in a flood of tears.

PEACE ACCORD SIGNED

P.W. Botha and Mozambique's President Samora Machel sign the Nkomati Accord to crown South

Unlikely partners: Machel and Botha stride the path to peace.

The Eighties

SOUTH AFRICA in the 20th CENTURY

WHAT'S NEW IN 1984

- **South African politics:** P.W. Botha is elected South Africa's first executive State President.
- SA's **National Union of Mine Workers** is formed.
- Computers take a sophisticated leap forward with the launch of **Apple's Macintosh**, the most user-friendly product to date.
- The terms **virtual reality** and **cyberspace** come into common use.
- **Black humour:** US President Ronald Reagan jokingly orders a nuclear strike against the Soviet Union – unaware that he's on live television.
- The word **yuppie** (young, upwardly mobile professional) enters the English language.

DIED

International: Indian leader Indira Gandhi; Russian leader Yuri Andropov; Second World War military men Arthur 'Bomber' Harris and Mark Clark; poet John Betjeman; comedian Eric Morecambe; writers Truman Capote and J.B. Priestly; actors Richard Burton, Johnny Weismuller, Jackie Coogan and James Mason; actress Diana Dors (born Diana Fluck); musicians William 'Count' Basie and Marvin Gaye; jogging expert James F. Fixx, author of bestseller The Complete Guide to Running, from a heart attack while jogging. *South Africa:* Thelma Gutsche, doyenne of the South African theatre world.

Africa's campaign for reconciliation with black Africa. The agreement recognizes 'the responsibility of states is not to allow their territory to be used for acts of aggression against other states'.

Nkomati ends the once-bitter relationship between the two neighbours, establishes a working relationship between Marxism and capitalism within the region, and paves the way for future peace agreements with other African nations.

LOW TURN-OUT AT POLLS

Coloured and Indian South Africans go to the polls to elect their representatives to the new three-chamber parliament. The turn-out is low, due largely to sustained opposition from the United Democratic Front. The UDF's Patrick 'Terror' Lekota tells a Cape Town rally that 'the laws will be made in the white House. The so-called coloured and Indian houses will be there only to put a rubber stamp on the laws made by the bosses'. Lekota, his colleague Archie Gumede and a number of other UDF figures are detained by police.

The Rev. Alan Hendrickse's Labour Party gains a majority in the House of Representatives; there is no clear winner in the Indian election.

SHOWBUSINESS

- Capetonian Anthony Sher makes a splendid entrance into British theatre in the title role of Shakespeare's *Richard III*. The performance, which draws comparisons with that of Laurence Olivier (and earns him the Laurence Olivier award) leads to further critical acclaim. He goes on to star in major stage, film and television productions, to write books, and to hold exhibitions of his paintings. He is also a talented musician.

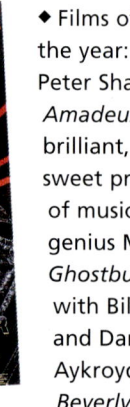

- Films of the year: Peter Shaffer's *Amadeus*, a brilliant, bittersweet profile of musical genius Mozart; *Ghostbusters*, with Bill Murray and Dan Aykroyd; *Beverly Hills Cop*, with Eddie Murphy; the ultra-violent *A Nightmare on Elm Street*; and Arnold Schwarzenegger as the terrifying android in *The Terminator*.
- Top television: *Miami Vice*; *The Cosby Show*; *The Jewel in the Crown*.
- Hit singles: 'Dancing in the Dark': Bruce Springsteen; 'Do They Know It's Christmas?': Band Aid; 'Ghostbusters': Ray Parker Jnr; 'I Just Called To Say I Love You': Stevie Wonder; 'Last Christmas': Wham!; 'Two Tribes': Frankie Goes to Hollywood. Dishy crooner Julio Iglesias, once a top Spanish footballer, releases his 56th album, *1100 Bel Air Place*.

Coloured voters elect representatives for the tricameral parliament.

SOUTH AFRICA in the 20th CENTURY

1985

PW DIGS A DEEPER HOLE

Pretoria, 21 July. President P.W. Botha, claiming that law-abiding South African blacks are falling victim to 'thuggery and violence', imposes a state of emergency on 36 magisterial districts. The move, which the South African Council of Churches condemns as a desperate attempt to stem 'the tide of liberation', comes after mounting township unrest that has left at least 500 people dead this year. Nobel laureate Bishop Desmond Tutu says that there is now virtually no chance of a peaceful solution to the country's race crisis.

A few weeks later, on 15 August, Botha delivers his disastrous 'Rubicon' speech. The world expects Botha to 'cross the Rubicon' and announce the dawn of a new era of radical reform. International press and broadcasting services are in full attendance; 300 million television viewers are tuned in; anticipation runs high.

But the finger-wagging Botha lets his vast audience down. It hears him berate those who dare tell him what to do; it hears him declare his intention to continue the reform process but, he thunders, he will not give in to 'hostile pressure and agitation from abroad'. He warns the world not to 'push us too far'.

Disappointment runs deep. The rand plunges; an alarmed government shuts down the money markets and the stock exchange for a full week, and declares a moratorium on foreign debt repayments.

> 'I am not prepared to lead white South Africans... on a road to abdication and suicide.'
> *President P.W. Botha*

Botha's Rubicon speech triggers renewed rioting; thousands grieve for loved ones caught in crossfire.

WHITE BUSINESS MEETS ANC

In a ground-breaking move, top South African businessmen meet exiled African National Congress leaders in Lusaka, the Zambian capital, for talks which Anglo American's Gavin Relly describes as 'useful' and, if followed up, 'might lead to some fruitful conclusions'. Oliver Tambo heads the ANC delegation.

LUCKLESS CURREN BOWS TO YOUTHFUL MAGIC

Wimbledon, 7 July. South African expatriate tennis star Kevin Curren falls victim to the wizardry of 17-year-old German Boris Becker in the final of the Men's Singles. The remarkably agile Becker, who wins 6-3, 6-7, 7-6, 6-4, is the first German, the first unseeded and the youngest player to take the title. He goes on to retain the championship in 1986 and wins it again in 1988.

Townships burn as the unrest continues.

Kevin Curren: no answer to teenage Boris Becker's flair.

SOUTH AFRICA in the 20th CENTURY
The Eighties

Horrors pile up as activists 'make the country ungovernable'.

MANDELA TURNS DOWN BRIBE

Nelson Mandela, the world's best-known political prisoner, rejects South African premier P.W. Botha's conditional offer of freedom – that he buy his release from Cape Town's Pollsmoor prison by renouncing violence. 'Let Botha renounce violence,' he replies. 'Let him say that he will dismantle apartheid.'

LOCAL SHOW BRINGS DISTRICT SIX TO LIFE

Kat and the Kings, a scintillating new musical created by David Kramer and Taliep Petersen, premieres in Cape Town. The two-hour rock extravaganza features Salie Daniels as Kat Diamond, an ageing shoeshine man who reminisces about himself as a youngster (played by Jody Abrahams) in the old South Africa, and about the talented kids (the 'kings') of District Six. Much later the show wins two Laurence Olivier awards in London, for best new musical and 'best actor' (presented to the entire cast). It opens on Broadway in August 1999 – just three weeks after Daniels, the original Kat, dies of bone cancer.

SOUND AND SCREEN

◆ Bob Geldof's 16-hour Live Aid concert in London's Wembley stadium, linked (after half-time) to the JFK stadium in Philadelphia, is watched by a worldwide audience of two billion and raises millions for starving Ethiopians (one million of whom die during the year). The star-studded cast includes Status Quo, Madonna, Queen, David Bowie, Duran Duran, Phil Collins (who plays both concerts, jetting off to the US by Concorde), U2 and Led Zeppelin.

◆ Compact discs are now cheap enough to begin replacing vinyl recordings.

WHAT'S NEW IN 1985

◆ **Labour:** The Congress of South African Trade Unions (Cosatu) is formed.
◆ **Street committees** make their appearance in South Africa's townships.
◆ The **Koeberg** nuclear power station, north of Cape Town, comes on stream.
◆ Churchman and UDF activist **Allan Boesak** receives the R.F. Kennedy Human Rights award.
◆ **Science and technology:** Genetic 'fingerprinting', from blood and body fluids, is developed by Dr Alec Jeffreys of Leicester University; lasers are used in surgery for the first time, in the US; DTP (desktop publishing) makes its appearance; mobile telephones (cellphones) are launched in Europe.
◆ **Commercial whaling** is banned by an international commission.
◆ The wreck of the ill-fated **Titanic**, which sank in 1912, is located, at a depth of 4,000 metres.
◆ The Church of England approves the ordination of **women priests**.
◆ The word **wannabe** (a 'want-to-be' imitator) enters the English language.

Kat and the Kings by talented duo David Kramer and Taliep Petersen.

SOUTH AFRICA in the 20th CENTURY — 1980s

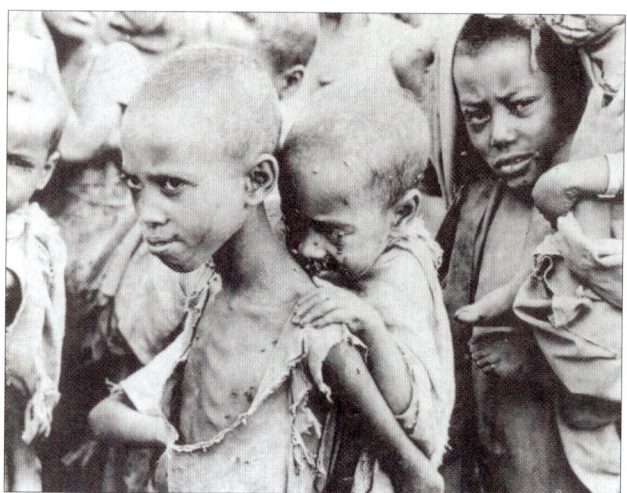

Hunger stalks Ethiopia; Live Aid helps – a little.

1986

SADF STRIKES AT NEIGHBOURS

20 May. The South African Defence Force mounts raids on alleged ANC targets in Botswana, Zimbabwe and Zambia, killing several people and injuring others.

According to the Air Force, fighter jets 'successfully attacked the ANC's operational headquarters 15 kilometres south-west of Lusaka'. An Army spokesman reveals that other major targets are 'a terrorist transit facility' in the Harare suburb of Ashdown Park, a site in the centre of that city, and a base 5 kilometres west of Gaborone, Botswana. Western governments condemn the incursions, which have effectively torpedoed the work of the Commonwealth Eminent Persons' Group that is on a delicate peace mission to South Africa.

MACHEL KILLED IN PLANE CRASH

October. Mystery surrounds the death of Mozambique's President Samora Machel, who is killed when his Russian-piloted aircraft crashes in a lonely part of the eastern Transvaal. Just why the plane, bound for Mozambique, was so

♦ Hit singles: 'We Are the World': USA for Africa; 'The Power of Love': Jennifer Rush; 'Into the Groove' and 'Like a Virgin': Madonna; 'Money for Nothing': Dire Straits; 'Careless Whisper': George Michael and Wham. South Africa: Reggae artist, Rastafarian and one-time *mbaqanga* singer Lucky Dube's first album, *Rastas Never Die*, is banned.
♦ The big screen: Diminutive former teenage idol Michael J. Fox stars in *Back to the Future*, a quirky, feel-good sci-fi movie that is a box-office success. Other top films are *The Color Purple*, *Out of Africa*, *Witness*, and *St Elmo's Fire*.

DIED
International: Poet and author Robert Graves; artist Marc Chagall; actors Orson Welles, Rock Hudson (of AIDS), Yul Brynner and Michael Redgrave. **South Africa**: Nurse and lawyer Victoria Mxenge, widow of attorney Griffiths Mxenge (both murdered); political novelist Alex la Guma; human rights activist Molly Blackburn, in a car smash; political leader James Moroka.

THE PASS LAWS

The government announces that it intends scrapping the influx control and pass laws, and a host of other discriminatory measures that prohibit the presence of 'unqualified blacks' in urban areas, bringing to an end forced removals and restoring freedom of movement to South Africa's black people.

No fewer than 34 statutes are to be either repealed or amended; the notorious Mixed Marriages Act and Section 16 of the Immorality Act, which criminalizes sex across the colour line, are abolished.

Old-timer shows his pass.

193

SOUTH AFRICA in the 20th CENTURY
The Eighties

WHAT'S NEW IN 1986

- **Apartheid rejected:** The Dutch Reformed Church condemns racism as a sin.
- **New-age disasters:** Part of the Ukraine's Chernobyl nuclear power plant explodes, raising levels of radioactivity over a wide area; the US space shuttle *Challenger* comes to grief just after lift-off, killing seven.

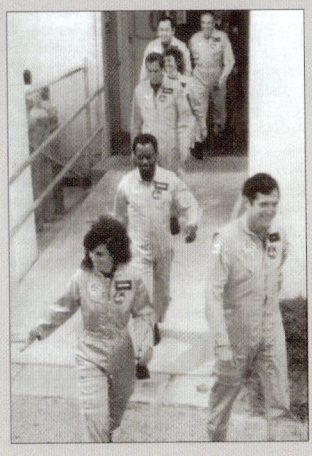

Challenger crew: seven killed.

- **Boxing:** South African Brian Mitchell wins the WBA world junior lightweight boxing title, beating Alfredo Layne in Panama. 'Iron Man' Mike Tyson, 20, becomes the youngest ever world heavyweight boxing champion when he knocks out Trevor Berbick in the second round.
- **Soccer:** Diego ('the hand of God') Maradona stars as Argentina wins the World Cup, defeating West Germany 3–1 in Mexico City.

'White Zulu' Johnny Clegg and his Juluka group.

far off course, and why it plunged to earth, is to be the subject of an intensive and inconclusive investigation. Machel was the co-architect of the crucial Nkomati Peace Accord signed two years ago by Mozambique and South Africa.

SPRINGBOK RUGBY IN GOOD HEALTH

After years of isolation the Springbok rugby team performs surprisingly well against the touring (unofficial) New Zealand Cavaliers. Some of South Africa's best, however, are seen on overseas fields. Naas Botha, Carel du Plessis, Danie Gerber, Rob Louw and the outstanding Errol Tobias, first player of colour to be selected for the national squad, are among those invited to play for Barbarians-type international sides.

At Twickenham, Du Plessis scores a brilliant try against the Northern Hemisphere team: it starts on the Southern's goal line and ends with a classic 50-metre sprint; two other South Africans, Botha and Gerber, have a hand in the movement, which the British press hails as the finest ever seen at the ground.

SA MUSICIANS MAKE GOOD

- Africa enters the charts with Paul Simon's top-selling *Graceland* album, created in association with local vocal group Ladysmith Black Mambazo.

Ladysmith Black Mambazo: music for the world.

The group, led by Joseph Shabalala, goes on to produce its own album (based on the *Shaka Zulu* television epic) and to win a Grammy award. Simon has been blacklisted for his contacts with South African artists, but pleads that his music is for the 'global village'.

- Meanwhile 'white Zulu' Johnny Clegg, whose Juluka group rode high on its tours of Europe, is proving equally popular with his recently formed Savuka. Savuka made its first single recording – 'Asimbinanga', a tribute to the heroes of the South African liberation movement – last year.
- Versatile musician Sipho 'Hotstix' Mabuse (who plays drums, flute and keyboard) also refashions his group, Harari, to produce the album *Burnout*, a lively mix of *mbaqanga* and funk.

LOCAL SHOWBIZ SHINES

- Local film director Jamie Uys's *The Gods Must be Crazy* is among the top-grossing non-Hollywood movies of the year. Uys

194

SOUTH AFRICA in the 20th CENTURY 1980s

created a number of successful Boer-versus-Brit satirical comedies (with Bob Courtney as his Anglo co-star) in the 1960s, followed these with a serious drama, *Dingaka* (starring Stanley Baker, Juliet Prowse and Ken Gampu), *Beautiful People* (about the Bushmen of the Kalahari) and the hilarious candid-camera *Funny People* and its sequel, *Crazy People*.

♦ Another Uys, the drag artist Pieter-Dirk – aka Evita Bezuidenhout, ambassador to the 'homeland' Bapetikosweti – continues to convulse audiences, lampooning the stuffy white establishment generally and the finger-wagging President P.W. Botha in particular.

♦ Soccer player turned actor Henry Cele stars in Bill Faure's television epic *Shaka Zulu*; Briton Edward Fox plays Francis Farewell; the series receives wide international exposure.

DIED

International: The Duchess of Windsor (the former Mrs Wallis Simpson, mistress to and later wife of ex-King Edward VIII); politician Harold Macmillan; sculptor Henry Moore; actress Anna Neagle; actors James Cagney and Cary Grant; jazzman Benny Goodman; writer Simone de Beauvoir; cricketer Jim Laker; film director Otto Preminger. *South Africa:* Writer Bessie Head; Cecil Higgs, considered one of the country's finest woman painters; Moses Mabhida, trade union leader and General Secretary of the SA Communist Party; composer Priaulx Rainier.

1987

ELECTIONS: WHITE SA LURCHES TO THE RIGHT

White South Africans go to the polls to re-elect P.W. Botha's Nationalists to power – but Andries Treurnicht's Conservative Party, despite being written off by the English-language press, gains 22 parliamentary seats and, for the first time since 1948, the government stands to the left of the official Opposition. Moreover, the Conservatives would have done even better had the right-wing vote not been split. Many whites accuse the Nats of being 'soft on security', despite Botha's hardline stance in the run-up to the election. The issues he targeted were not, as might have been expected, political progress and social reform but, rather, foreign meddling in South Africa's internal affairs, sanctions, the menace of communism and the spectre of revolution. He has repeatedly stated that he will not negotiate with those who regarded the limpet mine, the petrol bomb and the 'necklace' as instruments of change; force will be met by force.

Van Zyl Slabbert: crucial contacts.

Nevertheless the results hold a glimmer of hope. There is clearly an element within the National Party that is both progressive and significant. The left-of-centre independents put up a surprisingly good showing against their Nat opponents; not a few white South Africans, it seems, do indeed want change.

ANC TALKS TO WHITES

Senegal, 12 July. A group of more than 50 mainly Afrikaans-speaking business, academic and professional people meet ANC leaders in Dakar. Dr Frederick van Zyl Slabbert, leader of the mission, says that the group does not profess to support the ANC but recognizes the importance of starting a dialogue. The ANC team is led by the young Thabo Mbeki.

Dr Slabbert confesses that the debates are 'some of the toughest I have heard in a long time', but it becomes clear that the two groups are in broad agreement on the single most important issue: the need for non-racial democracy in South Africa.

The ANC admits that it admires the white delegates for their courage in breaking ranks with the ruling establishment. President Botha condemns them as 'political terrorists'.

TZANEEN GRANDMOTHER MAKES MEDICAL HISTORY

Pat Antony becomes the world's first surrogate mother to the children of her daughter and son-in-law – in effect, to give birth to her own grandchildren.

The 48-year-old grandmother, a resident of Tzaneen in the northern Transvaal, makes medical history by carrying in her womb the fertilized ova of her daughter Karen Ferreira-Jorge, and successfully producing triplets: David, José and Paula.

SA THEATRE ALIVE AND WELL

This is a good year for South African theatre – with New York the focus.

SOUTH AFRICA in the 20th CENTURY

The Eighties

> 'How do we prevent the use of nuclear weapons? By threatening the use of nuclear weapons. And we can't get rid of nuclear weapons because of nuclear weapons.'
> *Writer Martin Amis*

Sipho 'Hotstix' Mabuse continues to charm music-lovers.

- Local actress Yvonne Bryceland makes her US debut in Athol Fugard's *The Road to Mecca* – at the prestigious Spoleto Festival. Technically she is still forbidden to appear on stage in America, but the United States Equity organization has no jurisdiction over the festival. She will go on to appear on Broadway in 1988.
- Mmbongeni Ngema's *Sarafina*, a sparkling musical set in Soweto, is staged in New York (and later filmed, but with less success). Earlier in the decade Ngema travelled to Britain and the States with Percy Mtwa to produce (and act in) *Woza Albert!*, which was adjudged the 1983 Play of the Year by the prestigious London periodical *City Limits*.
- Back home in Johannesburg Janet Suzman, who received an Oscar nomination for her part in the 1971 film *Nicholas and Alexandra*, stages Shakespeare's tragedy *Othello* with leading black actor John Kani in the title role. The casting proves controversial; but the production is acclaimed.
- *District Six: The Musical*, created by locals David Kramer and Taliep Petersen, plays to packed houses in Cape Town and is set to become the longest-running show in the city's theatrical history. It is billed as 'a love story filled with music, song and dance and throbbing life – set against the political background'.
- Drag artist Pieter-Dirk Uys savages conservative South Africa with his one-man (woman) show *Rearranging the deckchairs on the SS Bothatanic*.

WHAT'S NEW IN 1987

- **Aviation disaster:** South African Airway's Boeing 747 airliner *Helderberg* plunges into the sea near the Indian Ocean island of Mauritius, killing all the passengers on board. There is speculation about a mysterious cargo.
- **Financial woes:** The New York Stock Exchange crashes, the Dow Jones index plummeting 22 percent. Bourses worldwide, including the Johannesburg Stock Exchange, tumble in sympathy.
- **SA publishing:** J.M. Coetzee's *Foe*; Nadine Gordimer's *A Sport of Nature*; Dalene Matthee's *Kringe in 'n Bos (Circles in the Forest)*.
- **International publishing:** The year's bestseller is Tom Wolfe's wickedly satirical *Bonfire of the Vanities*. Gnomes replace politically incorrect golliwogs in reprints of Enid Blyton's Noddy books.
- **Technology:** Digital audio tapes (DAT) are developed in Japan, by Aiwa; active suspension is developed by Ford, for Lotus Formula 1 racing cars.
- **Arts:** Whitney Houston becomes the first woman singer to top the Billboard charts with an album simply entitled *Whitney*.

SOUTH AFRICA in the 20th CENTURY 1980s

HENDRICKSE MAKES WAVES
5 January. Labour leader the Rev. Alan Hendrickse, accompanied by 150 supporters, takes to the sea off a Port Elizabeth beach that is set aside for whites only. This 'illegal' swim is in protest against the arrest of 18 black beach-lovers at Humewood on Friday.

DIED
Nazi leader Rudolf Hess; pop-artist Andy Warhol; film director John Huston; actress Rita Hayworth; actors Lee Marvin and Danny Kaye; classical guitarist Andrés Segovia; violinist Jascha Heifetz; dancer Fred Astaire; over-the-top pianist Liberace, from AIDS-related causes.

1988

MOVES TO RELEASE MANDELA?
17 August. Nelson Mandela's lawyer, Ismail Ayob, reports that his client has tuberculosis, is coughing up blood and looks 'very thin' and 'suddenly looks very old. It is clear that his condition has been deteriorating for some time'.

Mandela receives hospital treatment. Last month, on the occasion of his seventieth birthday, he was offered but refused a six-hour visit from wife Winnie and other family members. A spokesman for the Mandelas said that the decision was taken 'to focus attention on the thousands of mothers, sisters and daughters who have never had the chance of spending a day with their loved ones who are incarcerated for their opposition to apartheid'.

Later in the year Mandela is transferred to a pleasant three-bedroom house in the grounds of Victor Verster prison in Paarl. There is speculation that the move is a step towards his complete release.

Well-wishers at the hospital where Mandela is treated for tuberculosis.

WALLY, 79 AND STILL GOING STRONG
Wally Hayward completes the 90-kilometre Comrades marathon – at 79 the oldest ever entrant to do so. Hayward, described by sports scientists as a 'genetically superior' athlete, won the Comrades five times between 1930 and 1954. He also set new world 24-hour and 100-mile marks during the 1950s, when he was well over 40.

JUMBO JET CRASHES ON LOCKERBIE
A Pan Am jetliner explodes and plunges down on the small southern Scottish town of Lockerbie, killing all 259 on board and another 11 on the ground. Flames from the impact engulf two rows of houses. The Boeing 747 was en route from Frankfurt via London to New York.

The cause of the disaster is not known, but there is speculation that terrorists planted a bomb on the aircraft in retaliation for the recent accidental downing of an Iranian airliner, by missiles from a US cruiser, over the Persian Gulf. There are reports that American embassies received prior warning that a Pan Am flight would be targeted.

END OF COLD WAR IN SIGHT?
East-West tensions continue to ease as embattled Soviet leader Mikhail Gorbachev calls for a 'new world order' and reaffirms his intention to pursue *glasnost* (transparency) and *perestroika* (reform). He then cuts the size of the Red Army by half a million men. Late last year Gorbachev and US President Ronald Reagan made history when they agreed to reduce their nuclear arsenals.

Reagan visits Moscow, capital of what he once called the 'evil empire', in May and praises Gorbachev for his reforms. Gorbachev acknowledges that their meetings have made 'huge breaches in the walls of the Cold War fortress'.

ARTS AND ENTERTAINMENT
◆ This is the Year of the Woman, certainly on celluloid. Lovely Michelle Pfeiffer proves she really can act with a powerful performance in *Dangerous Liaisons*; Jodie Foster is superb as the rape victim

Wally Hayward strides out.

SOUTH AFRICA in the 20th CENTURY

The Eighties

in *The Accused*; tough-as-nails Jamie Lee Curtis keeps several steps ahead of John Cleese in the rollicking comedy *A Fish Called Wanda*. Dustin Hoffman and Tom Cruise score top marks in *Rain Man*, the moving story of an autistic genius.
◆ Hit singles: 'Mistletoe and Wine': Cliff Richard; 'I Should Be So Lucky': Kylie Minogue; 'I Think We're Alone Now': Tiffany; 'Faith': George Michael; 'Need You Tonight': INXS; 'Simply Irresistible': Robert Palmer
◆ Books: Disabled scientist Stephen Hawking's *A Brief History of Time*, which few can understand, becomes an improbable bestseller.

DIED
International: British spy (the 'third man') Kim Philby; footballer Jackie Milburn; heiress Christina Onassis; singer Roy Orbison; car designer Enzo Ferrari; actors Trevor Howard and Kenneth Williams. **South Africa:** Author Alan Paton; palaeoanthropologist and archaeologist Raymond Dart; circus clown Tickey (Eric Hoyland).

Alan Paton: acclaimed author.

1989

BOTHA OUT, DE KLERK IN

January. President P.W. Botha suffers a mild stroke and, a few weeks later, resigns the leadership of the ruling National Party in favour of Transvaal strongman Frederick Willem de Klerk. De Klerk is generally regarded as a political hardliner.

In August Botha also resigns the State Presidency, after fighting a bitter, unseemly rearguard action – against party progressives who think his anti-communist 'Total Strategy' has no place in the modern world, that the age of the 'securocrats' is over, that apartheid is well past its sell-by date, and that the time has come for an entirely new political dispensation.

P.W. Botha: forced to resign.

F.W. de Klerk: dawn of a new era.

The general election that follows confirms that white opinion has polarized. The Nats launch a 'smear and fear' campaign in a last-ditch effort to stampede voters back into the laager. But the party loses ground, both to the right, and to the growing body of realists who are convinced that the country is heading for all-out anarchy.

Time is on the side of the moderates: pressures to release ANC leader Nelson Mandela, now the world's best-known political prisoner – and to reach an accommodation with South Africa's black majority – have become irresistible.

BERLINERS OPEN GATEWAY TO FREEDOM

November. The Berlin Wall, for decades the symbol of East-West confrontation, comes crashing down, paving the way for an end to the Cold War.

Pressures for reform in the communist Eastern

The first of the massive, now-legal peace marches enlivens Cape Town's Adderley Street. From left: Sheik Nazeem Mohammed, Anglican Archbishop Desmond Tutu, Mayor of Cape Town Gordon Oliver and activist cleric Alan Boesak.

SOUTH AFRICA in the 20th CENTURY 1980s

The end of the Russian empire, and of the Cold War: a young Berliner helps smash the infamous Wall.

Bloc – notably in East Germany, Poland, Czechoslovakia and Romania – have been building up for months. Mass demonstrations, in East Berlin and other cities, call for free movement across borders; thousands of East Germans find their way to the West via Austria; what started out as a lively trickle quickly becomes a flood, and on 9 November all border restrictions are lifted.

Next day cheering Berliners from both sides of the hitherto divided city storm through the abandoned checkpoints to hug each other; others clamber onto the wall and begin breaking off chunks; still others arrive with sledgehammers to complete the job. Berlin, at last, is united and free.

Walter Sisulu.

SISULU RELEASED FROM PRISON

October. Former ANC secretary-general Walter Sisulu and six other ANC leaders – among them Oscar Mpetha, Raymond Mhlaba and Ahmed Kathrada – are released from prison. More than 70,000 jubilant supporters welcome them at a rally at Soccer City outside Soweto. Sisulu tells them that the liberation movement would be prepared to negotiate a suspension of hostilities once the government lifts the state of emergency, unbans the ANC and other bodies, and returns political exiles to their homes.

WHAT'S NEW IN 1989

Democratic supporters in high spirits as Jannie Momberg (centre) captures Simon's Town.

- **South African politics:** Democratic Party formed.
- **US politics:** George Bush succeeds Ronald Reagan as President.
- **Tiananmen Square, Beijing:** The Chinese army massacres several hundred pro-democracy demonstrators.
- **European Commission** orders total ban on CFC gases (contained in spray cans, refrigerators) by the end of the century.
- **Faked:** Milli Vanilli's song 'Girl, You Know It's True', rides high on the charts, but it is revealed that the group have mimed ('lip-synched') all their hits.
- **Britain:** In Europe's worst football disaster, 94 fans are crushed to death at Liverpool's Hillsborough ground during the FA Cup semifinal between Liverpool and Nottingham Forest.
- **Cinema:** The Japanese firm Sony buys Hollywood's Columbia Pictures.

DIED

International: Japanese emperor Hirohito; Romanian leader Nicolae Ceausescu, executed (with his wife) on Christmas Day; Iranian leader Ruholla (Ayatollah) Khomeini; actresses Lucille Ball and Bette Davis; actors Laurence Olivier and Anthony Quayle; songwriter Irving Berlin; painter Salvador Dali; conductor Herbert von Karajan; conservationist George Adamson (murdered, in Kenya); naturalist Peter Scott; aviation pioneer Thomas Sopwith, at age 101; boxer Sugar Ray Robinson; writers Samuel Beckett, Daphne du Maurier and Georges Simenon. *South Africa:* Painter May Hillhouse.

1990s

ELEVATED
1990: Slobodan Milošević, to the presidency of Serbia.
1991: Boris Yeltsin, to the presidency of the Russian Federation.
1992: The Democratic Party's Bill Clinton, to the US presidency, in succession to George Bush. He is re-elected in 1996.
1997: Labour leader Tony Blair, to British premiership.

GAINING INDEPENDENCE
1990: The Russian Federation, Lithuania and Uzbekistan, all from the former Soviet Union.
1992: Slovakia and the Czech Republic, from the former Czechoslovakia.

OUSTED
1990: British Tory premier Margaret Thatcher. She is succeeded by the colourless John Major.

COLLAPSED
1992: Public order in Somalia; UN and US troops intervene, with disastrous results. Ethnic warfare (between Serbs, Croats and Bosnians) continues to plague the former Yugoslavia.
1994: Public order in Rwanda; nearly a million die in the genocide that follows.

HONOURED
1991: SA novelist Nadine Gordimer, with the Nobel Prize for Literature.
1993: Nelson Mandela and F.W. de Klerk, with the Nobel Prize for Peace.
1998: Nelson Mandela, with the Congressional Gold Medal, the US's highest award.

ROYALS
1996: Prince Charles and Princess Diana are divorced; so too are Prince Andrew and wife Fergie.
1997: Princess Diana dies in a car smash, in Paris.

CHAMPIONS
1991: Australia win the Rugby World Cup, beating England in the final.
1994: Brazil win the Soccer World Cup, beating Italy in the final.
1995: South Africa win the Rugby World Cup, beating New Zealand in the final.
1996: SA swimmer Penny Heyns and marathon runner Josiah Thugwane win gold at the Atlanta Olympics, in the US.
1997: SA golfer Ernie Els wins the US Open.
1998: France win the Soccer World Cup, beating Brazil in the final; the Springboks win the Tri-Nations rugby championship.
1999: Australia win both the Rugby World Cup (beating France in the final) and the Cricket World Cup (beating Pakistan in the final).

PATHWAY TO PEACE
1990: SA President F.W. de Klerk unbans liberation organizations; Nelson Mandela released from prison. Namibia becomes an independent republic.
1991: The ANC, National Party and 17 other political groups meet under the auspices of the Convention for a Democratic SA, or Codesa. The US lifts sanctions; SA re-enters the sporting arena.
1992: White South Africans, voting in a referendum, give a massive 'yes' to the reform process. Massacres at Boipatong (near Johannesburg) and on the Ciskei border threaten peace talks, but chief negotiators sign a 'record of understanding'.
1993: Liberation hero Chris Hani assassinated. Talks continue. Transitional Executive Council replaces parliament as supreme authority.
1994: SA holds first democratic elections; ANC forms government of national unity; Nelson Mandela sworn in as state president.

South Africa's 'rainbow' flag first flutters in 1994.

Bill Clinton and White House intern Monica Lewinsky: the scandal of the decade.

THE NEW SA
1996: Truth and Reconciliation Commission (TRC) begins hearings.
1999: Mandela retires; Thabo Mbeki becomes President following second general election. The TRC produces its final report.

The Nineties

SOUTH AFRICA in the 20th CENTURY

1990

ANC UNBANNED: DAWN OF A NEW ERA

Cape Town, 2 February. In an astonishing speech at the opening of Parliament, President F.W. de Klerk announces the unbanning of 34 organizations, including the African National Congress, the imminent release of political prisoners and the lifting of media emergency regulations.

Political observers and ordinary South African people, nervous but hopeful, expected De Klerk simply to indicate how serious he is about change, but the radical extent of the reforms takes even the most optimistic of them by surprise.

The crowd waiting on the Cape Town's Grand Parade hears the news with disbelief, and then with euphoria. A convoy of cars and buses makes its way through the city with hooters blaring; the lead vehicle carries the ANC and Soviet flags. In Johannesburg, demonstrators outside the Cosatu offices shout 'Viva Comrade de Klerk', though the celebrations are marred when police fire teargas canisters.

Senior ANC leaders hold an emergency meeting in Stockholm, Sweden; the ANC's foreign affairs secretary Thabo Mbeki confirms that the address 'goes a very long way to meeting the ANC's demands'. Walter Sisulu says that De Klerk 'is a man the ANC can talk to'. In London, Prime Minister Margaret Thatcher describes the speech as 'an historic landmark on the road to a new South Africa'.

MANDELA WALKS TO FREEDOM

11 February. Nelson Mandela, incarcerated for the past 26 years, is unconditionally released and, with his wife Winnie at his side, walks to freedom through the gates of Victor Verster prison near Cape Town.

The emergence of the grey-suited, white-haired, dignified leader is witnessed by millions around the world, and greeted with rapture by black, and many white, people throughout South Africa.

Mandela is driven to Cape Town's Grand Parade, where a vast crowd has gathered. Some have been waiting for up to twelve hours. He finally appears on the balcony of the City Hall to roars of 'Viva' and 'Amandla', but there are few fireworks in his address. He stresses that he remains a loyal and disciplined member of the ANC, and that the armed struggle must go on, but strikes a conciliatory note in acknowledging that President de Klerk has taken 'real steps to normalize the situation'. He calls on 'our white compatriots to join us in the shaping of a new South Africa'.

Nelson Mandela, clasping wife Winnie's hand, ends his long walk to freedom.

SOUTH AFRICA in the 20th CENTURY
The Nineties

DIED
International: Composer Aaron Copland; actresses Barbara Stanwyck, Greta Garbo, Ava Gardner, Margaret Lockwood; actor Rex Harrison; singer and comedian Sammy Davis Jr; boxer Rocky Graciano; writers Irving Wallace, Roald Dahl; cricketer Len Hutton. *South Africa:* Actor Richard Haines; amateur Pretoria astronomer Jack Bennet, the only modern skywatcher to have made a visual discovery of a supernova (he also gave his name to two comets).

AGREEMENT AT GROOTE SCHUUR TALKS

Cape Town, 5 May. After years of bitter hostility, leaders of the African National Congress and the white Nationalist government emerge from their first meeting, held in the historic Groote Schuur mansion, confident of reaching an accord.
The talks were convened to define obstacles to formal negotiations.

The ANC delegation at the historic Groote Schuur talks. Front row from left: Ruth Mompati, Alfred Nzo, Nelson Mandela, Joe Slovo, Walter Sisulu, Cheryl Carolus. Back row: Archie Gumede, Ahmed Kathrada, Joe Modise, Beyers Naudé, Thabo Mbeki.

WHAT'S NEW IN 1990

- After 23 years of armed struggle, **Namibia** becomes a fully independent republic.
- **Iraq:** Saddam Hussein sends his armies into oil-rich Kuwait; US president George Bush commits troops to neighbouring Saudi Arabia.
- **Britain:** Premier Margaret Thatcher is ousted in a palace revolt, to be succeeded by John Major.
- The **Hubble space telescope**, designed to peer into the farthest reaches of the universe, is launched – but fails to deliver: its mirror has the wrong curvature.
- **Top films:** Ghost; Home Alone; Dances With Wolves; Pretty Woman.
- **Hit singles:** 'Unchained Melody': Righteous Brothers; 'Nothing Compares 2 U': Sinead O'Connor.

1991

SADDAM HUSSEIN DEFEATED IN HIGH-TECH GULF WAR

24 February. Saddam Hussein's armies are thrown out of Kuwait, with huge losses in men and material, by a half-million strong, 28-nation, American-led coalition force.

The ground phase of Operation Desert Storm lasts a bare 100 hours: the tough but battle-weary Iraqi soldiers, trained for defensive infantry warfare, have no answer to the tanks that come crashing over the Saudi border, or to the aircraft that swarm overhead, or to the banks of computers that guide the invaders.

The Gulf War started six weeks ago when Allied planes and missiles began pounding Baghdad, the Iraqi capital. High technology, including 'smart bombs' delivered by the new, radar-proof Stealth fighter, are a feature of this 'softening up' phase. The war – the air campaign at least – is also the first in history to be witnessed, blow by blow, by billions of ordinary people from the safety and comfort of their armchairs. The CNN television service is on hand to record the first missiles to explode, and keeps its cameras focused for the duration.

US President George Bush calls off the ground offensive after just three days, by which time Saddam's forces are in full flight. It is reckoned that up to 150,000 of his soldiers have been killed; Allied losses total fewer than 250. The retreating Iraqis, though, bequeath an environmentally disastrous legacy: they have set fire to Kuwait's oil wells, leaving behind them great clouds of billowing black smoke and an oil-polluted Gulf.

Kuwait's oilfields burn; firefighters battle the blazes.

SOUTH AFRICA in the 20th CENTURY — 1990s

De Klerk, Mandela and Buthelezi appear together for the first time.

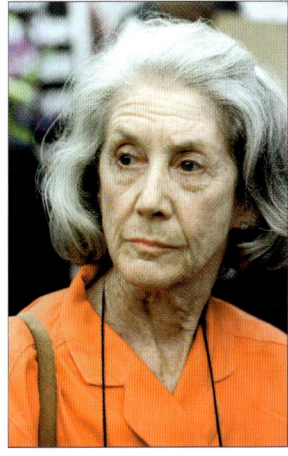

Nobel laureate Gordimer.

CODESA BEGINS PROBING FOR PEACE

South African political leaders come together to launch the super-talkshop, called the Convention for a Democratic South Africa (Codesa), and to sign a keynote declaration of intent to create a post-apartheid constitution 'by consensus'. There are 19 different groups represented; notable absentees are the Pan-Africanist Congress and Chief Mangosuthu Buthelezi's Inkatha Freedom Party.

The issues are complex. President F.W. de Klerk rejects simple majority rule in favour of a power-sharing formula with checks against 'domination of one group by another'. By this he means built-in protection for whites. He also advocates a federal arrangement. By contrast, the ANC and its partners want a unitary state, an all-powerful central government and a winner-takes-all electoral system.

WINNIE SENTENCED ON KIDNAPPING CHARGE

Winnie Mandela, wife of the ANC leader, is sentenced to six years' imprisonment for her involvement in the 1989 abduction and assault of four black youths, from a Soweto mission house, by her so-called 'football club'. One of the youths, 14-year-old Stompie Moeketsi Sepei, was later found murdered. The sentence is later reduced to a R15,000 fine.

SANCTIONS LIFTED; SA SPORTSMEN RE-ENTER WORLD ARENA

July. The US Congress, recognizing 'a profound transformation in South Africa', repeals the Comprehensive Anti-Apartheid Act and all remaining US sanctions.

The sporting embargoes also disappear. South Africa is welcomed back into the arena, and Colin Cowdrey, who was at the crease when the very last England-South Africa match ended, announces the end of the International Cricket Council's boycott.

GORDIMER WINS TOP AWARD

South African novelist Nadine Gordimer is awarded the 1991 Nobel Prize for Literature. Gordimer published her first notable book, a collection of short stories entitled *The Soft Voice of the Serpent*, in 1952, and her output since then – of profoundly thoughtful works written in studied, unsentimental style – has kept her in the top international literary ranks. Her last two books

DIED

International: Film director David Lean; ballet dancer Margot Fonteyn; author Graham Greene; cricket commentator John Arlott. **South Africa:** Writers Jack Cope and Uys Krige; dancer and choreographer David Poole.

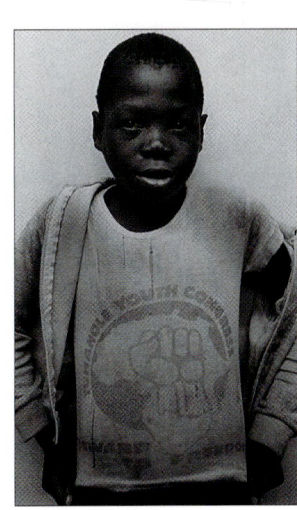

Murder victim Stompie Sepei.

WHAT'S NEW IN 1991

- **USSR:** The Union of Soviet Socialist Republics dissolves after member countries – including Estonia, Latvia, Azerbaijan and Armenia – declare their independence. Boris Yeltsin replaces Mikhail Gorbachev as Russian leader.
- **Sport:** Manchester United win the European Cup Winners' Cup, defeating Barcelona 2-1 in Rotterdam; American sprinter Carl Lewis sets a new world 100-metre mark of 9.85 seconds.

Boris Yeltsin takes over.

203

SOUTH AFRICA in the 20th CENTURY

The Nineties

Freddie Mercury: AIDS casualty.

are *A Sport of Nature*, published in 1987, and *My Son's Story*, which appeared last year.

ARTS AND ENTERTAINMENT

AIDS: Freddie Mercury, charismatic lead singer of the immensely successful pop group Queen, is the latest victim of the growing AIDS menace. Queen's *Bohemian Rhapsody*, the first video to promote a single recording, captivated viewers in 1975. Basketball star Erving 'Magic' Johnson reveals that he is HIV-positive and announces his retirement from the sport.

Movies of the year: Kevin Costner's sensitive *Dances with Wolves*, released last year, sweeps the board at the Oscars ceremony; Costner also scores with *Robin Hood: Prince of Thieves*; Jodie Foster and Anthony Hopkins (as the psychopath Hannibal 'the Cannibal' Lecter) keep audiences on the edge of their seats in *Silence of the Lambs*; so does Arnold Schwarzenegger, with the help of ground-breaking special effects, in *Terminator 2: Judgment Day*.

On the charts: Canadian Bryan Adams occupies top spot for a record 16 weeks with his '(Everything I do) I do it for You'. Other leaders are 'Bohemian Rhapsody' (resurrected): Queen; 'The Shoop Shoop Song': Cher; and 'The One and Only': Chesney Hawkes.

1992

MASSACRES, BUT PEACE PROCESS MOVES FORWARD

17 March. White South Africans flock to the voting booths to give overwhelming support to the 'continuation of the reform process which the State President began on 2 February 1990, and which is aimed at a new constitution through negotiation'.

There is a new air of hope, even confidence, in the corridors of power and among ordinary people. But matters suddenly take a turn for the worse.

On 17 June a 200-strong gang armed with guns and pangas attack the Boipatong informal settlement near Johannesburg; 39 residents are killed, many more injured. Suspicion falls on a shadowy 'third force' of conservative whites, and on elements in the predominantly Zulu Inkatha Freedom Party.

Inkatha Freedom Party supporters flourish 'cultural weapons'.

On 7 September Ciskei security forces fire on a crowd of ANC marchers, killing 28 and wounding more than 200.

The negotiations are in danger of collapse, but Mandela and De Klerk, their eyes set firmly on the ultimate prize, move to diffuse the crisis, signing a 'record of understanding'. This commits the parties to the creation of a non-racial transitional government, which is to be followed by the democratic election of a constituent assembly.

Thousands attend the funerals of the Boipatong victims.

SPORTING HIGHLIGHTS

This is a joyful year for South African sportsmen. The green-and-gold squad strides into the Barcelona Olympic stadium to a roar of welcome from the packed and sunlit stands, but the years of isolation have taken their toll and only Elana Meyer, second to the Ethiopian runner Tulu in the 10,000 metres, comes away with a track medal. Hand in hand, Meyer and Tulu complete a lap of honour.

SOUTH AFRICA in the 20th CENTURY 1990s

DIED
International: German leader Willie Brandt; Israeli leader Menachem Begin; jazz trumpeter Dizzy Gillespie; actors Robert Morley, Denholm Elliott and Anthony Perkins, who played the insane Norman Bates in Alfred Hitchcock's chilling classic Psycho; German actress Marlene Dietrich; comedians Benny Hill and Frankie Howard; authors Isaac Asimov, Alex Haley and Monica Dickens. *South Africa:* Human rights campaigner Helen Joseph; artist Gerard Bhengu; operatic singer Joyce Barker; Yvonne Bryceland, who acted in many of Athol Fugard's plays.

Queen Elizabeth and Prince Philip: a horrible year.

Weather defeats the country's cricketers, Down Under to contest their first World Cup. They start well, beating Australia by nine wickets (skipper Kepler Wessels scores 81 not out), fail against New Zealand and Sri Lanka but eventually squeak into the semifinals – against England and the darkening clouds. England, sent in to bat, make a little over 250 runs; South Africa chase and stand a good chance of overhauling this figure when rain comes down. When play resumes, the rule book sets a target of 22 runs in 13 balls and then, after a second shower, a laughable 22 runs off one ball. South Africa bow out with honour; England go though to the final, and are defeated by Pakistan.

Boxing says farewell to its favourite son when Brian Mitchell retires. Mitchell, a fighter of true class and unusual modesty, won the WBA junior lightweight championship when he beat Alfredo Layne in 1986 and went on to defend the title on a record ten occasions.

ROYALS EMBARRASS QUEEN

For Britain's Queen Elizabeth, it's been an 'annus horribilis' – a horrible year. The increasingly obvious rift between son Charles and his wife Diana stirs up a media feeding frenzy; biographer Andrew Morton reveals that Charles has returned to his long-time mistress Camilla Parker-Bowles, and that Diana developed an eating disorder and tried to kill herself. Not to be outdone, Fergie, Duchess of York and wife to Prince Andrew, is caught by the camera, in topless pose, with her 'financial adviser', American businessman John Bryan.

SIGHT AND SOUND

Top movies: *Unforgiven* (with Clint Eastwood); *Basic Instinct* (with Sharon Stone); *Howard's End*; *A Few Good Men*; *Lethal Weapon 3*; *Wayne's World*; *The Player*; and *The Crying Game*.

Hit singles: 'I Will Always Love You': Whitney Houston (from the film *The Bodyguard*); 'Please Don't': KWS; 'Stay': Shakespears Sister; 'Tears in Heaven': Eric Clapton; 'Save the Best for Last': Vanessa Williams.

WHAT'S NEW IN 1992

- **Bill Clinton** is elected US president.
- World heavyweight boxing champion **Mike Tyson** is convicted of raping Désirée Washington, a Miss Black America contestant, and is sentenced to 10 years in prison.
- **US:** Rioting in Los Angeles leaves 58 dead, thousands injured and buildings burnt. The trouble is triggered by the video-taped beating of Rodney King, a black motorist, by white cops.
- **Cricket:** South African strike bowler Alan Donald is adjudged Wisden's Cricketer of the Year. Donald made his international debut last year, and will go on to take well over 200 Test wickets.
- **Virtual reality** is developed as a 3-D video game, in the US.
- The phrase **ethnic cleansing** enters the English language.

Alan Donald: cricketer of the year.

SOUTH AFRICA in the 20th CENTURY

The Nineties

Hani with Cuban flag: a hero to the radicals.

1993

CHRIS HANI ASSASSINATED

10 April. Charismatic South African Communist Party boss Chris Hani, 50, died in a hail of bullets outside his Johannesburg home this morning.

Police act quickly, arresting Polish-born Janusz Wallus and right-wing political figure Clive Derby-Lewis in connection with the crime.

The tragedy puts the crucial constitutional talks in jeopardy, and threatens to trigger widespread unrest: Hani has been a hero to young black radicals, and was one of the few political personalities of stature capable of controlling the extremists of the left. In his last speeches before his death he urged the more militant elements in his huge audiences to work rather than fight for peace.

ANC and white Nationalist leaders avert disaster when they urge calm and agree to continue the talks. The two suspects, they say, appear to have acted on their own and there is no evidence of a wider conspiracy.

Martin Thembisile (better known as Chris) Hani joined the ANC in 1957 and was exposed to Marxist thinking at Fort Hare University, where he also developed a love for the classics and for literature. He underwent military training in the Soviet Union, took part in the low-key but savagely fought Rhodesian bush war, and was then based in Lesotho, his special task the reorganization of ANC structures in the eastern Cape. He became chief of staff of Umkhonto we Sizwe ('spear of the nation') in 1987, and five years later, on his return to South Africa, was elected secretary-general of the SACP.

WHAT'S NEW IN 1993

- President F.W. de Klerk reveals that South Africa built six **atomic bombs** but destroyed them two years ago.
- The first **Internet** program, or 'browser', is devised. It's called Mosaic.
- **US:** A massive bomb explodes in the parking garage of New York's World Trade Center.
- **IT:** Cellular phones become standard accessories rather than status symbols; the first voice-operated TV/radio remote control is launched.

Bomb damage at the World Trade Center.

TALKS ACHIEVE BREAKTHROUGH: LEADERS SHARE BIG PRIZE

The Kempton Park negotiators burn the midnight oil, and in June finally agree on an interim constitution for the country, on the need to bring the 'homelands' back into the South African fold, and on a date for national elections. The polls, which are scheduled for next April, are to be held on a one-person-one-vote, proportional representation basis; the people will choose a central government and nine regional governments.

In September, Nelson Mandela calls for the removal of all remaining international sanctions.

IN THE CHARTS
- Turn the Beat Around: Gloria Estefan
- Can't Help Falling in Love: UB40
- Dreams: Gabrielle
- All that She Wants: Ace of Base
- I Would Do Anything for Love: Meat Loaf

SOUTH AFRICA in the 20th CENTURY 1990s

The peacemakers: Mandela and De Klerk share the Nobel Prize.

macho roots of South African humour, a commodity as rawboned and physical as ourselves – whether we care to own up to it or not'. In the hugely popular *There's a Zulu on My Stoep*, Schuster swops skin pigmentation with black actor John Matshikiza. Close on the heels of this romp is *Panic Mechanic*, which breaks all local box-office records.

Steven Spielberg's *Jurassic Park*, setting new standards in computer simulation, is the international box-office hit of the year. In a quite different class is *Schindler's List*, Spielberg's moving tribute to the wartime German businessman who saved the lives of 1,200 Polish

Two months later ANC leader Nelson Mandela and President F.W. de Klerk share the Nobel Peace prize. The two stand on opposite sides of the racial divide but, together, they have piloted the ship of state to safe harbour.

In December, Parliament is effectively replaced by a multi-party Transitional Executive Council.

IN FASHION

For the young, 'grunge' is the name of the game when it comes to both clothes and music. The man's look is deliberately grubby – torn t-shirt, baggy knee-length shorts, heavy boots, no hairstyle to speak of, baseball cap turned back to front. Ugly, and deliberately so. It all began in the disillusioned Eighties with Kurt Cobain and Nirvana, Pearl Jam and other groups that produced a kind of tired and very loud punk sound. In part it's thumbing one's nose at smart yuppiedom, in part a reaction against the strictures of high fashion.

But the couture industry has hit back, elevating its coathangers to icon status. Supermodels like Cindy Crawford, Kate Moss, Naomi Campbell, Christy Turlington and Linda Evangelista are as well known as the top pop stars – and just about as well paid.

ON CIRCUIT

Leon Schuster's films are all the rage, at least in a country where, in columnist Charlotte Bauer's words, they 'tap the

Supermodels Naomi Campbell (left) and Kate Moss.

207

SOUTH AFRICA in the 20th CENTURY

DIED
International: South African-born scientist Lord Zuckerman; dancer Rudolph Nureyev; actresses Lilian Gish and Audrey Hepburn; actor River Phoenix; authors William Golding and Leslie Charteris; tennis player Arthur Ashe; footballer Bobby Moore; racing driver James Hunt. *Southern Africa:* Liberation leader Oliver Tambo; violinist Pierre de Groote; cricketer Eric Rowan; actor and director Simon Sabela; most of the Zambian national soccer squad, in a plane crash in Gabon.

Nelson Mandela takes the presidential oath of office.

Jews. Tom Hanks gives a star performance in *Philadelphia*, the first major Hollywood feature about AIDS. Other top movies include *Mrs Doubtfire* (Robin Williams in drag); *The Fugitive* (Harrison Ford on the run) and the tear-jerking *Sleepless in Seattle* (with Meg Ryan and, again, Tom Hanks).

##

ELECTIONS USHER IN NEW SOUTH AFRICA

The miracle unfolds; South Africans of all colours cast their votes in the country's first ever fully democratic elections – and do so free of fear.

Most people expected trouble, and indeed the run-up to the polls is marred by bombings and acts of sabotage, allegedly the work of right-wing white groups, that kill 21 and injure hundreds more. And, as election fever mounts, ANC snipers fire on a massive Zulu procession that, bristling with 'cultural weapons', is wending its way through Johannesburg's streets. At least 18 are killed; many more are wounded. Generally speaking, though, the election process unfolds in lively, often chaotic but – astonishingly in view of past antagonisms – good-humoured fashion. There are no incidents on the day itself, and millions wait patiently in long lines to exercise their long-denied rights.

The ANC gains just under a two-thirds majority in the new National Assembly. It also captures six of the nine regional parliaments, shares the honours in a seventh (the Northern Cape), loses the Western Cape to the Nationalists (the conservative coloured vote proves decisive) and KwaZulu-Natal to Mangosuthu Buthelezi's Inkatha Freedom Party.

On a sunny May day bright with hope, Nelson Rolihlahla Mandela mounts the podium in front of Pretoria's Union Building and takes the oath of office as the first president of a free and democratic South Africa. There to witness the historic event is the largest assembly of foreign luminaries ever to come together in Africa. 'Let there be peace for all,' says

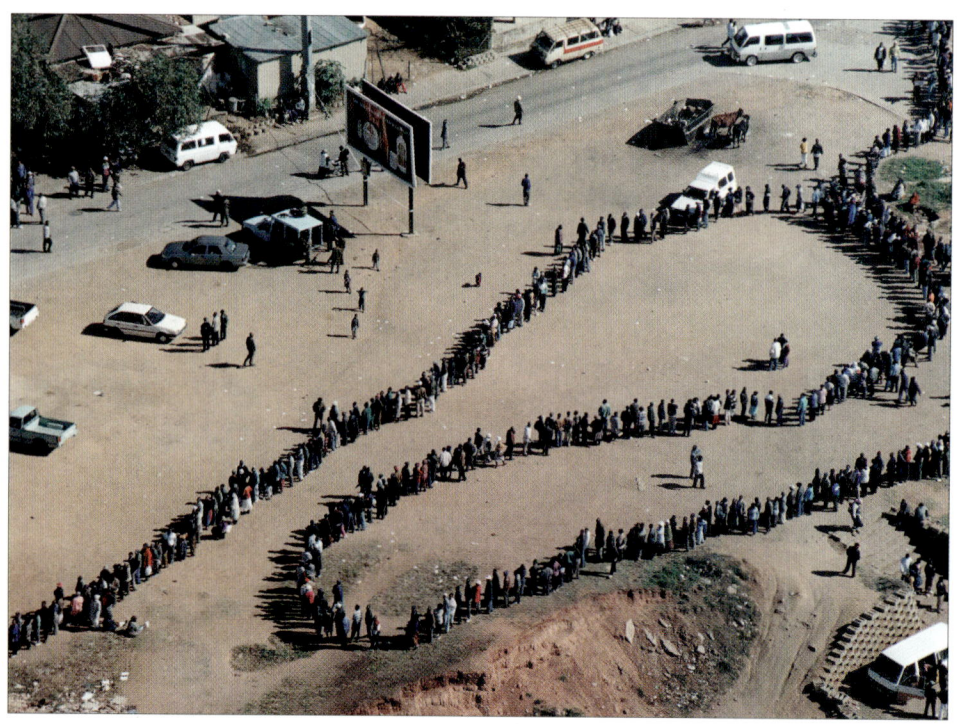

Long lines of voters wait patiently to launch democracy in South Africa.

SOUTH AFRICA in the 20th CENTURY — 1990s

Mandela in his address. 'Let there be work, salt and bread for all. The time for healing has come.'

GENOCIDE IN RWANDA

Rwanda, 21 April. More than 100,000 Tutsis and moderate Hutus are slaughtered during two weeks of mindless violence following the death, in a plane crash, of President Habyarimana. Among the victims are Roman Catholic priests and nuns, aid workers, and eleven Belgian members of the United Nations force deployed earlier to monitor the fragile peace. In the months to come an estimated 700,000 more people will lose their lives in what develops into Africa's worst-ever orgy of killing.

DIED
International: US politician Richard Nixon; Jacqueline Onassis, widow of the late US president John F. Kennedy; actor Burt Lancaster; Kurt Cobain, lead singer of the group Nirvana, by his own hand; Brazilian racing driver Ayrton Senna, killed during the Imola Grand Prix in Italy. **South Africa:** Lawyer and jurist Izrael ('Izzy') Maisels; trade unionist and community leader Oscar Mpetha; cricketer Hugh Tayfield; Danie Craven, universally known as 'Mr Rugby'.

Rugby wing Chester Williams: three Test tries.

Racing driver Ayrton Senna: killed at Imola.

SPORT AND ENTERTAINMENT

Boxing: Stylish junior featherweight Vuyani Bungu wins the IBF title, beating hard-hitting American Kennedy McKinney. Heavyweight George Foreman comes back, at age 47, to win the world title – 20 years after losing it to Muhammad Ali.

Rugby: Wing Chester Williams, the first rugby player of colour to represent the Springboks since Errol Tobias broke the mould 14 years ago, scores three tries against Wales in Cardiff.

Cricket: West Indian batsman Brian Lara sets a world record by scoring 375 in a Test match (against England) and 501 in a county game (for Warwickshire against Durham).

Soccer: Brazil win the World Cup, defeating Italy in a penalty shoot-out; Colombian soccer player Andres Escobar, whose own-goal eliminated his side from the Cup, is shot to death on his return to home town Medellin.

Top movies: *Pulp Fiction* (with John Travolta and Uma Thurman); *Forrest Gump* (with Tom Hanks); *Speed* (with Sandra Bullock), and Disney's animated tour de force, *The Lion King*.

On the charts: 'Love is All Around': Wet Wet Wet; 'All for Love': Bryan Adams, Sting, Rod Stewart.

Publishing: New books include J.M. Coetzee's *The Master of Petersburg*; Nadine Gordimer's *None to Accompany Me*. James Redfield's *The Celestine Prophecy* is the international best-seller.

WHAT'S NEW IN 1994

- The **UN tribunal for war crimes** is established in The Hague, Netherlands.
- **The Chunnel** – the Channel Tunnel linking Britain and France – is inaugurated.
- Weird superstar **Michael Jackson** weds Lisa Marie, daughter of rock legend Elvis Presley; he answers 'Why not?' instead of 'I do' at the ceremony. Earlier in the year Jackson is investigated by Los Angeles police for the sexual abuse of a minor.
- The first **women priests** are ordained into the Church of England.
- The phrase **road rage** enters the language.

SOUTH AFRICA in the 20th CENTURY

The Nineties

Moment of triumph: captain Pienaar receives the Cup from Madiba.

1995

SPRINGBOKS TRIUMPH IN WORLD CUP

The Springboks, aided by 'Madiba Magic', pride in the new South Africa and a vast and fanatical home crowd, power their way to victory in their first Rugby World Cup.

The fairy-tale begins at Newlands, Cape Town, where the hosts take on current world champions Australia (who are unbeaten in twelve months) and, against all expectations, win 27-18. But the occasion is much more than the opening match in a 16-nation contest. This is South Africa's real return to the international sporting arena; the stadium is festive with rainbow flags, noisy with song, and millions around the world watch as Nelson Mandela, the charismatic new State President, walks onto the field to inaugurate the tournament. For one magic month, the peoples of South Africa are united.

Mandela is there again, at the final, wearing François Pienaar's No. 6 jersey, to cheer Kitch Christie's boys in their battle with the mighty All Blacks. It's a gritty war of attrition between titans; honours are even, the fulltime score 9-9. Extra time, an exchange of penalties, and there is exhaustion and courage in equal measure as the minutes tick away. Then the miracle drop-goal: pivot Joel Stransky receives close to New Zealand's 22-metre line, steadies himself, and sends the ball sailing high and handsome between the posts.

Rugby great Morné du Plessis recalls that although he feels ecstatic he is also 'filled with sadness. I knew I would never experience anything like that again. It was a once-in-a-lifetime moment. That was it for me. I knew I had had my moment. It was gone'.

DEATH OF A GIANT

Joe Slovo, a giant of the liberation struggle, dies of leukemia. Lithuanian-born Slovo (he arrived in the country at age nine) was a lawyer, a leading member of the Communist Party and one of the architects of the seminal Freedom Charter. He also helped form Umkhonto we Sizwe (MK), the ANC's military wing, and later served as its chief of staff. During the 1980s he worked in Maputo, London and Lusaka, from where he masterminded MK's operations. Last year he was appointed Minister of Housing in the Government of National Unity. His wife, Ruth First, was murdered by letter-bomb in 1982.

Joe Slovo: key party member.

Joe Slovo confers with his leader Nelson Mandela.

SOUTH AFRICA in the 20th CENTURY

NEW SOFTWARE LAUNCHED

Home and office computers reach a new level of sophistication, say Bill Gates' fans, with the launch of Microsoft's Windows 95, a refinement of Windows 3.x that introduced menus and icons to the DOS operating software. Many other users, though, remain loyal to the Apple Macintosh system that appeared, far ahead of its time, in the late 1980s. Seattle-born genius Gates, who designed a traffic-control program for his home city at the age of 15, and then (in 1981) licensed DOS to personal computer giant IBM, is the world's richest man.

WHAT'S NEW IN 1995

- *Illustrious visitors to South Africa include **Pope John Paul II** and **Queen Elizabeth II**.*
- *SA bans **capital punishment**.*
- *Israeli premier **Yitzhak Rabin**, co-architect of the Camp David peace accord, is assassinated.*
- ***Space:** In an historic link-up, the US shuttle* Discovery *docks with the Russian space station* Mir.
- ***Banking:** Rogue trader Nick Leeson, 26, single-handedly brings down Barings, Britain's most venerable bank, when he runs up losses of around R6 billion.*
- ***US:** 158 people are killed in a massive bomb blast that destroys Oklahoma City's Alfred P. Murrah federal building.*
- *British serial killer **Frederick West**, accused of murdering 12 people (including daughter and stepdaughter), hangs himself in his cell.*

Historic moment: the late Yitzhak Rabin (left) and Palestinian leader Yasser Arafat shake on the Camp David peace deal; US President Bill Clinton smiles approval.

JURY ACQUITS OJ

Los Angeles, 3 October. After a mammoth nine-month trial, watched by televiewers in South Africa and around the world, football great and sometime actor O.J. Simpson is acquitted of murdering his ex-wife Nicole and her acquaintance Ronald Goldman. Two years later Simpson is found guilty, on the balance of probability, by a civil court.

O.J. Simpson: acquitted.

MANDELA TARGETS MILITARY REGIME

South Africa's president Nelson Mandela leads the campaign to suspend Nigeria's membership of the Commonwealth. The move follows outrage at the public execution of Ken Saro-Wiwa, the Nigerian poet and human-rights activist, by the military regime.

NOTABLES PART COMPANY

This has been a year of marital separations in the world of the rich and famous. Among the more prominent: Earl Spencer (brother of Princess Diana) and his wife Victoria, who are living in Cape Town, finally part company to conclude a messy divorce. Camilla Parker Bowles, mistress of Prince Charles, splits from husband Anthony. Actors Melanie (*Working Girl*) Griffith and Don (*Miami Vice*) Johnson end their second go at marriage. Onetime screen goddess Elizabeth Taylor sends seventh husband Larry Fortensky packing.

SIGHT AND SOUND

Top movies: *Dead Man Walking* (with Sean Penn and Susan Sarandon); *Babe* (with the pig, or rather pigs, of that name); *The Madness of King George*; *Apollo 13*; *Muriel's Wedding*; and *Four Weddings and a Funeral* (with British actor Hugh Grant – who also hits the headlines when he is arrested, in Hollywood, for lewd conduct with a prostitute in a public place).
On the charts: 'I Believe': Robson and Jerome; 'Kiss from a Rose': Seal; 'All I Really Want': Alanis Morissette; 'Think Twice': Céline Dion; 'Back For Good': Take That; 'Gansta's Paradise': Coolio.

DIED

International: Author Kingsley Amis; actor and singer Dean Martin; dancer and actress Ginger Rogers, who made more than 80 films but is best remembered for her partnership with Fred Astaire; Jerry Garcia, leader of Sixties group The Grateful Dead; author James Herriott. **South Africa:** Musician and big-band leader Gerry Bosman, a feature of the local airwaves for the past three decades; boxer Vic Toweel.

The Nineties

SOUTH AFRICA in the 20th CENTURY

1996

TUTU'S COMMISSION GETS GOING

April. South Africa's Truth and Reconciliation Commission, chaired by Archbishop Desmond Tutu and convened to expose (and, when asked to do so, forgive) the crimes of the past, holds the first of its hearings, in East London.

The commission's task promises to be difficult, not least because its very purpose is under debate. Its mission is based on the Biblical principle that 'the truth shall set you free', yet there are many who think the investigations will simply open up old wounds and thus impede the process of national reconciliation.

It must also be careful not to show bias. Already the ANC draws a distinction between actions committed in the name of apartheid and those 'defending not an evil system but a movement dedicated to democracy'.

The process will gain momentum over the next three years and the commission's hearings will, by and large, be seen as fair and valuable to national reconciliation.

Desmond Tutu: towards national reconciliation.

Elvis Presley and Juliet Prowse in the 1960 movie GI Blues.

STARS BOW OUT

Juliet Prowse, the Indian-born, South African trained dancer and actress, has died at the age of 59. She made a name for herself in Hollywood in the 1950s and 1960s. She appeared with Frank Sinatra and Shirley MacLaine in *Can Can*, her first major feature film (Russian leader Nikita Kruschev, visiting the set, gave her priceless publicity when he denounced the dancing as 'immoral'); topped the entertainment bill at Las Vegas, and was romantically linked to Frank Sinatra, to whom she was briefly engaged, and to Elvis Presley. Her major contribution to South Africa's film industry was her performance in Jamie Uys' *Dingaka*.

Another star of the stage makes a final exit: Siegfried Mynhardt, widely known for his Shakespearean roles, played with London's Old Vic and with practically every South African theatre company during his long and illustrious career. He twice won the Best Actor award (in 1963 and 1967), for his performances in *The Affair* and *Heartbreak House*), and was the first to present an Afrikaans version of a Shakespearean play to Johannesburg audiences. He also appeared in a number of feature films.

Prowse during her London stage career.

SOUTH AFRICA in the 20th CENTURY 1990s

SPORT: SOUTH AFRICANS ON WINNING STREAK

Boxing great Muhammad Ali, who could once 'float like a butterfly, sting like a bee' but now crippled by Parkinson's disease, lights the Olympic Flame in Atlanta. South Africans perform with honour; Durban swimmer Penny Heyns breaks the world 100-metre breast-stroke record and also takes gold in the 200 metres; Hezekiel Sepeng gains silver in the men's 800 metres (he becomes the country's first black Games medallist), and the diminutive Josiah Thugwane wins the closest marathon in Olympic history.

Thugwane's is a rags-to-riches story. Abandoned at birth, he grew up illiterate and, before the race, worked as a mine janitor, living in a humble shack with his wife and four children – not the ideal environment for an athlete in training. And the odds lengthened even more, a few months before his departure for Atlanta, when he was shot in the face by car hijackers. His Olympics victory makes him an instant millionaire.

And, to cap a good year, the national soccer team, Bafana Bafana, wins the African Cup of Nations.

MASSACRE OF THE INNOCENTS

Two senseless killing sprees capture the headlines. In the Scottish village of Dunblane, 43-year old scoutmaster Thomas Hamilton walks into the local primary school and shoots 16 children. Hamilton is a loner with a suspect background. In Port Arthur, Tasmania, 28-year-old Michael Bryant methodically guns down 20 patrons of a crowded café.

Mandela cheers as Bafana captain Neil Tovey holds the Cup aloft.

Josiah Thugwane: victor in the closest marathon.

WHAT'S NEW IN 1996

◆ The **Dalai Lama** visits South Africa.
◆ **Medical:** An estimated 30 million people worldwide will die of tuberculosis within the next ten years, predicts the World Health Organisation.
◆ **UK:** Prince Charles and Princess Diana divorce. So too do the Duke and Duchess of York (Andrew and Fergie).
◆ **Same-sex marriages** are prohibited in terms of the Defence of Marriage Act, US.
◆ The word **cyberspace** enters the English language.

Fergie: divorced.

SOUTH AFRICA in the 20th CENTURY
The Nineties

DIED
International: French politician François Mitterrand; comedian George Burns, aged 100; actress Claudette Colbert; jazz singer Ella Fitzgerald; Timothy Leary, doyen of the Sixties 'psychedelic revolution'; South African-born Air Marshall Sir Arthur McDonald, a key figure in the development of radar; cricket commentator Alan McGilvray. **South Africa:** Human rights campaigner Jean Sinclair; champion jockey Tiger Wright, who rode 2,454 race winners, including four in the Durban July.

Jazz queen Ella Fitzgerald.

BEST SELLERS
Movies: Shine; Emma; The First Wives Club; Independence Day; 101 Dalmations (a remake with both real and computer-animated dogs); Secrets and Lies.
Hit singles: 'Wannabe': Spice Girls; 'Forgiven, Not Forgotten': The Corrs; 'Killing Me Softly': Fugees; 'Say You'll Be There': Spice Girls; 'Return of the Mack': Mark Morrison; 'Where the Wild Roses Grow': Kylie Minogue and Nick Cave.
Books: John Grey's Men Are From Mars, Women Are From Venus.

1997

PRINCESS DI KILLED IN CAR CRASH

Tragedy strikes the beleaguered British Royal Family and millions around the world mourn when Diana, Princess of Wales and former wife to Prince Charles, dies in a midnight car smash in a Paris underpass. Also killed are her constant companion, millionaire playboy Dodi Al Fayed, and Henri Paul, driver of the armoured Mercedes. Bodyguard Trevor Rees Jones is badly injured but survives.

The accident occurs after a late-night dinner at the Ritz, when the departing couple are chased through the city streets by paparazzi on motorbikes. The car, travelling at high speed, veers out of control on a slight curve and slams into a concrete column.

Condolences pour in from across the continents; the pavement outside Kensington Palace is transformed by an ocean of flowers. A week later Diana's funeral cortège, watched by thousands in silence and broadcast to countries all around the world,

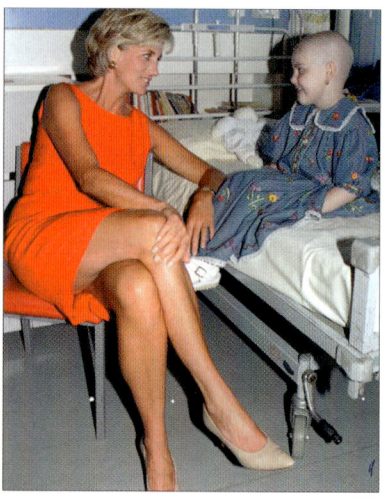
Diana cheers up a young AIDS patient.

The men in Di's life follow her coffin: (from left) former father-in-law Prince Philip, elder son Prince William, brother Earl Spencer, younger son Prince Harry and former husband Prince Charles.

winds its slow way to Westminster Abbey. The service is simple and dignified; pop star Elton John, a personal friend of the Princess, sings a revised version of his hit 'Candle in the Wind'. Nearly 32 million copies of the song, recorded directly after the funeral, are sold during the next four weeks.

The coffin is borne through Westminster Abbey.

SOUTH AFRICA in the 20th CENTURY 1990s

ON THE CHARTS
- Barbie Girl: Aqua
- Bittersweet Symphony: The Verve
- MMMBop: Hanson
- I'll Be Missing You: Puff Daddy
- Don't Speak: No Doubt

WHAT'S NEW IN 1997

- Visitors to South Africa include **Mother Teresa** and **Princess Diana**, both of whom die later in the year.
- **South Africa:** F.W. de Klerk quits politics.
- South African troops invade **Lesotho**.
- British scientists succeed in **cloning** a sheep: Dolly is an exact replica of a donor adult animal.
- **UK politics:** Tony Blair's Labour Party win a landslide victory at the polls.
- The British colony of **Hong Kong** reverts to the People's Republic of China.

Cherie and Tony Blair.

DIED
International: Mother Teresa of Calcutta, saintly head of the Missionaries of Charity; explorer Jacques Cousteau; poet Allen Ginsberg; singers John Denver and Michael Hutchence; actors James Stewart and Robert Mitchum; fashion designer Gianni Versace. **South Africa:** Quinten Smythe, last surviving recipient of the Victoria Cross (for gallantry in the Western Desert, in 1942); movie-maker Jamie Uys; author Laurens van der Post; trade unionist Frances Baard; actor, producer and playwright Brian Brooke; activist Barney Desai. Also //Am//Op, leader of the //Khomeni clan of the southern Kalahari (and known to outsiders for the sound of his mouth-bow), whose name, which means 'Survivor', was given him by his parents who had escaped a party of German Bushman-hunters from Namibia in 1899; says musicologist Cait Andrews: 'His personal song was the survivor's song. He is gone now and with him an era has died, a language and a lot of knowledge.'

Among the year's other sporting highlights: field athlete Marius Corbett comes from nowhere to win the javelin at the world championships in Athens; IBF lightweight champion Philip Holiday successfully defends his title, against hard-hitting Australian Jeff Fenech, to record his 28th consecutive ring victory; stylish cricketer Peter Kirsten scores his 57th first-class century in the last inter-provincial match of his long career (he made his debut in 1973); wicket-keeper Dave Richardson claims his 141st Test dismissal, in the Melbourne match against

BIG ERNIE BEATS THE BEST

Golfing great Ernie Els, affectionately known to the press as 'The Big Easy', enjoys his best year yet on the world circuit, winning the Johnnie Walker Classic in Australia, the US Open and, a week later, the Buick Classic. He then helps South Africa to victory in the Alfred Dunhill world team event at St Andrews, Scotland, and goes on to take the PGA Grand Slam of Golf title in Hawaii, beating the year's three other grand-slam winners (he also breaks the course record).

South Africa's Ernie ('The Big Easy') Els: best year on circuit.

SOUTH AFRICA in the 20th CENTURY

The Nineties

Australia, to beat Johnny Waite's long-standing South African record.

Jockey Michael Roberts, the first local boy to win 200 races in a season, left in 1988 to become Britain's leading rider – but had never won the Rothman's (Durban July); this year he remedies the omission when he returns to Greyville to bring Super Quality to victory.

STAGE AND SCREEN

Alice Krige, one of South Africa's more successful foreign-based actresses, stars in the hugely popular Hollywood spectacular *Star Trek, First Contact*. Krige was born in the Kalahari desert (her father was a flying doctor), trained as a dancer, qualified as a psychologist but took up acting instead. She made her screen debut as the charming Sybil in the award-winning *Chariots of Fire*. Another South African, actor, artist and writer Anthony Sher, makes his Broadway debut.

Also in the news is Anant Singh, the young Durban producer who is handling Nelson Mandela's autobiographical *Long Walk to Freedom*. Singh has brought some of the best anti-apartheid movies to international screens, including the film version of Alan Paton's *Cry the Beloved Country* and Mbongeni Ngema's *Sarafina*. Last year he became the first South African admitted to the Academy of Motion Picture Arts and Sciences (the body which organizes the Oscar awards).

Alice Krige in Chariots of Fire.

Richard Harris (left) and James Earl Jones in Cry the Beloved Country.

Two fine troupers bow out during the year. Stage director Leonard Schach presented more than 250 plays during his illustrious career, including Arthur Miller's *After the Fall* – staged in 1964 and the last play during the apartheid era to be legally performed before a multiracial South African audience. Among his other notable productions was *The Comedians*, which defied the old censorship laws and proved a triumph for Johannesburg's young Market Theatre.

Eve Boswell, who became an international star with such hit numbers as 'Sugarbush' ('Suikerbossie') and 'Pickin' a Chicken', will sing no more. Voted Britain's 'Forces' Favourite' in the 1950s, she gave numerous radio and television performances in Europe and the US, and later hosted her own TV shows, among them *Eve and Song*, *The Eve Boswell Show* and *The Song's the Thing*.

1998

EVE'S FOOT-PRINT FOUND

Stunning discoveries are made by South African scientists investigating humankind's distant past.

Cape Town archaeologist Dave Roberts finds 'Eve's footprint', a perfectly preserved impression on the dune rock near Langebaan on the West Coast. The fossilized print, dating back 117,000 years, is the oldest sign yet found of an anatomically modern human, indicating that the region was the cradle of *Homo sapiens*, and that the genes that mutated here slowly spread to become dominant everywhere.

Farther north, the scientific world sits up when Ron Clarke discovers the almost complete skeleton of a 3.5-million-year-old hominid in the palaeontological treasure-house of the Sterkfontein cave complex. Clarke is a Wits University colleague of the renowned Philip

Ngema's Sarafina*: brought to the big screen by Anant Singh.*

SOUTH AFRICA in the 20th CENTURY

Digging up the past: Ron Clarke (centre) and helpers.

Tobias, who sparked a row in archaeological circles in the 1980s with his theory that humankind's ancestor of two million years ago, long thought incapable of language communication, was in fact 'a jabbering, chattering, talking and teaching hominid'. Later, after the 1994 discovery of the 3.5 million-year old 'Little Foot' at Sterkfontein, he advanced brand new theories on how, why and when ape-men began walking upright.

DISASTERS ARE WORST EVER; MORE PREDICTED
Nature turns nasty during the year: the International Federation of the Red Cross says that natural disasters have caused more damage and driven more refugees from the land than all the regional wars and conflicts combined.

And the future looks just as grim: the developing world will continue to be hit by 'super-disasters' as global population spirals, and human activity changes the climate and degrades the environment.

El Niño, declining soil fertility and deforestation have chased 25 million 'environmental refugees' from their land, swelling the cities of the poorer regions. Fires, droughts and floods caused by El Niño kill 21,000 people; 180 million others are displaced by floods in China's Yangtse basin. Among the hardest hit countries is Indonesia, where crops fail, the price of rice quadruples, the currency loses 80 percent of its value and vast forest fires burn out of control, polluting much of southeast Asia.

THE PASSING OF TWO LOCAL LEGENDS
The renowned composer and jazz musician Basil 'Manenberg' Coetzee dies, in Cape Town, at the age of 54. Coetzee, who grew up in District Six, first mastered the pennywhistle, went on to play (saxophone, flute) with Pacific Express and Sabenza, and recorded 'Manenberg', his best-known piece, on his friend Abdullah Ibrahim's album *Manenberg – Where it's Happening*. The moving 11-minute number became one of the anthems of the liberation struggle. But the composer's often experimental music, and his refusal to allow political correctness to intrude into his work, limited his following, and he died in relative poverty.

Quite different but just as renowned in his own field was Soweto entrepreneur Godfrey Moloi, former gangster and shebeen king who made news in 1987, when he was reported to have been murdered by the dreaded 'necklace' method. The reports, however, were greatly exaggerated and he popped up again, unscathed and in prime health, to write his autobiography. *My Life, Volume One* dwelt on Durban's shebeen culture in the 1940s, the Orlando gangs of the '50s, the development of township jazz and Moloi's friendship with acclaimed singer Miriam Makeba.

Shebeen king Godfrey Moloi lives it up.

217

SOUTH AFRICA in the 20th CENTURY
The Nineties

WHAT'S NEW IN 1998

◆ Among heavyweight politicians to visit South Africa are US President **Bill Clinton** and British Prime Minister **Tony Blair**.
◆ **Nelson Mandela** marries **Graça Machel**, widow of former Mozambique president Samora Machel, on his 80th birthday. In September, Mandela bids farewell to the UN, and is awarded the US's highest honour, the Congressional Gold Medal.

Nelson Mandela and Graça Machel marry on his 80th birthday.

◆ South African playwrights **Mbongeni Ngema**, **Athol Fugard** and **Percy Mtwa** are inducted into the New York Playwrights' Sidewalk, American theatre's version of the Hollywood Walk of Fame. Local author **Pamela Jooste** wins the Best First Book award in the Commonwealth Writers Prize for her *Dance with a Poor Man's Daughter*.
◆ The potency drug **Viagra** cheers up millions of under-performing men around the world; one Dutchman is hospitalized after suffering a 36-hour erection.
◆ **France** wins the Soccer World Cup, beating a surprisingly lacklustre Brazil 3–0 in the final, in Paris.
◆ **Britain:** A survey reveals that 40 percent of pupils entering secondary school are functionally innumerate.

Bill Clinton and Monica Lewinsky: lurid details emerge.

SLICK WILLIE IN TROUBLE

Embattled US President Bill Clinton solemnly informs pressmen and televiewers that he has not, definitely not, 'had sexual relations with that woman'.

The woman in question is nubile White House intern Monica Lewinsky, who then tells the grand jury all about their affair. The lurid details involve, among other things, cigars and semen stains. Special Investigator Kenneth Starr's report becomes an instant bestseller; Clinton, known universally as Slick Willie, eventually apologizes to his wife and the world and escapes impeachment – just.

SPORTING HIGHLIGHTS

South African boxer Vuyani Bungu mounts his twelfth defence of the world junior lightweight title, against American challenger Danny Romero. The national soccer team, Bafana Bafana, compete in the World Cup finals for the first time (in France),

DIED
International: Churchman and anti-apartheid campaigner Fr. Trevor Huddleston; British right-wing politician Enoch Powell; child-care guru and anti-war campaigner Benjamin Spock; actresses Eva Bartok and Maureen O'Sullivan, who played Jane to Johnny Weismuller's Tarzan; photographer and Beatle wife Linda McCartney; sprinter Florence Griffith Joyner; country music star Tammy ('Stand by your Man') Wynette; 'singing cowboy' Roy Rogers; convicted murderer Karla Faye Tucker, first woman to be executed in the US since 1863. **South Africa:** Television director Edgar Bold; activist Archie Gumede; cricketer Athol Rowan; rugby player Keith Oxlee; rugby coach Kitch Christie.

SOUTH AFRICA in the 20th CENTURY — 1990s

Bafana Bafana's Benni McCarthy: World Cup debut.

Songs: 'Never Ever': All Saints; 'Torn': Natalie Imbruglia; 'My Heart Will Go On': Céline Dion. Pop megastar George Michael admits he's gay after he is arrested, in a Beverly Hills public toilet, for an alleged 'lewd act'. Britain's five cute Spice Girls, who make up in verve what they lack in talent, become four when Ginger leaves the group, but they continue to tour (there's mutual enchantment when they meet Mandela Nelson Mandela in Johannesburg) and crowds that gather to look and listen are bigger than ever.

with modest success. The Springboks win the Tri-Nations rugby cup, remaining unbeaten against Australia and New Zealand; their finest hour: the Kings Park game when sheer never-say-die grit turns a 5-23 deficit into a 24-23 last-gasp triumph. They also beat the visiting (and under-strength) Wales team by a record 96-13.

Long-serving wicketkeeper Dave Richardson retires from international cricket, after playing in 42 Tests, scoring 1 359 runs and a record 151 catches (plus one stumping). Fast bowler Makhaya Ntini is the first black African to be selected for the national team; he takes 2/31 and holds a good catch in his debut match, against New Zealand.

Elana Meyer breaks her own world half-marathon record (her time: 67 minutes 29 seconds) in Kyoto, Japan.

SIGHT AND SOUND
Films: *Saving Private Ryan*; *The Truman Show*; *The Wedding Singer*. The blockbuster *Titanic* wins 11 Oscars (14 nominations).

Elana Meyer on track.

The original five Spice Girls: pulling in the crowds.

SOUTH AFRICA in the 20th CENTURY

1999

FAREWELL TO A GIANT OF OUR TIMES

June. Nelson Rolihlahla Mandela, Madiba, father of post-apartheid South Africa and among the century's most respected statesmen, relinquishes the burden of presidential office to his protégé Thabo Mbeki. His final gift to the world: an agreement from maverick Libyan leader Muammar Gadaffi to commit to trial two suspects in the 1989 Lockerbie air disaster.

Freed in 1990 after 26 years in prison, Mandela, in tandem with F.W. de Klerk, embarked on a marathon series of all-party talks that led, four years later, to the country's first fully democratic elections and to his own elevation to the presidency. Thereafter, he steered the country through the difficult years of transition – a process driven by his passionate advocacy of racial harmony, and concluded by what is widely regarded as a miracle of national reconciliation.

Vision, moral authority, humanity, charisma, a charming sense of humour, genuine humility (a rare grace among politicians) – Mandela embodied these and more. He will be remembered with affection, and gratitude, by the millions he so well served.

Nelson Mandela campaigns for his successor.

Mandela and president-to-be Thabo Mbeki salute their supporters.

Madiba at home

Above and below: Nelson Mandela and Graça Machel with their extended family at his home at Qunu in the Eastern Cape.

For all his stature as a statesman, Nelson Mandela is very much a family man. Indeed his whole demeanour, whatever preoccupies his mind at a given moment, is that of one's favourite uncle, though of course he has a sterner side – which colleagues who don't quite come up to scratch, and political opponents who underestimate the power of his will, know only too well.

'With women', he writes in his autobiography *Long Walk to Freedom*, 'I found I could let my hair down and confess to weaknesses and fears I would never reveal to another man'. He has been married three times and has an enormous extended family. He and his first wife, Evelyn, parted company in 1958 under the stresses (and dangers) that come with political activism in an authoritarian state. Shortly afterwards he met, and married, a beautiful young social worker named Nomzamo Winifred Madikizela. This union withstood the long years of harassment and imprisonment, only to crumble in the heady days of liberation. The third love of his life, whom he married on his 80th birthday, is Graça, widow of Mozambique's President Samora Machel, and a woman of both intelligence and, as befitting her name, rare grace.

SOUTH AFRICA in the 20th CENTURY

The Nineties

Penny Heyns: eleven world records.

SPORTING HIGHLIGHTS

Swimming great Penny Heyns breaks eleven world breast-stroke records in the space of a few weeks.

South Africa's cricketers fail – by the proverbial hair's-breadth – in their bid for the World Cup, held in England. They could so easily have triumphed but for one, crucial dropped catch against Australia (it went to hand but the culprit, Herschelle Gibbs, celebrated too soon) and an oh-so-near winning run in the semi-final (the match is tied; South Africa lose on run rate). All-rounder Lance Klusener totals 280 runs at an average of just over 140, takes 17 wickets at 20.6 apiece, and wins the Man of the Series award. Earlier in the year the South Africans whitewash the Windies 5-0 in the Test and win the one-day series 6-1.

The Springboks, disrupted by injury and low in self-confidence, beat a talented England side but bow out in the semi-finals of the Rugby World Cup, losing in extra time to Australia. In the upset of the century, France run the All Blacks off their feet but cannot rise to the same heights in the final. Australia carry away the William Webb Ellis trophy.

MOVIES AND MUSIC

Top films: *The Matrix*; *You've Got Mail* (Tom Hanks and Meg Ryan cashing in on their *Sleepless in Seattle* weepie); *Eyes Wide Shut* (the late Stanley Kubrick's final masterpiece); *Notting Hill* (with Hugh Grant and Julia Roberts); *Star Wars – The Phantom Menace*; *The Blair Witch Project*. Antonio Benigni's *Life is Beautiful*, a deeply moving tale of a father's attempts to make a game of wartime horrors, steals the Oscars show.

Hit singles: 'Dolphins Cry': Live; 'A Beautiful Stranger': Madonna; 'You Drive Me Crazy': Britney Spears; 'Mambo No.5': Lou Bega.

WHAT'S NEW IN 1999

- The **gold price** plummets to $255 an ounce, threatening thousands of miners' jobs, before rising towards year's end to break the $300 barrier.
- Average **life expectancy** in South Africa is expected to drop from 60 to 40 years by 2008 as a result of AIDS mortality.
- **Theatre:** Agatha Christie's play The Mousetrap, longest running in theatre history, is to have its third new set – after 19,400 performances. The show premiered in 1952.
- Superstar **Michael Jackson** and his second wife, Debbie Rowe, agree to divorce after three years of marriage; they have two children.
- British entrepreneur **Richard Branson** plans a hotel in space by 2005 (if a reusable rocket can be developed).

Richard Branson: space hotel.

John F. Jnr. (John-John) and his mother Jackie Onassis confer beneath a portrait of the late John F. Kennedy.

DIED
International: The 'curse of the Kennedys' continues to exact its toll when the late President John F. Kennedy's son John-John dies in his light aircraft, off the US east coast. Tanzanian leader Julius Nyerere; author Mario Puzo; Dusty Springfield, the Swinging Sixties singer (her first contact with South Africa, a tour, was an unhappy one: she was thrown out of the country within days of her arrival for performing before a mixed audience); writers Gunter Grass and Morris West; violinist Yehudi Menuhin; actors Oliver Reed and Dirk Bogarde; singer Frankie Vaughan; cricketers Cyril Washbrook, Godfrey Evans, and three great West Indian players: Sylvester Clarke, Conrad Hunte and Malcolm Marshall; soccer guru Alf Ramsey; American author Joseph Heller, whose 1961 novel Catch 22 became a bestseller. *Southern Africa:* Politician Sir de Villiers Graaff; Zimbabawe vice-president Joshua Nkomo; singer Gé Korsten (by his own hand); Dmitri Tsafendas, deranged killer of prime minister Hendrik Verwoerd in 1966; singer Simon Mahlatini Nkabinde, the 'Lion of Soweto'; travel writer T.V. Bulpin; anti-apartheid activists Baruch Hirson and Marius Schoon; sports writer A.C. Parker; film and theatre critic Percy Baneshik; artist and sculptor Lucky Sibaya.

AIDS:
THE SCOURGE OF AFRICA

According to World Health Organisation estimates, AIDS killed two million people in sub-Saharan Africa in 1998. About half the patients that lie in the medical wards of the Witwatersrand's mine hospitals have AIDS-related illnesses. Half of South Africa's rapidly growing number of tuberculosis victims are HIV-positive. By 1995, one in five residents of KwaZulu-Natal were infected with the virus, and the incidence is rising.

These horrific figures darken the dawn of the new millennium. Life expectancy in South Africa (and in the rest of the continent) is set to plummet; the very fabric of social and family life is under threat; the economy will come under mounting pressure as the disease hits its most active human components.

Grim prospects indeed. Nor are there any discernible lights on the horizon: even if a vaccine is found – unlikely in the foreseeable future, since the virus mutates so fast that researchers can barely keep up – Africa's crisis will not be resolved quickly. Any new medication will be difficult to distribute on a mass scale and prohibitively expensive: the combination drugs that hold HIV at bay in the developed world cost $17,000 (about R100,000) per patient per year; many African countries are able to spend no more than an annual R50 on each patient.

So, for the time being, prevention remains more relevant than cure. Uganda, where the risk of infection has slowed down, has shown that health promotion campaigns can work – a lesson that South Africa's decision makers seem, at last, to have learnt.

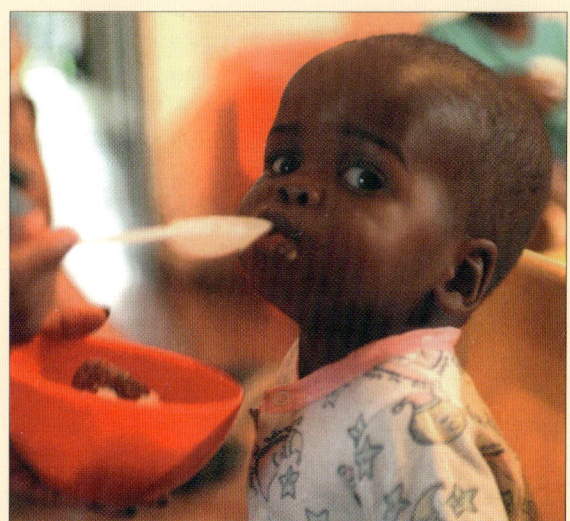

An HIV-infected baby: prevention is better than cure.

SOUTH AFRICA in the 20th CENTURY

Opposite: Capetonians celebrate the millennium at their glittering Waterfront.

Top left: Cape Town's Table Mountain sends the message.

Above: One second to go, Grand Parade, Cape Town.

Left: Nelson Mandela returns to his Robben island cell for one joyful, poignant moment.

Below: Mandela, President Thabo Mbeki and friends raise their glasses to the future on Robben Island.

SOUTH AFRICA in the 20th CENTURY

Two thousand

Above: Fireworks illuminate Dresden's Catholic cathedral; 10,000 merrymakers party in the street below.

Right: Berlin's famed Brandenburg Gate, once the symbol of East-West division, at the last midnight of the old millennium.

Opposite: The Eiffel Tower, Paris, in celebratory guise.

226

SOUTH AFRICA in the 20th CENTURY

Opposite: Times Square, New York, at the magical moment.

Right: Crowds of celebrants at the Great Pyramid, west of Cairo, are treated to a dazzling light-and-sound show created by renowned French musician Jean-Michel Jarre.

Below: Muslim and Christian come together in Istanbul, Turkey, when the sky above the Blue Mosque is lit by a firework display, marking both the millennium and the holy time of Lailatul Qadr.

SOUTH AFRICA in the 20th CENTURY

Two thousand

Above: Australia's Sydney harbour bridge and the city's Opera House glow in an extravaganza of ephemeral lights.

Right: The front pages of some of Britain's national newspapers.

Opposite: Fireworks explode over the Century Altar in Beijing. During the festivities President Jiang Zemin pushes a button to reveal the 'Sacred Flame of China'. The flame, reports the local press, has been brought to the city, by torch runner, from the nearby site where the remains of the million-year-old 'Peking Man' were unearthed in the 1920s.

SOUTH AFRICA in the 20th CENTURY Index

Note to the Index
Page numbers in **bold type** indicate the main discussion of the topic. Those in *italic type* indicate illustrations.

CHRONOLOGICAL INDEX
1900 6, **7–9**, 174
1901 6, **10–13**, *17*, 25
1902 6, **14–15**
1903 6, **15–18**, 35
1904 6, **18–20**
1905 6, **20–2**
1906 6, **22–3**
1907 6, **24–5**
1908 6, 17, *17*, **25–6**, 30
1909 6, **26–7**
1910 28, **29–33**, *30*
1911 16, 28, **33–4**
1912 28, 30, **34–6**
1913 28, **37–8**, 42
1914 28, *35*, **39–41**
1915 28, **41–2**, 59–60
1916 28, **42–3**
1917 28, **44–6**
1918 16, 28, **46–7**
1919 16, 28, **48–9**
1920 50, **51–3**
1921 50, **53–4**
1922 50, **55–8**
1923 50, **58–60**
1924 50, **60–3**
1925 50, **64–5**
1926 50, **66–9**
1927 50, **69–70**
1928 50, **71–3**
1929 50, **73–5**
1930 76, **77–9**
1931 76, **80**
1932 76, **81–2**
1933 76, **82–3**
1934 76, **83–5**
1935 16, 76, **86**, 182
1936 76, **87–8**
1937 76, **89**
1938 76, 89, **90–1**
1939 76, **92–3**
1940 94, **95–7**
1941 94, **98–100**, 115
1942 94, **100–1**
1943 94, **101–3**
1944 94, **103–4**
1945 94, **105–7**
1946 94, **107–8**
1947 94, **108–10**
1948 94, 109, *109*, **110–11**
1949 94, **111**
1950 112, **113–15**
1951 112, **116–18**, 128
1952 112, **119–20**, 132
1953 112, **121–3**, 185
1954 112, **123–5**
1955 112, **125–8**
1956 112, **128–31**
1957 112, 130, **131–2**
1958 112, **132–4**, 176
1959 112, **134–7**
1960 138, **139–41**, *212*
1961 138, **142–4**
1962 138, **144–5**
1963 138, **146–8**, 185

1964 138, **149–50**, 216
1965 138, **151–2**
1966 138, **153–4**
1967 138, **154–6**, *159*
1968 138, **156–7**
1969 138, **158–9**
1970 157, 160, **161–3**
1971 160, **163–5**
1972 160, **165–6**, 181
1973 160, **167–8**
1974 137, 160, **169–70**
1975 160, **170–1**, 204
1976 160, **172–3**
1977 160, **174–6**
1978 160, **176–8**, 184
1979 160, **178–9**
1980 180, **181–3**
1981 180, **183–5**, 211
1982 180, **185–7**
1983 137, 180, **187–9**
1984 180, **189–90**
1985 180, **191–3**
1986 180, **193–5**
1987 180, **195–7**, 217
1988 180, **197–8**
1989 180, **198–9**
1990 200, **201–2**
1991 200, **202–4**
1992 200, **204–5**
1993 200, **206–8**
1994 200, **208–9**, 217
1995 200, **210–11**
1996 200, **212–14**
1997 200, **214–16**
1998 200, **216–19**
1999 200, **220–3**
2000 **224–31**

NON-ALPHABETICAL CHARACTERS
1820 Settlers' Memorial 169
2001: A Space Odyssey 157
//Am//Op (Survivor) 215

A
Abba 172
Abdurahman, Abdullah 27, *27*, 97
Abominable Snowman 117
abortion 157
Abrahams, Jody 192
Abrahams, Lionel 71
Abyssinia *see* Ethiopia
Academy of Motion Picture Arts and Sciences
 establishment of **70**, 75
 first South African in 216
 Oscar awards 70, 75, 97, 149, 187, 188
Ackerman, Raymond 80, 156
Action Man 149
Adam and the Ants 185
Adams, Bryan 204, 209
Adams, Paul 175
Adamson, George 199
Adamson, Joy 182
aeroplanes *see* aviation
African Cup of Nations 213, *213*
African League of Rights (ALR) 74
African Mirror 42
African National Congress (ANC)
 see also South African Native National Congress
 1994 elections **208**
 Alfred Xuma as leader **97**, *97*
 banned 139
 in Cape 50
 Codesa talks 203
 and Communists 74, **77**
 Defiance Campaign **119**, *119*, 132
 going underground **132**
 Groote Schuur talks **202**, *202*
 honouring Lilian Ngoyi **186**, *186*
 meetings with white delegates **191**, 195
 PAC split from **134**
 SADF raids on **193**
 unbanned 201
African National Congress Women's League 16
African National Congress Youth League 102, 176
African Peoples' Organisation 6
Afrika, Patience 100
Afrikaans Bible 76
Afrikaans language
 in Bantu education 173
 development/promotion of 6, 24, 65, 113
 first Shakespearean play 212
Afrikaner Broederbond 28
Afrikaner Weerstandsbeweging (AWB; Afrikaner Resistance Movement) 168, 182, *182*
After the Fall 216
Aggett, Neil **186**, *186*
AIDS (HIV)
 development of 180, **184**, *184*
 Erving Johnson retires 204
 first major film 208
 Freddie Mercury's death 204
 Liberace's death 197
 life expectancy in SA 222
 outlook and statistics **223**, *223*
 Princess Di with patient *214*
 Rock Hudson's death 193
Airport 163
airships **78**
Albu, George 86
Alcock, John 48
Alcock, William 17
alcohol prohibition 25, **51**, *51*, 53
Aldrin, 'Buzz' 158
Alexandra 136
Algeria 145
Alien 179
All Africa Convention (AAC) 16, **86**, *86*
All Saints 219
Allen, Woody 86, 168, 176
Allende, Salvador 168
Altrincham, Lord 126
Amadeus 179, 190
Amin, Idi 164, **165**, *165*, 179
Amis, Kingsley 58, 125, 211
Amis, Martin 196
Amnesty International 143
//Am//Op (Survivor) 215
Amos, Stanley 189
Amundsen, Roald 34
ANC *see* African National Congress

Anderson, Kevin **178**
Andes aircraft crash 181
Andress, Ursula 148
Andrew, Duke of York 213
Andrews, Cait 215
Andrews, Julie 130, 149, 152, *152*, 187
Angel, Bobby 89
Anglican Church **122**
Anglo American Corporation 28, 191
Anglo-Boer War
 action 6, **7–9**, *8*, *9*, **11**, *11*
 black/coloured people 7, *7*, 11, 12, *12*, 14
 Boer War Show 19
 books 75
 discovery of gold 18
 heroes *15*
 peace and recovery **14**, *14*, 15
 prisoners-of-war *12*
 rugby 13
 scorched-earth policy **11**, *11*
 songs 43, *43*
Angola
 freedom fight 112, 138
 independence 171
 Portuguese dictator's death 160
 SA raids on **170**
Anne of Green Gables 25
Anne, Princess 115
Annecke, David 128
anthem, national 13
anthropology *see* palaeoanthropology
Anti-Apartheid Movement 130
anti-apartheid protests/demos
 international **131**, 135, 139, **158–9**, 163, **183**, *183*, 184
 sanctions 175, **184**, 189, 203, 206
 sport 156, 161, 163, 203
Antony, Pat 195
apartheid and race laws
 see also forced removals
 1911 race laws 33
 1927 race laws 69
 1948 Nat victory 110
 1950s race laws **112**, 113, 116
 in action 113, 122, 160, **164**, 166, 168, *168*, 172, **178**, 179, **182**, *182*, 197
 Asian policy **162**, *162*, 164
 Asiatic Land Tenure Act 94
 Bantu Authorities Act 116
 Bantu Education Act **122**
 Fagan Commission 94
 foreign protests *see* anti-apartheid protests/demos
 'grand apartheid' **146**
 Group Areas Act 113, 153, 162, 179
 homelands system 116, 146
 Immorality Act **69**, 113, 162, 164, 193
 Indian Representation Act 94
 Lagden report 6, **20**
 Mixed Marriages Act 162, 193
 Native Affairs Act 50
 Native Resettlement Bill **124**
 Natives' Land Act 32, **37–8**, 81
 Natives (Urban Areas) Act 59
 Population Registration Act 113, 162
 Prevention of Illegal Squatting Act 116
 reform of 177, **178**, 179, 180, **181**, 184, 193

Index

SOUTH AFRICA in the 20th CENTURY

Representation of Natives Act 76
Sauer report 94
Separate Registration of Voters Act 116, **128**
sport **156**, **162**, **164**, 168, 172, 177
white protests **116**, *116*
white woman treated as black **178**
apartheid reforms 177, **178**, 179, 180, **181**, 184, 193
ape-men *see* palaeoanthropology
Apple company 172, 175
Apple Macintosh 190, 211
Arab-Israeli peace accords 177
Arafat, Yasser 158, *211*
Arbuckle, Roscoe 'Fatty' **54**, *54*
archaeology
   see also palaeoanthropology
   Chinese terracotta soldiers 169
   Dead Sea Scrolls **109**
   Inca city 34
   Knossos **8**
   Tutankhamen's tomb **57**, *57*
Ardrey, Robert 182
Argentina 186
armaments race **145**, 196
armaments reduction 197
Armstrong, Louis 'Satchmo' 9, 157, 165, *165*
Armstrong, Neil 79, **158**, *158*
Armstrong-Jones, Anthony 140, *140*
Art Deco 65
Art Nouveau 14, 19
Ascot **38**
Ashe, Arthur 164, *164*, 171, 208
Asians *see* black, coloured and Asian people
Asiatic Land Tenure Act 94
Asmal, Abdul Kadar 84
aspirin 21, *21*
assassinations
   Anwar Sadat 184
   Chris Hani **206**
   Franz Ferdinand 39
   Indira Gandhi 180
   king and queen of Serbia 18
   Malcom X 152
   Martin Luther King **157**
   Michael Collins 58
   Mohandas Gandhi 109, *109*
   Pope John Paul II (attempted) 184, *184*
   Ruth First **185**
   Umberto of Italy 9
   US President Kennedy **147**, *147*
   US President McKinley 12
   US President Reagan (attempted) 184
   US Senator Kennedy **157**
   Verwoerd **153**, *153*
   Verwoerd (attempted) 140
   Yitshak Rabin 211
Astaire, Fred 85, *85*, 197
astronomy
   comets 115, **162**
   galaxies **60**
   Hubble telescope 202
   Pluto 78
   rings around Uranus 175
   R.P. de Kock **115**
   supernovas 162
Aswan Dam 14, 161

Atlantic Charter **99**
Atomic Energy Corporation 186
atomic power/weapons
   armaments race **145**, 196
   armaments reduction 197
   Campaign for Nuclear Disarmament (CND) 134
   Chernobyl 194
   first US power plant 130
   Hiroshima and Nagasaki 107, *107*
   Koeberg 192
   Martin Amis on 196
   Nuclear Non-Proliferation Treaty 157
   Reagan's joke about nuclear strike 190
   in SA **161**, 192, 206
   scientific progress 49, 76, 92, 101
Attenborough, Richard 59, 120, 188
Attlee, Clement 106, *106*, 156
Australia
   commonwealth 12
   franchise for aborigines 168
   massacre in Tasmania **213**
   millennium celebrations 230, *230*
Automobile Club of South Africa 12
aviation
   in 1919 **48–9**
   accidents/crashes **133**, 135, 138, 175, 181, **193–4**, 196, **197**, 208, 220, 223
   air speed records 60
   airports 106, 112
   airships **78**
   balloonists 80
   Boeing 747 aircraft 158
   Concorde 158
   first across Atlantic **48**, *49*
   first across Channel 26
   first air raid 34
   first airline 41
   first airlines in SA 49, **74–5**
   first dogfight 41
   first international airline 69
   first parachute jump 36
   first passenger aeroplane 25
   first passenger in SA 26
   first powered flight **16**, *16*
   first seaplane 33
   first trans-Africa **51**, *51*
   flying doctors 72
   Flying Matchbox **26**, *26*
   hijackings 160
   jet aircraft 94, 119
   John Household 22, *22*
   John Weston 26, *26*
   mail service **33–4**, *33*, *34*
   national airline **84**, *84*
   New York to Paris 70
   round-the-world flights 67
   Royal Air Force 47
   Royal Flying Corps 36
   sound barrier 109
   warplanes 97, 103
   wartime **96**, **114**, *114*
   women pilots **71**, 79
   women selling petrol 62
Aykroyd, Dan 190

B

Baader-Meinhoff gang 166
Baard, Frances 215
Babe 211

Bacher, Ali 101, 161
Back to the Future 193
Baden-Powell, Agnes 32, *32*
Baden-Powell, Robert 7, **24**, 32, 101
Bader, Douglas 187
Bafana Bafana 213, *213*, 218–19, *219*
Bailey, David 151
Bailey, Gary 134
Bailey, Lady Mary **71**, *71*, 141
Baird, John Logie **67–8**, *67*, 108
bakelite 27
Baker, Herbert 14, 108
Baker, Norma Jean *see* Monroe, Marilyn
Baker, Stanley 149, 195
Balewa, Abubakar Tafawa 154
Ballinger, Margaret 182, *182*
Ballington, Kork 178
Bambatha, Zulu chief **22**
Banana, Canaan 181
Band Aid 190
Banda, Hastings 121, 163, *163*
Baneshik, Percy 223
Bangladesh 160
banks 211
Bannister, Roger 125, *125*
Banoobhai, Shabbir 111
Bantu Authorities Act 116
Bantu Education (Act) **122**, 172, 173
Bantu Women's League 16
Bantustans *see* homelands
Barbie dolls 135
Bardot, Brigitte 84, 124, *124*, 131
Barings bank 211
Barker, Joyce 80, 205
Barlow, Eddie 97, 161
Barnard, Christiaan 58, **154**, *154*
Barrie, James 19, 34
Bart, Lionel 141
Basie, William 'Count' 20, 190
Battiss, Walter 22, 187
Battle of Blood River centenary **91**, *91*
Bauer, Charlotte 207
Baum, L. Frank 9, 18
Bay City Rollers 171
Bay of Pigs 143
Beano 91
Beatles, The
   Apple boutique 157
   breaking up 163
   emergence 144
   films 149
   MBEs 152
   memorabilia 138
   songs 145, 148, 149, 152, 153, 155, 157
   on top 149, 150, *150*
   turned down by Decca 145
Beatniks 126, *126*
Beatrix, Gonda 103
Beautiful People 195
Becker, Boris **191**
Beckett, Samuel 22, 128, 199
Bega, Lou 222
Beijing
   millennium celebrations 230, *231*
   Tiananmen Square 199
Beit, Alfred 22
Bell, Alexander Graham 58
Bell, Charles 108
Bell, William 108

Ben Hur 69, 135
Benigni, Antonio 222
Bennet, Jack **162**, 202
Benz motor cars 15, *17*
Benz Voiturette 10, *10*
Bergman, Ingrid 42, 101, *101*, 106, 187
Berlin, millennium celebrations 226, *226*
Berlin Wall 143, *143*, **198–9**, *199*
Berndt, Florrie 67, *67*
Bernhardt, Sarah **60**, *60*
Bernstein, Lionel 146
Berry, Chuck 68, 126, *126*
Best, Pete 145
Beyers, Christiaan 40
Bezuidenhout, Evita *see* Uys, Pieter-Dirk
Bhengu, Gerard 33, 205
Bibles
   Afrikaans 76
   Gideon company 25
   New English 163
bikinis 108, *108*, 152
Biko, Steve
   birth 108
   Black Students' Organisation **158**, *158*
   death in police custody **174**, *174*
   on oppression 173
   South African Students' Organization 166, *166*
Bilk, Acker 145
Bill Haley and the Comets 126
Biocchi, Hugh 108, 168
bird, national 138
birth control 41, 54, *54*
Bizos, George 71
black, coloured and Asian people
   Anglo-Boer War 7, *7*, 11, 12, *12*, 14
   church bars mourners 158
   first boxing champion 26
   first national cricket player 219
   first national rugby player 194
   first novel published by woman 171
   first nurse 6
   first Transvaal lawyer **129**
   first university **43**
   first in White House 12
   first Wimbledon titles 130, *130*, 171
   Oscars 97, 149
   township talent **136–7**, *136*, *137*, 188, 217
   World War I **45**, *45*, 47
   World War II **101**, *102*
black, coloured and Asian rights
   see also African National Congress; apartheid and race laws; pass laws
   Asian policy **162**, *162*, 164
   Atlantic Charter 99
   Australian aborigines 168
   Charlotte Maxeke **16**
   Congress of the People 125, *125*
   Defiance Campaign **119**, *119*, 132
   education **122**, *122*, 172, 173
   first urban location 6
   franchise in SA 25, 27, 116, **128**, 187
   Freedom Charter **125**, 128, 210
   Gandhi 6, 7, **24**, **38**, *38*, 50, 80, 109, *109*
   'native policy' 6, **20**
   political organizations 6, 16, **34–5**, **74**, **86**, *86*, **102**, 112, **158**, 166

233

SOUTH AFRICA in the 20th CENTURY Index

treason charges/trial 112, **128**, **142**, *142*
   in US 19, **27**, **126**, **131**, **146**
black consciousness **158**, 166
Black Labour Regulation Act 33
'Black Monday' 180, 196
Black Peoples' Convention 166
'Black Pimpernel' *see* Mandela, Nelson Rolihlahla
Black Sash 112
Black September group 166
Black Students' Organisation 158
Blackburn, Molly 193
Blaiberg, Philip 159
Blair, Cherie *215*
Blair, Linda 168
Blair, Tony 215, *215*, 218
Blatty, William 165
Bleriot, Louis 26
Bloemfontein
   British occupation 8
   judicial capital 27
Blood Knot, The 147
Bloom, Claire 120
Bloom, Harry 136
Bluebird **73–4**, *74*, 80
Blyton, Enid 157, 196
BMW (Bayerische Motoren Werke) 46, 184
bobbysoxers 115
Boeing 747 aircraft 158
Boer War *see* Anglo-Boer War
Boerevrou, Die 80
Boers
   in America **19**
   in Europe **15**
   fleeing scorched-earth tactics *11*
   World War I **40**, 41
Boesak, Alan 108, 192, *198*
Bogarde, Dirk 152, 223
Bogart, Humphrey 101, *101*, 132
Bohemian Rhapsody 204
Boipatong massacre **204**, *204*
Bold, Edgar 218
Bolt, Robert 141
bombs
   see also atomic power/weapons; guerrilla campaign in SA; letter bombs
   Oklahoma City 211
   World Trade Center **206**, *206*
Bond, James 112, 128, 145, 149, 152
Bonnie and Clyde 84, *84*
Boonzaier, Daniël *61*, 115
Boonzaier, Gregoire 27
Bophuthatswana 175, 179
Borg, Bjorn 130, 172, *172*, 178
Bosman, Gerry 211
Bosman, Herman Charles 21, 70, 118
Boswell, Eve 58, 216
Boswell's Circus 83
Botha, Louis 7, 8, **15**, 24, 29, 33, 41, **48**, *48*
Botha, Naas 134, 194
Botha, Pik 82
Botha, P.W.
   in 1987 election 195
   becomes prime minister **176**, *176*
   birth 44
   first SA executive President 190
   freedom of Mandela 192

new constitution 187
Nkomati Accord 189–90, *189*
Pieter-Dirk Uys's lampooning 195, *196*
reform programme **178**, 181, 184
resignation after stroke **198**, *198*
'Rubicon' speech 191
states of emergency 191
'total strategy' **178**
on white delegates to ANC 195
Botswana
   independence 138
   SA raid on **193**
Bouwer, Gerry **71**
Bowie, David 192
bowls 160
boxing
   1948 Olympics 111
   Andrew Jeptha 24
   Arnie Taylor **167**
   Brian Mitchell 194, 205
   first black champion 26
   George Foreman 209
   Gerrie Coetzee 189
   Joe Louis 89
   legalization 12
   Mike Tyson 194, 205
   Muhammad Ali (Cassius Clay) 101, 149, *149*, 169, 213
   Philip Holiday 215
   Pierre Fourie 168
   Rocky Marciano 130, 159
   Vic Toweel **113**, 211
   Vuyani Bungu 209, 218
Boy Scout Association **24**
Boycott, Geoff 186
boycotts *see* sanctions; sport, international isolation
Bradman, Donald 79, *79*, 83
Braine, John 133
Brand, Quintin **51**, *51*
Brando, Marlon 62, 118, 123, 124, 165, 179
Branson, Richard 222, *222*
bras **40**, *40*, 88, *88*
Braun, Eva 106
Breytenbach, Breyten 93, 171
Brickhill, Joan 170
Bridges, Bles 110
Briers, Theunis 126
Brink, André 86, 171, 179
Brink, George 97, *97*, 98
Britain
   see also Anglo-Boer War; Festival of Britain; London
   anti-apartheid protests/demos **131**, **158–9**
   Falkland Islands **186**, *186*
   last executions 128
   millennium celebrations 230, *230*
   post-war conditions 106, *107*, **117**, **124**
   space exploration 131
   spy scandals **117–18**, 148, 198
British Commonwealth of Nations 12, 68, **142**
broadcasting *see* radio
Brook, Clive 115
Brooke, Brian 215
Brooke, Rupert **41**, *41*
Broom, Robert 76, 108–9, *109*, 118

Brotherhood of Man 172
Brown, Arthur 48
Brown, Louise 177, *177*
Bryant, Michael 213
Bryceland, Yvonne 68, 196, 205
Brynner, Yul 130, 193
Buchan, John 41
Buck, Pearl S. 81, 168
Budd, Zola 154, **189**, *189*
Bugs Bunny 97
Buick motor cars 25, *128*
Bullitt 157
Bullock, Sandra 209
Bulpin, T.V. 223
Bungu, Vuyani 156, 209, 218
Burgess, Anthony 46, 145
Burgess, Guy 118, *118*
Burke, Louis 170
Burne, Gary 172
Burroughs, Edgar Rice 41, 115
Burton, Richard 125, 148, 153, 190
Busby's Babes 133
Bush, George 199, 202
Bushman musicians 215
business, meetings with ANC **191**, **195**
Buthelezi, Mangosuthu
   on apartheid **168**
   birth 71
   Codesa talks 203
   with De Klerk and Mandela *203*
   in *Zulu* (film) 149
Butler, Jonathan 144

C

Cabbage Patch Kids 188
Cadillac Motor Company 12
Caine, Michael 149
Cairo 229, *229*
Callaghan, James 168
Cambodia 163
cameras *see* photography
Cameron, Jock 86
Cameron, Margaret (Kathleen Lindsay) **167**, *167*
Camp David 177, 211, *211*
Campaign for Nuclear Disarmament (CND) 134
Campbell, Malcolm **73–4**, *74*, 80
Campbell, Naomi 207, *207*
Campbell, Roy 13, 63, 118, *118*, 132
Can Can 212
Canary Islands aviation disaster 175
cancer
   'microbe' discovered 36
   and smoking 117, 130
'Candle in the Wind' 214
Canessa, Roberto **181**
Cango Caves 182
cannibalism **181**
Cape, forced removals 112, 146, *146*, **153**, *153*
Cape Argus 96, *153*
Cape Corps **47**
Cape of Good Hope Nature Reserve 76
Cape Times 10, *29*
Cape Town
   Adderley Street *13*, *29*, *78*, *198*
   ANC unbanned 201
   aviation 34, 51
   bikinis 152
   cigarette manufacturers 20

Grand Parade *18*, 225, *225*
Groote Schuur hospital 154, 169
heart transplants **154**, *154*
legislative capital 27
Mandela's release 201
millennium celebrations 224, 225, *225*
motor cars 10, 12, 17, 21
Nico Malan theatre 172
peace marches *198*
Pick 'n Pay 156
Pinelands 50
radio 61
royal visits 64, 108
Salt River station 168, *168*
Table Mountain 114, 225, *225*
Tivoli theatre *18*, *18*
trams *13*, *13*
trolley-buses *78*, *78*
Waterfront 224, 225
Cape-to-Rio yacht race 164, *164*
capital punishment *see* executions
Capone, Al 51, **75**, **80**, *80*, 110
Capote, Truman 62, 153, 190
Cara, Irene 187
Carlton Hotel **23**, *23*
Carnarvon Castle 67, *67*
Carnegie, Andrew 13
Carolus, Cheryl **202**
Carpenter, Karen 115, 188
cars *see* motor cars
Carson, Rachel 148
Carter, Howard 57, *57*
Carter, Jimmy 62, 183
Caruso, Enrico 18, 54
Casablanca 101, *101*
Castle Mail Packets Company **8–9**, 174
Castro, Fidel 70, **134**, *134*
Catch 22 223
Catcher in the Rye 118
Cato Manor **111**, *111*
Cats 185
Cave, Nick 214
Cavell, Edith **42**, *42*
Ceausescu, Nicolae 199
Cele, Henry 195
Celestine Prophecy, The 209
cellphones 192, 206
censorship
   television 140
   Wilbur Smith 149
Central African Federation **121**, 147
Central African Republic 140
CFC gases 199
Chad 140
Chaka-Chaka, Yvonne 154
Challenger space shuttle 194
Chamberlain, Neville **90**, *90*
Champion, George 171
Chanel, Coco 36, 54, 165
Channel Tunnel 209
Chaplin, Charlie **40**, 46, 49, 65, 79, 97, 120, 175
Chariots of Fire 185, 187, 216, *216*
charity walks 178
Charles, Prince of Wales *180*, **185**, *185*, 205, 213, *214*
Charleson, Ian 185
Checker, Chubby 141
Cheetham, Jack **182**
Chekhov, Anton 13, 20

Index

SOUTH AFRICA in the 20th CENTURY

Cher 204
Chernobyl 194
Chesterton, G.K. 34
Chevrolet Motor Car Company 34
Chikane, Frank 118
Childers, Erskine 58
Chile 168
China
  archaeological discoveries 169
  cultural revolution 138
  earthquakes 172
  emperor 6
  floods 217
  foot-binding 14
  Hong Kong reverts to 215
  Japanese invasions of 76
  millennium celebrations 230, *231*
  People's Republic declared **111**
  rebellions 6
  Tiananmen Square 199
Chinese citizens, and apartheid 162, *162*, 164
Chinese immigrants 6, **19**, *19*
Chisholm, Erik 132, 152
Christie, Agatha **51**, 85, 120, 172, 222
Christie, Julie 152
Christie, Kitch 210, 218
Christie, Reginald **122–3**
churches
  Anglican Church **122**
  Dutch Reformed Church 33, **158**, 194
Churchill, Winston
  Anglo-Boer War 7, **8**, *8*
  death and funeral 152, *152*
  Iron Curtain **108**
  leisure times 9, 25
  voted out 106
  World War II 90, 95, 96, 99, 100
  after World War II 117
cigarettes *see* smoking
cinema *see* film
circuses 19, **83**, *83*, **114**
Ciskei
  independence 180
  violence 204
Citizen Kane 100
Clapton, Eric 205
Clark, Petula 126, 152
Clarke, Ron 216–17, *217*
Clavell, James 171
Clay, Cassius *see* Muhammad Ali
Clayton, Geoffrey 132
Cleese, John 198
Clegg, Johnny 122, 194, *194*
Clemens, S.L. (Mark Twain) **32**
Clinton, Bill
  becomes US president 205
  birth 108
  Camp David talks 211
  Monica Lewinsky affair 200, **218**, *218*
  visit to SA 218
Clockwork Orange, A 145, 165
Cloete, Stuart 89, 172
cloning 215
Close Encounters of the Third Kind 176
CNN 202
coal mine disasters **140**
Cobain, Kurt 209
Cobb, John 120
Cobham, Alan 67
Coca-Cola **43**

Codesa (Convention for a Democratic SA) **203**
coelacanth **91**, *91*
Coertze, Mimi 82
Coetzee, Basil 'Manenberg' **217**
Coetzee, Gerrie 189
Coetzee, J.M. 97, 183, 188, 196, 209
Coetzer, Amanda 165
Coetzer, Willem 188
coffee, instant 12, **91**, *91*
Cold War
  Berlin Wall **143**, *143*, **198–9**, *199*
  Iron Curtain **108**
  nearing end **197**, **198–9**
  as a phrase 109
Cole, Bobby 169
Collins, Michael 58
Collins, Mike 158
Collins, Phil 192
coloured people *see* black, coloured and Asian people
Coloured People's Organisation 112
Comedians, The 216
comets (astronomy) 115, **162**
Commonwealth, British 12, 68, **142**
Commonwealth Eminent Person's Group 193
communist organizations in SA
  early years 55, 74
  South African Communist Party 112, 206, 210
  Suppression of Communism Act 112
compact discs (CDs) 183, 192
computer technology
  Apple company 172, 175
  Apple Macintosh 190, 211
  in cars 184
  DTP (desktop publishing) 192
  ENIAC 108
  first mass-produced computers 175
  floppy disks 163
  Gates on memory capacity 185
  hacking 188
  integrated circuits 134
  Internet 206
  laser printers 171
  microchips 164, 186
  mouse 140
  Olsen on home computers 175
  Univac 117
  Windows operating system **211**
Comrades Marathon 50, 57, 197
concentration camps
  in Anglo-Boer War 6, **11**, *11*
  Nazi 82, 105, *105*, 120
  as new English word 9
Concorde 158
Congo (Brazzaville) 140
Congo (Kinshasa/Belgian) 25, **140**, *141*, *141*
Congress of Democrats 112, 185
Congress of the People **125**, *125*
Congress of South African Trade Unions (Cosatu) 192
Connaught, Duke of 29, *29*
Connery, Sean 79, 145, 149, 152
Connors, Jimmy 120
Conrad, Joseph 9, 15, 25, 41
Conran, Terence 151
Conservative Party **185**, 195
constitutions of SA **187**, 203, 204, 206

continental drift **36**
Convention for a Democratic SA (Codesa) **203**
Coolio 211
Cooper, Gary 13, 100
Cope, Jack 203
Coppola, Francis Ford 179
Corbett, Marius 215
Cormack, Alan 179
Corrs, The 214
Cosatu (Congress of South African Trade Unions) 192
Costner, Kevin 204
Coué, Emile 60
coups
  Chile 168
  Nigeria 154
  Seychelles (attempted) **184**
  Uganda 164
Court, Margaret 163
Courtenay, Bryce 82
Courtney, Bob 195
Cousteau, Jacques 33, 103, 215
Covington, Julie 176
Coward, Noël 100, *100*, 168
Cowdrey, Colin 203
Crabbe, Buster 155
Cranko, John 70, 168
Craven, Danie 33, **89**, *89*, 209
Crawford, Cindy 207
Crazy People 195
Cream 150
Creedence Clearwater Revival 159, 162
Cresswell, Frederick 61, *61*
Crick, Francis 122
cricket
  in the 1900s **23**, 26
  in the 1920s 60
  in the 1930s 79, **83**, *83*, 91, 182
  in the 1940s 109, 110
  in the 1950s 122, 128, 130
  Alan Donald 205, *205*
  apartheid in action **156**, 164
  Australian one-day internationals 175, 178
  Australian tour (1970) **161**
  bodyline **83**, *83*
  Brian Lara 209
  Dave Richardson 215–16, 219
  D'Oliviera's selection **156**
  Dudley Nourse 110, **117**, *117*, **182**
  first black African on national team 219
  Garth le Roux 178
  Graeme Pollock 104, **140**, *140*
  Herbert Wade 182
  international isolation 161, 203
  Jack Cheetham **182**
  Mike Proctor 161, *161*, 164
  Peter Kirsten 215
  rebel tours 186
  World Cup 205, 222
Crippen, Dr Hawley **31**
Cronjé, Hansie 159
Cronjé, Piet 19
Crosby, Bing 20, 101, 175
Cross, Ben 185
Cruel Sea, The 118, *118*
Cruise, Tom 198
Cry, the Beloved Country 111, **115**, 216, *216*

Cuba **134**, **143**, 145
Cullinan diamond **20**
Cullinan, Thomas 87
cults and sects **53**, *53*, **177**, *177*
Culture Club 189
Cundill, John 172
Curie, Marie 6, 16, 33, *33*
Curie, Pierre 16
Curren, Kevin **191**, *191*
currency (notes/coins) **55**, *55*
Currie, Donald 8, 174
Curtis, Jamie Lee 198
custody, deaths in *see* deaths in detention
Czechoslovakia 138, 200

D

D-Day **103–4**, *103*
Dadoo, Yusuf 188
Dagwood and Blondie 78, *78*
Daily Illustrated Mirror, The 19
Dalai Lama 135, 213
Dallas 183, 187
Dambuuzu, T.M. 32
dance
  ballet **64–5**
  Cakewalk 22
  Charleston 65, *65*, 66
  Jitterbug 103, *103*
  Saturday Night Fever 176, *176*
  Tango **31**, *31*
  Twist 141
  Volkspele 91
Dance with a Poor Man's Daughter 218
Dances with Wolves 204
Daniels, Salie 192
Darnley, June (Kathleen Lindsay) **167**, *167*
Darracq motor car *17*
Dart, Raymond **61**, *61*, 198
Darwin, Charles **65**
Davidson, Emily 38
Davis, Bette 26, 97, 199
Davis, Miles 133, *133*
Dawn 168
Dawson, Charles 36
Day of the Triffids, The 118
Dayan, Moshe 42
De Dion motor car *17*
De Gaulle, Charles 106
De Groote, Pierre 208
De Klerk, F.W.
  ANC unbanned **201**
  atomic bombs 206
  becomes President **198**, *198*
  birth 87
  Codesa talks 203
  with Mandela and Buthelezi 203
  Mandela's release **201**, *201*
  Nobel Prize 207, *207*
  peace process 204
  quits politics 215
De Kock, R.P. **115**
De la Rey, Koos **11**, 15, *15*, 40
De Melker, Daisy 82
De Morgan, Michael 172
De Niro, Robert 172, 179, 182
De Villiers, Dawie 158, 162
De Villiers, Mr Justice Johann (Lord) **32**, *32*

235

SOUTH AFRICA in the 20th CENTURY Index

De Wet, Christiaan R. 11, 15, *15*, 40, 57, *57*
Dead Sea Scrolls **109**
Dean, James 80, 123–4, 126–8, *126*
death penalty *see* executions
deaths in detention
    Neil Aggett **186**
    Steve Biko **174**
decimal system 143
Decker, Mary **189**, *189*
Dee, Kiki 172
defections, of British agents **117–18**
Defiance Campaign **119**, *119*, 132
Delville Wood **42–3**, *42*
DeMille, Cecil B. 70
Democratic Party (1973) 168
Democratic Party (1989) **199**, *199*
Dennison, Tommy **35**
Denver, John 215
Derby-Lewis, Clive 206
Desai, Barney 215
Desmond, Hugh (Kathleen Lindsay) **167**, *167*
detention *see* deaths in detention
Dexy's Midnight Runners 187
Dhlomo, Herbert 130
Dhlomo, Rolfes 165
diamonds **20**, *20*, 40, **64**, **66**, *66*, 76
Diana, Princess of Wales (Lady Diana Spencer)
    with AIDS patient *214*
    death and funeral **214**, *214*
    differences with Charles 205
    divorce 213
    engagement *180*
    marriage **185**, *185*
    visit to SA 215
Diary of Anne Frank, The **120**, *120*
Diary of a Cape Housewife 15
Die Burger 28
Diet Coke 186
Dietrich, Marlene 13, 79, *79*, 205
Digital Equipment Corporation 175
Dillinger, John 84, *84*
DiMaggio, Joe 41
Dinuzulu, Zulu chief 22, *22*, 38
Dion, Céline 211, 219
Dior, Christian 21, 110, *110*, *123*, 132
Dire Straits 193
disabled sports 33
disasters
    in the 1990s **217**
    earthquakes 6, **23**, **138**, 172
    meteorite in Russia **26**
    Mount St Helen's volcano 183
discotheques 150
Disney, Walt 13, **73**, *73*, 89, 97, 149
Disneyland 126
District Six **153**, *153*, 192
District Six: The Musical 196
DNA molecule 122
dogs, in World War II 105
D'Oliviera, Basil 80, **156**, *156*
Dollar Brand (Abdullah Ibrahim) 84, 136, 169, 188, *188*
Dolly (sheep) 215
domestic servants 15, *15*
Donald, Alan 154, 205, *205*
Donald Duck 85
Doyle, Arthur Conan 9, 15, **18**, 38, 79
Dr Zhivago 152
Dresden cathedral 226, *226*
Driver, Evelyn 108
drugs
    crippled babies **133**, *133*
    hippies 155
    Timothy Leary 151, 214
Drum magazine **112**, *112*
Du Plessis, Carel 141, 194
Du Plessis, Menan 188
Du Plessis, Morné 111, 210
Du Preez, Frik 86
Du Toit, Nellie 74
Du Toit, Stephanus 34
Dube, John 35, *35*, 108
Dube, Lucky 148, 193
Duckitt, Hildagonda 15
Dumile, Mslaba 101
Dunblane **213**
Duncan, Isadora 58
Dunjwa, Jeremiah 86
Dunkirk **95–6**, *95*, *96*
Duran Duran 192
Durban
    bikinis 152
    'Lady in White' 165
    motor cars 17
    ocean-going ships 6
    protest marches 116
    radio 61
    riots **111**, *111*
Dutch Reformed Church
    barring black mourners 158
    condemning racism 194
Dutch Reformed Churches Union Act 33
Duzi river canoe marathon 112
Dylan, Bob 100, 144, 148, *148*
Dziomba, Elsa 163

E

Earhart, Amelia **71**, *71*
earthquakes
    China 172
    Messina, Sicily 6
    San Francisco **23**
    Tulbagh 138
East London, motor cars 84
Eastwood, Clint 79, 165, 205
Ebony magazine 106
Eden, Anthony 129, 175
Edinburgh Castle 174
Edison, Thomas 14, 33, 78, *78*
education, black **122**, *122*, 172, 173
Edward VII, King of England 10, 14, 29, 74
Edward VIII, King of England **64**, *64*, 80, **87**, *87*, 166
Edwardes, Michael 179
Egan, Eric 113, *113*
Egypt
    Aswan Dam 14, 161
    millennium celebrations **229**, *229*
Eichmann, Adolf 145
Einstein, Albert 6, 92, 128
Eisenhower, Dwight (Ike) 103, 119, *119*, 131, 132, 159
El Alamein **100**
El Niño 217
elections
    1970 (NP reduced minority) 161
    1984 (tricameral parliament) **190**, *190*
    1987 (move to the right) **195**
    1989 (De Klerk as President) 198
    1992 (peace process approved) 204
    1994 (new SA) **208**, *208*
Elgin, Lord 23
Eliot, T.S. 57, 152
Elizabeth II, Queen of England
    birth 68
    coronation **121**, *121*
    father's death 119–20
    horrible year 205
    Lord Altrincham on 126
    with Prince Philip 205
    visits to SA 108, *108*, 211
Elizabeth, queen to George VI 108, *108*
Ellis, Ruth 128
Els, Ernie 159, **215**, *215*
embargoes *see* sanctions
Embury, John 186
Eminent Person's Group 193
Entebbe hijacking 160
epidemics
    see also AIDS (HIV)
    influenza 28, **47**
Erasmus Commission 176
Esau, Abraham **12**, *12*
Escobar, Andres 209
ET: The Extra-Terrestrial 187
Ethiopia (Abyssinia) 86, 98, *98*, 169, 192, *193*
ethnic cleansing
    see also genocide
    as a phrase 205
Eurovision song contest 129
Evangelista, Linda 207
Evans, Arthur 8
Evans, Timothy 123
Everard, Bertha 152, *152*
Everest, Mount 62, **121**, *121*, 171
Everley Brothers 133
'Eve's footprint' **216**
evolution, theory of **65**
executions (capital punishment)
    by guillotine 92
    last in Britain 128
    public **114**
    in SA 82, 152, 211
    in US 70, 218
Exodus 140
Exorcist, The 165, 168

F

facelifts 12
Fagan Commission 94
Fagan, Gideon 182
Fair Lady magazine 152, *152*
Fairbanks, Douglas 49, **52**, 75
Faith, Adam 151
Falkland Islands **186**, *186*
famine *see* starvation
fashions and trends
    see also dance
    in the 1900s **19**, 22
    in the 1910s **30**, *30*, **40**, *40*, 45
    in the 1920s **56**, *56*, 69, 72
    in the 1930s 80, *80*, **88**, *88*
    in the 1940s **102**, *102*, **108**, *108*, **110**, *110*
    in the 1950s 115, **123–4**, *123*, *124*, 126, *126*, **133**, *133*
    in the 1960s **150**, *150*, **151**, 158
    in the 1970s **166**, *166*, 172
    in the 1980s 188, 207
    in the 1990s 207
    Chanel 36, 54, 165
    stockings 33, 45, 86, *86*, 97, *97*, 102
Faulkner, Aubrey 79, *79*
Faure, Bill 195
feathers, ostrich 19, **21**, *21*, 30, *30*
Federation of the Rhodesias and Nyasaland **121**, 147
Fellini, Federico 140
Fenton, Elizabeth (Kathleen Lindsay) **167**, *167*
Ferguson, Sarah 205, **213**, *213*
Festenstein, Hillard 146
Festival of Britain **117**, *117*
Fighting Talk 185
film
    in the 1930s 76, *79*, 85, **93**
    in the 1940s 100, **101**, 102–3, **104**, 111
    in the 1950s **115**, 118, **123**, 124, 126–8, 130, 131
    in the 1960s **140**, 145, 148, 149, 152, 153, 157, *212*
    in the 1970s 163, 165, 168, 171, 172, 176, 179
    in the 1980s 182, 185, 187, 188, 190, 194–5, 197–8
    in the 1990s 202, 204, 205, 207–8, 209, 211, 214, **216**, 219, 222
    Academy of MP Arts and Sciences **70**
    of Anglo-Boer War **9**
    cinema in SA **31**, *31*, **33**
    companies founded 36, 63
    Cry the Beloved Country **115**, 216, *216*
    drive-in movies 115
    first SA epic **43**
    first war coverage **9**
    first Western 18
    in Hollywood **32**, 49, 69
    Juliet Prowse **212**, *212*
    million-dollar contract 46
    nudity 131, 148
    Rudolph Valentino 67, *67*
    special effects 14, 60, 85, 131
    talking 33, **69**, 76, **79**
    in World War I **42**
fingerprints 6, 12
First, Ruth **185**, *185*
Fischer, Bram 171
fish, ancient **91**, *91*
Fitzgerald, Ella 214, *214*
Fitzgerald, F. Scott 65
FitzGerald, Mary 37
FitzPatrick, Sir Percy 24, 80
FitzSimons, Frederick William 118
Fixx, James F. 190
flagpole sitting 59
flags, national **71–2**, *71*, 200, *200*
Fleming, Alexander **72**, *72*
Fleming, Ian 26, 128
flower children (hippies) 152, **155**, *155*
    see also Woodstock
flying *see* aviation
'Flying Cheetahs' **114**, *114*
flying saucers **109**
Flynn, Errol 101, 135
FNLA 170
football *see* rugby; soccer

Index

SOUTH AFRICA in the 20th CENTURY

'football club' (of Winnie Mandela) 203
forced removals
   District Six **153**, *153*
   end of 193
   Johannesburg **124**
   Sophiatown **127**, *127*
   Western Cape 112, 146, *146*
Ford, Harrison 185, 208
Ford, Henry 19, 26, 110
Ford motor cars
   10-millionth car 63
   active suspension 196
   Model A 16, 17, 72
   Model T (Tin Lizzy) 17, *17*, **26**, 62
   in SA 62
Fordyce, Bruce 128
Foreman, George 209
Forster, E.M. 63, 163
Forsyth, Frederick 165
Foster, Bob 168
Foster gang **40**
Foster, Jodie 172, 184, 197–8, 204
Fourie, Jopie 40, *40*
Fourie, Pierre 168
Fournier, Louis 12
Fowles, John 163
Fox, Edward 195
Fox, Michael J. 193
France
   Allied liberation **103–4**, *103*, *104*
   Angola 170
   millennium celebrations 226, *227*
franchise
   in Australia 168
   in SA 25, 27, 116, **128**, 187
   in US 19
   for women 6, 25, 47, 72, 83
Franco, General Francisco 88, *88*, 92, 171
Frank, Anne 74, **120**, *120*
Frankie Goes to Hollywood 190
Franz Ferdinand, Archduke 39, *39*
Freedom Charter **125**, 128, 210
French Connection, The 165
Freud, Sigmund 9
Friedan, Betty 148
Frisbees 65
Frost, David 135
fuel plants, sabotage of **181**
Fugard, Athol
   birth 82
   plays **132**, 137, **147**, *147*, 169, 171, 182, 196
   Playwrights' Sidewalk 218
Fugees 214
Funny People 195
Future Shock 163, *163*

G

Gable, Clark 13, 93, *93*, 141
Gadaffi, Muammar 158, 220
Gagarin, Yuri **143**, *143*, 157
Galsworthy, John 81
gambling 179
Gampu, Ken 79, 195
Gandhi (film) 188
Gandhi, Indira 46, 180, 190
Gandhi, Mohandas
   Anglo-Boer War 7
   anti-pass campaigns 6, **24**, *24*
   assassinated 109, *109*
   imprisoned 6, **38**, *38*, 50
   meets King George V 80
   partition of India 109
Garbo, Greta 21, 79, 202
Gardiner, Margaret 177, *177*
Gardner, Ava 135, 202
Garland, Judy 58, 93, 159
Garlick, Charles 17, *17*
Garlicks company 10
Garson, Greer 101
gas, poison **41**
gas chambers 63
Gates, Bill 185, 211
gay and lesbian rights/issues
   lesbian novels 72
   in US 169, 213
Gay Liberation Front 161
Geldof, Bob 192
General Motors 25
genocide, in Rwanda **209**
George V, King of England 34, 80, 87
George VI, King of England 87, 108, *108*, **119**, *119*
Gerber, Danie 134, 194
Gerdener, Theo 168
Gere, Richard 182
Germany
   Baader-Meinhoff gang 166
   millennium celebrations 226, *226*
   Nazi Party 53–4, **58–9**, 75, **78**, **82**
   after World War I *58*, 59
Geronimo 27
Gerry and the Pacemakers 148
Gershwin, George 63, 70, 89
Ghana (Gold Coast) 119, **132**
Ghostbusters 190
GI Blues 212
Gibbons, Stella 81
Gibson, Althea 130, *130*
Gibson, Perla Seidle 165
Gideon company 25
Gilbert, John 79
Gill, Sir David 41
Gillette, King 12
Ginwala, Frene 82
Gitsham, Christopher 35
glasnost 197
Glenn, John 54, 145
Glitter, Gary 168
Gluckman, Leon 136
Goddard, Trevor 80
Godfrey, Freda 64, *64*, 182
Gods Must be Crazy, The 194
Godspell 136
Goering, Hermann 58–9, 96, 108
gold, discovery of 18, **62–3**
Gold Coast *see* Ghana
gold mines
   Chinese immigrants 6, **19**, *19*
   'flu epidemic 28
   record output 112
   strikes **37**, *37*, **55**, *55*, **107**
gold price 180, 222
Goldberg, Dennis 146, *146*, 149
Goldblatt, David 79
Golding, William 125, 208
Goldreich, Arthur 146
Goldreich, Hazel 146
Goldstone, Richard 91
golf
   Bobby Cole and Dale Hayes 169
   Bobby Jones 79
   Ernie Els **215**, *215*
   Gary Player 135, *135*, 162
   Hugh Biocchi 168
   Sally Little 163, *163*
   Sewsunker 'Papwa' Sewgolum **162**, **177**
   Vincent Tshabalala 172
Gone with the Wind 88, 93, *93*, 97
Gooch, Graham 186
'Good-bye Dolly Gray' 43, *43*
Goodbye Mr Chips 86
Goodman, Benny 27, 195
Gool, Cissie 148
Goons, The 125
Gorbachev, Mikhail 180, 197
Gordimer, Nadine
   birth 59
   Nobel prize **203–4**, *203*
   on Sarah Gertrude Millin 52
   works 120, 133, 169, 179, 184, 196, 209
Graaff, De Villiers 175, 223
Grace, Princess of Monaco (Grace Kelly) 74, 124, **131**, *131*, 187
Grace, W.G. **26**
Graceland 136, 194
Grahame, Kenneth 25
Grahamstown, 1820 Settlers' Memorial 169
Grandmaster Flash and the Furious Five 187
Grant, Cary 20, 135, 195
Grant, Hugh 211, 222
Graves, Robert 85, 193
Gray, Stephen 100
Great Depression 76, **77**, *77*, **81**, *81*
Great Train Robbery 148
Great Train Robbery, The 18
Great War *see* World War I
Green, Lawrence 9, 165, *165*, 166
Greene, Graham 20, 91, 97, 111, 203
greenhouse effect 156
   see also CFC gases
Greenpeace 164
Greer, Germaine 163
Grey, John 214
Grey, Sir Edward 40
Griffith, D.W. 32, 42, 49
Griffith, Melanie 211
Grogan, Tony *182*
Groote Schuur hospital 154, 169
Groote Schuur talks **202**, *202*
Group Areas Act 113, 153, 162, 179
Grove, Stefan 58
grunge 207
Guam, Japanese WWII soldier 166
guerrilla campaign in SA
   fuel plants **181**
   making SA ungovernable *192*
   pre-1994 election 208
   Pretoria bomb **187–8**, *188*
Guevara, Ernesto 'Che' 71, 134, 156
Guinness Book of Records, The 128
Gulf War **202**, *202*
Gumede, Archie 41, 190, **202**, 218
Gumede, Josiah 74, *74*, 77, 110

guns
   AK-47 109
   'Long Cecil' 9
   'Long Tom' 9, *11*
   Tommy-Gun 53
Gutsche, Thelma 190
Guyana, Jonestown 177, *177*

H

Hackman, Gene 165
Haile Selassie (Ras Tafari) 72, 98, 169, 171
Hailey, Arthur 163
Haines, Richard 202
Hair 156, *156*
Haley, Bill 126, 184
Hall, Elsie 132, 172
Hall, Radclyffe 72
Hamilton, Thomas 213
Hammerskjöld, Dag 138, 144
Hammerstein II, Oscar 70
Hancock, Tony 125, 157
Handcock, Peter 14
Handley, Tommy 99
Hanekom, Hendrik 120, *120*
Hani, Chris 103, **206**, *206*
Hanks, Tom 208, 209, 222
Harari 136, 194
Hardy, Oliver 69
Harley-Davidson 16, *16*
Harlow, Jean 89, *89*
Harris, Frederick 152
Harris, Richard *216*
Harris, Rolf 141
Harrison, George (musician) *see* Beatles
Harrison, George (prospector) **62–3**
Harrison, Rex 130, 149, 202
Harry, Prince *214*
HART (Halt All Racist Tours) 183
Hart, William S. 42
Hartman, Anton 187
Hartzenberg, Ferdi 185
Harvey, Lawrence 74, 118, *118*, 133, 168
Hawkes, Chesney 204
Hawking, Stephen 198
Hayes, Dale 169
Hayward, Wally 27, **197**, *197*
Head, Bessie 89, 195
Heart of Darkness 9, 15
heart transplants **154**, *154*, 159
Helderberg aircraft 196
Heller, Joseph 223
Hemingway, Ernest 75, 81, 97, 125, 144
Hendrickse, Alan 190, **197**
Hendrik Verwoerd Dam 160
Hendrix, Jimi 101, **155**, 157, 163
Hepburn, Audrey 74, 123, 149, 208
Herenigde Nasionale Party (HNP) 83, **110**
Herero people **20**, *20*
Hertzog, J.M.B. 'Barry' **38**, **61**, *61*, 83, *83*, 93, *93*, 101
Herzog, Heidi **156**
Heston, Charlton 59, 135
Het Volk 6, 24
Heyerdahl, Thor 41
Heyns, Penny 213, 222, *222*
Higgins, Jack 171
Higgs, Cecil 195
highway robberies 35
hijackings 160

Hillary, Edmund **121**, *121*
Hillhouse, May 199
Hilton, James 85
Hinckley, Warnock 184
Hindenburg, Paul von 82, *82*
hippies (flower children) *152*, **155**, *155*
 see also Woodstock
Hirohito, Emperor of Japan 72, 107, 199
Hiroshima 107
Hirson, Baruch 223
Hitchcock, Alfred 69, 79, 106, 124, 135, 140, 182
Hitler, Adolf
 see also Holocaust
 lampooning of 97
 Mein Kampf 65, *76*
 Olympic Games 87
 rise to power 53–4, **58**–9, *58*, 65, 78, **82**, *82*
 suicide **106**
 World War II 90, *90*, 92, 95–6
HIV see AIDS
Hoare, 'Mad Mike' **184**
hoaxes **36**
Hobbit, The 89
Hobbs, Mike 172
Hobhouse, Emily **68**, *68*
Hoefling, Rita **178**, *178*
Hoffman, Dustin 172, 187, 198
Hofmeyr, Jan Hendrik 'Onze Jan' 27
Hoft, Dennis 158
Hogan, Barbara 186, *186*
Holiday, Philip 215
Holland, Allied liberation of *104*
Holly, Buddy 133, 135
Hollywood **32**, *32*
 see also film
Holmes, Sherlock **18**
Holocaust *92*, **105**, *105*, 120
Holomisa, Bantu 128
homelands
 Bophuthatswana 175, 179
 Ciskei 180, 204
 policy 116, 146, 206
 Transkei 172
 Venda 179
 white 182
Hong Kong 215
Hoogenhout, Casparus 58
Hoover, Herbert 72
Hopkin, Mary 157
Hopkins, Anthony 204
Hornby, Lesley (Twiggy) **151**, *151*
horse racing 162, 189, 214, 216
hot pants 166, *166*
Houdini, Harry 68
Hound of the Baskervilles, The 15
House of Assembly 187
House of Delegates 187, 190
House of Representatives 187, 190
Household, John Goodman **22**, *22*
Houston, Thelma 176
Houston, Whitney 196, 205
hovercraft 145
Hoyland, Eric (Tickey the clown) **83**, *83*, 198
Hubble, Edwin **60**, *60*
Hubble telescope 202
Huddleston, Fr Trevor 38, 130, *130*, 218
Hudson, Rock 193
Huguenet, André 22, 117, 144

hula hoops 133, *133*
human ancestors see palaeoanthropology
Human League 185
Hungary **129**–30, *129*
hunger see starvation
Hussein, Saddam 180, **202**
hut tax **22**
Hutchinson, Mavis 178
Huxley, Aldous 81, 148

I
'I have a dream' speech **146**
IBM (International Business Machines) 63
Ibrahim, Abdullah (Dollar Brand) 84, 136, 169, 188, *188*
Idasa (Institute for a Democratic SA) 180
identity books see pass laws
Ifield, Frank 145
IFP see Inkatha Freedom Party
Iglesias, Julio 190
Ilanga Lase Natal 35
Imbruglia, Natalie 219
immigration
 Chinese 6, **19**, *19*
 restrictions 76
Immorality Act **69**, 113, 162, 164, 193
Imvo Zabantsundu 43
Inca city 34
Incredible Shrinking Man, The 131
India, independence of **109**
Indian Representation Act 94
Indian rights **24**, **38**, *38*
 see also black, coloured and Asian rights
Indonesia, natural disasters in 217
Industrial and Commercial Workers' Union (ICU) 49
Industrial Conciliation Acts 50, 160
influenza pandemics 28, **47**
'Info Scandal' **176**
informal settlements
 see also townships
 riots in **111**, *111*
Inkatha Freedom Party (IFP)
 1994 elections 208
 Boipatong massacre 204
 Codesa 203
 cultural weapons 204
inkblot tests 53
Institute for a Democratic SA (Idasa) 180
Internet 206
Interpol 60
INXS 198
Ipi Tombi 137
IQ tests 21
Iran 180
Iraq 180, **202**
Ireland (Northern) 161
Irish Coffee 103
Iron Curtain **108**
irons, electric 53, *53*
Irons, Jeremy 185
Irwin, James 164
Iscor (SA Iron and Steel Corporation) 50
Israel
 advances of 129
 Arab strike on Yom Kippur **167**

 founding of **110**, *110*
 peace accords 177
 school bus attacked 163
 six-day war **155**, *155*
Israelite sect **53**, *53*
Istanbul 229, *229*
Italy, Allied liberation of **104**
'It's a Long Way to Tipperary' **38**
Ivanov, Captain Eugene 148

J
Jabavu, Davidson 135, *135*
Jabavu, Helen 'Noni' 148
Jabavu, John Tengo 43, *43*, 54, *54*
Jackson, Jesse 100
Jackson, Michael 134, 187, *187*, 189, 209, 222
Jagger, Mick *150*
Jaguar motor cars 86
James, Sid 172
Jameson, L.S. 29, 46
Japan
 atomic bombs 107, *107*
 invasion into China 76
 World War II 94, 99, 102
 WWII soldier surrenders 166
Japanese citizens, and apartheid 162
Jarre, Jean-Michel 229
Jaws 171
jazz
 Glenn Miller 20, 93, 101, *101*, 104
 international 133
 township 136–7, *136*, *137*, 188, 217
Jazz Singer, The 50, 69–70
Jeep 97
Jeptha, Andrew **24**
Jews
 see also Israel
 persecution of 76, *92*, **105**, *105*, 120
Joan of Arc 27, *27*
Jock of the Bushveldt **24**, *24*
jockeys 162, 189, 214, 216
Joel, Billy 189
jogging 190
Johannesburg
 see also gold mines
 ANC unbanned 201
 British occupation 8
 first urban location 6
 Flying Matchbox **26**, *26*
 forced removals **124**
 Market Theatre 169, 216
 motor cars 10, **17**, *17*
 OK Bazaars **70**, *70*
 radio 61
 riots **37**, *37*, **55**, *55*, 208
 sewerage system 6
 snow 149
 trams 6, 13
John, Elton 168, 172, 179, 214
John Paul II, Pope 184, *184*, 211
Johnson, Amy 79, *79*, 100
Johnson, Don 211
Johnson, Erving 'Magic' 204
Johnson, Jack **26**, 31
Johnson, Lyndon 147, 152, 168
Jolobe, James Ranisi 172
Jolson, Al **50**, 69, 115
Jones, Bobby 79
Jones, James Earl 216
Jones, 'Reverend' Jim 177

Jones, Tom 153
Jonestown, Guyana 177, *177*
Jonker, Ingrid 152
Jooste, Pamela 218
Joplin, Janis **155**, 163
Joplin, Scott 168
Jordan, Pallo 103
Joseph, Helen 21, 128, 129, *129*, 142, 205
Joubert, André 149
Joubert, Elsa 183
Joubert, Piet 9
Joyce, James 41, 57, 100
judges, in the peerage **32**
Juluka **194**, *194*
Junkin, Ava 162
Jurassic Park 207
Just Nuisance (dog) **105**
Just So Stories 15

K
Kadalie, Clements 49, *49*, 66, 118
Kafka, Franz 62, 65
Kalahari Gemsbok National Park 76
Kane, Nigel 172
Kani, John 103, 137, 170–1, *171*, 196
karate 164
Kariba Dam 140
Karpov, Anatoly 118
Kat and the Kings **192**, *192*
Kathrada, Ahmed 142, 146, *146*, 149, 199, *202*
Kaunda, Kenneth 121, 170
Keeler, Christine 148, *148*
Kekana, Steve 134
Kellogg, William 23
Kelly, Gene 36, 120
Kelly, Grace (Princess of Monaco) 74, 124, 131, *131*, 187
Kelsey, Ken 145
Kemp, J.C.G. 40
Kennedy, Jackie (Jacqueline Onassis) 122, *122*, 147, *147*, 209, 223
Kennedy, John F.
 assassinated **147**, *147*
 Bay of Pigs **143**
 becomes US president **141**, *141*
 birth 46
 Cuban missile crisis **145**, *145*
 marriage 122, *122*
 portrait *223*
Kennedy, John F. Jnr. 223, *223*
Kennedy, Robert 157
Kente, Gibson 82, 137, 187
Kentridge, Sydney 174
Kentridge, William 128
Kenya
 independence 148
 Kenyatta released **143**
 Mau Mau 94, **120**, *120*
Kenyatta, Jomo **143**, 178
Kern, Jerome 70
Kerr, Deborah 123, 130
Kerzner, Sol 86, 179
Keynes, John Maynard 48
Kgosana, Philip 87
Khama, Seretse 182
Kim 13
Kimberley
 big hole **40**
 siege 7, 9

Index

Kimmerling, Albert 26
Kindergarten, the 15, *15*
King, Coretta *157*
King and I, The 130
King Kong (film) 85, *85*
King Kong (musical) 136, *136*, 138
King, Martin Luther 74, 126, **146**, *146*, 157
King, Rodney 205
King, Steven 179
Kingsley, Ben 188
Kinski, Nastassja 185
Kipling, Rudyard 9, 13, 14, 15, 25
Kirsten, Peter 128, 215
Kissinger, Henry 59
Kitchener, H. Herbert 9, **11**, 43–4
Kitt, Eartha 166
Klaaste, Aggrey 97
Klaaste, Sol *137*
Klatzow, Peter 106
Kleenex tissues *63*
Kliptown rally **125**, *125*
Klug, Aaron 183
Klusener, Lance 222
Knossos, Crete **8**
Koch, Robert **22**
Koeberg 192
Korda, Zoltan 115
Korean war **114**, *114*, **117**
Korsten, Gé 70, 223
Kotane, Moses 178
Kramer, David 118, 192, 196
Kriel, Anneline 170, *170*
Krige, Alice 128, 185, 216, *216*
Krige, Uys 203
Kruger, Jimmy 174
Kruger, Paul 8, **18**, *18*
Kruger National Park **66–7**
Krugerrands 138
Kruschev, Nikita 122, 131, 145, *145*, 165, 212
Ku Klux Klan **59–60**, *59*
Kubrick, Stanley 157, 165, 222
Kumalo, Sidney 87
Kuwait **202**, *202*
kwela 136
KWS 205

L

La Guma, Alex 193
Labour Party 190
labour reforms **178**
Labram, George 9
Lady Chatterley's Lover 72, 141, *141*
'Lady in White' (Perla Gibson) 165
Ladysmith, siege of 7–8
Ladysmith Black Mambazo 136, 194, *194*
Lagden, Sir Godfrey 20
Laker, Jim 130, 195
Lancaster, Burt 123, 209
Land Bank 28
Langebaan, 'Eve's footprint' **216**
Langenhoven, C.J. 69, 82, *82*, 83
Langley, Noël 182
Langtry, Lillie 74
language *see* Afrikaans language
Lara, Brian 209
laser printers 171
lasers **141**, *141*, 192
Laubser, Maggie 168

Laurel, Stan 69, 152
Laurence Olivier awards 190, 192
Lawrence of Arabia 145
Lawrence, D.H. 34, 38, 72, 79, 141
Lawrence, T.E. ('of Arabia') **47**, *47*, 69, 86
lawyers, first black **129**
Le Carré, John 80, 148, 179
Le Mans racetrack 60, 128, *128*
Le Neve, Ethel 31, *31*
Le Roux, Etienne 179
Le Roux, Garth 128, 178
League of Nations 28, **48**, *48*
Lean, David 145, 152, 203
Leary, Timothy 151, 214
Led Zeppelin 192
Lee, Bruce 100, 168
Lee, Canada 115
Lee, Harper 141
Leeson, Nick 211
Lego 134
Leibbrandt, Robey **99**, *99*, 154
Leigh, Janet 140
Leigh, Vivien 93, *93*, 118, 156
Leipoldt, C. Louis 110
Lekota, Patrick 'Terror' 111, 190
Lembede, Anton 102, 110
Lenglen, Suzanne 60, *60*
Lenin 44, 44, 62, *62*
Lennon, John 97, 163, 182, *182*
 see also Beatles
Leon, Tony 130
Leonard, Cessie 26
Leonardo da Vinci 34
Leoniv, Alexei 152
Lepers, Jacob *137*
lesbian rights/issues *see* gay and lesbian rights/issues
Lesotho
 independence of 138
 SA invasions of **186–7**, 215
letter bombs **185**
Lewinsky, Monica 200, **218**, *218*
Lewis, Carl 203
Liberace 197
Liberal Party 112
Liddell, Eric **63**, *63*
lie detectors 54
Life is Beautiful 222
Linda, Solomon 136
Lindberg, Des and Dawn 168
Lindbergh, Charles **70**, *82*, 170
Lindsay, Kathleen *167*, *167*
Lion King, The 209
Lister, Moira 62, **165**
'Little Foot' 217
Little Rock, Arkansas **131**
Little, Sally 163, *163*
Live 222
Live Aid 192
Lloyd George, David 11, 31, 106
Lloyd-Webber, Andrew 185
Locke, Bobby 46
Lockerbie air disaster **197**, 220
Lolita 128, 145
London
 blitz *96*
 Carnaby Street 151, *151*
 funeral of George VI 119
 Muslims marching *109*

 St Paul's Cathedral *96*
 swinging 151, *151*, 153
Loneliness of the Long-distance Runner 145
Long Walk to Freedom 216, 221
Loren, Sophia 84, 187
'Louisville Lip' *see* Muhammad Ali
Louw, Juliet Marais 73
Louw, N.P. van Wyk 163
Louw, Rob 194
Love Story 163
Lumumba, Patrice 141, 144
Lusitania 23, **41**
Luthuli, Albert 124, **143**, *143*, 156
Lynn, Vera 101

M

*M*A*S*H* 188
Mabasa, Lemmy 'Special' 108, 136
Mabhida, Moses 195
Mabuse, Sipho 'Hotstix' 120, 194, *196*
MacArthur, Douglas 114, 117
Macbeth, Zulu (*uMubatha*) 137, **161**
Machel, Graça 218, *218*, 221, *221*
Machel, Samora
 death in plane crash **193–4**
 Nkomati Accord 189–90, *189*
MacKenzie, Nigel (Kathleen Lindsay) *167*, *167*
MacLaine, Shirley 188
Maclean, Don 166
MacLean, Donald 118, *118*
Macmillan, Harold 130, **140**, *140*, 195
Macnab, Roy 59
Madikizela-Mandela, Winnie
 birth 84
 'football club' assaults 203
 house arrest and prison 161, *161*
 at Mandela's release 201, *201*
 marriage to Mandela 221
 at Rivonia Trial 146
Madonna 134, 189, 192, 193, 222
Mafeking
 court in *7*
 siege of **7**
 soup kitchen in *7*
Mafia 51, **75**, **80**
Magubane, Peter 82
Mah Jong 59
Maharaj, Mac 80
mail service
 by air **33–4**, *33*, *34*
 by sea 67, *67*, 174
 by women 37
Maisels, Izrael 'Izzy' 209
Major, John 103, 202
Makeba, Miriam 82, 108, 136
Makipela, Thomas 35
Makiwane, Cecilia 6
Malan, Adolph 'Sailor' 116, 148
Malan, Daniël F. **83**, 110, *110*, 113, 135
Malan, Magnus 79
Malawi (Nyasaland) **121**, 138, **147**
Malcom X 152
Malherbe, Mabel **80**
Malinga, Sugarboy 132
Mallett, Nick 132
Mallory, George 62, *62*
Mamas and the Papas, the 153
man, ancestors of *see* palaeoanthropology

Man and Superman 18
Mandela, Nelson Rolihlahla
 80th birthday 218, *218*
 African Cup of Nations 213
 ANC Youth League 102
 autobiography 216, 221
 becomes president 208–9, *208*
 birth 47
 'Black Pimpernel' **142**, 144
 campaign for release 181, *181*, 198
 conditional offer of freedom 192
 Congressional Gold Medal 218
 with De Klerk and Buthelezi *203*
 Defiance Campaign 119
 Groote Schuur talks **202**
 at home **221**, *221*
 jailed 144
 with Joe Slovo *210*
 marriages 218, *218*, 221
 meets Spice Girls 219
 millennium celebrations 225, *225*
 Nigeria condemned **211**
 Nobel Prize 207, *207*
 outside SA 144, *144*
 peace process 204
 release imminent **197**
 released from prison 201, *201*
 resigns presidency 220, *220*
 Rivonia arrests/trial 146, *146*, 149
 rugby World Cup 210, *210*
 on sanctions 206
 treason charges/trial **128**, **142**, *142*
 tuberculosis treatment 197, *197*
 Umkhonto we Sizwe 142
Mandela, Winnie *see* Madikizela-Mandela, Winnie
'Manenberg' 217
Mangena, Alfred 62
Mann, Thomas 38, 128
Manthey, Anne *60*, 61
Manuel, Trevor 130
Manvers, Betty (Kathleen Lindsay) *167*, *167*
Mao Tse-tung 111, 138, 144, 172
Maponya, Maishe 120, 179
Maradona, Diego 194
Marais, Dave 162
Marais, Eugène 87, *87*, 89
Marais, Saré 13
Marciano, Rocky 130, 159
Marconi, Guglielmo 12
Maree, Sidney 184, *184*
Margaret, Princess 108, *108*, 140, *140*
Marion Island 111
Maritz, S.G. 'Manie' 13, 40
Market Theatre 169, 216
Marks, J.B. 166
Marley, Bob 106
Marquez, Gabriel Garcia 176
Mars
 exploration 138, 164
 invasion scare **90**
Mars Bar 81, *82*
Martienssen, Rex 101
Martin, Steve 106
Marx Brothers 79, 149, 175
Mary Poppins 85, 149, 152
Masekela, Hugh 93, 136, 165
Mashiyane, Spokes 136
Mason, James 145, 190
mass murderers 27

SOUTH AFRICA in the 20th CENTURY Index

massacres
   Australia **213**
   Boipatong **204**, *204*
   Ciskei 204
   Scotland **213**
Mata Hari **46**, *46*
Mathis, Johnny 172
Mathlala, Baby Jake 145
Matshikiza, John 207
Matshikiza, Todd 58, 136, 157
Matthee, Dalene 196
Matthews, Z.K. 157
Mau Mau 94, **120**, *120*
Maugham, W. Somerset 41
Mauriat, Paul 157
Maxeke, Charlotte **16**
mayors, women as **80**
Mbeki, Govan 33, 146, *146*, 149
Mbeki, Thabo
   ANC unbanned 201
   becomes president **220**, *220*
   birth 101
   Groote Schuur talks *202*
   meetings with white delegates 195
   millennium celebrations 225, *225*
   outside SA 144
Mboweni, Tito 134
mbube 136
McArthur, Kenneth 35, *35*
McBride, Willie-John 169
McCarthy, Benni 178, *219*
McCarthy, Senator 123
McCartney, Linda 218
McCartney, Paul 101, 163
   see also Beatles
McCullough, Colleen 176
McDonald, Arthur 214
McDonald, Hattie 97
McGlew, Jackie 74, 128
McKinley, William 12
McLuhan, Marshall 167
McQueen, Steve 157, 182
Mda, Zakes 111, 179
medical science
   in 1900s 12, 16, **25**, 27
   in 1912 36
   in 1920s 54, 55, 67, 69, **72**
   in 1940s 97
   in 1950s 115, 117, 122, **124**, 130
   in 1960s 148, **154**
   in 1970s 177, 179
   in 1980s 192
Mein Kampf 65, **76**
Melba, Nellie 51, *51*, 80
Melies, Georges 14
Men Are From Mars, Women Are From Venus 214
Mencken, H.L. 53
Mercedes 12
Mercury, Freddie 204, *204*
Merensky, Hans 64, *64*
Meropal KwaZulu 170
meteorites, in Russia **26**
metric system 143
Meyer, Elana 154, 204, 219, *219*
Mgijima, Enoch 53, *53*
Mgudlandu, Gladys 179
Mhlaba, Raymond 146, *146*, 149, 199
Mhlongo, George 171
Michael, George 193, 198, 219
Mickey Mouse **73**, *73*

Microsoft 185, 211
millennium celebrations **224–31**, *224–31*
Miller, Allister 49, **74–5**, 118
Miller, Arthur 42, 131, 182, 216
Miller, Glenn 20, 93, 101, *101*, 104
Miller, Henry 85
Milli Vanilli 199
Millin, Sarah Gertrude **52**, *52*, 157
Milne, A.A. 63, 69, 130
Milner, Alfred (Lord) 15, *15*, 24
Milošević, Slobodan 200
mines *see* coal mine disasters; gold mines
Mines and Works Act 33, 50
mini-skirts 151, 156
Minogue, Kylie 198, 214
Miss America 54
Miss Universe 177, *177*
Miss World 117, 170, *170*
Mitchell, Brian 144, 194, 205
Mitchell, Charles 73
Mitchell, Margaret 88, 93
Mitford, Nancy 81, 168
Mixed Marriages Act 162, 193
Mlambo, Johnson 97
Mlangeni, Andrew 146, 149
Mobutu, Joseph-Désiré 141
Model A Ford 16, 17, 72
Model T Ford (Tin Lizzy) 17, *17*, **26**, 62
Modisane, William 'Bloke' 59
Modise, Joe 74, *202*
Moeketsi, Kippie 62, 136, 188
Mogothlana, Frank 146
Mohammad Ali *see* Muhammad Ali
Mohammed, Sheik Nazeem 198
Mokaba, Peter 134
Mokolo, Philip 146
Molefe, Popo 120
Moloi, Godfrey **217**, *217*
Momberg, Jannie *199*
Mompati, Ruth *202*
Mona Lisa 34, *34*
Monet, Claude 68, *68*
money (notes/coins) **55**, *55*
Monongoaha, Oriel 108
Monroe, Marilyn
   birth 68
   career 120, 122, 123, *123*, 128, 131, 135, 145
   death 145, *145*
Monsarrat, Nicholas 118
Montgomery, Lucy Maud 25
Moodley, Strinivasa 97
moon landings **158**, *158*, 164
Moosa, Mohammed Valli 132
Moosa, Rahima 129
Morant, Harry 'Breaker' **14**
Morissette, Alanis 211
Morkel family 37, *37*, 53
Moroka, James 94, 119, *119*, 193
Morris Minor 135, *135*
Morrison, Herbert 117
Morrison, Mark 214
Morse code 23, 100
Morton, Andrew 205
Mosego, Job **101**
Mosheu, John 'Shoes' 152
Moss, Kate 207, *207*
Mostert, Mr Justice 176
motor cars
   see also Ford motor cars

   accident death rate 115
   active suspension 196
   Cape Town to Cairo **71**
   Cape Town rally **12**
   car of the century 17
   companies founded 25, 34, 46, 65, 72, 86
   computers on board 184
   Durban to Amanzimtoti 15
   first accident 17, *17*
   first air-conditioning 92
   first electric windows 111
   first motor show 17
   first in SA 10, *10*
   first SA Grand Prix **84**
   first SA world champion **178**, *178*
   first safety belts 119
   first speeding fine 21
   first trans-Africa 62
   first used in robbery 12
   Ford's ambition for **26**
   largest ever built 78
   Le Mans races 60, **128**, *128*
   mechanical problems 21
   Napier **32**
   new in 1900s 10, 12, 16, 21
   new in 1948 111
   new in 1950s **128**, *128*, 135, *135*
   petrol pumps 62
   pioneers **17**, 75
   speed limits 21
   speed records 12, 19, **73–4**, *74*, 80
   women champion drivers 178
motorcycles 16, *16*, **35–6**, *36*, 178
Motsoaledi, Elias *146*, 149
Mouillot, Frederick 31
Mount Nelson hotel 9, *9*
Mountbatten, Lord 179
Mousetrap, The 120, 222
mouth-bow musicians 215
Mozambique
   civil war 138
   independence 171
   Nkomati Accord **189–90**, *189*
   Portuguese dictator's death 160
Mpanza, James 163
Mpetha, Oscar 199, 209
MPLA 170
Mqhayi, Samuel 106
'Mrs Ples' 109
Mrwebi, Ben *137*
Msane, Saul *35*
Msomi, Welcome 100, 137, **161**
Mtshali, Oswald 97, 165
Mtwa, Percy 135, 137, 196, 218
Mugabe, Robert 177, *177*, 181, *181*
Muhammad Ali (Cassius Clay) 101, 149, *149*, 169, 213
Muir, Karen 120, **151**
Mulder, Connie 176
Muller, Hennie 175
Muller, Hilgard 170
Mullin, Emil 71
Munich conference (1938) **90**
Murdoch, Rupert 80
Muriel at the Metropolitan 171
Murphy, Eddie 190
Murray, Bill 190
music
   see also jazz; recorded sound
   broadcasting 6

   township **136–7**, *136*, *137*, 188, 217
Mussolini, Benito 86, 90, *90*, 97, **106**, *106*
Mutwa, Credo 54, 153
Muzorewa, Abel 177, *177*, 179
Mxenge, Griffiths 193
Mxenge, Victoria 193
My Fair Lady 130, 149
Mynhardt, Patrick 82
Mynhardt, Siegfried 212

N

NAACP (National Association for Advancement of Coloured People) 27
Nabokov, Vladimir 128, 175
Nagasaki 107
Naidoo, Jay 124
Namibia (South West Africa)
   German settlers **20**
   Herero rebellion **20**
   independence 202
   SA's mandate to govern 28, 53, 138
   UN Resolution on elections 160
   World War I 41
Napier motor car *32*
Nasser, Gamal Abdel 160
national anthems, flags, emblems, etc.
   anthems 13
   bird 138
   flags **71–2**, *71*, 200, *200*
   money (coins/notes) **55**, *55*
National Association for Advancement of Coloured People (NAACP) 27
National Association for Public Morality and Welfare 156
National Convention **25**, 27, 32
national parks/reserves *see* Cape of Good Hope Nature Reserve; Kalahari Gemsbok National Park; Kruger National Park
National Party
   see also Herenigde Nasionale Party; South African Nationalist Party
   in 1970 election 161
   in 1977 election 175
   in 1987 election 195
   in 1989 election 198
   in 1994 election 208
   founded 38
   fusion government 83
   Groote Schuur talks **202**
National Union of Mine Workers 190
National Velvet 104, *104*
Native Administration Act **69**
Native Affairs Act 50
Native Resettlement Bill **124**
Natives' Land Act 32, **37–8**, 81
Natives (Urban Areas) Act **59**
Natref 181
Naudé, Beyers 42, *202*
Navratilova, Martina 130, 178
Nazi Party 53–4, **58–9**, 75, **78**, **82**
Ndaba My Children 153
Nerina, Nadia 70, 154, *154*
Nesbitt, Murrogh **33**, *33*
netball 12
New English Bible, The 163
New Republic Party 175
New Seekers, The 166
New York
   Empire State Building 80

240

millennium celebrations *228*, 229
Playwrights' Sidewalk 218
New Zealand **183**, *183*
Newman, Paul 168
newspapers
  see also *Cape Argus*; *Cape Times*; *Daily Illustrated Mirror*; *Die Burger*; *Ilanga Lase Natal*; *Imvo Zabantsundu*; *Rand Daily Mail*; *Star*; *Sunday Times*
  colour photos 19
  millennium celebrations 230, *230*
Newsweek 200
Newton, Arthur **57**
Newton-John, Olivia 178, 187
Ngatane, Ephraim 91
Ngema, Mbongeni 128, 137, 196, 216, 218
Ngoyi, Lilian 128, 129, *129*, 142, **186**, *186*
Nicholas II, Tsar of Russia 44, **47**, *47*
Nicholson, Jack 188
Nico Malan theatre 172
Nigeria 138, 140, 154, 159, *159*, 161, **211**
Nightmare on Elm Street, A 190
Nike 166, 179
Niven, David 130, 171, 188
Nixon, Richard 38, 141, 158, 167, 169, *169*, 209
Nkabinde, Simon Mahlatini 223
Nkomati Accord **189–90**, *189*
Nkomo, Joshua 121, 144, 177, *177*, 223
Nkosi, Lewis 87
'Nkosi Sikelel' iAfrika' 13
Nkrumah, Kwame 119, **132**, 166
Nobel Prize
  for chemistry 16, 183
  first awarded 12
  for literature 25, 65, 81, 125, 157, **203–4**
  for medicine **22**, 179
  for peace **143**, *143*, 184, **189**, *189*, 207, *207*
  for physics 6, 16
Noddy books 196
Noether, Weiyien Wong 162
Nokwe, Philemon **129**
Nomis, Syd 162
Non-European Unity League 102
Normandy **103–4**, *103*
North Pole 6, **32**
Northern Rhodesia see Zambia
Nourse, Dave 23
Nourse, Dudley 110, **117**, *117*, **182**
novelists
  first black woman published 171, *171*
  world's most prolific **167**, *167*
Novello, Ivor 118
Ntini, Makhaya 175, 219
Ntshona, Winston 137
Nuclear Non-Proliferation Treaty 157
nuclear physics see atomic power/weapons
Nuremburg rallies 75, *75*
Nurmi, Paavo 63, 72, *72*
nursing 6, **34**, 42
Nyasaland see Malawi
Nylon 86, *86*, 97, *97*
Nzo, Alfred 202

O'Connor, Sinead 202
Ofarim, Esther and Abi 157
oil companies, Vacuum 6
oil prices 168
oilfields, in Kuwait 202, *202*
Ojukwa, Odumegwu 159
OK Bazaars **70**, *70*
Oklahoma City bomb 211
Oldsmobile 25
Olive Schreiner prize 188
Oliver! 141, 157
Oliver, Gordon 198
Olivier, Laurence 104, 111, 199
  see also Laurence Olivier awards
Olsen, Ken 175
Olympic Games
  1908 (London) **25**, *25*
  1912 (Stockholm) **35**, *35*
  1920 (Antwerp) **52**, *52*
  1924 (Paris) **63**, *63*
  1928 (Amsterdam) **72**, *72*
  1936 (Berlin) **87**, *87*, 99
  1948 (London) 111
  1952 (Helsinki) **120**
  1956 (Melbourne) 130
  1960 (Rome) **141**
  1972 (Munich) **166**
  1984 (Los Angeles) **189**, *189*
  1992 (Barcelona) 204
  1996 (Atlanta) 213
  hostage drama **166**
  SA leaves **141**
  SA returns 204
Omar, Dullah 84
On the Beach 135
Onassis, Jacqueline see Kennedy, Jackie
One Flew Over the Cuckoo's Nest 145, 171
O'Neal, Ryan 168
O'Neal, Tatum 168
Ono, Yoko 182
Onze Jan see Hofmeyr, Jan Hendrik
OPEC (Organization of Petroleum-Exporting Countries) 168
Operation Desert Storm 202
Oppenheimer, Ernest 132
Oppenheimer, Harry 26
Orange Free State (Orange River Colony)
  gold mines 112
  independence struggles 6, 14, **24**
  pass laws 28
Orangia-Unie 24
Orbison, Roy 149, 198
Organization of Petroleum-Exporting Countries (OPEC) 168
Orwell, George 18, 85, 89, 91, 106, 115
Osborne, John 74, 133
Oscar awards 70, 75, 97, 149, 187, 188
Osler, Bennie 80, *80*, 98, 145
Osmond, Donny 166
Osmond, Jimmy 166
Ossewa-Brandwag (ox-wagon sentinel) 76, 99, *99*
ostrich feathers 19, **21**, *21*, 30, *30*
O'Sullivan, Maureen 218
Oswald, Lee Harvey 147, *147*
O'Toole, Peter 145
'Oubaas' see Smuts, Jan
Outspan magazine 72, **131**, *131*

Owens, Jesse 38, **87**, *87*, 182
Oxford English Dictionary, The 72
Oxlee, Keith 218

PAC see Pan-Africanist Congress
Packer, Joy 21, 128, 175
Packer, Kerry 175, 178
Pacman 186
Pagel's Circus **114**
Pakistan **109**
palaeoanthropology
  australopithecines 76
  Eve's footprint **216**
  Little Foot 217
  Mrs Ples **108–9**
  Piltdown Man 36, *36*
  Sterkfontein hominid 216–17
  Taung skull **61**, *61*
Palmer, Robert 198
Pan-Africanist Congress (PAC)
  Codesa 203
  formation **134**, 176
  Sharpeville 139
Panic Mechanic 207
Pankhurst, Emmeline 38
Paris
  fashions **30**, *30*
  German troops 95, *95*
  millennium celebrations 226, *227*
  underground railways 9
Parker, A.C. 223
Parker Jnr, Ray 190
Parker-Bowles, Camilla 205, 211
Parks, Rosa **126**
parks/reserves see Cape of Good Hope Nature Reserve; Kalahari Gemsbok National Park; Kruger National Park
Parliament, tricameral 187, 190
pass laws
  abolition of **193**, *193*
  comments on 23
  Indians protests against 6, 24, 28
  protests/demonstrations against 50, **139**
  reference books replace 112
  for women 16, 28, **129**
passive resistance 24
Paton, Alan 18, 111, 115, 198, *198*, 216
Pavlova, Anna **64–5**, *64*, 80
peace marches, legalized 198
Peanuts 115
Pearl Harbor 27, **98**, 99
Peary, Admiral R.E. 6
Peck, Gregory 106, 123, 135
Peking see Beijing
Pele 97
Penguin books 86
Penicillium **72**
Penn, Sean 211
Pepsi-Cola 16
perestroika 197
Perkins, Anthony 140, 205
Personality magazine 131
Petacci, Clara 106, *106*
Peter Pan 19, 34
Peter, Paul and Mary 148
Peters and Lee 168
Petersen, Hector 173
Petersen, Taliep 118, 192, 196
Pfeiffer, Michelle 197

Phantom of the Opera, The 65
Philadelphia 208
Philby, Kim 198
Philip, Duke of Edinburgh 54, 108, *205*, 214
Phosa, Mathews 120
photography
  Box Brownie camera 9
  first colour 41
  first newspaper colour 19
  Instamatic cameras 157
  Polaroid 109
Piaf, Edith 42, 148, *148*
Picasso, Pablo 13, **88**, 168
Pick 'n Pay 156
Pickford, Mary 42, 49, **52**, 179
Picture Post magazine 91
Piel, Albert *17*
Pienaar, François 156, *210*
Pierneef, Jacob 132, *132*
Pietermaritzburg Philharmonia Society 166
Pietri, Dorando 25
Piggot, Lester 125
Pilgrim's Rest 35
Pill, the **143**, *143*
Piltdown Man 36, *36*
Pimville 6, 108
Pinter, Harold 79
Pius X, Pope 42
pizzas 21
Plaatje, Sol 35, **81**, *81*
Planck, Max 9
Planet of the Apes, The 157
plastics 27
Platters, The 126
Playboy magazine 122
Player, Gary 86, 135, *135*, 162
Plomer, William 168
Pluto 78
plutonium 50
Poiret, Paul 30
Poirot, Hercule **51**
Poitier, Sidney 115, 149
Poland 92, *92*, 183
Polanski, Roman 82, 185
pole sitting 59
police custody, deaths in see deaths in detention
Police, The 182, 189
polio **124**
Pollock, Graeme 104, **140**, *140*, 161
Pollock, Peter 161
Pollock, Shaun 166
Poole, David 203
Popeye 75
Popham, Glen 164
Popova, Madame 27
Popular Front for Liberation of Palestine 163
Population Registration Act 113, 162
Port Elizabeth, motor cars in *17*
Porter, Anne 145
Portugal 160
postcards, airmail 33–4, *34*
Potgieter, Gert 141
Potter, Beatrix 9
Pratt, David 140
Pravda 37
Preller, Alexis 34, 171

SOUTH AFRICA in the 20th CENTURY — Index

Preller, Gustav 43, *43*
President's Council 181
Presley, Elvis
  birth 86
  death **175**, *175*
  with Juliet Prowse 212, *212*
  marriage 156
  songs 125, 128, 130, 133, 141, 144, 162, 175
Presley, Lisa Marie 209
Presley, Priscilla 156
Pretoria
  administrative capital 27
  bomb 187–8, *188*
  British occupation 8
  declared a city 76
  first lady mayor **80**
  motor cars 10, *10*
  peace after Anglo-Boer War 14
  petty apartheid **182**
  trams 13
  women's march **129**
Prevention of Illegal Squatting Act 116
priests, women as 192, 209
Prince 134
Prince Edward Island 111
prison deaths *see* deaths in detention
Private Eye 143
Proctor, Mike 108, 161, *161*, 164
Profumo, John 148
Progressive Federal Party 175
Progressive Party 134
Progressive Reform Party 171, 175
prohibition of alcohol 25, **51**, *51*, 53
Prowse, Juliet 195, **212**, *212*
Psycho 140
Puccini, Giacomo 9, 19, 62
Puck of Pooks Hill 15
Pulitzer Prize 46, 81
Pussycat 172

Q
Quant, Mary 84, 103, 150, *150*, 151
quantum theory 9
Queen 171, 192, 204
Quota Act 76

R
Rabin, Yitzhak 211, *211*
race relations *see* apartheid and race laws; black, coloured and Asian rights
radar 166, 214
Radebe, Dorothy 136
Radebe, Jeff 122
Radebe, Lucas 159
radio
  British sitcoms 125
  capture of Crippen **31**
  first commercial programmes 86
  first live election coverage 51
  first music/voice broadcast 6
  first professional performer 51
  first transatlantic signal **12**
  Martian scare **90**
  national broadcasters 61, **69**, 113
  pictures transmitted **67**–8
  SA stations 60–1, *61*, **113**
  transistor 94
  World War II 99–100, 101
Radziwill, Princess 100

railways
  Paris underground 9
  in Russia 19
  in SA **65**
Rain Man 198
Rainier, Priaulx 195
Rainier, Prince of Monaco 130–1, *131*
Ramaphosa, Matamela Cyril 120
Ramphele, Mamphela 110
Rand Daily Mail 15, 26, 73, 176
rap music 187
Ras Tafari (Haile Selassie) 72, 98, 169, 171
Rasputin 44, *44*
Raubenheimer, Marc 188
Ray, James Earl 157
Rayne, Leonard **64**
Reader's Digest, The 57–8, *58*, 117
Reagan, Nancy 183
Reagan, Ronald
  attempted assassination 184
  becomes US President 180, 183, *183*
  birth 34
  'constructive engagement' policy 180
  and Gorbachev 197
  joke about nuclear strike 190
Rebel Without a Cause 126, *126*
rebellions, revolts and riots
  see also massacres
  the 1900s 6
  anti-apartheid 112, 180, *191*
  anti-German 41
  gold mines 37, *37*, **55**, *55*
  Herero 20
  informal settlements 111, *111*
  Los Angeles 205
  Natal 38
  pre-1994 election 208
  Russian **22**
  Sharpeville **139**, *139*
  Soweto 173, *173*
  Zulu **22**, *22*
recorded sound 10, 54, 179, 183, 192, 196
Red Revolt **55**, *55*
Redeemer, The *see* Nkrumah, Kwame
Redfield, James 209
Redford, Robert 168, 172
Reeve, Christopher 120
Reeves, Jim 153
referendum **187**, *187*
Reform Party *see* Progressive Reform Party
Reitz, Denys 11, 75, 104
Relly, Gavin 191
Remarque, Erich Maria 75
removals *see* forced removals
Renault, Mary 188
Representation of Natives Act 76
Republic of South Africa
  constitutions **187**, 203, 204, 206
  declared a republic **142**
  détente with Africa 163, *163*, **170**
  first executive President 190
  first President 142
  franchise 187
  invasions of Angola **170**, *170*
  invasions of Lesotho 186–**7**, 215
  pathway to peace 200, 201, 202, 203, 204, 206, 208–9

raids on ANC targets 193
referendum **187**, *187*
royal visits 211
revolts *see* rebellions, revolts and riots
Rhodes of Africa 86
Rhodes, Cecil John 9, **14**, *14*, 100
Rhodes, Jonty 159
Rhodes memorial building 14
Rhodesia, Northern *see* Zambia
Rhodesia, Southern *see* Zimbabwe
Rice, Clive 111
Richard, Cliff 97, 133, 135, 141, 145, 198
Richard, Mary (Kathleen Lindsay) **167**, *167*
Richards, Barry 106, 161
Richardson, Dave 215–16, 219
Riekert commission 178
Righteous Brothers 202
Riotous Assemblies Amendment Act 160
riots *see* rebellions, revolts and riots
Ritchie, Lionel 185
Rivonia arrests/trial **146**, *146*, 149
Robben Island 225, *225*
Roberts, Dave 216
Roberts, Julia 222
Roberts, Michael 216
Robson and Jerome 211
'Rock Around the Clock' 126
Rocky 172
Rocky Horror Picture Show, The 171
Rogers, Ginger 85, *85*, 211
'Rolling Stone' 118
Rolling Stones, The 150
Rolls-Royce motor cars 19
Romania 199
Romeo and Juliet 157
Rommel, Erwin 100, *100*
Room at the Top 133
Rooney, Mickey 97, 104
Roos, Paul 23
Roosevelt, Franklin D. 81, *81*, 99, 100, 106
Roosevelt, Theodore 12, 49
Roots 176
Rorschach, Hermann 53
Rosemary's Baby 157
Rosenberg, Julius and Ethel 123
Rosenkowitz sextuplets **169**, *169*
Ross, Diana 104, 185
Rotary Club 21
Roux, Mannetjies 162
Rowan, Athol 218
Rowan, Eric 208
Royal Air Force 47
Royal Flying Corps 36
Royal Navy, and Just Nuisance (dog) *105*
Royal Scots Dragoon Guards Band 166
'Rubicon' speech 191
Rubik's Cube 183
Rubusana, Walter **35**, 87
Ruby, Jack 147, *147*
Rudd, Bevil 52, **52**
Rudolph, Wilma 141
rugby
  against All Blacks 53, **89**, **162**, *162*, 210
  during Anglo-Boer War 13
  anti-apartheid demos 158–**9**, **183**, *183*
  against Australia **89**, 210

  against Britain **80**, **126**, **158**–9, **169**
  Chester Williams 209, *209*
  first national player of colour 194
  first overseas tour 23
  first player sent off 65
  first radio commentary 61
  international isolation 194
  local progress **16**
  Morkel family **37**, *37*, 53
  national emblem 23
  Roberto Canessa **181**
  Tom von Vollenhoven **132**, *132*
  Tri-Nations cup 219
  against unofficial NZ side **194**
  World Cup 200, **210**, *210*, 222
running
  see also jogging
  100-metre record 203
  1952 Olympics **120**
  1996 Olympics 213
  Budd and Decker **189**, *189*
  Elana Meyer 204, 219, *219*
  four-minute mile 125, *125*
  Josiah Thugwane 213, *213*
Rupert, Anton 44
Rush, Jennifer 193
Russell, Jane 103, *103*
Russia
  Bolsheviks 44
  collectivization 50
  Cuban missile crisis 145
  fighting Japan 21
  first soviet 21
  first western rock star 179
  glasnost and *perestroika* 197
  Iron Curtain 108
  meteorites 26
  purges 76
  railways 19
  revolts 22
  royal family murdered 47
  space exploration **131**, 132, **143**, 148, 164
  Stalin 50, 76, **122**
  USSR dissolves 203
  World War II **98**–9, 102
Russian Communist Party 47
Rwanda 209
Ryan, Meg 208, 222

S
Sabela, Simon 208
Sabotage Act 138
sabotage campaign *see* guerrilla campaign in SA
Sacco, Nicola 70, *70*
Sadat, Anwar 160, 184
safari suits 150
Sagan, Leontine 170
Saint Laurent, Yves 87, 133, 134
Sakharov, Andrei 54
Salazar, Antonio 160
Salinger, J.D. 49, 118
Salk, Jonas 124
Salvation Army 25
sanctions 175, **184**, 189, 203, 206
Sarafina 137, 196, 216, *216*
Sarandon, Susan 211
'Sarie Marais' 13
Saro-Wiwa, Ken 211
Sasol *see* Sasolburg; Secunda

Index

SOUTH AFRICA in the 20th CENTURY

Sasolburg
    founded 112
    sabotage **181**
Sassoon, Vidal 151
Saturday Night Fever 176, *176*
satyagraha 24
Saudi Arabia 202
Sauer report 94
Savimbi, Jonas 138
Savuka 194
Sayer, Leo 176
Sayers, Dorothy 99
Scaffold 157
Schach, Leonard 216
Scheckter, Jody 115, **178**, *178*
Schiaparelli 80
Schindler's List 207–8
Schlesinger 69, *69*
Schmidt, Uli 144
Schoeman, Karel 165
Schonland, Basil 166, *166*
Schoon, Marius 223
Schreiner, Olive 34, **51–2**, *52*
    see also Olive Schreiner prize
Schreiner, William 27, *27*
Schultz, Charles 115
Schuster, Leon 120, 207
Schwarzenegger, Arnold 190, *190*, 204
Scofield, Paul 153
Scopes, John 65, *65*
Scotland, massacre in **213**
Scott, David 164
Scott, Robert Falcon 32, 34
Seal 211
Secret Agent, The 25
sects and cults **53**, *53*, **177**, *177*
Secunda **181**, 186
Seekers, The 152, 155
Segogela, Mashego 87
Sekoto, Gerard 38
Sellers, Peter 182
Seme, Pixley ka Isaka 33, *33*, 34, 77, 118
Senna, Ayrton 209, *209*
Sepamla, Sipho 184
Separate Registration of Voters Act 116, **128**
Sepei, Stompie 203, *203*
Sepeng, Hezekiel 170, 213
Serbia 18, 200
serial killers 122–3, 211
Serote, Mongane Wally 104, 169
servants 15, *15*
Seven Year Itch, The 123, 128
Sewgolum, Sewsunker 'Papwa' **162**, **177**
sex-change operations 115
Sexwale, Gabriel 'Tokyo' 122
Seychelles, attempted coup **184**
Shabalala, Joseph 97, 194
Shaffer, Peter 179, 190
Shaka Zulu 195
Shakespears Sister 205
Sharif, Omar 152
Sharpeville **139**, *139*
Shaw, George Bernard 18, 25, 65, *65*, 115
Shaw, Irwin 163
Shawaddywaddy 172
Sheen, Martin 179
Shell petrol 62
Shepard, Alan 59, 143

Sher, Anthony 190, 216
Sherwell, Percy 23, *23*
Sherwood-Kelly, John **49**
Shilowa, Sam 135
shipping
    Lusitania 23, **41**
    mailships 67, *67*, 174
    passenger liners 91
    settlers and immigrants 174
    Titanic **35**, 192
    Union-Castle line **8–9**, 67, *67*, **174**, *174*
    Waratah disappears 6
    Windsor Castle **174**, *174*
Shipton, Eric 117
Shrimpton, Jean 151
Sibaya, Lucky 101, 223
Sibeko, David Maphgumzana 171
Sidney 230, *230*
Silence of the Lambs 204
Simon, Carly 168
Simon, Paul 136, 194
Simon's Town
    DP victory in *199*
    Just Nuisance (dog) *105*
    SA Navy base 112
Simplon tunnel 21
Simpson, O.J. **211**, *211*
Simpson, Wallis 80, 87, *87*, 195
Sinatra, Frank 42, 94, 115, *115*, 123, 135, 153, 212
Sinatra, Nancy 153
Sinclair, Jean 214
Singana, Margaret 91, 137
Singh, Anant 216
Sirhan Sirhan 157
Sisulu, Albertina 49
Sisulu, Walter
    ANC unbanned 201
    ANC Youth League 102, *102*
    birth 36
    Groote Schuur talks 202
    release from prison **199**, *199*
    Rivonia arrest/trial 146, *146*, 149
    treason charges/trial 128, 142
Sita, Nana 119
Six-Day War **155**, *155*
Sizwe Bansi is Dead 137, **171**, *171*
Skukuza (James Stevenson-Hamilton) **66–7**
Skylon 117, *117*
Slabbert, Frederick van Zyl 97, 195, *195*
Slade 168
Slovo, Joe 68, 185, **202**, **210**, *210*
Smith, Alfred Aloysius 80
Smith, Ian 49, 149, *149*, 151, *151*, 170, 177
Smith, J.L.B. 91, *91*
Smith, Pauline 69, 135
Smith, Wilbur 82, **149**
Smith, Willie 63, *63*
smoking
    cigarette manufacturers **20–1**
    health warnings on packets 152
    linked to cancer 117, 130
    protection against plague 10
Smuts, Jan Christiaan
    cartoons *61*
    death **114–15**
    Het Volk 24
    League of Nations 48

    loses 1948 election 110
    prime minister **48**, **53**
    Royal Air Force 47
    with Royal family 108, *108*
    South African Party 33, 83, *83*
    on Table Mountain 114
    United Nations 107, *107*
    World War I 41, **44–5**
    World War II 93, *93*
Smythe, Quinten 215
snow, in Johannesburg 149
Snow White and the Seven Dwarfs 89, *89*
Snyman, Harold 174
Sobukwe, Robert 62, 134, *134*, 139, **176**
soccer (football)
    African Cup of Nations 213, *213*
    Bafana Bafana 213, *213*, 218–19, *219*
    Busby's Babes **133**
    Diego Maradona 194
    disasters 199
    first floodlighting 126
    World Cup 69, 79, 91, 125, **154**, *154*, 163, 169, 178, 186, 194, 209, 218–19, *219*
Soga, John Henderson 100
Soga, Jotello 22
'Soldier', 'The' 41
Solidarity 183
Solomon, Bertha **83**, *83*, 159
Solzhenitsyn, Alexander 145, 157
Somalia 200
Somme, battle of **42–3**, *42*
Sontonga, Enoch 13
Sophiatown **127**, *127*, 130, 136
Soul Brothers 136
Soul, David 176
Sound of Music, The 152, *152*
South Africa *see* Republic of South Africa; Union of South Africa
South African Airways 75, **84**, *84*
South African Broadcasting Company (SABC) 61, 113, 171
South African Communist Party 112, 206, 210
South African Lady's Pictorial 88
South African Land Bank 28
South African Nationalist Party 29
South African Native Affairs Commission 6, 20
South African Native Labour Corps **45**, *45*
South African Native National Congress (SANNC) 28, **34–5**, *35*
South African Party (1911) 33, 83
South African Party (1977) 175
South African Students' Organization 166
South African War *see* Anglo-Boer War
South Pole **32**, **34**
South West Africa *see* Namibia
South West African Peoples' Organisation (SWAPO) 138
Southern Rhodesia *see* Zimbabwe
Soweto
    Pimville 6, 108
    student uprisings **173**, *173*
Soweto Students' Representative Council 172
space exploration
    see also astronomy

    accidents 156, 194
    British 131
    docking of space craft 211
    end of space race 171
    first man in space **143**
    first space walk 152
    first woman 148
    Mars 138, 164
    moon landings **158**, *158*, 164
    Russia 131, 132, **143**, 148, 152, 164
    shuttles 184, 194
    US 54, 59, 132, 134, 138, 143, 145, 152, 157, 158, *158*, 164, 184, 194
space hotel 222
Spain **88**, 92
spam 89, *89*
Sparman, Professor and Mrs *31*
Spears, Britney 222
Speer, Albert 184
Spencer, Diana *see* Diana, Princess of Wales
Spencer, Earl 211, 214
Spice Girls 214, 219, *219*
Spielberg, Steven 171, 176, 185, 187, 207–8
spies
    British scandals **117–18**, 148, 198
    Julius and Ethel Rosenberg 123
    Mata Hari **46**, *46*
Spioenkop **7**, *8*
Spock, Benjamin 108, 218
sport
    see also bowls; boxing; cricket; golf; jockeys; karate; netball; Olympic Games; rugby; running; soccer; surfing; swimming; tennis; yachting
    anti-apartheid demos **158–9**, **183**, *183*
    apartheid in action 156, 162, 164, 168, 172, 177
    international isolation 156, 161, 163, 203
    rebel/unofficial tours 186, 194
    wheelchair athletes 33
Springbok, as rugby emblem 23
Springbok Radio 113, *113*
Springbok tobacco 20
Springfield, Dusty 148, 152, 223
Springfield, Rick 185
Springsteen, Bruce 190
Sputnik programme **131**, 132
squatter camps, riots in **111**, *111*
St Helena, prisoners-of-war on *12*
St Helen's, Mount 183
St Valentine's Day massacre **75**, *75*
Staff, Frank 165
Stalin, Josef 50, 76, **122**
Stallone, Sylvester 172
Stamp, Terence 151
Stansfield, Julia 26
Star, The 37, 105, *105*, 142
Star of Africa 20, *20*
Star Trek series 153, 216
Star Wars series 176, 182, 188, 222
Starr, Kenneth 218
Starr, Ringo *see* Beatles
starvation
    in Ethiopia 192, *193*
    in Nigeria 159
states of emergency 191

243

Status Quo 192
Steinbeck, John 89, 106, 120, 157
Sterkfontein caves 76, **108–9**, *109*, 216–17
Stern, Irma 49, *49*, 154
Stevenson-Hamilton, James **66–7**
Stewart, Rod 165, 171, 179, 209
Steytler, Jan 134
Sting 209
stock exchange crashes 73, *73*, **77**, 196
Stockdale, Henrietta **34**, *34*
stockings 33, 45, 86, *86*, 97, *97*, 102
Stone Age paintings 97
Stone, Sharon 205
Stopes, Marie 54, *54*, 134
Story of an African Farm, The **51–2**
Stransky, Joel 156, 210
Streep, Meryl 185
Streisand, Barbra 101, 182, 188
Strijdom, J.G. **61**, 128, 129, 134
strikes
    anti-apartheid 38, 139, 142
    in gold mines 37, *37*, 55, *55*, **107**
student organizations **158**, *158*, 166, *166*, 172
student uprisings **173**, *173*
Stylistics 171
submarines 19
Suez Canal **129**, *129*, 160
suffragettes *see* women's rights
'Suikerbossie' ('Sugarbush') 216
Sun City **179**, *179*
Sunday Times 201
supermodels 207, *207*
Supernature **168**, *168*
Suppression of Communism Act 112
surfing **175**, *175*
surrogate motherhood **195**
Survivor (//Am//Op) 215
Survivor (group) 187
Susann, Jacqueline 153
Suzman, Helen 46, **134**, *134*, 175
Suzman, Janet 93, 196
Swart, C.R. 114, 142
Swaziland 138
swimming
    English Channel **178**
    Karen Muir **151**
    Penny Heyns 213, **222**, *222*
    women in 67
Swindell, Madge 188
Synge, J.M. 25

T

Table Mountain
    Jan Smuts 114
    millennium celebrations 225, *225*
Taiwanese citizens, and apartheid 162
Take That 211
Talbot-Darracq 17
Tale of Peter Rabbit, The 9
Tam, Patricia 162
Tambo, Oliver 46, 102, 142, 191, 208
Tamm, Oscar 32
Tanzania (Tanganyika and Zanzibar) 138
Tarzan of the Apes 41, 218
Taung skull **61**, *61*
Tayfield, Hugh 209
Taylor, Arnie 167

Taylor, Elizabeth 82, 102, 104, *104*, 115, 148, *148*, 153, 211
Taylor, Herbie 168
Teichmann, Gary 156
telephone 58, 69, 76, 129, 148
    see also cellphones
television
    arrives in SA **171**, *171*, **172**
    banned in SA **140**
    milestones **67–8**, 72, 75, 76, 97, 117, 148
    O.J. Simpson trial 211
    war coverage 155, 167, 202
Temple, Shirley 71, 85, *85*
tennis
    Arthur Ashe **164**, *164*, 171
    Bjorn Borg **172**, *172*, 178
    Curren versus Becker **191**, *191*
    Davis Cup 9
    French Open 111
    Grand Slam 91
    Wimbledon 60, 85, 91, 111, 130, *130*, 157, 163, 171, 172, *172*, 178, **191**, *191*
Tensing, Sherpa **121**
Teresa, Mother 33, 215
Tereshkova, Valentina 148
Terminator films **190**, *190*, 204
Terre'Blanche, Eugene 100, 168, 182, *182*
Terrorism Act 174
terrorist groups
    see also bombs; guerrilla campaign in SA
    Baader-Meinhoff gang 166
    Black September group 166
test-tube babies **177**, *177*
Thalidomide **133**, *133*
Thatcher, Margaret 171, 179, 182, 201, 202
theatre
    Anthony Sher 190, 216
    Athol Fugard 82, **132**, 137, **147**, *147*, 169, 171, 182, 196, 218
    Godspell 168
    Joan Brickhill 170
    Kramer and Petersen 118, 192, 196
    Leonard Schach 216
    Market Theatre 169, 216
    Mbongeni Ngema 128, 137, 196, 216, 218
    Moira Lister 62, **165**
    Percy Mtwa 135, 137, 196, 218
    Pieter-Dirk Uys 106, 195, 196
    Sarah Bernhardt **60**, *60*
    Siegfried Mynhardt 212
    Tivoli Theatre **18**, *18*
    townships **136–7**
    uMabatha 137, **161**
    Zakes Mda 111, 179
Theiler, Arnold 87
Themba, Can **127**, 157
There's a Zulu on My Stoep 207
Thomas, Dylan 41, 125
Thompson, Shaun 175, *175*
Thorpe, Jim 35, *35*
Thugwane, Josiah 165, 213, *213*
Thurber, James 81
Thurman, Uma 209
Tiananmen Square 199
Tickey the clown (Eric Hoyland) **83**, *83*, 198

Tiffany 198
Tight Fit 187
Time Magazine 60, 153, 186
Titanic (film) 219
Titanic (ship) 35, 192
Tivoli Theatre **18**, *18*
Tlali, Miriam **171**, *171*
tobacco *see* smoking
Tobias, Errol 118, 194
Tobias, Philip 216–17
Tobruk **100**, *100*, 101
Todd, Garfield 166
Todd, Judith 166
Toffler, Alvin 163
Togo 140
Tolkien, J.R.R. 89, 125, 168
Tombaugh, Clyde 78
Tombouctou, Clyde
Torch Commando **116**
Tornados 145
'total onslaught' 178
Tovey, Neil 213
Toweel, Vic **113**, 211
townships
    see also informal settlements
    poverty 160
    street committees 192
    talent **136–7**, *136*, *137*, 188, 217
Trader Horn 80
trams 6, **13**, *13*
Transitional Executive Council 207
Transkei 172
Transkei Bill 146
transplants, of organs 27, 115, 148, **154**, *154*, 159
Transvaal
    Chinese immigrants 6, **19**, *19*
    diamonds discovered 66, *66*
    first black lawyer **129**
    gold discovered 18
    independence struggles 6, 14, **24**
    pass laws 23, 24
    president Kruger 18
Transvaal Native Congress 50
Travers, Pamela 85
Travolta, John 176, *176*, 178, 209
treason charges/trial 112, **128**, **142**, *142*
Treaty of Vereeniging 14
trends *see* fashions and trends
Tretchikoff, Vladimir 38
Treurnicht, Andries 185, 195
Tribune 164
trolley-buses **78**, *78*
Trotsky, Leon 97
Truman, Harry S. 106, 114, 117
Truth and Reconciliation Commission 200, **212**, *212*
Tsafendas, Dimitri 153, 223
Tshabalala, Vincent 172
Tshombe, Moise 141, 159
Tshwete, Steve 91
tuberculosis 22, 213
Tucker, Karla Faye 218
Tulbagh earthquake 138
Tulu 204
Turkey 229, *229*
Turlington, Christy 207
Turner, Tina 97
Tutankhamen's tomb **57**, *57*
Tutu, Desmond
    birth 80

    free Mandela campaign 181
    Nobel Peace Prize **189**, *189*
    peace marches *198*
    on peace in SA 191
    Truth and Reconciliation Commission **212**, *212*
Twain, Mark 32
Twiggy (Lesley Hornby) **151**, *151*
Tyler, Bonnie 189
Tyson, Mike 194, 205
Tzaneen, surrogate mother in **195**

U

U2 182, 192
UB40 189, 206
UDF (United Democratic Front) **187**, 190
Uganda
    AIDS 223
    Amin overthrown 179
    Amin's reign of terror **165**
    coup 164
    Entebbe hijacking 160
    independence 145
Umberto, King of Italy 9
Umkhonto we Sizwe 142, 146, 210
uMabatha 137, **161**
Underwood, Derek 186
Unidentified Flying Objects (UFOs) **109**
Union Airways **74–5**, 84
Union of South Africa
    changed to republic 142
    dominion 68
    formation 6, 25, 27, **28**, **29**, *29*
    legislative independence 76
    royal visits 64, *64*, **108**, *108*
Union of Soviet Socialist Republics (USSR), dissolution of 203
Union-Castle Mail Steamship Company **8–9**, 67, *67*, **174**, *174*
Unionist party 29
Unita 138, 170
United Democratic Front (UDF) **187**, 190
United Nations 107, *107*, 135, 163, 175
United Nations tribunal for war crimes 209
United Party (UP) 83, 134, 175
United States of America
    Angola 170
    anti-apartheid protests/demos **131**
    Bay of Pigs **143**
    Cambodia 163
    Chile coup 168
    civil rights 19, **27**, 63, **126**, **131**, 146
    Cuban missile crisis **145**
    entry into World War I **44**, *44*
    entry into World War II **98–9**
    Gulf War **202**
    Los Angeles riots 205
    millennium celebrations *228*, 229
    space exploration 54, 59, 132, 134, 143, 145, 152, 157, **158**, *158*, 164, 184, 194
    Vietnam War 152, 155, **158**, *158*, **167**, *167*, 171
    Watergate scandal 166, 169
University of Cape Town 28
University of Fort Hare 43
University of Orange Free State 112
University of Pretoria 76, 182
University of South Africa 28
University of Stellenbosch 28

Index

U

University of Witwatersrand 50
Updike, John 157
uranium 112, 161
Uranus 175
USA for Africa 193
Uys, Jamie 112, 194–5, 215
Uys, Pieter-Dirk 106, 195, 196

V

Vacuum oil company 6
Valentino, Rudolph 67, *67*
Van der Post, Laurens 22, 133, 215
Van der Schyff, Jack 126
Van der Westhuizen, Joost 165
Van Ryneveld, Pierre 51, *51*, 166
Van Wouw, Anton 106, *106*
Van Wyk, Piston 162, *162*
Vanne, Marda **61**
Vanzetti, Bartolomeo 70, *70*
'Vat Jou Goed en Trek Ferreira' 113
Vatican City 75
VE Day **105**, *105*
Venda 179
Verneukpan 73–4, *74*
Versace, Gianni 215
Versailles **48**, *48*
Verwoerd, Hendrik
  apartheid 116, *116*, 122
  assassination **153**, *153*
  assassination attempt 140
  birth 13
  forced removals 124, *124*
  with Macmillan 140
  prime minister **132**
  Republic of SA 142
  concerning television 140
Vespa 108
veterinary surgeons, first in SA 22
Viagra 218
Vicious, Sid 179
Vickers Vimy aircraft 48, *49*, 51, *51*
Victoria Cross 215
Victoria, Queen of England **10**, *10*
Vidal, Gore 157
Vietnam War 152, 155, 158, *158*, **167**, *167*, 171
Vietnam War movies 179
Viljoen, Ben 19
Villagers, The 172
violence *see* guerrilla campaign in SA; massacres; rebellions, revolts and riots
Vionet, Madeleine 30
Voight, John 179
volcanic eruptions, Mount St Helen's 183
Volkswagen beetle 88, *88*
Von Vollenhoven, Tom **132**, *132*
Voortrekkers, De 43
Vorster, B.J.
  atomic power/weapons 161
  becomes prime minister 138
  birth 42
  death 188, *188*
  détente with Africa 163, *163*, **170**
  D'Oliviera selection 156
  'Info Scandal' **176**
  lampooning of *162*
  Ossewa-Brandwag 99
  resigns as president 179
  Soweto uprising 173
voting rights *see* franchise

W

Wade, Herbert 182
wages and salaries (in 1924) **62**
Wagon Tracks and Orchards **73**
Walesa, Lech 103
Walker, Clarence 52, *52*
Walker, George **62–3**
Walker, Reggie **25**, *25*
walking for charity 178
Walkman 179
Wall Street crash 73, *73*, **77**
Wallace, De Witt 184
Wallace, Edgar 15, 34
Wallus, Janusz 206
Waltons, The 176
War in South Africa, The 15
War of the Worlds 90
Waratah 6
Ward, Stephen 148
Warhol, Andy 71, 157, 197
Waring, Molly (Kathleen Lindsay) **167**, *167*
Warner, Sir Pelham 'Plum' 23, *23*
wars
  see also Anglo-Boer War; Gulf War; Six-Day War; World War I *and* II
  first film coverage 9
  television coverage 155, 167, 202
Warsaw Pact 126
washing machines 23, *59*
Washington, Booker T. 12, 35
Washington, Désirée 205
Washkansky, Louis 54, *154*
Watergate scandal 166, 169
Watson, E.L.C. **35–6**, *36*
Watson, James 122
Watson, Lyall 168
Waugh, Evelyn 18, 106, 120, 154, 185
Weaver, Sigourney 179
Weight Watchers 143
Weismuller, Johnny 20, *58*, 63, 190
Welensky, Roy 121, *121*
Well of Loneliness, The 72, *72*
Welles, Orson 42, 90, 100, 102, 111, 193
Wells, H.G. 57, 90, 108
Wendt, Theo 118
Wessels, Kepler 132, 205
West, Frederick 211
West Side Story 144, *144*
Western Cape, forced removals 112, 146, *146*, **153**, *153*
Weston, John 26, *26*, 115
Wet Wet Wet 209
whaling 192
Wham! 190, 193
wheelchair athletes 33
When the Lion Feeds **149**
'White Christmas' 101
White, Edward 152
White, Gordon 23
white people
  delegations to ANC **191**, **195**
  homelands for 182
  poor whites 50, 77, *77*, 110
  protests against apartheid 116, *116*
  treated as black **178**
Who's Afraid of Virginia Woolf 153
Wiehahn commission 178
Wilder, Billy 135
Willem 172
William, Prince 214
Williams, Chester 163, 209, *209*
Williams, Pat 136
Williams, Robin 208
Williams, Sophie *129*
Williams, Tennessee 128, 188
Williams, Vanessa 205
Wilson, Désirée 178
Wilson, Harold 151
Wilson, Woodrow 36, *36*
'Wimoweh' 136
'wind of change' speech 140
Wind in the Willows, The 25
Windows operating system **211**
Windsor Castle 174, *174*
Wings 176
Winnie-the-Pooh 69
Winslow, Charles 52, *52*
Winslow, Paul 128
wireless *see* radio
witchdoctors 120
Witton, George 14
Wizard of Oz, The 9, 18, 93
Wolfe, Tom 196
women
  in aviation 71, 79
  aviatrixes selling petrol *62*
  delivering mail 37
  first mayor in SA 80
  first Nobel prize 6, 16
  first in space 148
  first to top Billboard charts 196
  first UK Conservative Party leader 171
  first UK prime minister 179
  motor-racing champions 178
  Mount Everest 171
  priests 192, 209
  protest marches 129, *129*
  smuggling alcohol *51*
  swimmers 67
Women and Labour 34, 52
women's rights
  Bertha Solomon **83**, *83*
  Charlotte Maxeke 16
  and fashions 56
  franchise in SA 83
  franchise in UK 47, 72
  Germaine Greer 163
  Mabel Malherbe 80
  Mary FitzGerald 37
  Olive Schreiner 34, **51–2**, *52*
  suffragettes 6, 25, **38**, *38*
Wonder, Stevie 115, 190
Wonderful Wizard of Oz, The 9, 18
Woodstock 159, *159*
Wooley, Richard 131
Woolf, Virginia 100, 153
World Trade Center, bomb 206, *206*
World War I
  armistice 46, *46*
  London bombed 45
  outbreak of 39–40, *39*, *40*
  SA forces in 41, *41*, 42–3, 44–5, *45*, 46, **47**
  US entry into 44, *44*
World War II
  air battles 96
  Allied advance 103–4, *103*, *104*
  German advance 95–6, *95*
  'join up now' *94*
  Just Nuisance (dog) 105
  last surviving VC recipient 215
  outbreak of 92, *92*
  post-war conditions 94, 106, **107**, **117**, **124**
  SA entry into 76, *76*, 93, *93*
  SA forces in 94, **96–7**, *97*, **98**, *98*, 100, *100*, 102, *104*
  soldier surrenders after 27 years 166
  songs 93, 99, 101
  summary 94
  turn of the tide 101–2, *102*
  Union-Castle ships 174
  US, Russian entry into **98–9**
  victory 105–6, *105*
  Western Desert **100–1**
World Wildlife Fund 143
Woza Albert! 137, 196
Wright brothers **16**, *16*
Wright, Frank Lloyd 135, *135*
Wright, Tiger 189, 214
Wyndham, John 118, 159
Wynette, Tammy 171, 218

X

Xuma, Dr Alfred **97**, *97*, 145

Y

yachting, Cape-to-Rio race 164, *164*
Yeltsin, Boris 203, *203*
Young, Andrew 177
Young, Neil 166
Yssel, Gert 156
Yugoslavia 200

Z

Zager and Evans 159
Zaire *see* Congo (Kinshasa/Belgian)
Zambia (Northern Rhodesia)
  Federation **121**, **147**
  independence 138
  SA raid on 193
Zanzibar *see* Tanzania
Zatopek, Emil 120
Ziegfeld, Florenz 70
Zimbabwe African People's Union (ZAPU) 144
Zimbabwe (Southern Rhodesia)
  arrest of Garfield Todd 166
  civil war **177**
  declared a republic 161
  détente with SA 170
  Federation **121**, **147**
  independence 181, *181*
  interim Zimbabwe-Rhodesia 160, 179
  named after Rhodes 14
  SA raid on 193
  self-governing colony 57
  state of emergency 135
  Unilateral Declaration of Independence **151**, *151*
  ZAPU banned **144**
Zinn, Corporal *105*
Zuckerman, Lord 208
Zulu (film) 149
Zulu Macbeth (*uMubatha*) 137, **161**
Zulu rebellion 22, *22*
Zuma, Jacob 101
Zuma, Nkosazana 111
Zwelithini, Goodwill 111

SOUTH AFRICA in the 20th CENTURY

AP=Associated Press; AS=Allsport; BAPA=Bailey's African Photo Archives; BC=Barnett Collection; BG/T=Benny Gool/Trace; CPNM=C.P. Nel Museum, Oudtshoorn; CPP=Central Press Photos Ltd; CL=Cory Library, Grahamstown; CP=Culver Pictures; CT=*Cape Times*; CTAR=Cape Town Archive Repository; DB=*Die Burger*; DCAS/Unisa=Documentation Centre for African Studies, University of South Africa; DLR=Dana Le Roux; DP=Doug Pithey; DR=David Rogers; EA=Equinox Archives; HG/G=Hulton Getty/Gallo; HT=Hannes Thiart; HWW=H.W. Wilson New York; Inpra=International Press Agency; IWM=Imperial War Museum; JBKC=J.B. Kramer Collection; JFN=John Frost Newspapers; JS=Jürgen Schadeberg; KC=Kobal Collection; KCC=Killie Campbell Collection; LF=London Features; LG/T=Louise Gubb/Trace; LHMC=Local History Museums' Collection, Durban; LoC=Library of Congress; LP=Lighthouse Pictures; MA = MuseumAfrica; MC=Mayibuye Centre; MEPL=Mary Evans Picture Library; MM=McGregor Museum; MMH=Museum of Military History; NA=National Archives; NELM = National English Literary Museum; NL=National Library; PB=Peter Beaumister; P/S=Popperfoto/Superstock; RF=Rex Features; RHL=Robert Hunt Library; ROC=Robert Opie Collection; RT=*Radio Times*; SABC=South African Broadcasting Corporation; S&G=Sport & General; SM=Science Museum, London; SP=Snap Photo; ST=*Sunday Times*; SU=source unknown; TA=*The Argus*; TS=*The Star* Newspaper; UPI/B/C=UPI/Bettman/Corbis; VM=The *Vintage* Magazine, London; WWP=Wide World Photos.

COVER: 1900 KCC; 1910 HG/G; 1920 VM; 1930 NL; 1940 Camera Press/Inpra; 1950 BAPA; 1960 TA; 1970 and 1980 MC; 1990 BG/T; 2000 PB/Trace.

1900s: Pages 6 KCC; 7 (top) NL, (centre SU, (bottom) MM; 8 (top) HWW, (centre CTAR Ref. No. J340, (bottom) NA; 9 (top) SA Pictorial Stage & Cinema, (centre) Mount Nelson Hotel, (bottom) NL; 10 (top) Johannes Meintjies Private Collection, (bottom, left and right) MA; 11 (top, and centre right) L. Hughes Collection, Johannesburg, (centre left) NA, (bottom) MA; 12 (top) SU, (bottom) CT; 13 (top) CTAR ref. no. E7862, (bottom) NL; 14 (top) NA, (bottom) HG/G; 15 (top and bottom) CTAR ref. no. AG15332, (centre) CT; 16 (top left) NL, (top right) LoC, (bottom) National Air & Space Museum, Smithsonian Institution (SI Neg. No. A-26767-B-2); 17 (all) MA; 18 (top) CTAR ref. no. E8308, (bottom) BC; 19 MA; 20 (top, left and right) Namibian Ministry of Information & Broadcasting, (bottom left) NA, (bottom right) United Tobacco Co.; 21 (top) MA, (centre) CPNM, (bottom) Science Society Picture Library, London; 22 (top) *Outspan* 1956/DB 1962, (centre and bottom left) LHMC, (bottom right) MA; 23 (top, left and right) SU, (right) MA; 24 (top) MC, (bottom) NELM; 25 MA; 26 (top) MA, (bottom) Transnet Heritage Museum; 27 (top) NL, (bottom left) CT, (bottom right) HG/G.

1910s: Pages 28 (top left) MA, (bottom right) KCC; 29 (top) CTAR ref. no. AG6286, (bottom left) MA, (bottom right) NL; 30 top) MEPL, (bottom, all) Dragon's World, Ltd, Limpsfield UK; 31 (top left) SM, (top right) HG/G, (bottom) TS; 32 (top) HG/G, (centre) CP, (bottom) CPNM; 33 (top left) EA, (top right, and bottom, left and right) NL; 34 (top) NL, (bottom left) MM, (right) Musée du Louvre, Paris (*Mona Lisa*, Leonardo da Vinci/ AKG London); 35 (left) MC, (top right) CTAR ref. no. SU, (bottom right) UPI/B/C; 36 (top left) MA, (top right) HG/G, (bottom) CP; 37 (all) SU; 38 (top, and bottom left) LHMC, (bottom right) HG/G); 39 (top and centre right) HG/G, (centre left) SU, (bottom, left and right) IWM; 40 (top) IWM, (centre) NL, (bottom) NA; 41 (top) CTAR ref. no. E9205, (bottom) MEPL; 42 (left) HG/G, (right) MMH; 43 (top) DCAS/Unisa, (bottom left) Commercial Print, (bottom right) MMH; 44 (top) LoC, (bottom left) SU, (bottom right) HG/G; 45 (top) MMH, (bottom) NA; 46 (top) NL, (centre left, and bottom) UPI/B/C, (centre right) JBKC; 47 (top) SU, (bottom) CP; 48 (left) CTAR ref. no. E2849, (right) UPI/B/C; 49 (top) CTAR, (bottom left) Irma Stern Museum, (bottom right) MA.

1920s: Pages 50 KC; 51 (top and bottom left) HG/G, (bottom right) UPI/B/C; 52 (top left) NELM, (top right) NL, (centre, and bottom, left and right) SU; 53 (top) Rowenta UK Limited, (centre and bottom) TA; 54 (top) UPI/B/C, (centre left) CL (picture scanned from *An Illustrated Dictionary of South African History*), (centre right) JFN, (bottom) RT/HG/G; 55 (top left) DB, (top right and bottom right) Mr Jimmy Lawrence, (bottom left) NA; 56 (top left) HG/G, (top right) LP, (bottom left) NL, (bottom right) Lee Creelman Erickson; 57 (top) Thomas Pakenham, (bottom) MEPL; 58 (top left) Reader's Digest, (top right and bottom) HG/G; 59 (top left) JFN, (top right) ADM International, (bottom left) Topham/ Inpra, (bottom right) SU; 60 (top and centre) HG/G, (left) Henry E. Huntington Library and Art Gallery, (bottom) SABC Archives; 61 (top, and bottom right) NL, (bottom left) HG/G; 62 (top) ST, (centre) TS, (bottom) HG/G; 63 (top) HG/G, (left) JFN, (bottom) SU; 64 (top, and bottom left) NL, (centre) Centre for Theatre and Performance Studies, (bottom right) HG/G; 65 (top left) VM, (top right) P/S, (bottom right) *Punch* Cartoon Library; 66 (top) LP, (bottom) MA; 67 (top left) SU, (top right) NL, (centre) CTAR ref. no. AG5639, (bottom) HG/G; 68 (top) SU, (bottom) NA; 69 (top) ROC, (bottom) SU; 70 (top) RT/HG/G, (centre and bottom) OK Bazaars; 71 (top) P/S, (centre) NL, (bottom) SU; 72 (top, and bottom right) HG/G, (bottom left) The Fallon Press; 73 (top) P/S, (left) HG/G, (bottom) *Boston Daily News*; 74 (top) MA, (bottom) Working Life; 75 (top and bottom) HG/G.

1930s: Pages 76 (left) Topham/Inpra, (bottom) republished with permission *The Star*; 77 (top) Carnegie Commission Reports/NL, (bottom) NA; 78 (top) G. Shields, (centre) HG/G, (bottom) Press Features (Pty) Ltd/ Magazine Features; 79 (top) NL, (left) P/S, (centre) LF/Inpra, (right) SU.; 80 (top) SU, (bottom left) VM, (bottom right) AP/Picturenet; 81 (top) P/S, (bottom left) HG/G, (bottom) NA; 82 (top left) Archives of the Centre for South African Literature, Pretoria, (top right) Mars Confectionery Ltd, (bottom, left and right) HG/G; 83 (top left) SU, (top right) HG/G, (centre) Archives of the Centre for South African Theatre, Pretoria, (bottom) CTAR ref. no. AG2887; 84 (top) LHMC, (bottom left) P/S, (bottom right) SU; 85 (top left and right) Topham/Inpra, (bottom) SP/Inpra; 86 (top) Keystone/HG/G, (bottom) DCAS/Unisa; 87 (top) Süddeutscher Verlag, (bottom left) HG/G, (bottom right) MA; 88 (top) DACS 1989 and Madame Maya Widmaier Picasso, Paris, (centre left) Topham/Inpra, (centre right) NL, (bottom) Stiftung AutoMuseum, Volkswagen; 89 (top) Fotos International/ Inpra, (centre left) SU, (centre right) Newforge Food Ltd, (bottom) SP/Inpra; 90 (top) HG/G, (bottom) P/S; 91 (top) J.L.B. Smith Institute of Ichthyology, (bottom left) DB, (bottom right) Nestlé SA; 92 (top and bottom) TS; 93 (top) TS, (centre) CT, (bottom) Topham/Inpra.

1940s: Pages 94 MMH; 95 (left) WWP, (right) SU; 96 (top) SU (bottom) Topical Press Agency London; 97 (top left) MMH, (centre) NL, (top

246

SOUTH AFRICA in the 20th CENTURY

right) Inpra, (bottom) HG/G; **98** (all) SU; **99** (top) SU, (bottom) SU; **100** (top) LHMC, (bottom left) RHL, (bottom right) SU; **101** (top) SP/Inpra, (bottom) HG/G; **102** (top, left and right) SU, (centre) P/S, (bottom left) BAPA, (bottom right) HG/G; **103** (top left) HG/G, (top right) HG/G, (bottom right) SU, (centre) Sygma/Inpra; **104** (top) S&G, (bottom left) SU, (bottom right) Topham/Inpra; **105** (top left) MMH, (top right) SU, (centre) republished with permission *The Star*, (bottom right) HG/G; **106** (top right) HG/G, (centre left) P/S, (bottom) National Cultural, Historical and Open-Air Museum, Pretoria; **107** (top left) AP/Picturenet, (top right) NA, (bottom) HG/G; **108** (left) SU, (bottom) NA; **109** (top left) NL, (top right, and bottom) HG/G; **110** (top left) Camera Press/ Magazine Features, (top right) Christian Dior, (bottom) P/S; **111** (top left) SU, (top right) SU.

1950s: Pages **112** BAPA; **113** (top) RHL, (centre and bottom) SABC Archives; **114** (top left) United States National Archives, (top right) NA, (bottom) HG/G; **115** (top) Winston Link, (bottom) LF/Inpra; **116** (top) *Daily News*, (bottom) CT; **117** (top) HG/G, (bottom) S&G; **118** (left top and centre left) HG/G, (top right) KC, (centre) Archives of the Centre for South African Theatre, (bottom right) Oxford University Press, UK; **119** (top left) TS, (top right) P/S, (centre) HG/G, (bottom left) JS; **120** (top) Tafelberg Publishers Ltd, (bottom left) CPP/Inpra, (bottom right) P/S; **121** (top left) SU, (top right) Topham/Inpra, (bottom) HG/G; **122** (top left) MC, (top right) HG/G, (bottom) SU; **123** (top) HG/G, (bottom left) RF/Inpra, (bottom right) Horst; **124** (top) Imapress/ Inpra, (centre) SU, (bottom) P/S; **125** (top) Peter Magubane, (bottom) Topham/ Inpra; **126** (top left) Yulsman/Globe Photos, (top right, and bottom) RF/Inpra; **127** (top left) JS, (top right) Bob Gosani, (bottom) SU; **128** (top) HG/G, (bottom) VM; **129** (top) SU, (centre and bottom) HG/G; **130** (left) Bob Gosani, (right) CPP/Inpra; **131** (top left) HG/G, (top right) NL; **132** (top) SU, (bottom) DB; **133** (top) SU, (bottom left) Redferns Music Picture Library, (bottom right) P/S; **134** (top right) HG/G, (centre) BAPA, (bottom right) CT; **135** (centre left) Gary Player Group, (centre) HG/G, (centre right) Department of Public Relations, University of Fort Hare, (bottom) National Motor Museum, UK; **136** and **137** (all) JS.

1960s: Pages **138** Action Press/Inpra; **139** (top and bottom) HG/G; **140** (top) NL, (bottom left) HG/G, (bottom right) S&G; **141** (top, and centre left) HG/G, (centre right) Heinemann Ltd, London, (bottom) P/S; **142** (top) TS, (centre and bottom) MC; **143** (top left) MC, (top right, centre, and bottom right) HG/G; **144** (left) P/S, (right) MC; **145** (top) HG/G, (bottom) AFP/Inpra; **146** (top) HG/G, (centre, left and right) MC, (bottom) DB; **147** (top) Sygma/Inpra, (bottom left) P/S, (bottom right) NL; **148** (top) Topham/Inpra, (centre) Universal Pictorial Press and Agency/Inpra, (bottom left) The International Press Agency/Inpra, (bottom right) HG/G; **149** (top) HG/G, (centre) Action Press/Inpra, (bottom) AS/Touchline; **150** (top right) Pictorial Press UK, (centre, top left) EA, (centre, top right) RF/Inpra, (centre, bottom left) RF/Inpra, (centre, bottom right and left) Topham/Inpra; **151** (top) ROC, (bottom left) UPI/B/C, (bottom right) Topham/Inpra; **152** (top right) Topham/Inpra, (top left) Henry Diltz/Corbis, (centre) Everard Group, (right, centre) Carmen Schaivone/*Fair Lady*, (bottom right) HG/G; **153** (top) TA, (bottom left) Cloete Breytenbach, (bottom right) Mike MacKenzie/TA; **154** (top) HG/G, (centre) Jim McLagan/TA, (bottom left) CT, (bottom right) HG/G; **155** (top left) HG/G, (top right) LF/Inpra, (centre left) RF/Inpra, (centre right) Topham/Inpra; **156** (left) LF/Inpra, (right) NL; **157** (top) P/S, (bottom) UPI/B/C; **158** (right top) UPI/B/C, (bottom) Sygma/Inpra, (right bottom) MC; **159** (top right and centre right) Topham/Inpra, (bottom) World Press Photos.

1970s: Pages **160** TA; **161** (top) MC, (bottom) SU; **162** (bottom left) SU, (bottom right) CT; **163** (top) TS, (centre) *Future Shock*, author Alvin Toffler, published by Bodley Head Publishers, the Random House Group; (bottom) NA; **164** (top) HT/TA, (bottom) Colour Sport UK; **165** (top) P/S, (centre) BAPA, (bottom) NL; **166** (top) P/S, (centre) MC, (bottom) CL (picture scanned from *S.A. Hall of Fame*); **167** (top) Black Star, (bottom) CT; **168** (top right) Hodder & Stoughton, (bottom left) MC; **169** (top left) TA, (bottom) RF/Inpra; **170** (top) Anneline Bacon, (bottom) Ashanti Publishing; **171** (centre left) TA, (centre right) SU, (bottom) CT; **172** HG/G; **173** (all) MC; **174** (top, both) Union-Castle Mail Steamship Co. Ltd, (centre) MC, (bottom) Norma Hudson; **175** (top left) Topham/Inpra, (top right) Jeff Hornbaker/*Zig Zag* Magazine; **176** (top) Orde Eliason/Link Photoreportage, (bottom) SP/Inpra; **177** (top left) HT/TA, (top right) UPI/B/C, (centre left) HG/G, (centre right) United Press International, (bottom left) WWP, (bottom right) TA; **178** (top) TA, (bottom) Gavin Stapleton; **179** (top) HG/G, (bottom) Herman Potgieter.

1980s: Pages **180** AP/Picturenet; **181** (top) SU, (bottom) MC; **182** (top) Tony Grogan/CT, (centre right) RF/Inpra, (bottom left) TS, (bottom right) CT; **183** (top) P/S, (bottom) DB; **184** (top left) TA, (top right) HG/G, (bottom) P/S; **185** (top) AP/Picturenet, (bottom) NL; **186** (top left) TA, (top right) HG/G, (centre) NL, (bottom) MC; **187** (left) Sam Emerson/ Sygma/Inpra, (right) TS; **188** (top) DB, (bottom left) TA, (bottom right) TS; **189** (top right) P/S, (centre left) TA, (bottom right) SU; **190** (top right) RF/Inpra, (bottom)TA; **191** (top) Leo Müller/TA, (bottom left) HT/TA, (bottom right) TA; **192** (top) Willie de Klerk/TA, (bottom) Press/R. Frankel/Inpra; **193** (top) HG/G, (bottom) P/S; **194** (top left) P/S, (top right) DP/TA, (bottom) World of Music; **195** AP/Picturenet; **196** (left) BAPA, (right) TA; **197** (top) *Natal Mercury*, (bottom) MC; **198** (top, and bottom left) DLR/TA, (bottom right) DP/TA, (centre) NL; **199** (top left) AP/ Picturenet, (top right) DLR/TA, (bottom) MC.

1990s: Pages **200** (right) AP/Picturenet; **201** (top) Picturenet, (bottom) Reuters/Trace; **202** (left) MC, (right) Topham/Inpra; **203** (top left) BG/T, (top right and bottom left) Picturenet (bottom right) AP/Picturenet, **204** (top left) RF/Inpra, (top right) Picturenet, (bottom) Paul Velasco/Gallo; **205** (top) AP/Picturenet, (bottom) TA; **206** (top) Picturenet, (right) Reuters/Bettman/Corbis; **207** (both) AP/Picturenet; **208** (top) LG/T, (bottom) Picturenet; **209** (top) DR/AS/Touchline, (bottom) Picturenet; **210** (right, top and bottom) Picturenet, (bottom left) DR/AS/ Touchline; **211** (both) AP/Picturenet; **212** (top, and bottom right) Aquarius/Inpra, (bottom left) Picturenet; **213** (top) Gallo Images, (bottom left and right) AP/Picturenet; **214** (all) AP/Picturenet; **215** (top) AP/Picturenet, (bottom) Picturenet; **216** (top) Photos International/Inpra, (centre) Ster Kinekor, (bottom) Picturenet; **217** (top) Picturenet, (bottom) JS; **218** (left) Themba Hadebe/TS, (top right) AP/Picturenet; **219** (top, and bottom right) Picturenet, (bottom right) AP/Picturenet; **220** (top) Jean-Marc Bujou/AP Photo, (bottom) Picturenet; **221** (both) BG/T; **222** (top) AP/Picturenet, (bottom) Picturenet; **223** (both) AP/Picturenet.

2000: Pages **224** PB/Trace; **225** (top left) TA, (top right, and bottom) DB; (centre) LG/T; **226–231** (all) AP/Picturenet.

Further Reading: SOUTH AFRICA in the 20th CENTURY

Alhadeff, V. (1990): *A Newspaper History of South Africa*. Don Nelson, Cape Town.

Coplan, D. (1985): *In Township Tonight!* Ravan, Johannesburg.

Davenport, R. (1987): *South Africa: A Modern History*. Macmillan, Johannesburg.

Financial Mail (supplement, 1999): *100 Years: The Century that Discovered Dignity*. Times Media, Johannesburg.

Hadland A. and Rantão, J. (1999): *The Life and Times of Thabo Mbeki*. Zebra Press, Johannesburg.

Harrison, D. (1981): *The White Tribe of Africa*. Macmillan, Johannesburg.

Ingham, K. (1986): *Jan Christiaan Smuts: The Conscience of a South African*. Jonathan Ball, Johannesburg.

Joyce, P. (1999): *Concise Dictionary of South African Biography*. Francolin, Cape Town.

Kane-Berman, J. (1978): *Soweto: Black Revolt, White Reaction*. Ravan, Johannesburg.

Kruger, R. (1983): *Goodbye Dolly Gray*. Cassell & Co., London.

Lodge, T. (1983): *Black Politics in South Africa since 1945*. Ravan, Johannesburg.

Luthuli, A. (1962): *Let My People Go*. Collins, London.

Mandela, N. (1994): *Long Walk to Freedom*. MacDonald Purnell, Johannesburg.

Mbeki, G. (1991): *The Prison Writings of Govan Mbeki*. David Philip, Cape Town.

Odendaal, A. (1984): *Vukani Bantu! The Beginnings of Black Protest Politics in South Africa to 1912*. David Philip, Cape Town.

Packenham, T. (1979): *The Anglo-Boer War*. Weidenfeld and Nicolson, London.

Pitts, J. (1989): *The Star: World War II*. Struik Publishers, Cape Town.

Plaatje, S. (1973): *The Boer War Diary of Sol. T. Plaatje*. J. Comaroff.

Plaatje, S. (1982): *Native Life in South Africa*. Ravan, Johannesburg.

Reader's Digest (1988): *Illustrated History of South Africa*. The Reader's Digest Association, Cape Town.

Reader's Digest (1981): *South Africa's Yesterdays*. The Reader's Digest Association, Cape Town.

Reitz, D. (1929): *Commando: A Journal of the Boer War*. London.

Sparks, A. (1990): *The Mind of South Africa – The Story of the Rise and Fall of Apartheid*. Mandarin, London.

Sparks, A. (1994): *Tomorrow is Another Country*. Struik Book Distributers, Johannesburg.

Sunday Times (supplement, 1999): *2000: Celebrating 100 Years in South Africa*. Times Media, Johannesburg.

Van der Ross, R. (1986): *The Rise and Decline of Apartheid*. Tafelberg, Cape Town.

Waldmeir, P. (1997): *Anatomy of a Miracle*. Penguin Books, London.

Walshe, P. (1970): *The Rise of African Nationalism in South Africa: The African National Congress, 1912–1952*. Hurst & Co., London.